SOUJŪ MATSUSHITA

FORMER JAPAN LEAGUE PLAYER

JOSUI JUNIOR HIGH

COACH

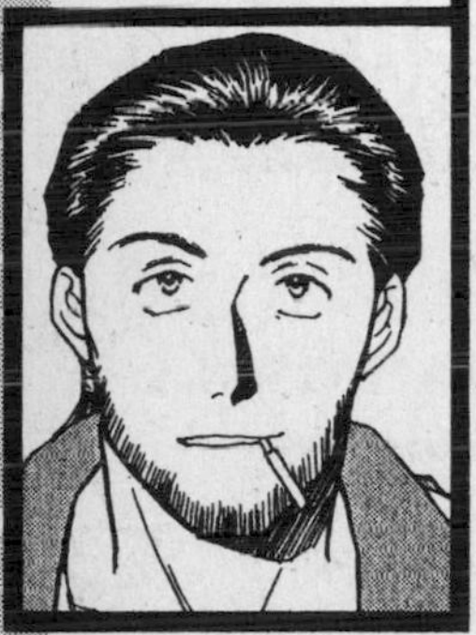

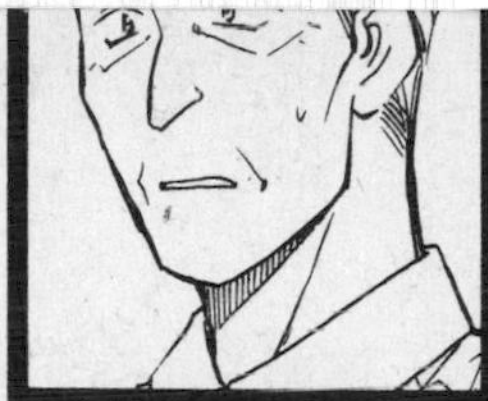

SOUICHIRO KIRIHARA

MUSASHINOMORI PRIVATE SCHOOL SOCCER TEAM

COACH

SHIGEKI SATŌ

JOSUI JUNIOR HIGH SOCCER TEAM

FORWARD

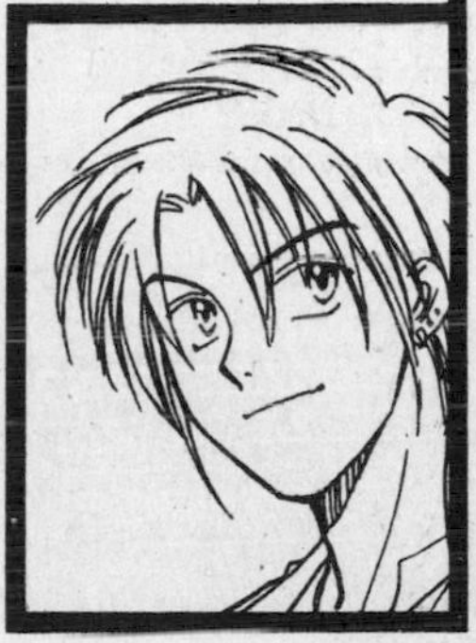

STORY

TO REALIZE HIS DREAM, SHŌ KAZAMATSURI, A BENCH WARMER AT SOCCER POWERHOUSE MUSASHINOMORI, TRANSFERRED TO JOSUI JUNIOR HIGH SO HE COULD PLAY THE GAME HE LOVES.

SOON AFTER SHŌ'S ARRIVAL, SOUJŪ MATSUSHITA, A FORMER JAPAN LEAGUE PLAYER, BECAME JOSUI'S COACH, AND THE TEAM HEADED INTO THE SUMMER CHAMPIONSHIP.

TEAMWORK ISSUES BETWEEN THE GOALKEEPER AND THE DEFENSE THREATENED TO SPOIL THE FIRST GAME AGAINST IWA TECH. JOSUI STRUGGLED EARLY ON: THEY SCORED AN OWN GOAL IN THE FIRST HALF AND REPEATEDLY FAILED TO PENETRATE THE OPPONENT'S SOLID DEFENSE.

AT THE END OF THE GAME, HOWEVER, JOSUI CAME TOGETHER AS A TEAM. THANKS TO SOME HEROIC EFFORTS AND A NOBLE, IF ILL-ADVISED, STRATEGY CHANGE BY IWA TECH, JOSUI MANAGED TO CARVE OUT A 2-1 LEAD AS THE LAST SECONDS OF STOPPAGE TIME TICKED DOWN...

WHISTLE!

**Vol. 8
RAIN CATS
AND DOGS**

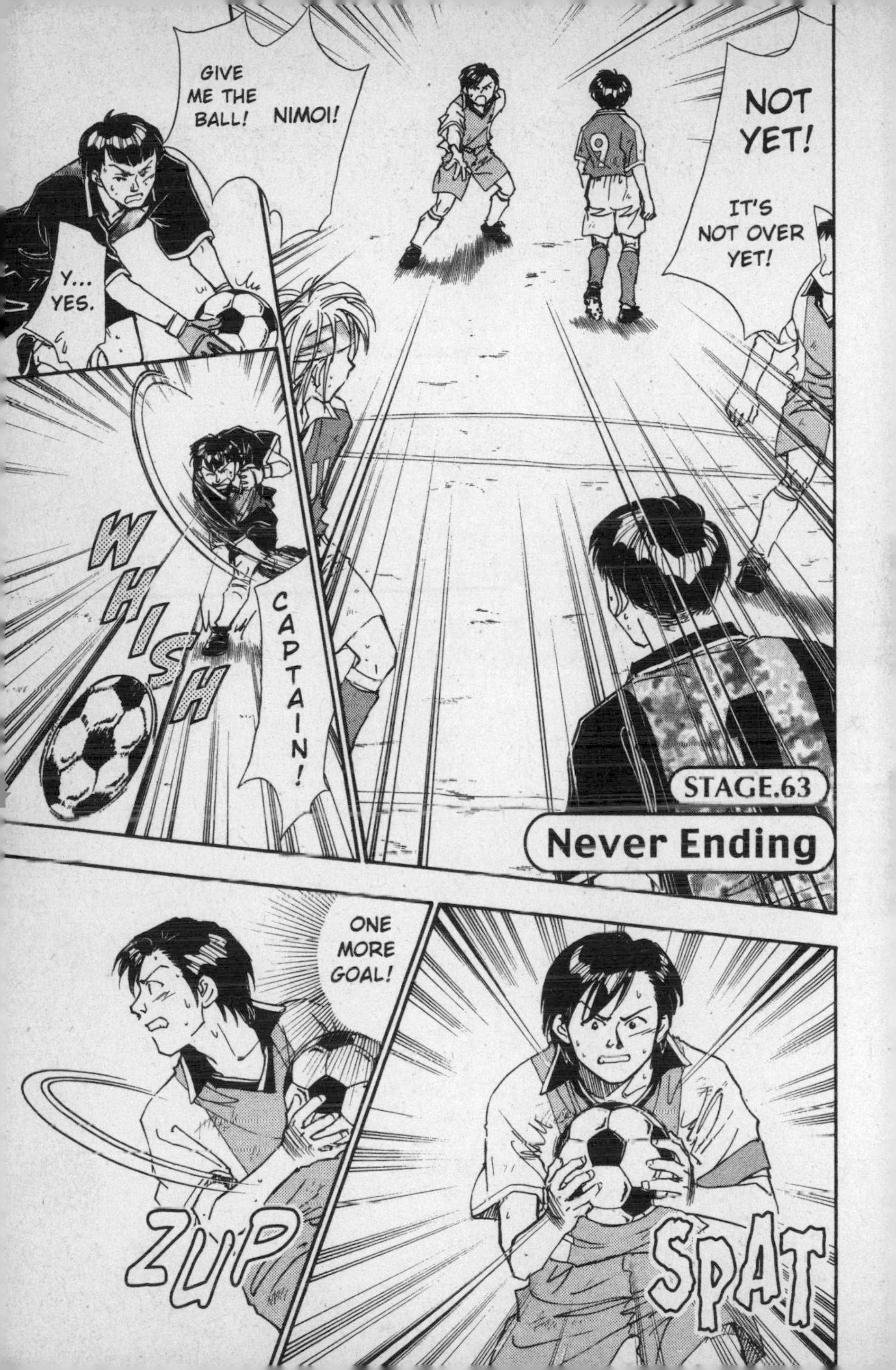
NOT YET!
IT'S NOT OVER YET!
STAGE.63
Never Ending
NIMOI!
GIVE ME THE BALL!
Y... YES.
CAPTAIN!
WHISH
SPAT
ONE MORE GOAL!
ZUP

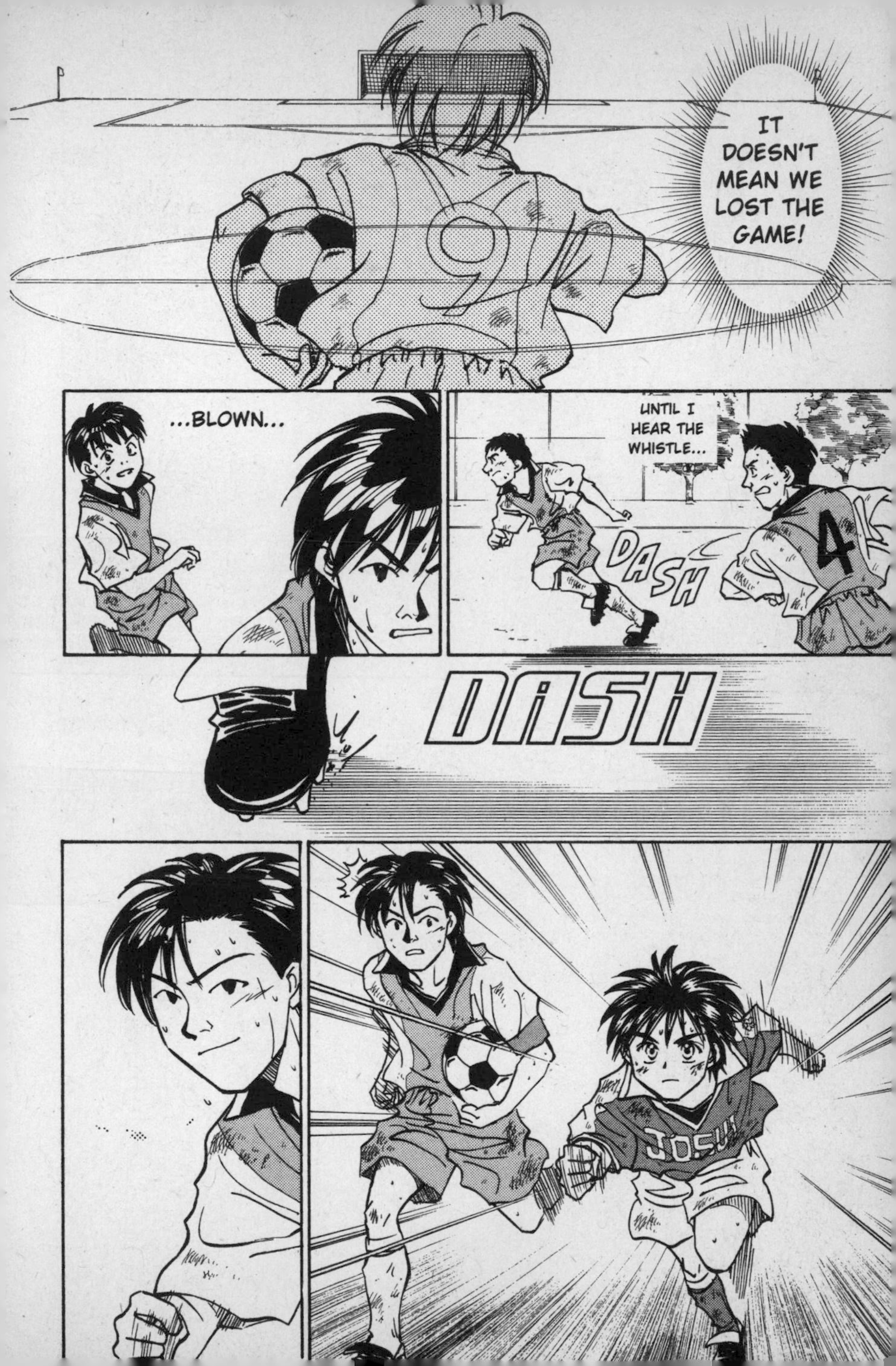
IT DOESN'T MEAN WE LOST THE GAME!
UNTIL I HEAR THE WHISTLE...
DASH
...BLOWN...
DASH

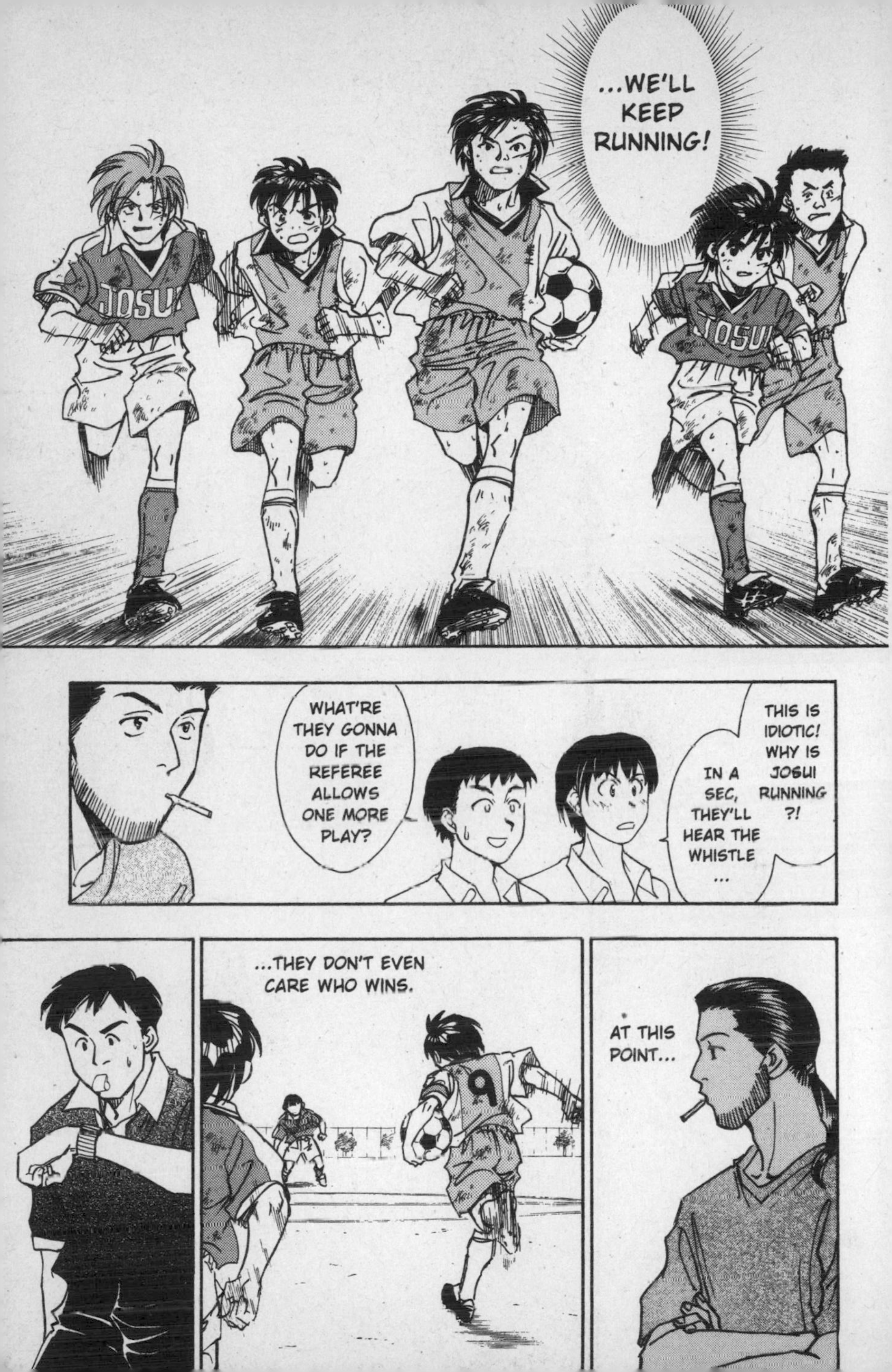
...WE'LL KEEP RUNNING!
THIS IS IDIOTIC! WHY IS JOSUI RUNNING ?!
IN A SEC, THEY'LL HEAR THE WHISTLE ...
WHAT'RE THEY GONNA DO IF THE REFEREE ALLOWS ONE MORE PLAY?
AT THIS POINT...
...THEY DON'T EVEN CARE WHO WINS.

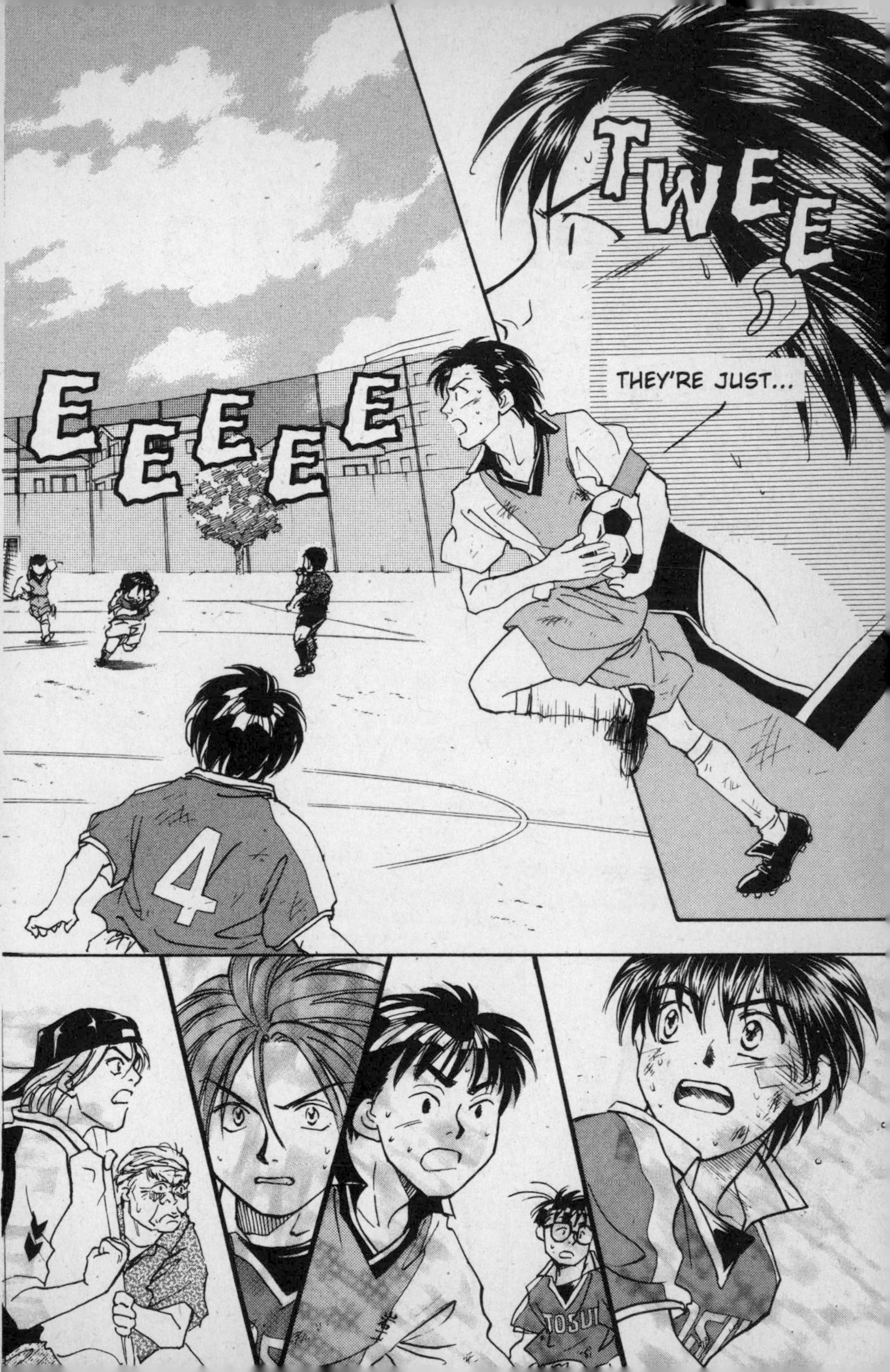
TWEE
THEY'RE JUST...
EEEEE
TOSUI

STAGE.63
Never Ending

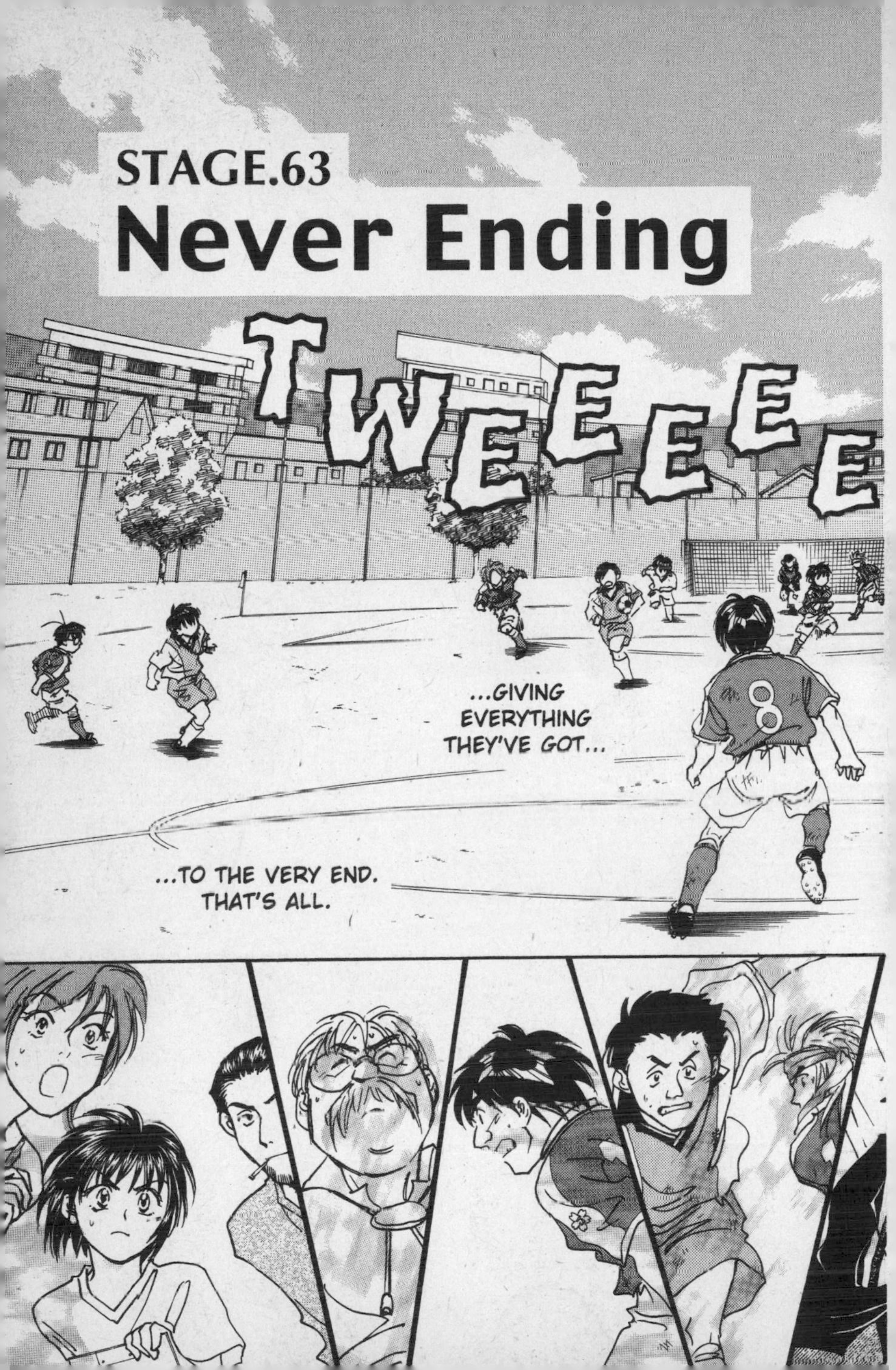
TWEEEEE
...GIVING EVERYTHING THEY'VE GOT...
...TO THE VERY END. THAT'S ALL.

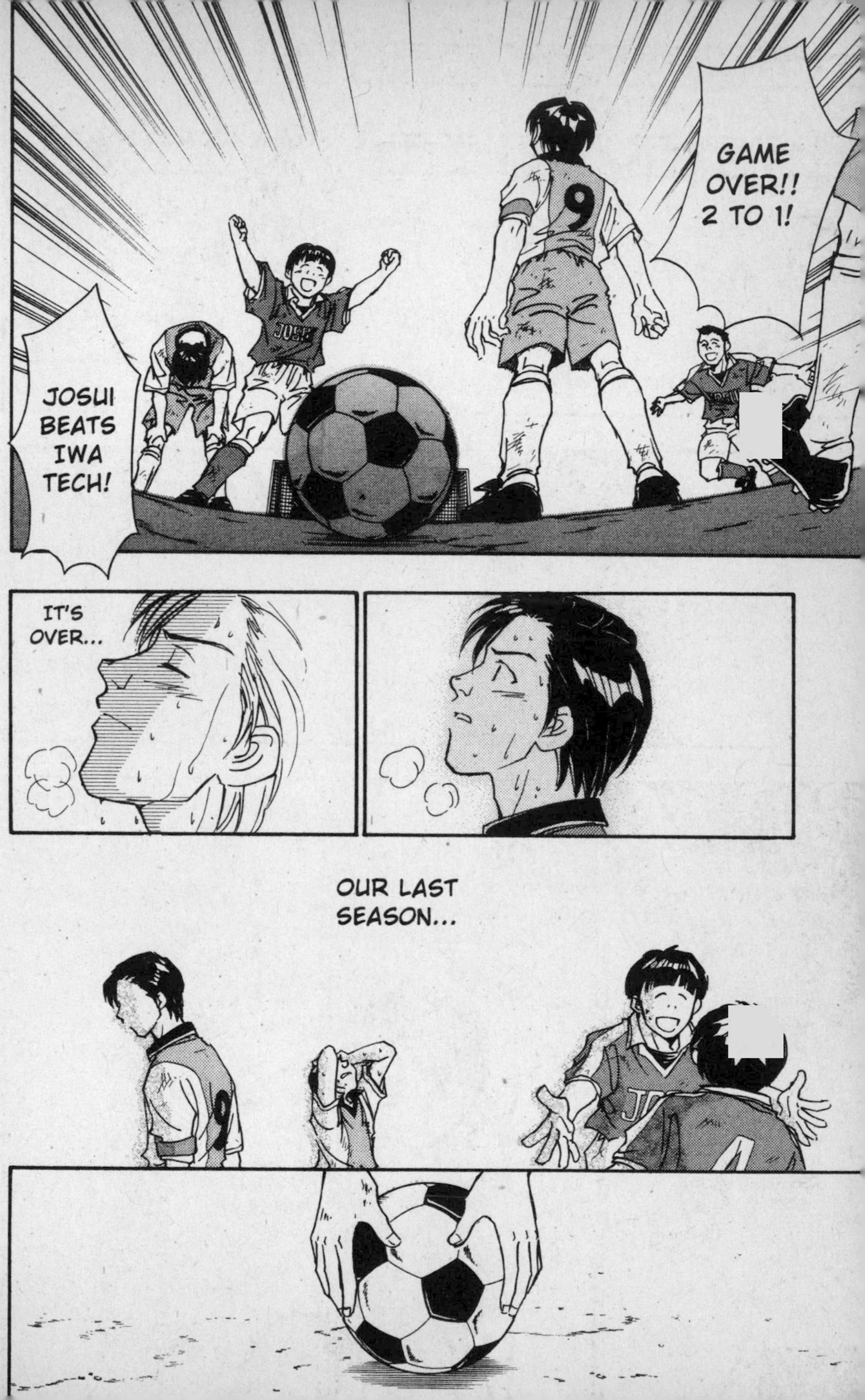
GAME OVER!! 2 TO 1!
JOSUI BEATS IWA TECH!
IT'S OVER...
OUR LAST SEASON...

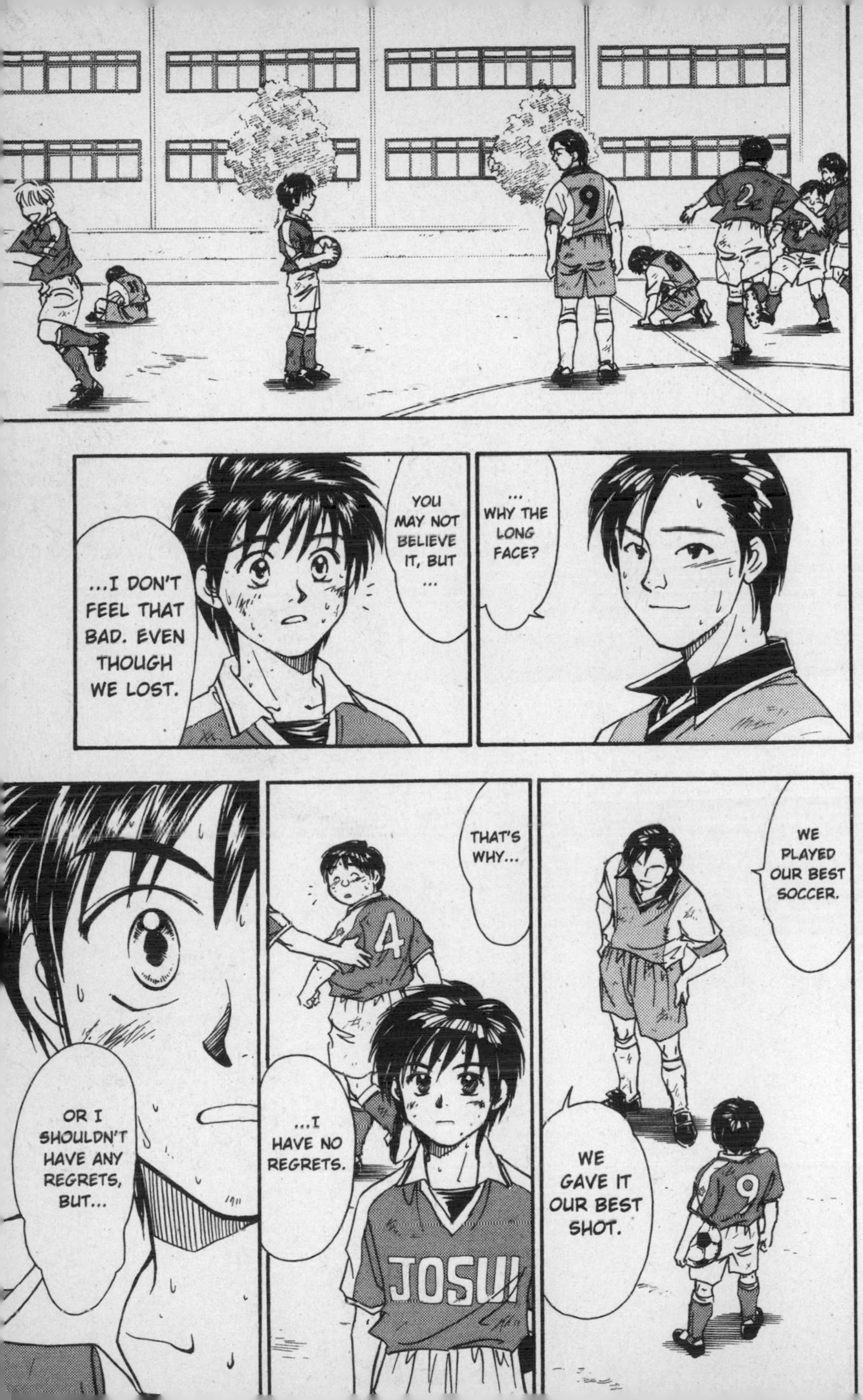
... WHY THE LONG FACE?
YOU MAY NOT BELIEVE IT, BUT ...
...I DON'T FEEL THAT BAD. EVEN THOUGH WE LOST.
WE PLAYED OUR BEST SOCCER.
WE GAVE IT OUR BEST SHOT.
THAT'S WHY...
...I HAVE NO REGRETS.
OR I SHOULDN'T HAVE ANY REGRETS, BUT...
JOSUI

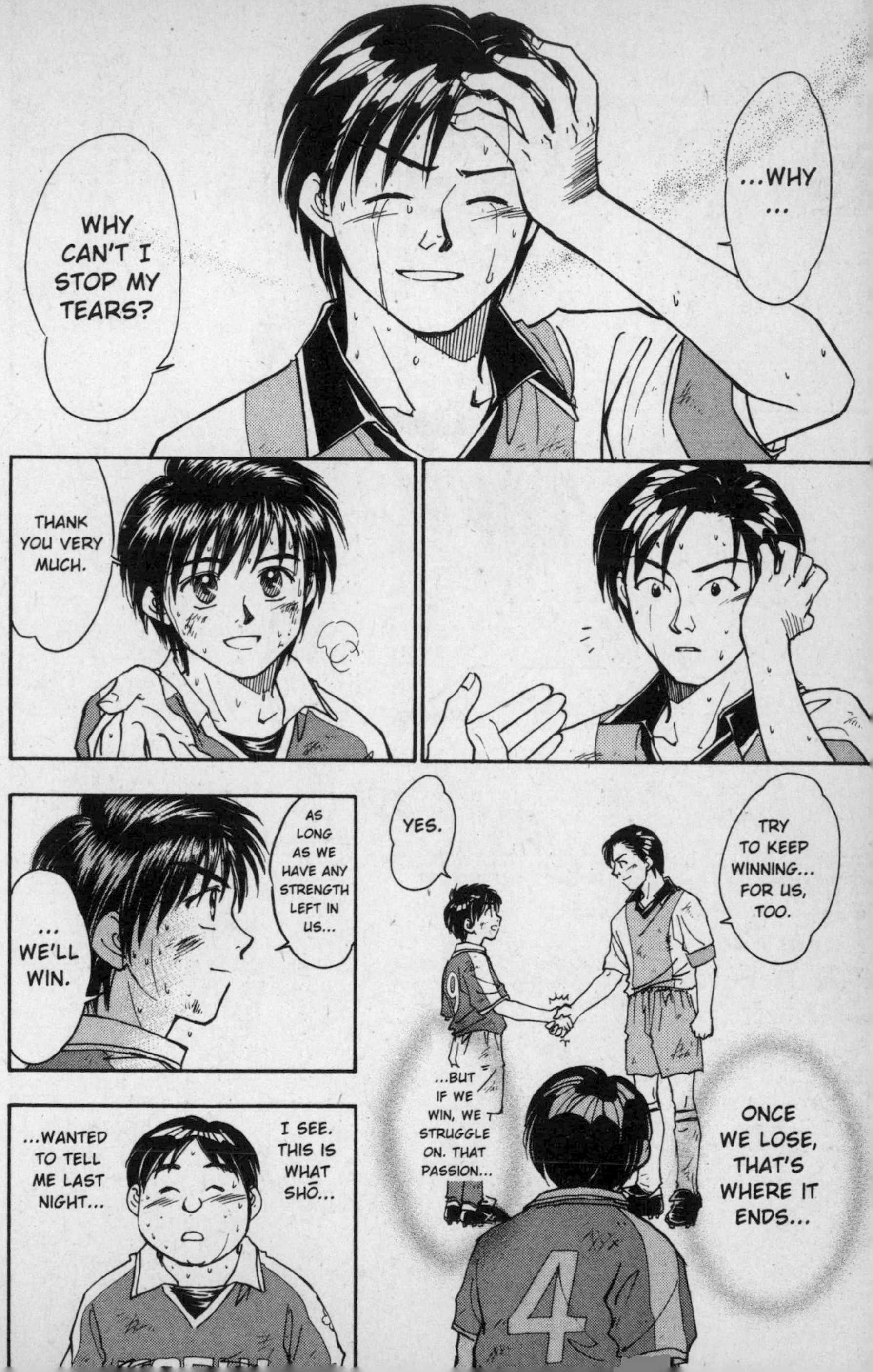
...WHY ...
WHY CAN'T I STOP MY TEARS?
THANK YOU VERY MUCH.
TRY TO KEEP WINNING... FOR US, TOO.
YES.
ONCE WE LOSE, THAT'S WHERE IT ENDS...
...BUT IF WE WIN, WE STRUGGLE ON. THAT PASSION...
AS LONG AS WE HAVE ANY STRENGTH LEFT IN US...
... WE'LL WIN.
I SEE. THIS IS WHAT SHŌ...
...WANTED TO TELL ME LAST NIGHT...

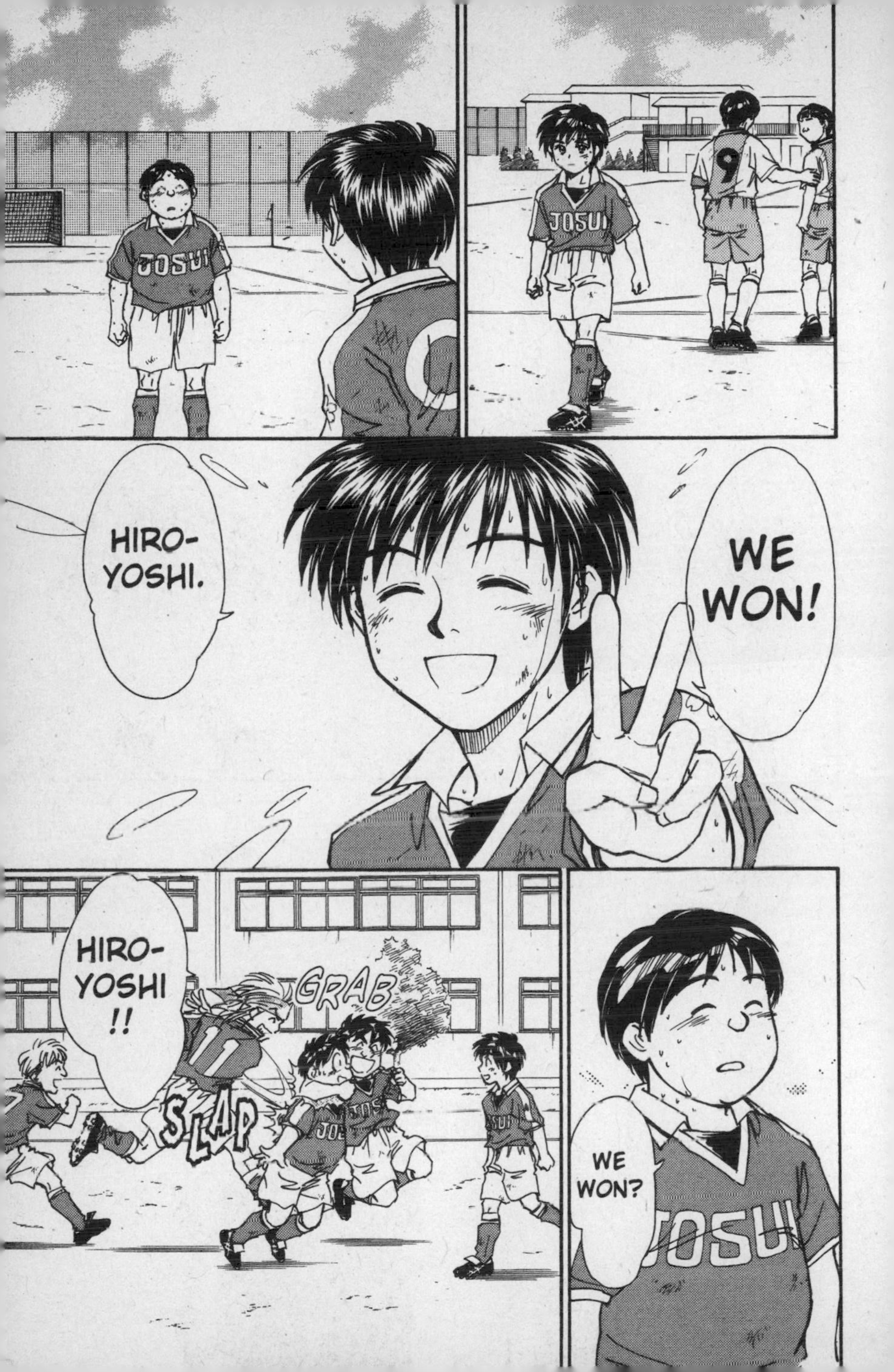
WE WON!
HIRO-YOSHI.
WE WON?
HIRO-YOSHI!!
GRAB
SLAP

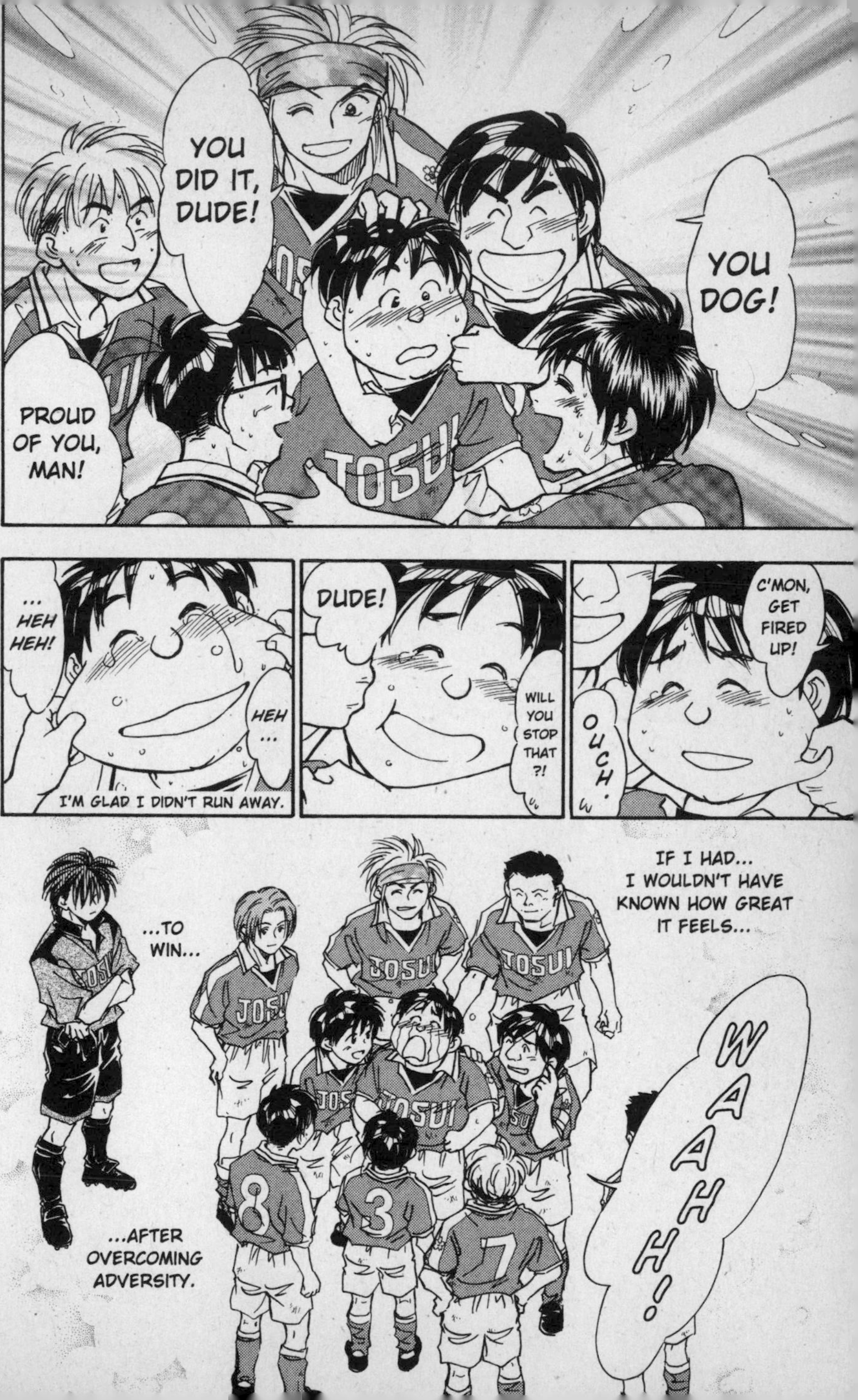
YOU DOG!
YOU DID IT, DUDE!
PROUD OF YOU, MAN!
C'MON, GET FIRED UP!
OUCH.
DUDE!
WILL YOU STOP THAT?!
...HEH HEH!
HEH...
I'M GLAD I DIDN'T RUN AWAY.
IF I HAD... I WOULDN'T HAVE KNOWN HOW GREAT IT FEELS...
WAAHHH!!
...TO WIN...
...AFTER OVERCOMING ADVERSITY.

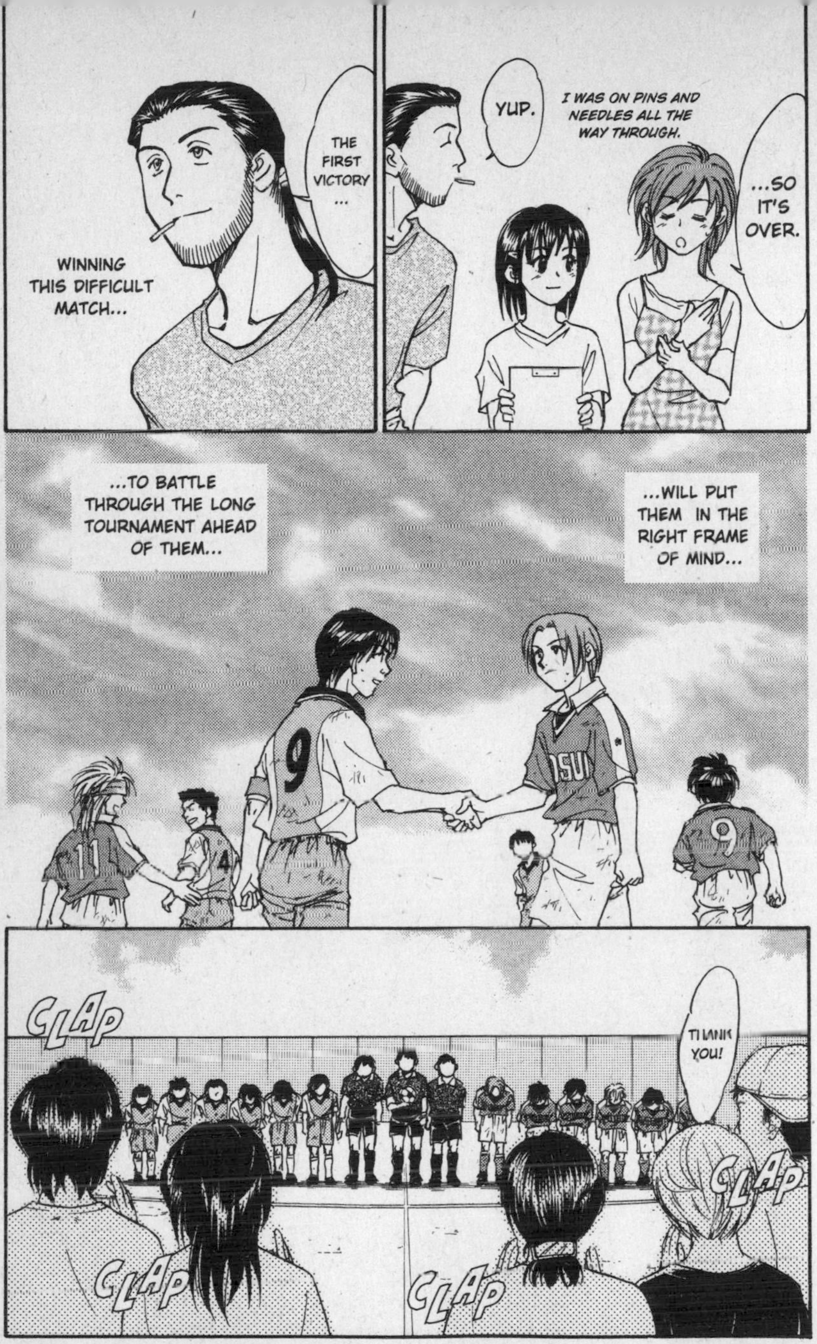

...SO IT'S OVER.
I WAS ON PINS AND NEEDLES ALL THE WAY THROUGH.
YUP.
THE FIRST VICTORY ...
WINNING THIS DIFFICULT MATCH...
...WILL PUT THEM IN THE RIGHT FRAME OF MIND...
...TO BATTLE THROUGH THE LONG TOURNAMENT AHEAD OF THEM...
THANK YOU!
CLAP
CLAP
CLAP
CLAP

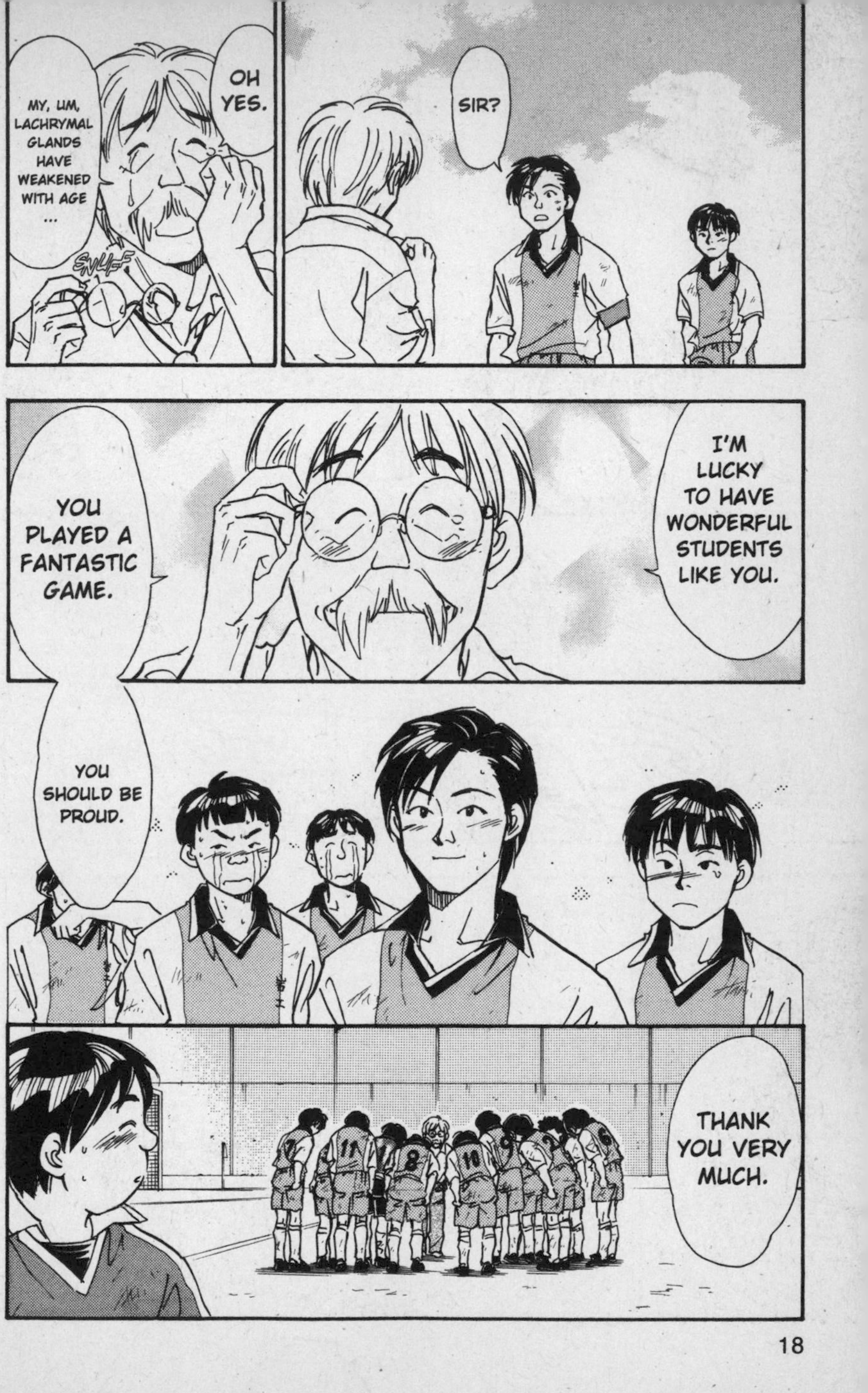
SIR?
OH YES.
MY, UM, LACHRYMAL GLANDS HAVE WEAKENED WITH AGE ...
I'M LUCKY TO HAVE WONDERFUL STUDENTS LIKE YOU.
YOU PLAYED A FANTASTIC GAME.
YOU SHOULD BE PROUD.
THANK YOU VERY MUCH.

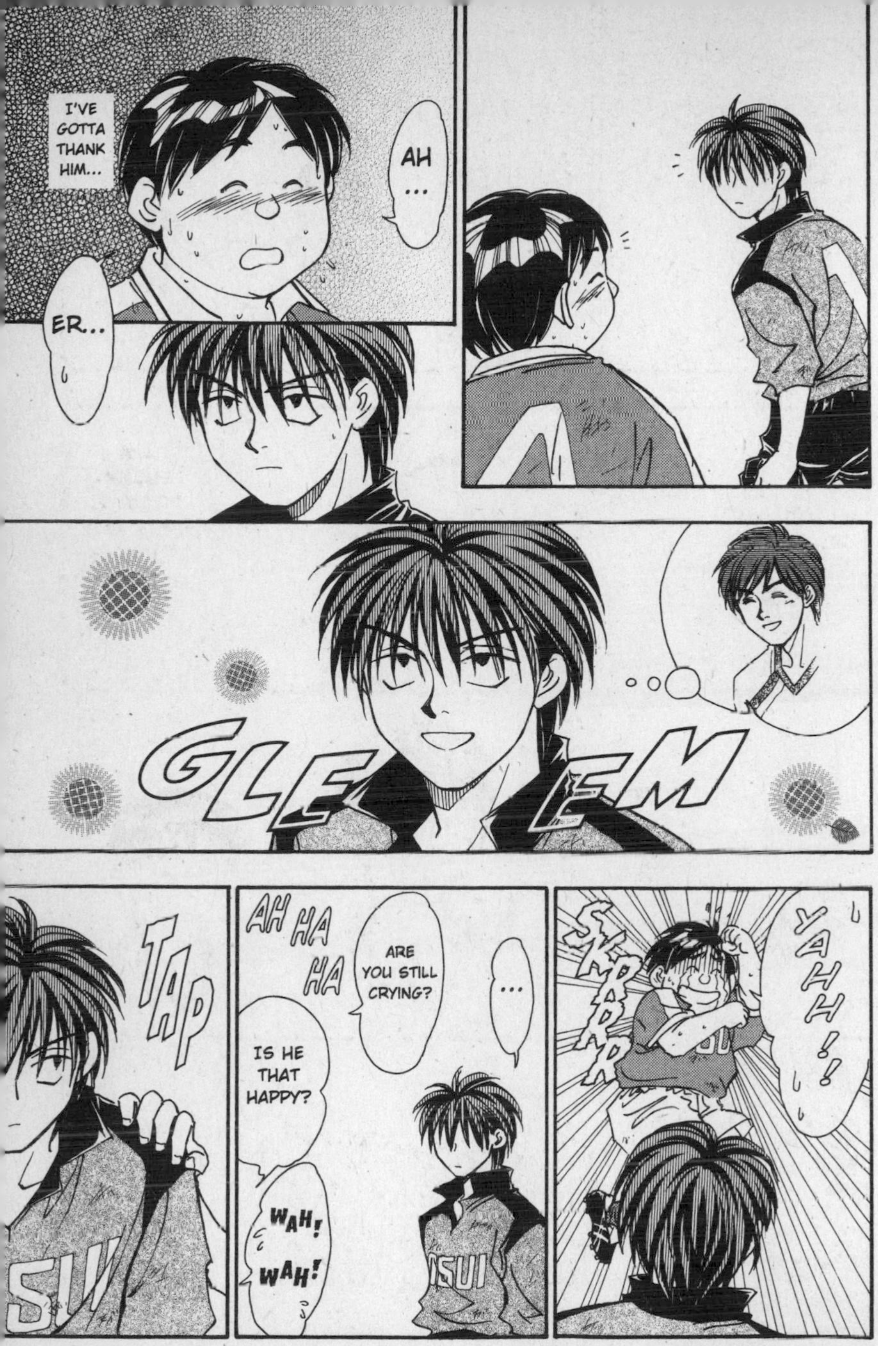
AH ...
I'VE GOTTA THANK HIM...
ER...
GLEEM
YAHH!!
SKRRRR
ARE YOU STILL CRYING?
AH HA HA
...
IS HE THAT HAPPY?
WAH! WAH!
TAP

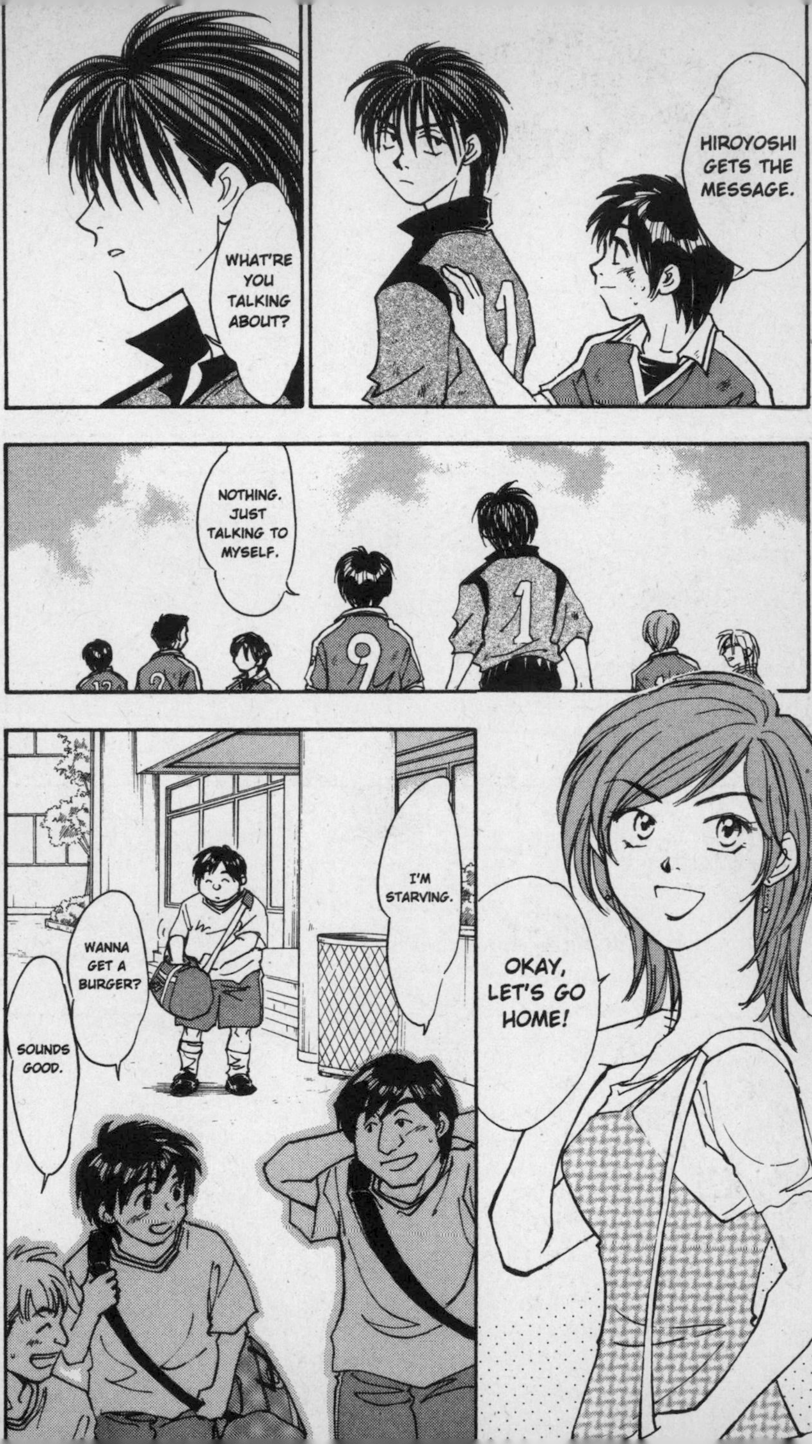
HIROYOSHI GETS THE MESSAGE.
WHAT'RE YOU TALKING ABOUT?
NOTHING. JUST TALKING TO MYSELF.
OKAY, LET'S GO HOME!
I'M STARVING.
WANNA GET A BURGER?
SOUNDS GOOD.

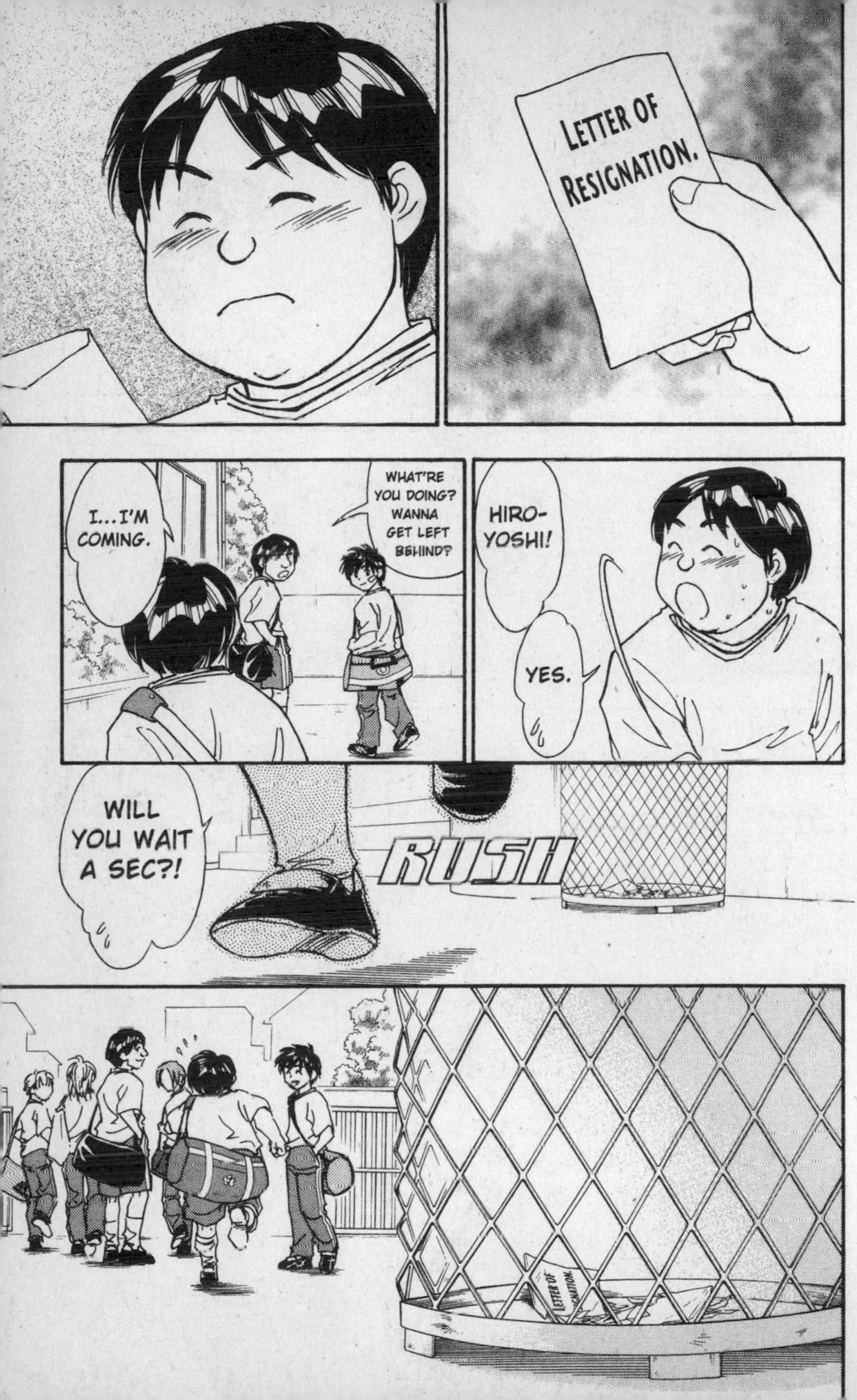
LETTER OF RESIGNATION.
HIRO-YOSHI!
YES.
WHAT'RE YOU DOING? WANNA GET LEFT BEHIND?
I...I'M COMING.
RUSH
WILL YOU WAIT A SEC?!

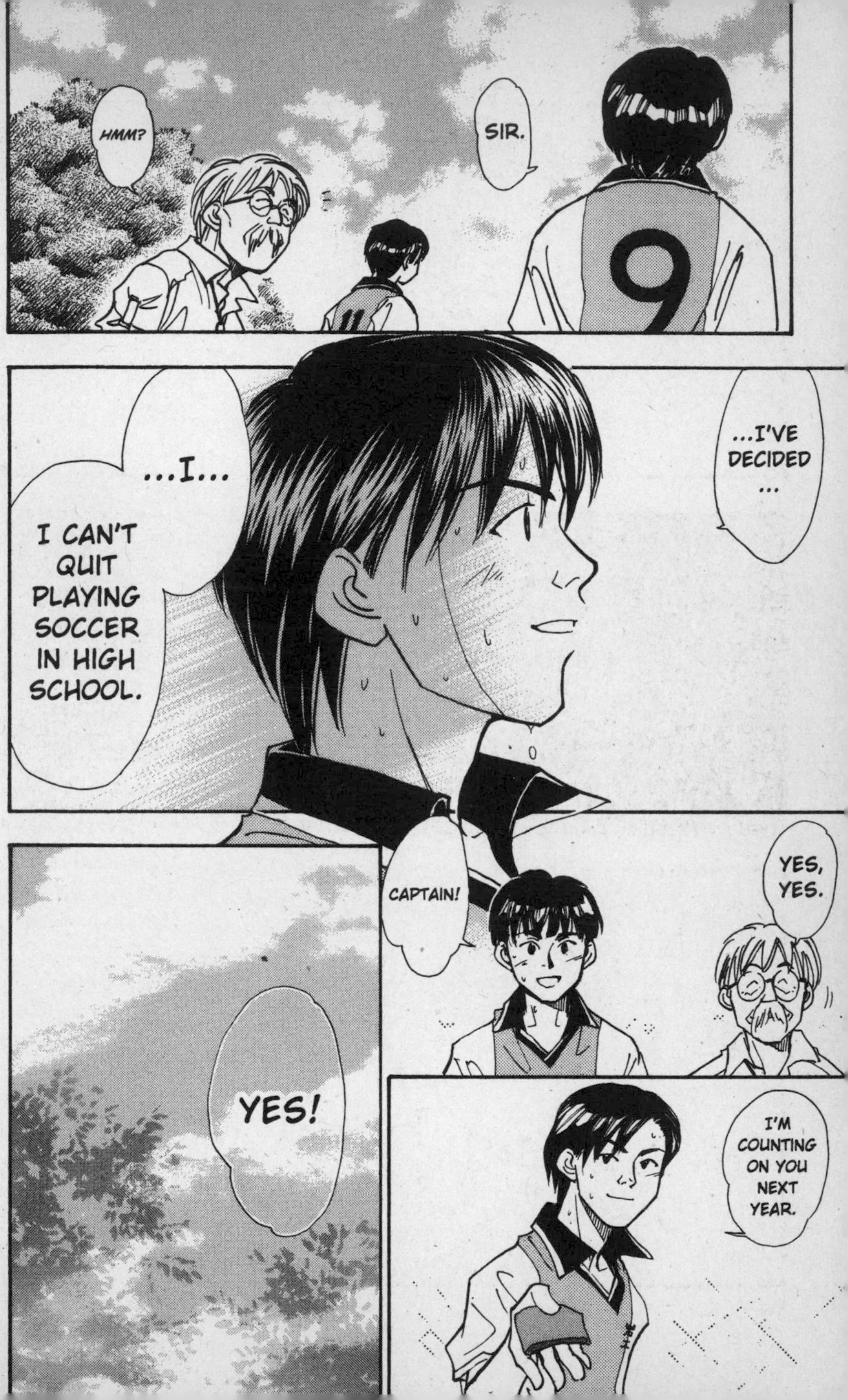
SIR.
HMM?
...I'VE DECIDED ...
...I...
I CAN'T QUIT PLAYING SOCCER IN HIGH SCHOOL.
YES, YES.
CAPTAIN!
I'M COUNTING ON YOU NEXT YEAR.
YES!

READ THIS WAY

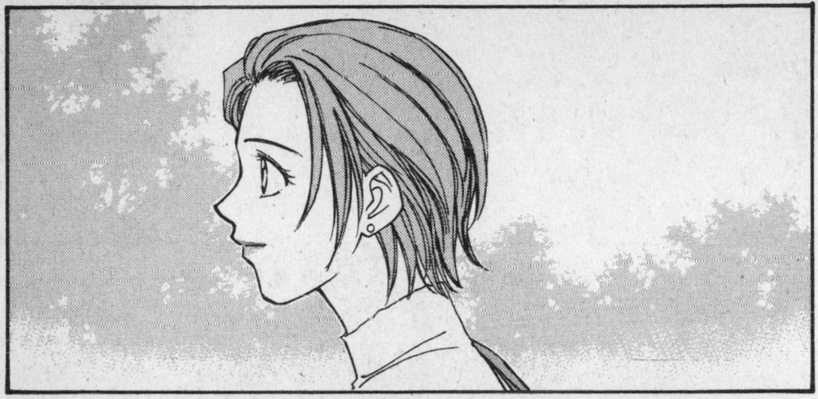

From Stage 63 to 64

Prologue ▷ Dark Clouds

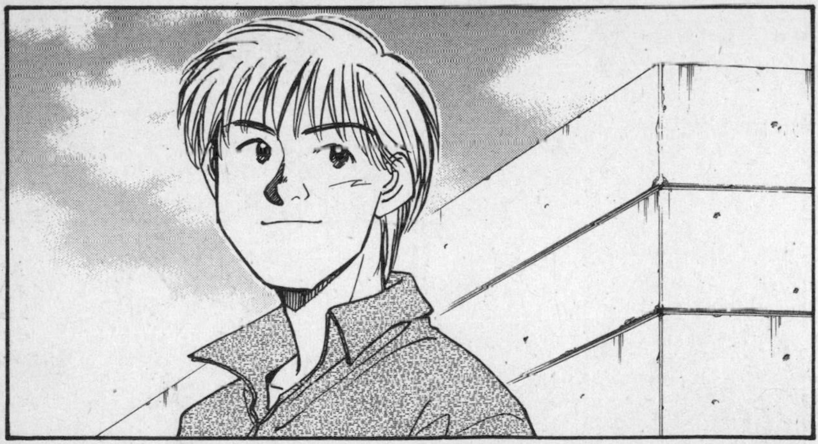

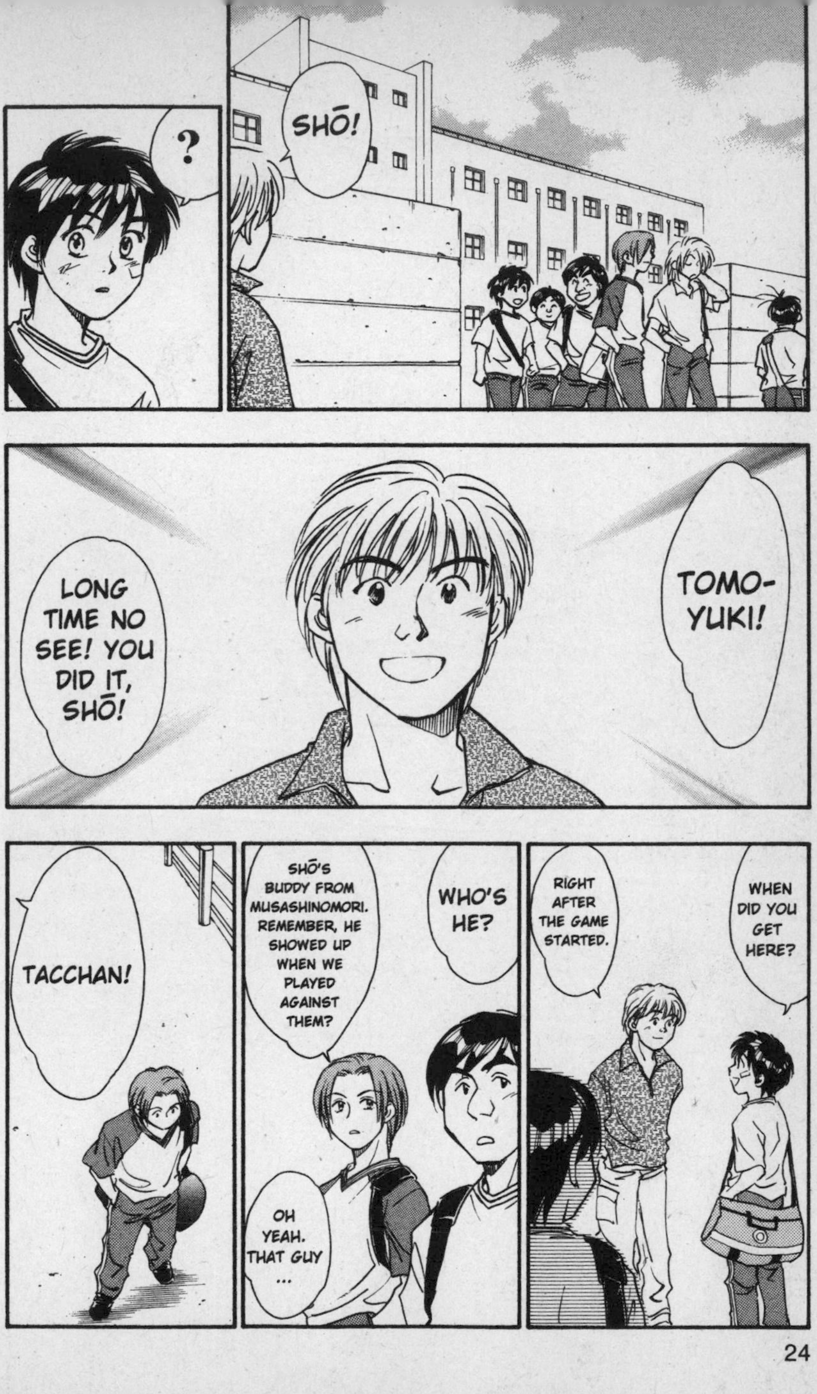
SHŌ!
?
TOMO-YUKI!
LONG TIME NO SEE! YOU DID IT, SHŌ!
WHEN DID YOU GET HERE?
RIGHT AFTER THE GAME STARTED.
WHO'S HE?
SHŌ'S BUDDY FROM MUSASHINOMORI. REMEMBER, HE SHOWED UP WHEN WE PLAYED AGAINST THEM?
OH YEAH. THAT GUY ...
TACCHAN!

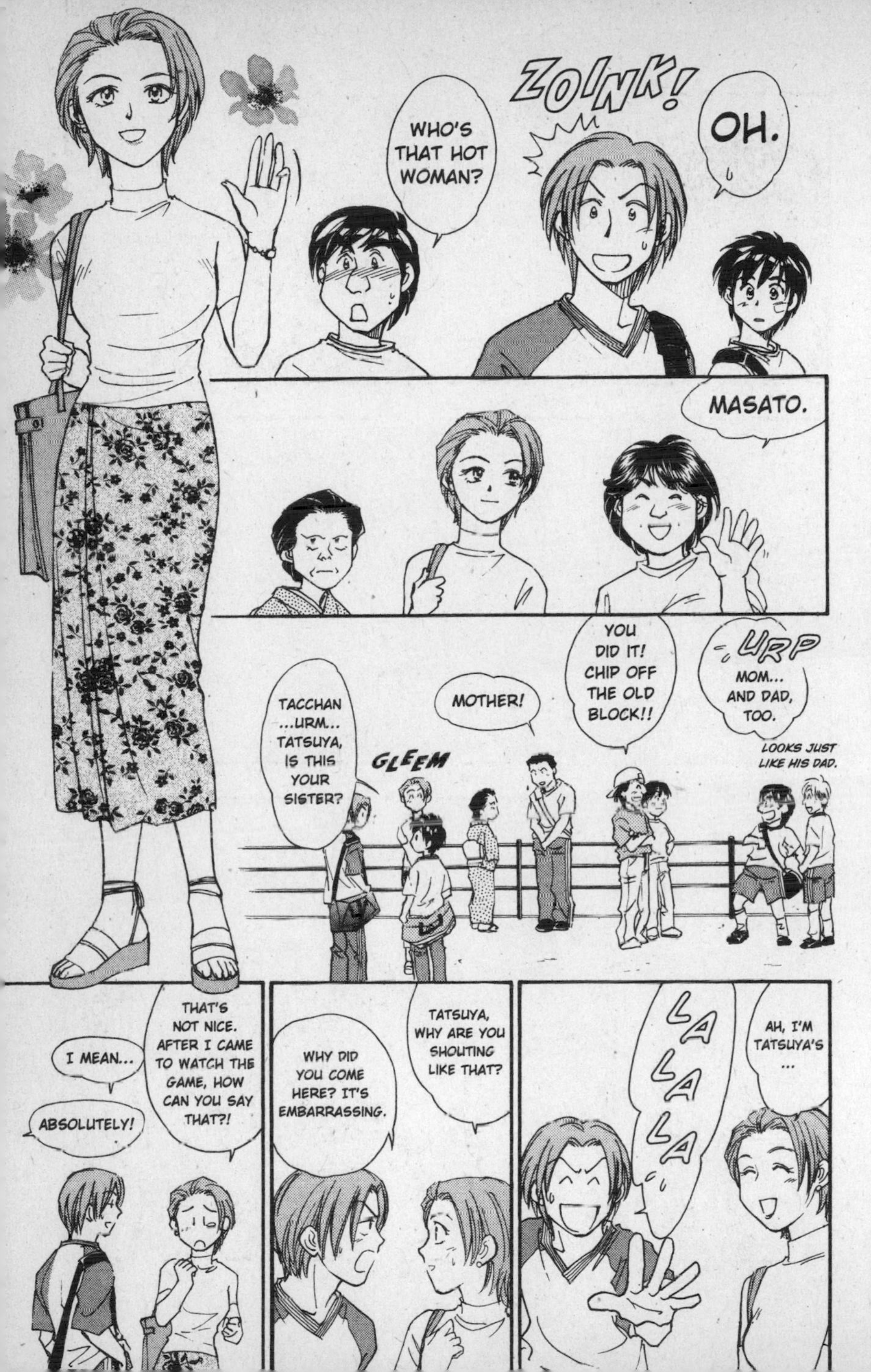
OH.
ZOINK!
WHO'S THAT HOT WOMAN?
MASATO.
URP
MOM... AND DAD, TOO.
LOOKS JUST LIKE HIS DAD.
YOU DID IT! CHIP OFF THE OLD BLOCK!!
MOTHER!
GLEEM
TACCHAN ...URM... TATSUYA, IS THIS YOUR SISTER?
AH, I'M TATSUYA'S ...
LA LA LA LA
TATSUYA, WHY ARE YOU SHOUTING LIKE THAT?
WHY DID YOU COME HERE? IT'S EMBARRASSING.
THAT'S NOT NICE. AFTER I CAME TO WATCH THE GAME, HOW CAN YOU SAY THAT?!
I MEAN...
ABSOLUTELY!

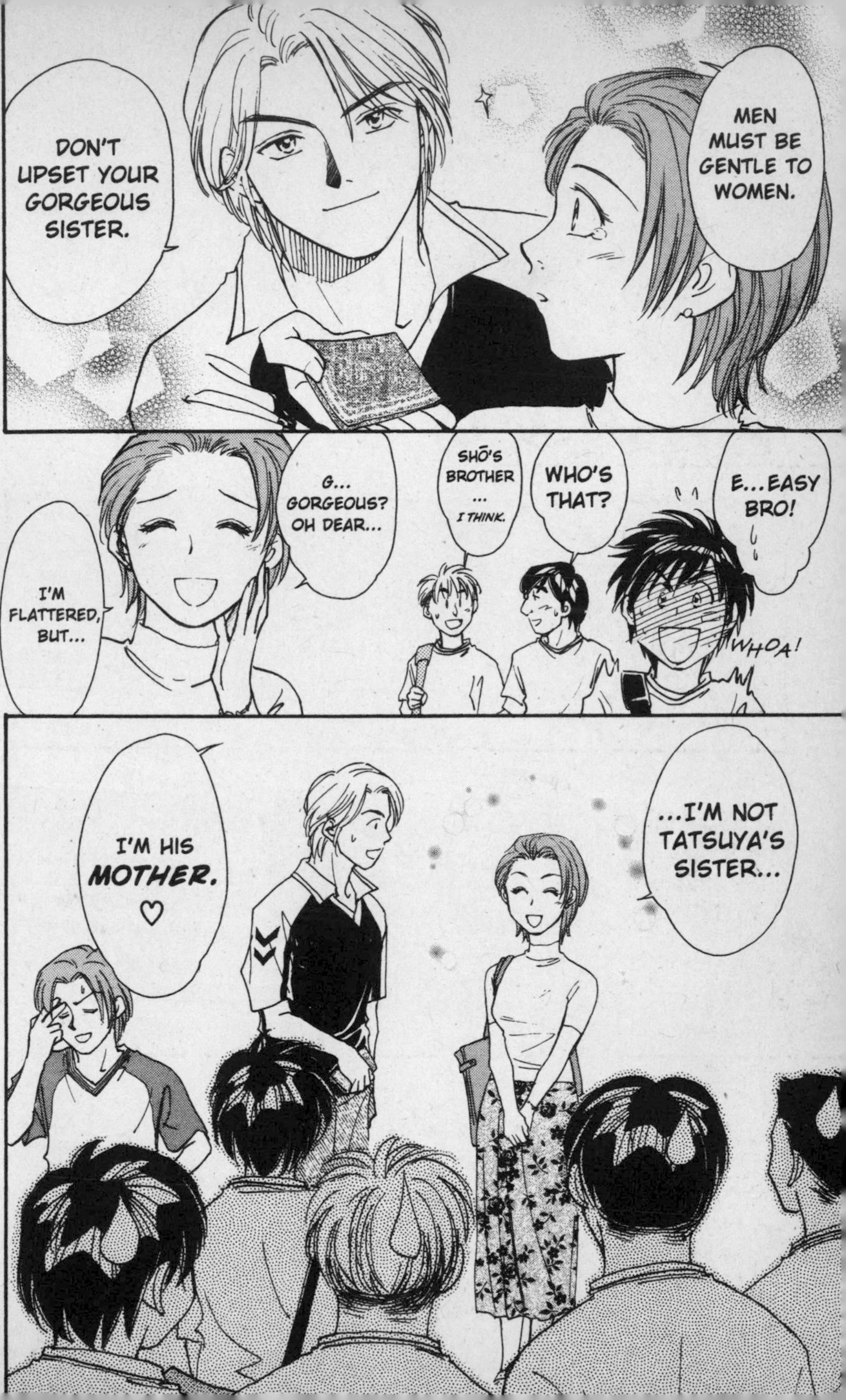
MEN MUST BE GENTLE TO WOMEN.
DON'T UPSET YOUR GORGEOUS SISTER.
E...EASY BRO!
WHOA!
WHO'S THAT?
SHŌ'S BROTHER ... I THINK.
G... GORGEOUS? OH DEAR...
I'M FLATTERED, BUT...
...I'M NOT TATSUYA'S SISTER...
I'M HIS *MOTHER.* ♡

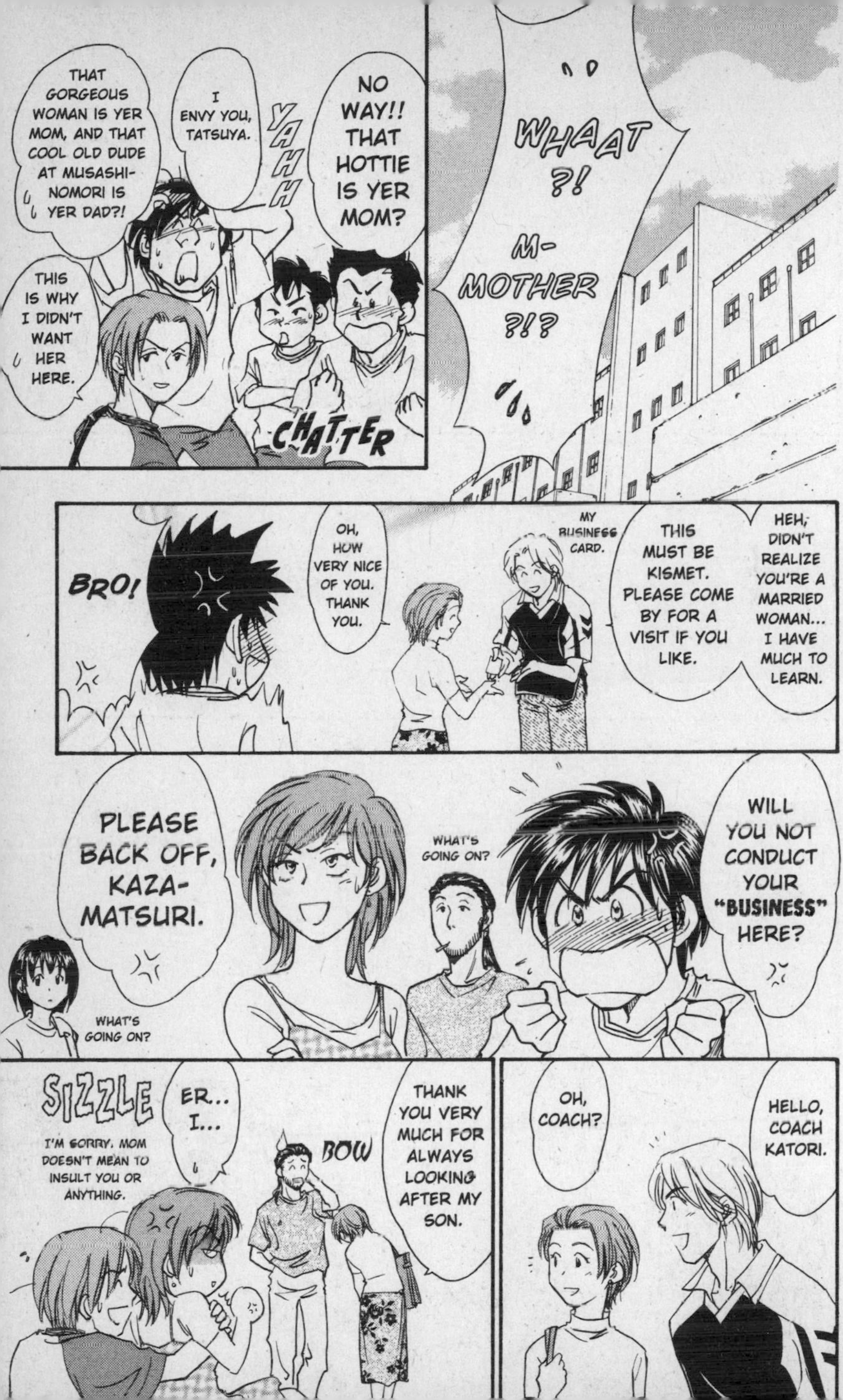
WHAAAT ?!
M-MOTHER ?!?
NO WAY!! THAT HOTTIE IS YER MOM?
YAHHH
I ENVY YOU, TATSUYA.
THAT GORGEOUS WOMAN IS YER MOM, AND THAT COOL OLD DUDE AT MUSASHI-NOMORI IS YER DAD?!
THIS IS WHY I DIDN'T WANT HER HERE.
CHATTER
HEH, DIDN'T REALIZE YOU'RE A MARRIED WOMAN... I HAVE MUCH TO LEARN.
THIS MUST BE KISMET. PLEASE COME BY FOR A VISIT IF YOU LIKE.
MY BUSINESS CARD.
OH, HOW VERY NICE OF YOU. THANK YOU.
BRO!
WILL YOU NOT CONDUCT YOUR "BUSINESS" HERE?
WHAT'S GOING ON?
PLEASE BACK OFF, KAZA-MATSURI.
WHAT'S GOING ON?
HELLO, COACH KATORI.
OH, COACH?
THANK YOU VERY MUCH FOR ALWAYS LOOKING AFTER MY SON.
BOW
ER... I...
SIZZLE
I'M SORRY. MOM DOESN'T MEAN TO INSULT YOU OR ANYTHING.

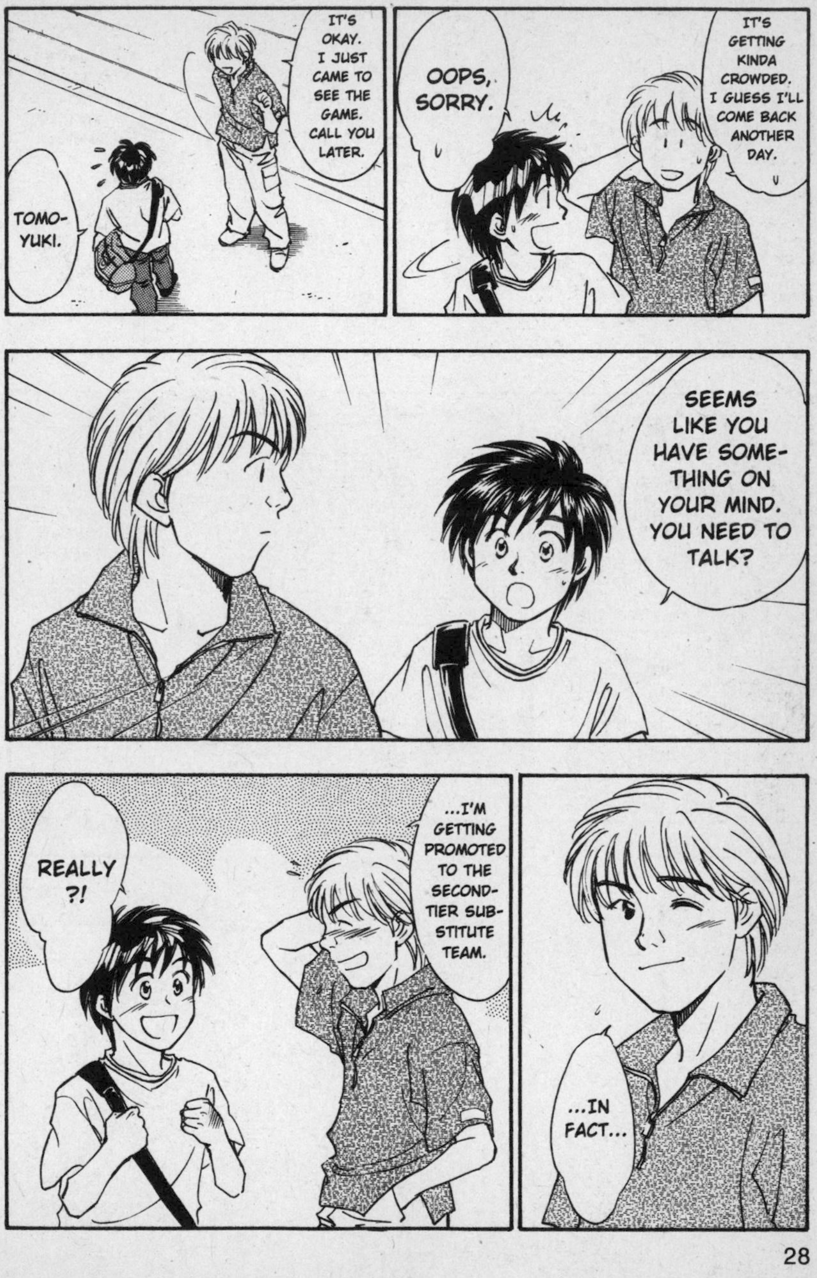
IT'S GETTING KINDA CROWDED. I GUESS I'LL COME BACK ANOTHER DAY.
OOPS, SORRY.
IT'S OKAY. I JUST CAME TO SEE THE GAME. CALL YOU LATER.
TOMO-YUKI.
SEEMS LIKE YOU HAVE SOME-THING ON YOUR MIND. YOU NEED TO TALK?
...IN FACT...
...I'M GETTING PROMOTED TO THE SECOND-TIER SUB-STITUTE TEAM.
REALLY ?!

READ THIS WAY

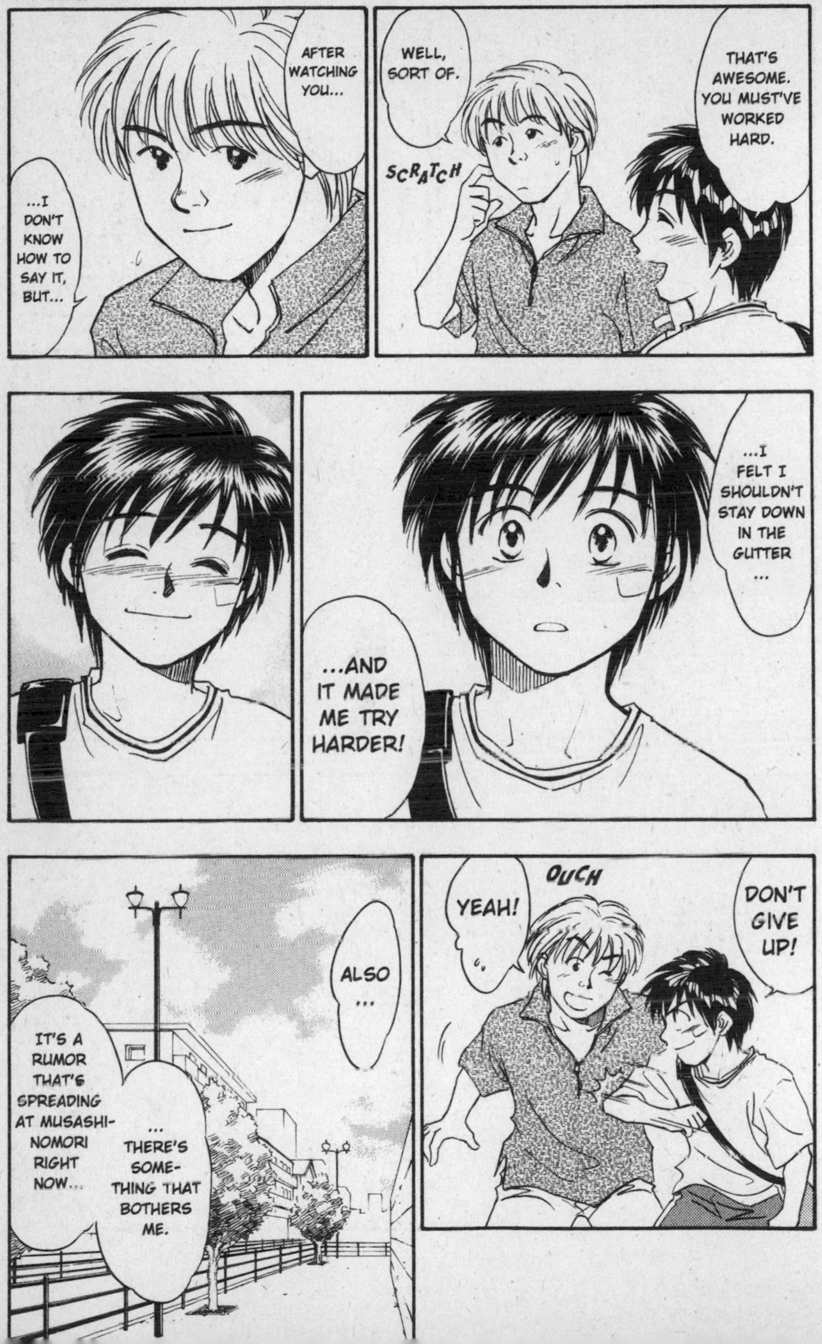

THAT'S AWESOME. YOU MUST'VE WORKED HARD.
WELL, SORT OF.
SCRATCH
AFTER WATCHING YOU...
...I DON'T KNOW HOW TO SAY IT, BUT...
...I FELT I SHOULDN'T STAY DOWN IN THE GUTTER ...
...AND IT MADE ME TRY HARDER!
DON'T GIVE UP!
OUCH
YEAH!
ALSO ...
... THERE'S SOME-THING THAT BOTHERS ME.
IT'S A RUMOR THAT'S SPREADING AT MUSASHI-NOMORI RIGHT NOW...

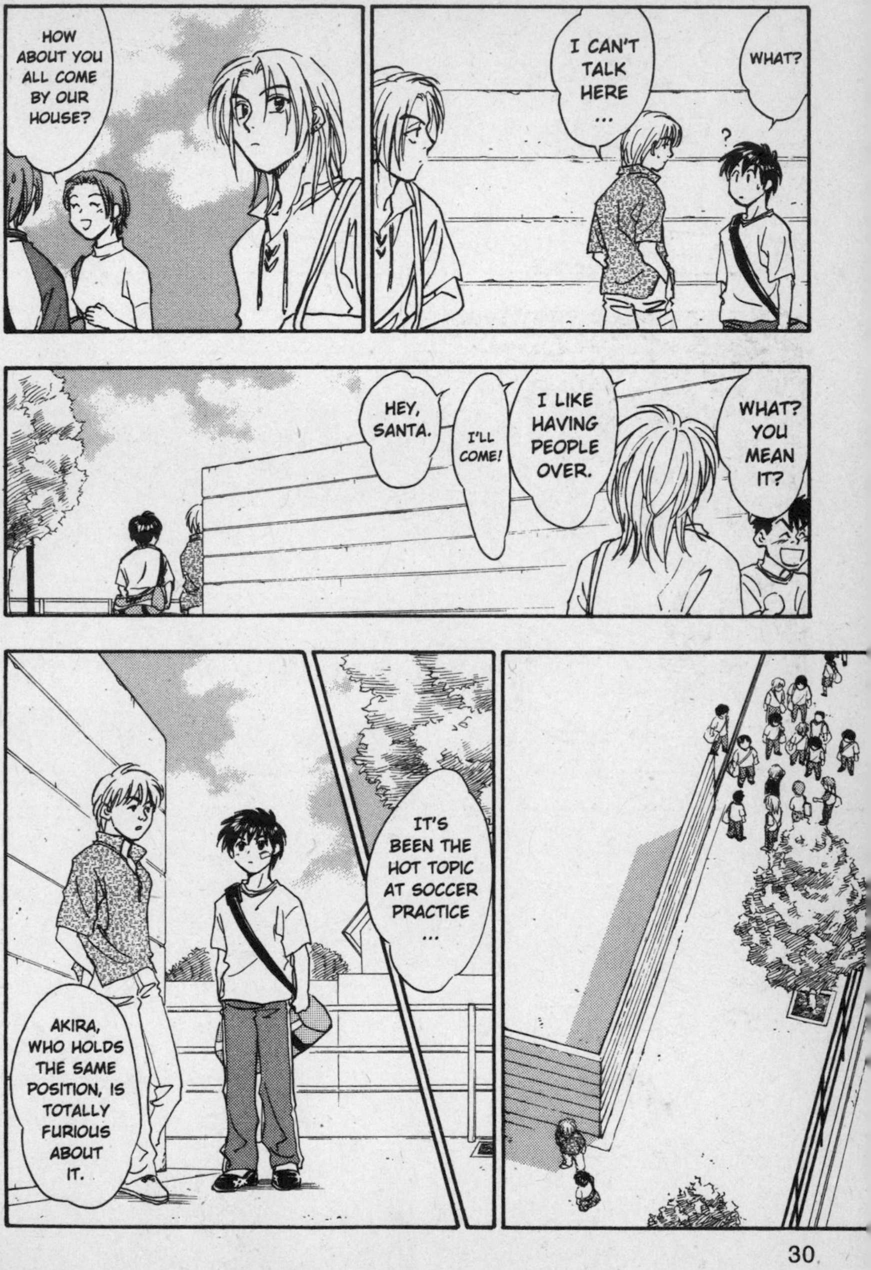
WHAT?
I CAN'T TALK HERE ...
HOW ABOUT YOU ALL COME BY OUR HOUSE?
WHAT? YOU MEAN IT?
I LIKE HAVING PEOPLE OVER.
I'LL COME!
HEY, SANTA.
IT'S BEEN THE HOT TOPIC AT SOCCER PRACTICE ...
AKIRA, WHO HOLDS THE SAME POSITION, IS TOTALLY FURIOUS ABOUT IT.

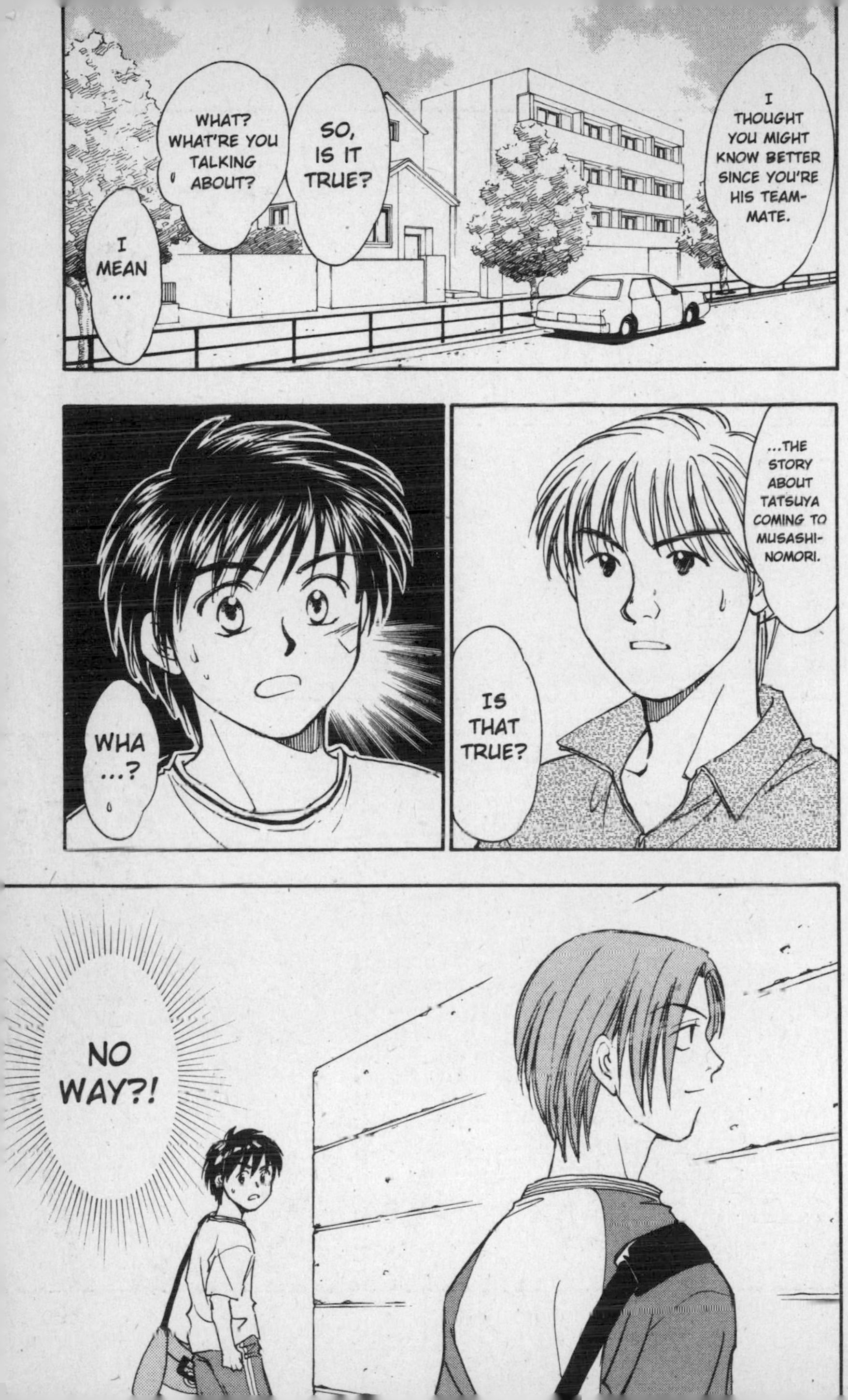
I THOUGHT YOU MIGHT KNOW BETTER SINCE YOU'RE HIS TEAM-MATE.
SO, IS IT TRUE?
WHAT? WHAT'RE YOU TALKING ABOUT?
I MEAN ...
...THE STORY ABOUT TATSUYA COMING TO MUSASHI-NOMORI.
IS THAT TRUE?
WHA ...?
NO WAY?!

◆ A few words from Daisuke Higuchi ◆

IN VOLUME 7, IN THE CHARACTER PROFILES, THE NAMES OF THE TWO PLAYERS FROM IWA TECH WERE MISSING. I'M SORRY. THEY'RE ***SATORU OGATA*** AND ***MASASHI HAYANO***. AND, A WORD ON THE VOLUME TITLE. I'VE BORROWED TITLES FROM MY FAVORITE SONGS OR USED SOME SOCCER TERMS SO FAR, BUT THIS TIME, I TRIED SOMETHING DIFFERENT. "RAINING CATS AND DOGS" MEANS "POURING RAIN."

WHISTLE!

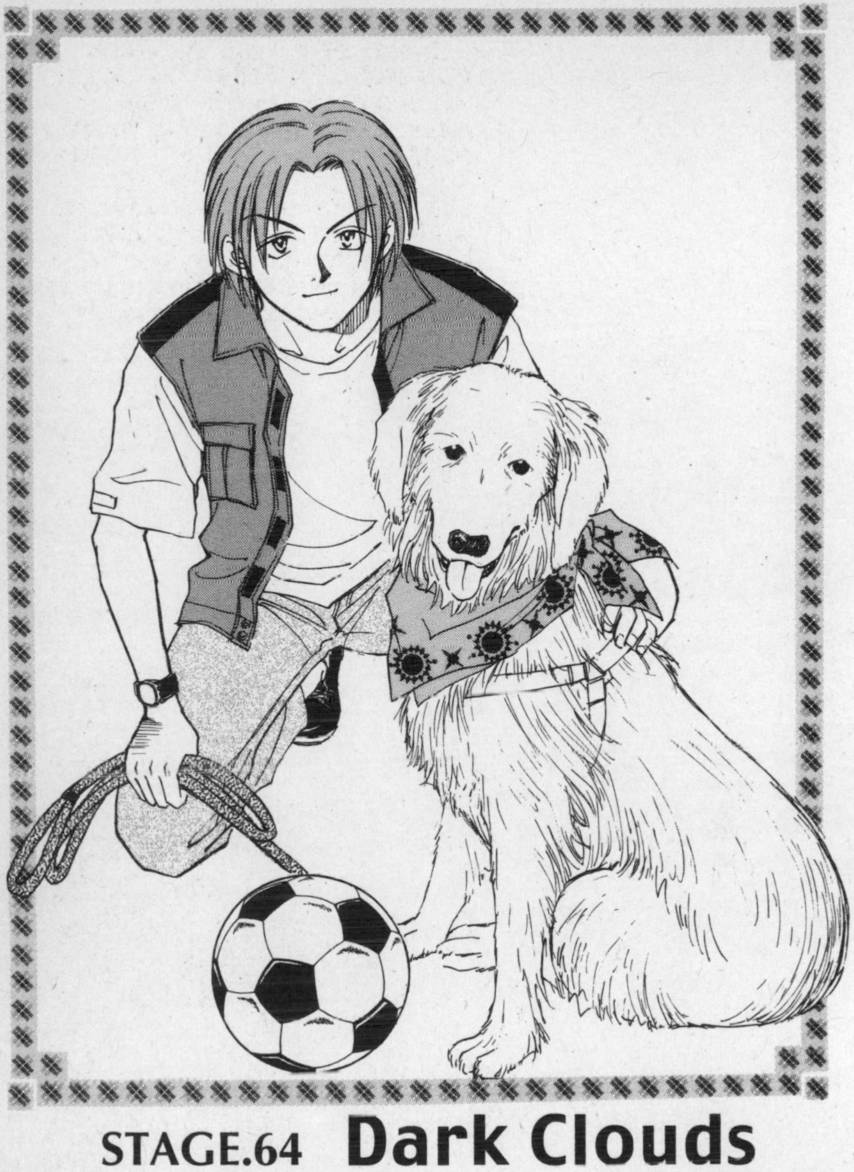

STAGE.64 Dark Clouds

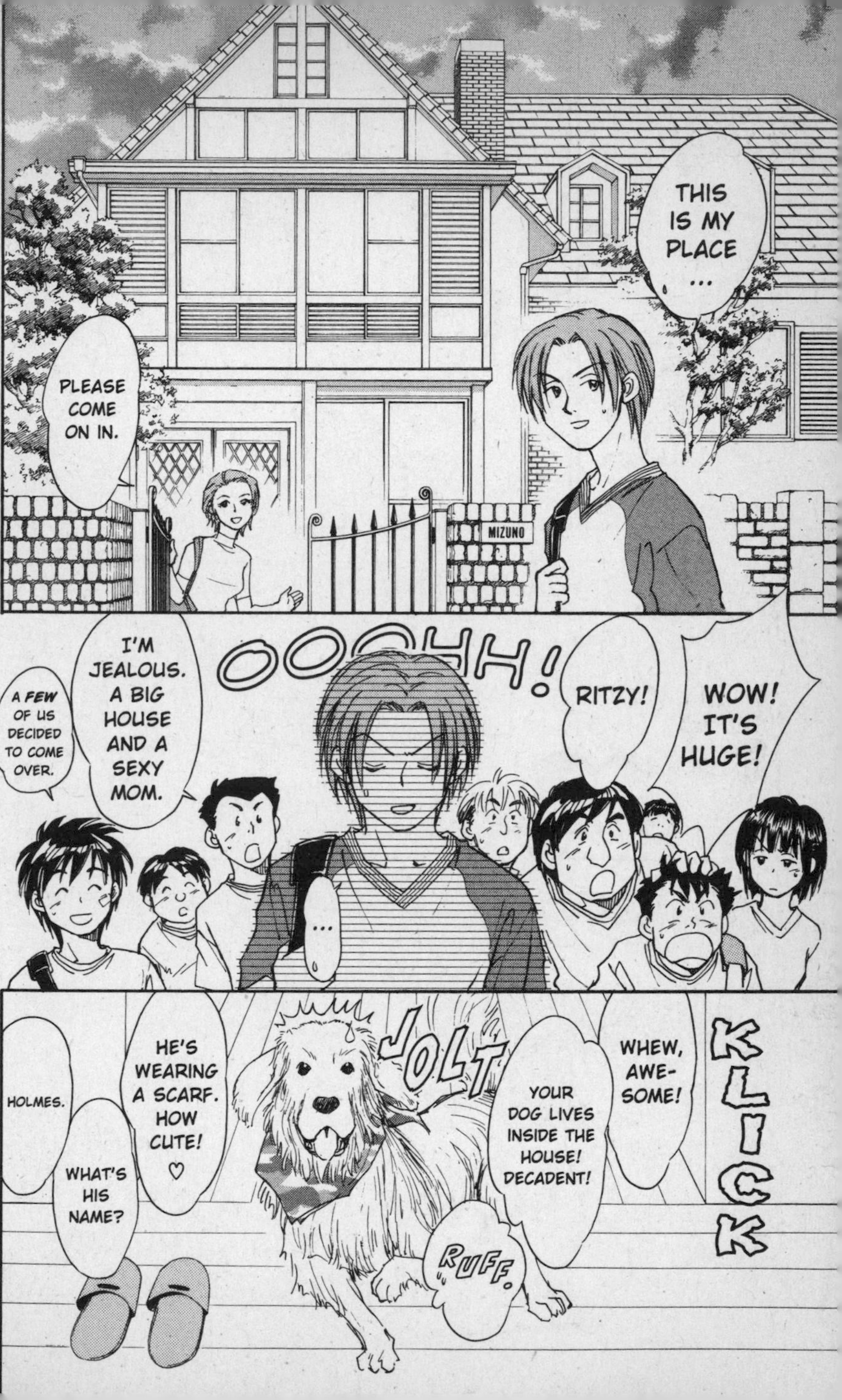
THIS IS MY PLACE ...
MIZUNO
PLEASE COME ON IN.
WOW! IT'S HUGE!
RITZY!
OOOHH!
I'M JEALOUS. A BIG HOUSE AND A SEXY MOM.
A *FEW* OF US DECIDED TO COME OVER.
...
KLICK
WHEW, AWE-SOME!
YOUR DOG LIVES INSIDE THE HOUSE! DECADENT!
JOLT
RUFF.
HE'S WEARING A SCARF. HOW CUTE! ♡
WHAT'S HIS NAME?
HOLMES.

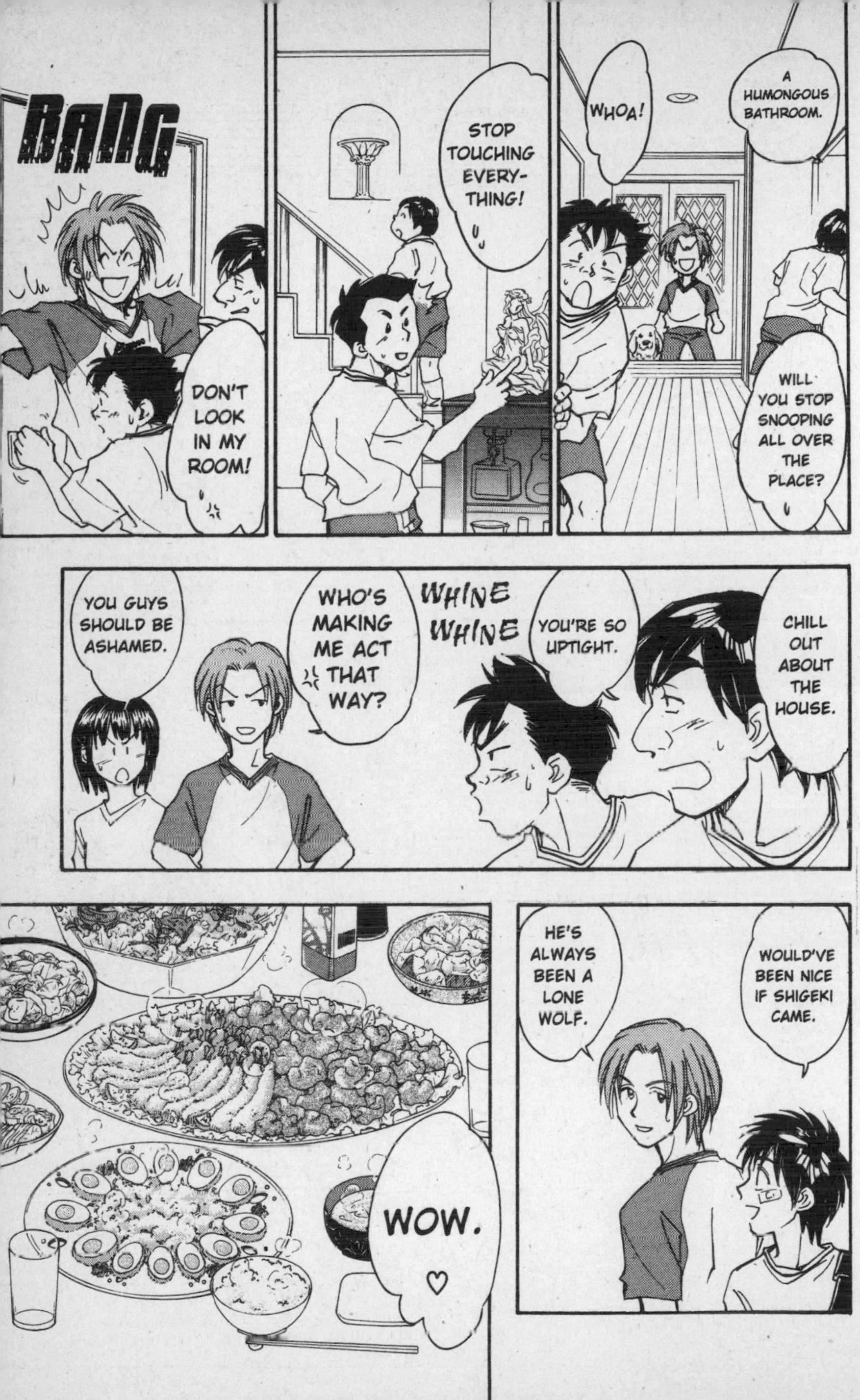
A HUMONGOUS BATHROOM.
WHOA!
WILL YOU STOP SNOOPING ALL OVER THE PLACE?
STOP TOUCHING EVERY-THING!
BANG
DON'T LOOK IN MY ROOM!
CHILL OUT ABOUT THE HOUSE.
YOU'RE SO UPTIGHT.
WHINE WHINE
WHO'S MAKING ME ACT THAT WAY?
YOU GUYS SHOULD BE ASHAMED.
WOULD'VE BEEN NICE IF SHIGEKI CAME.
HE'S ALWAYS BEEN A LONE WOLF.
WOW. ♡

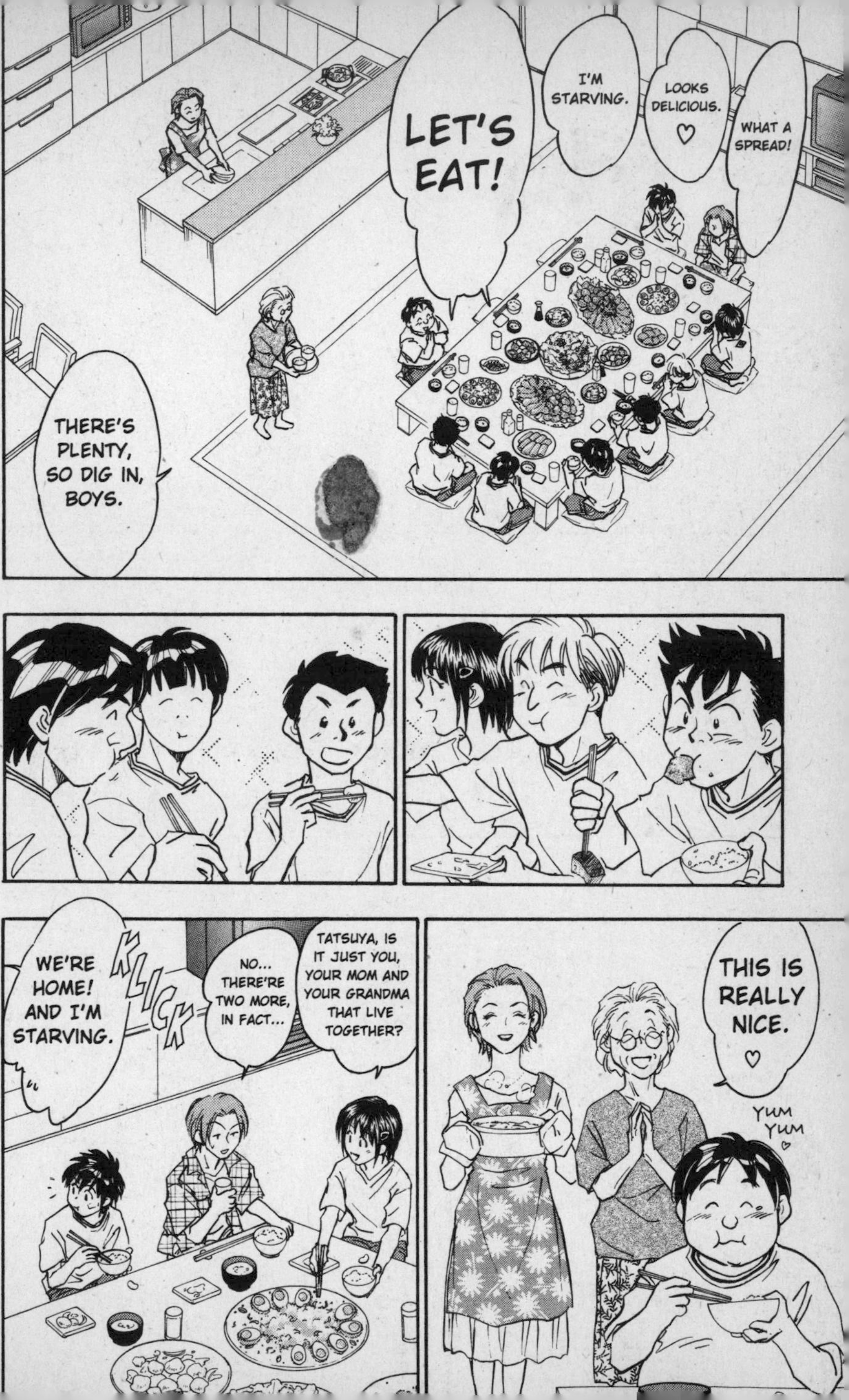
WHAT A SPREAD!
LOOKS DELICIOUS. ♡
I'M STARVING.
LET'S EAT!
THERE'S PLENTY, SO DIG IN, BOYS.
THIS IS REALLY NICE. ♡
YUM YUM ♡
TATSUYA, IS IT JUST YOU, YOUR MOM AND YOUR GRANDMA THAT LIVE TOGETHER?
NO... THERE'RE TWO MORE, IN FACT...
KLICK
WE'RE HOME! AND I'M STARVING.

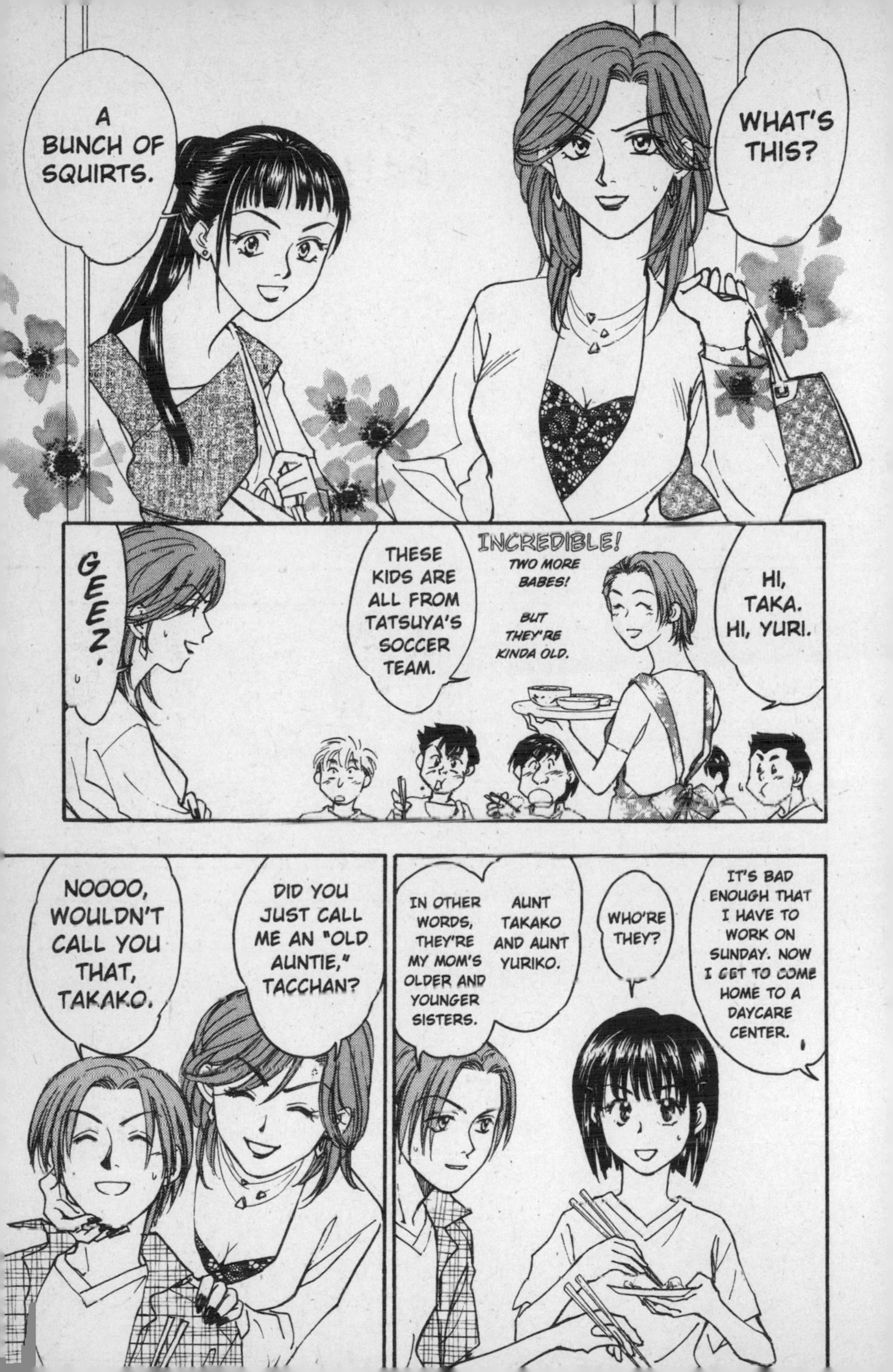
WHAT'S THIS?
A BUNCH OF SQUIRTS.
HI, TAKA. HI, YURI.
INCREDIBLE!
TWO MORE BABES!
BUT THEY'RE KINDA OLD.
THESE KIDS ARE ALL FROM TATSUYA'S SOCCER TEAM.
GEEZ.
IT'S BAD ENOUGH THAT I HAVE TO WORK ON SUNDAY. NOW I GET TO COME HOME TO A DAYCARE CENTER.
WHO'RE THEY?
AUNT TAKAKO AND AUNT YURIKO.
IN OTHER WORDS, THEY'RE MY MOM'S OLDER AND YOUNGER SISTERS.
DID YOU JUST CALL ME AN "OLD AUNTIE," TACCHAN?
NOOOO, WOULDN'T CALL YOU THAT, TAKAKO.

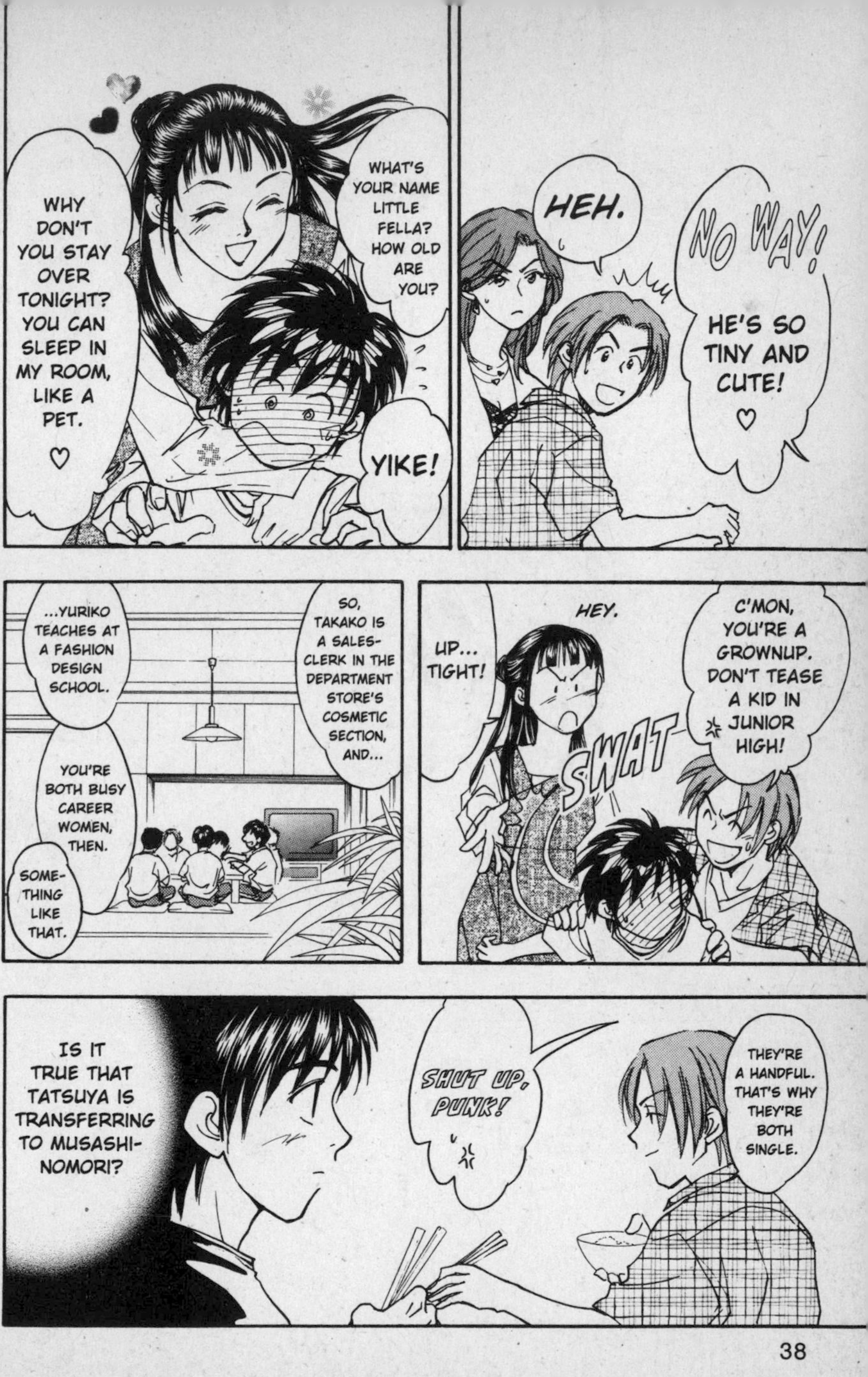
NO WAY!
HE'S SO TINY AND CUTE! ♡
HEH.
WHAT'S YOUR NAME LITTLE FELLA? HOW OLD ARE YOU?
WHY DON'T YOU STAY OVER TONIGHT? YOU CAN SLEEP IN MY ROOM, LIKE A PET. ♡
YIKE!
C'MON, YOU'RE A GROWNUP. DON'T TEASE A KID IN JUNIOR HIGH!
HEY.
UP... TIGHT!
SWAT
SO, TAKAKO IS A SALES-CLERK IN THE DEPARTMENT STORE'S COSMETIC SECTION, AND...
...YURIKO TEACHES AT A FASHION DESIGN SCHOOL.
YOU'RE BOTH BUSY CAREER WOMEN, THEN.
SOME-THING LIKE THAT.
THEY'RE A HANDFUL. THAT'S WHY THEY'RE BOTH SINGLE.
SHUT UP, PUNK!
IS IT TRUE THAT TATSUYA IS TRANSFERRING TO MUSASHI-NOMORI?

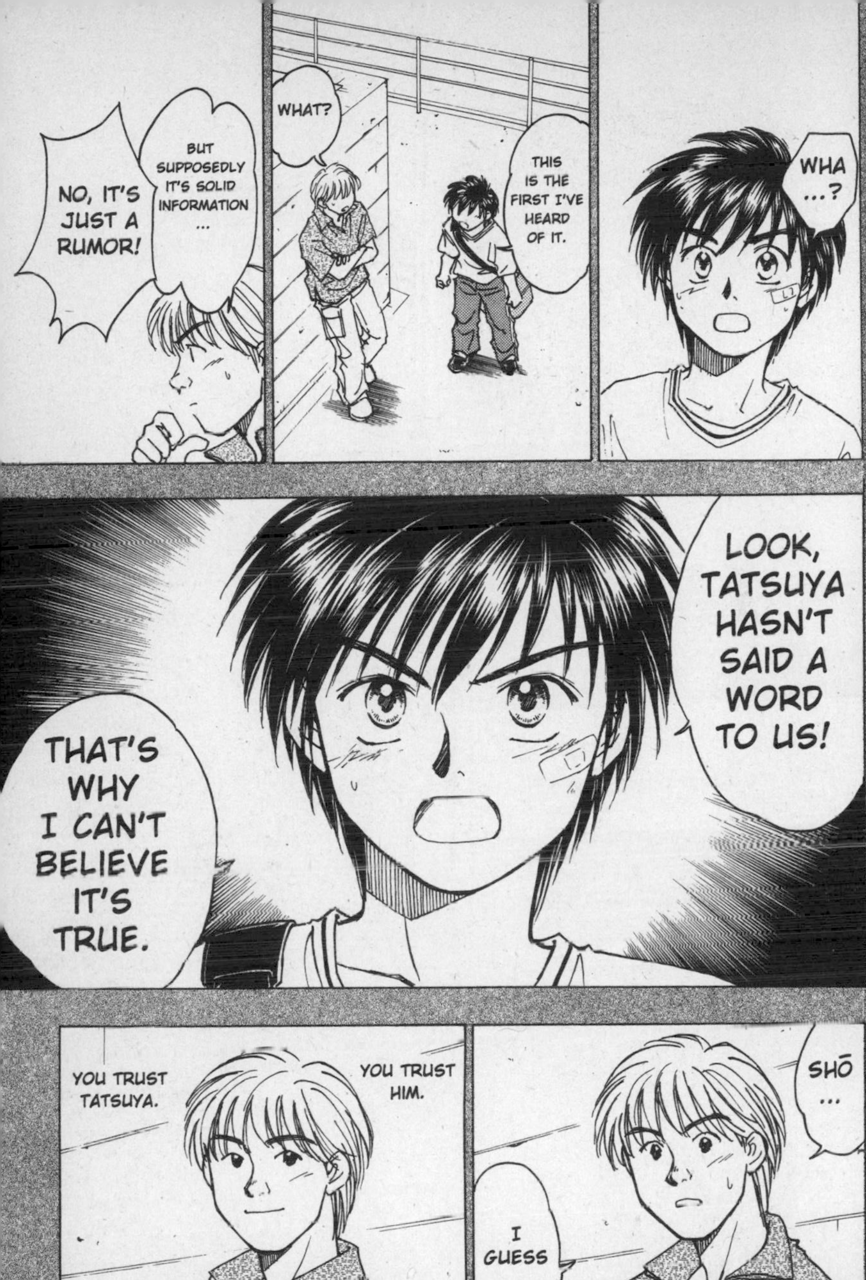
WHA ...?
THIS IS THE FIRST I'VE HEARD OF IT.
WHAT?
BUT SUPPOSEDLY IT'S SOLID INFORMATION ...
NO, IT'S JUST A RUMOR!
LOOK, TATSUYA HASN'T SAID A WORD TO US!
THAT'S WHY I CAN'T BELIEVE IT'S TRUE.
SHŌ ...
I GUESS ...
YOU TRUST HIM.
YOU TRUST TATSUYA.

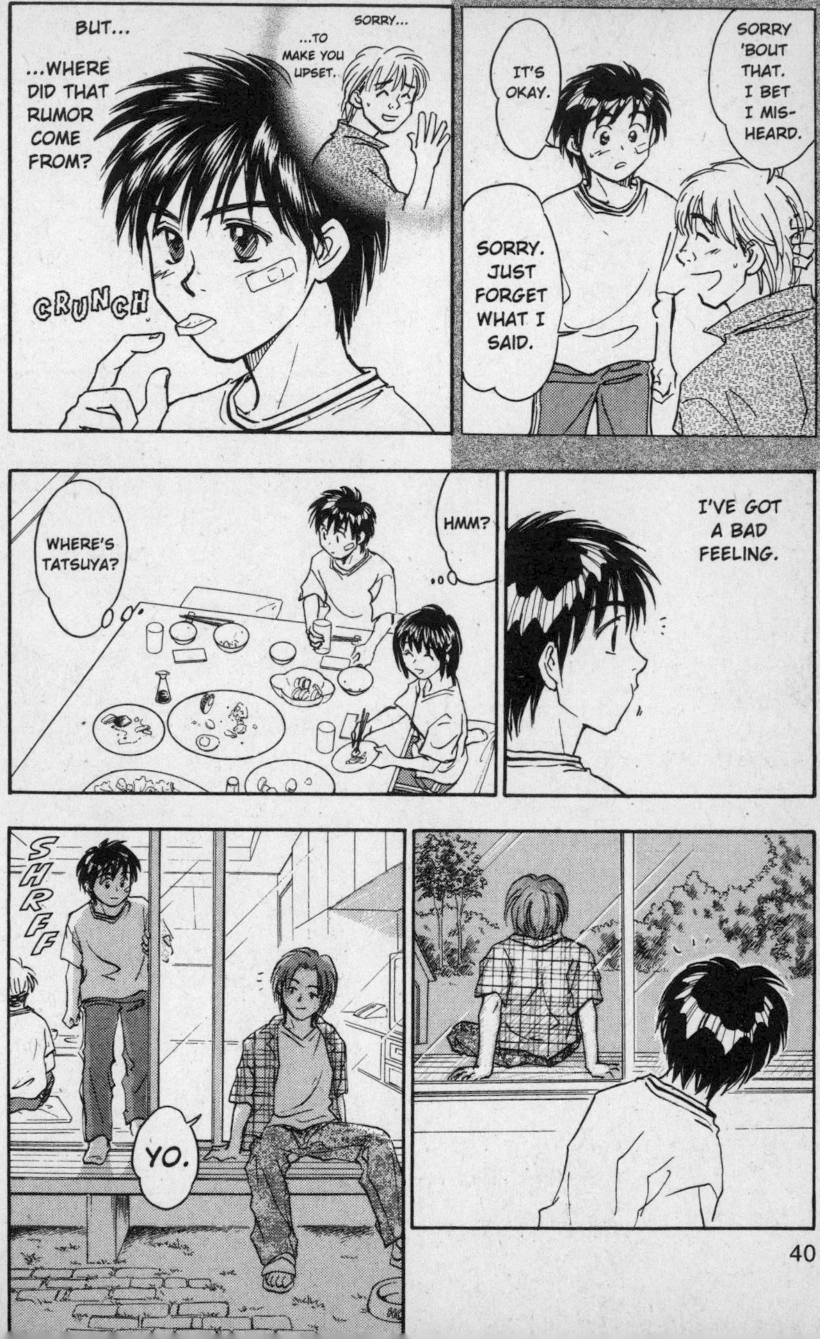
SORRY 'BOUT THAT. I BET I MIS-HEARD.
IT'S OKAY.
SORRY. JUST FORGET WHAT I SAID.
SORRY...
...TO MAKE YOU UPSET.
BUT...
...WHERE DID THAT RUMOR COME FROM?
CRUNCH
I'VE GOT A BAD FEELING.
HMM?
WHERE'S TATSUYA?
SHRFF
YO.

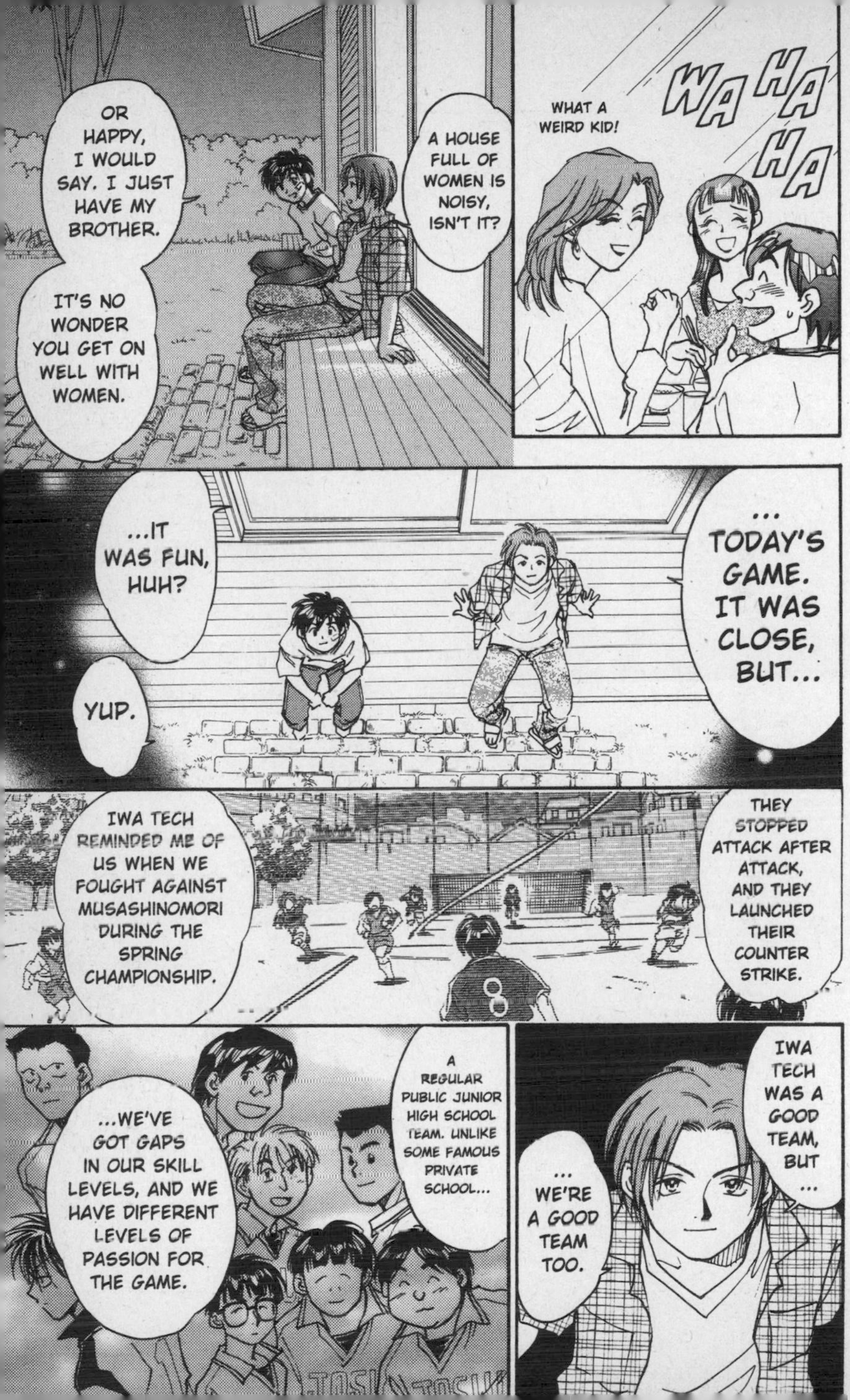
WAHAHAHA
WHAT A WEIRD KID!
A HOUSE FULL OF WOMEN IS NOISY, ISN'T IT?
OR HAPPY, I WOULD SAY. I JUST HAVE MY BROTHER.
IT'S NO WONDER YOU GET ON WELL WITH WOMEN.
... TODAY'S GAME. IT WAS CLOSE, BUT...
...IT WAS FUN, HUH?
YUP.
THEY STOPPED ATTACK AFTER ATTACK, AND THEY LAUNCHED THEIR COUNTER STRIKE.
IWA TECH REMINDED ME OF US WHEN WE FOUGHT AGAINST MUSASHINOMORI DURING THE SPRING CHAMPIONSHIP.
IWA TECH WAS A GOOD TEAM, BUT ...
... WE'RE A GOOD TEAM TOO.
A REGULAR PUBLIC JUNIOR HIGH SCHOOL TEAM. UNLIKE SOME FAMOUS PRIVATE SCHOOL...
...WE'VE GOT GAPS IN OUR SKILL LEVELS, AND WE HAVE DIFFERENT LEVELS OF PASSION FOR THE GAME.

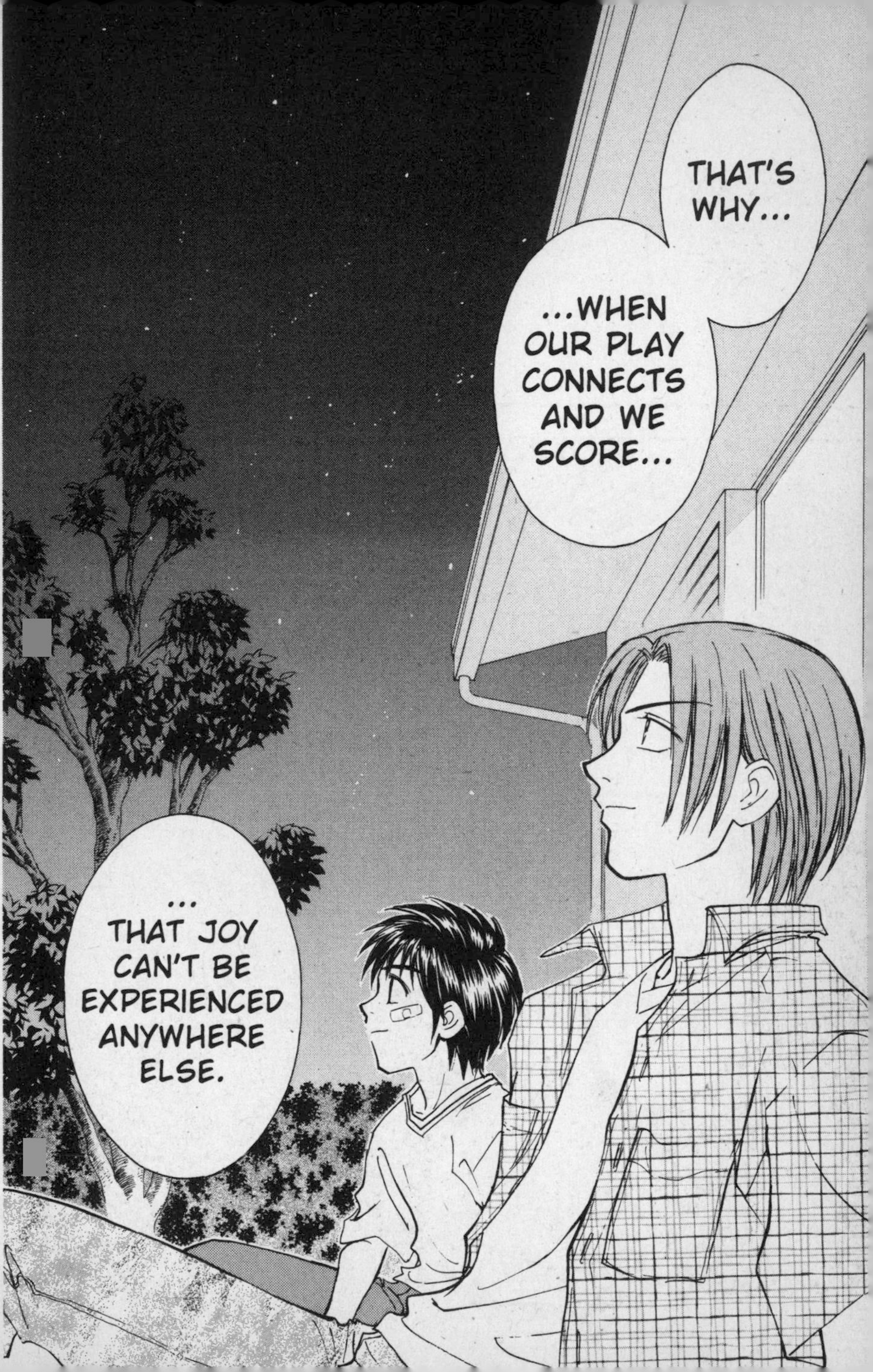
THAT'S WHY...
...WHEN OUR PLAY CONNECTS AND WE SCORE...
...THAT JOY CAN'T BE EXPERIENCED ANYWHERE ELSE.

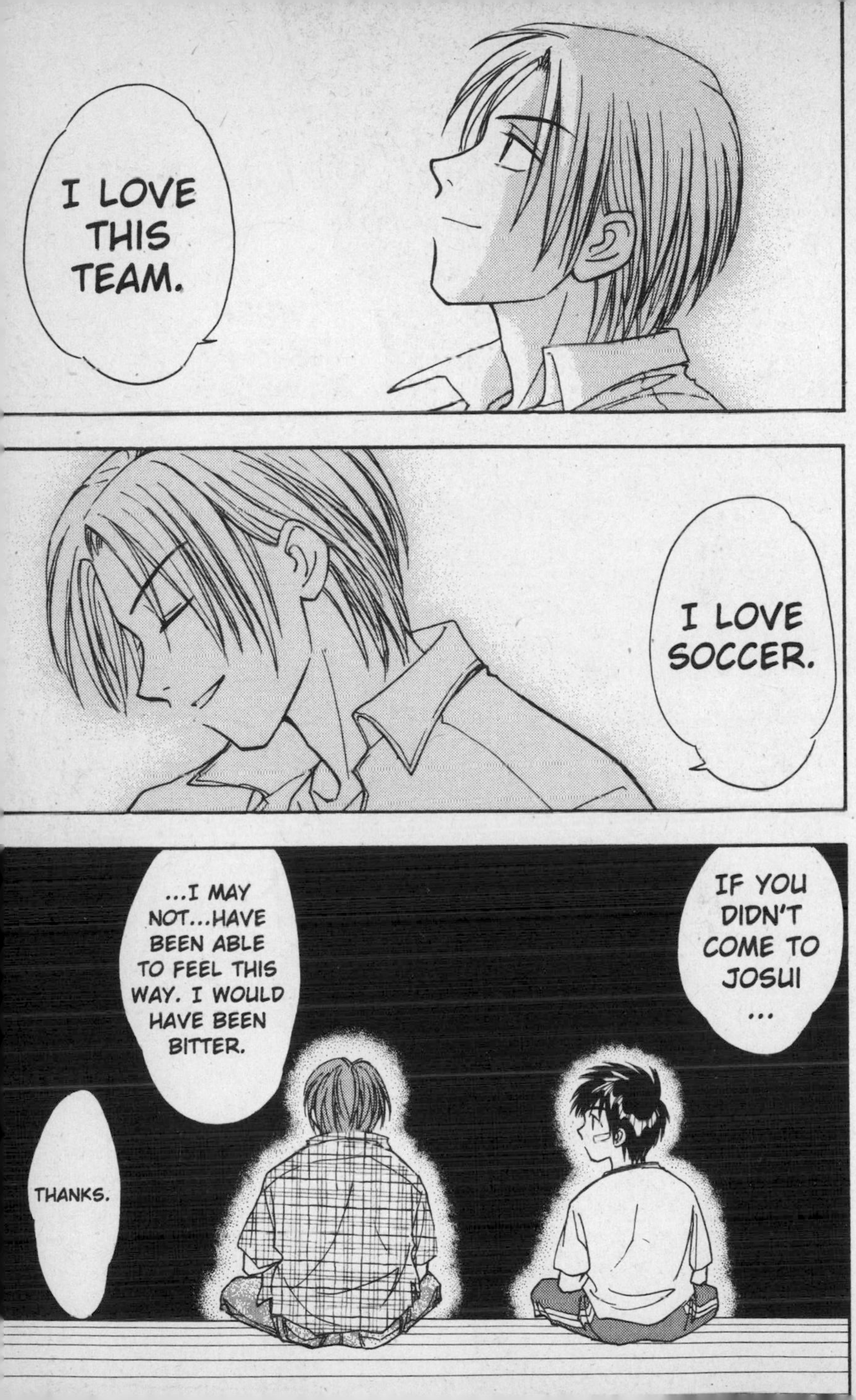
I LOVE THIS TEAM.
I LOVE SOCCER.
IF YOU DIDN'T COME TO JOSUI ...
...I MAY NOT...HAVE BEEN ABLE TO FEEL THIS WAY. I WOULD HAVE BEEN BITTER.
THANKS.

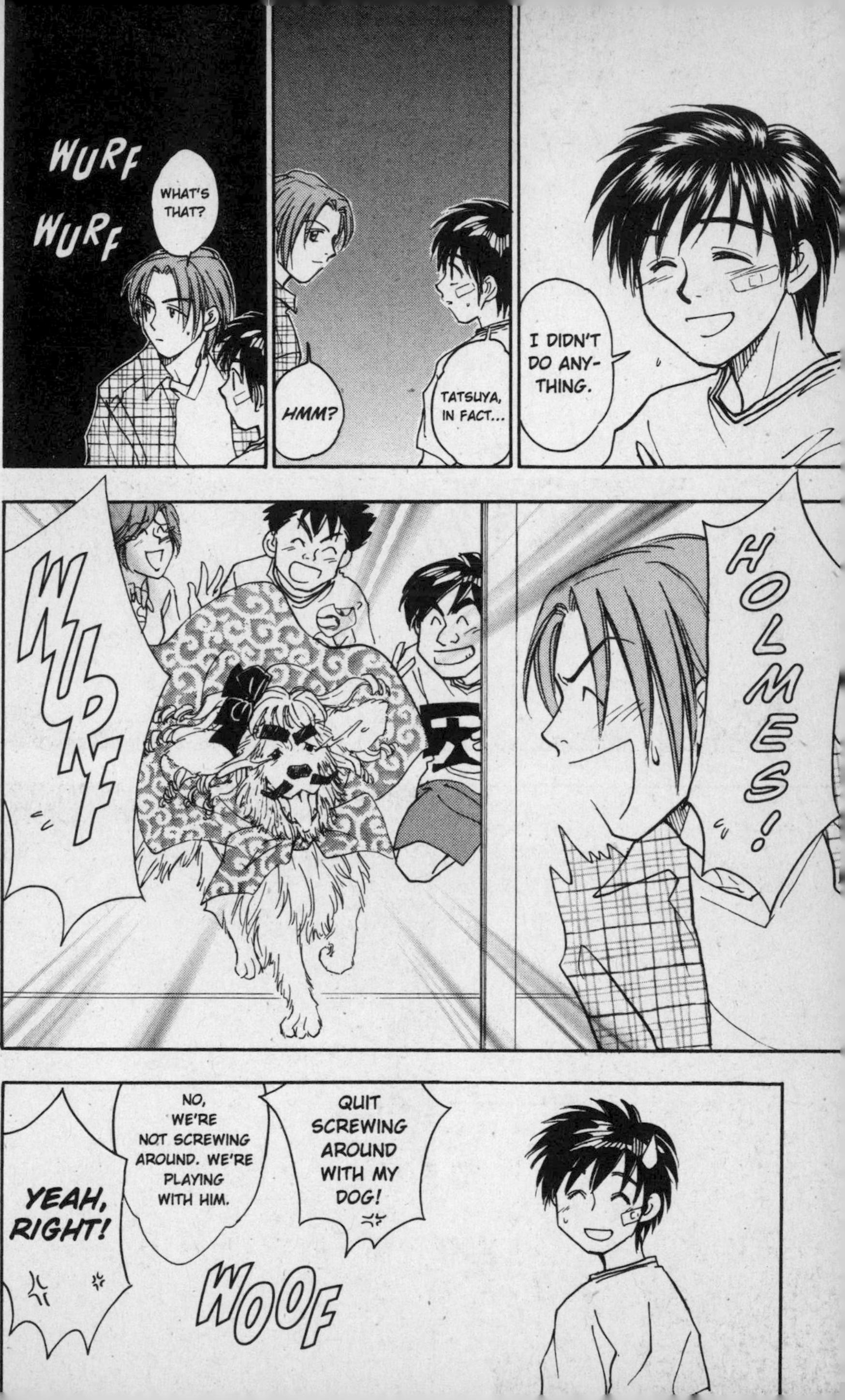
I DIDN'T DO ANY-THING.
TATSUYA, IN FACT...
HMM?
WURF WURF
WHAT'S THAT?
HOLMES!
WURF
QUIT SCREWING AROUND WITH MY DOG!
NO, WE'RE NOT SCREWING AROUND. WE'RE PLAYING WITH HIM.
YEAH, RIGHT!
WOOF

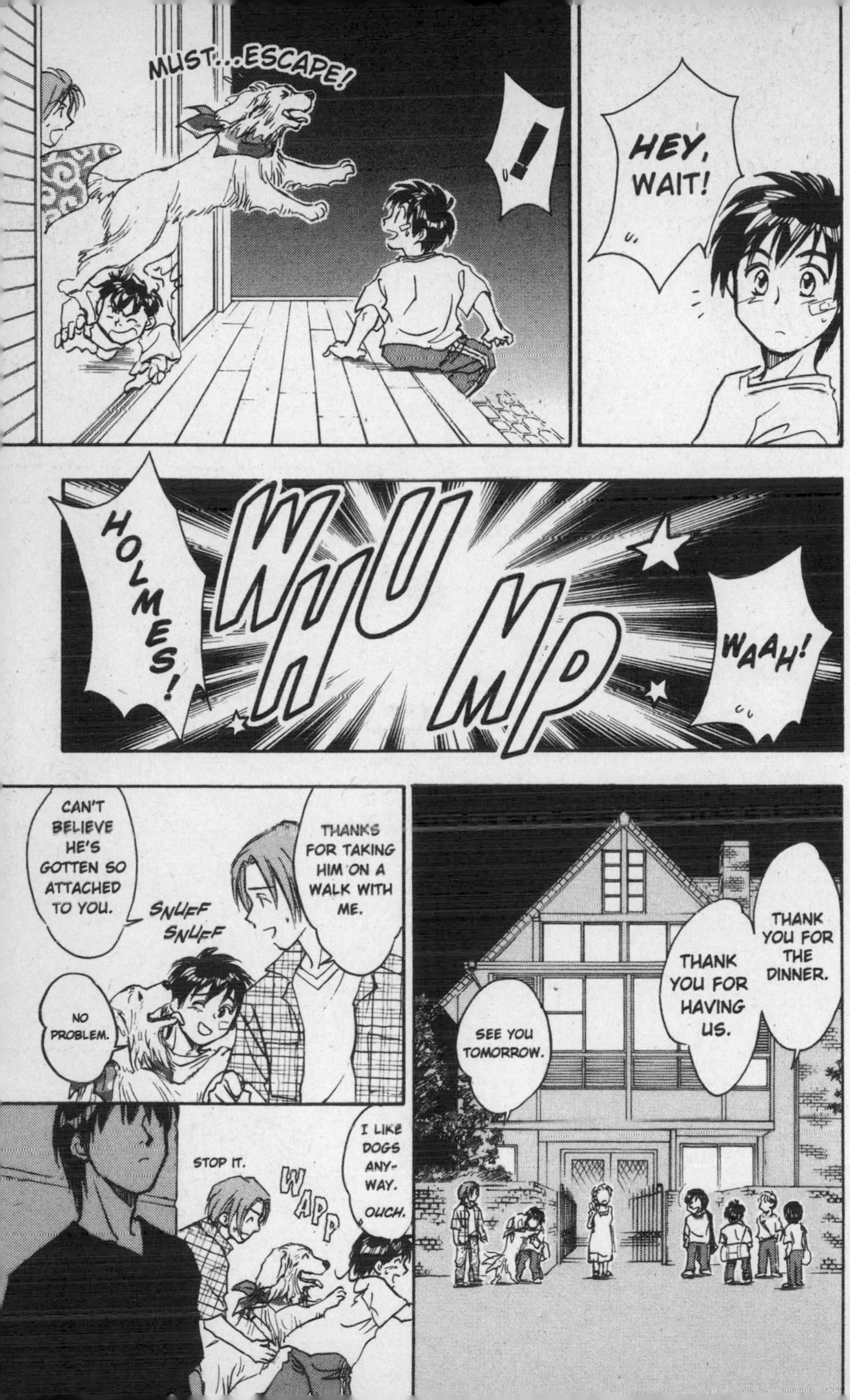
HEY, WAIT!
!
MUST...ESCAPE!
WAAH!
WHUMP
HOLMES!
THANK YOU FOR THE DINNER.
THANK YOU FOR HAVING US.
SEE YOU TOMORROW.
THANKS FOR TAKING HIM ON A WALK WITH ME.
CAN'T BELIEVE HE'S GOTTEN SO ATTACHED TO YOU.
SNUFF SNUFF
NO PROBLEM.
I LIKE DOGS ANY-WAY.
OUCH.
WAPP
STOP IT.

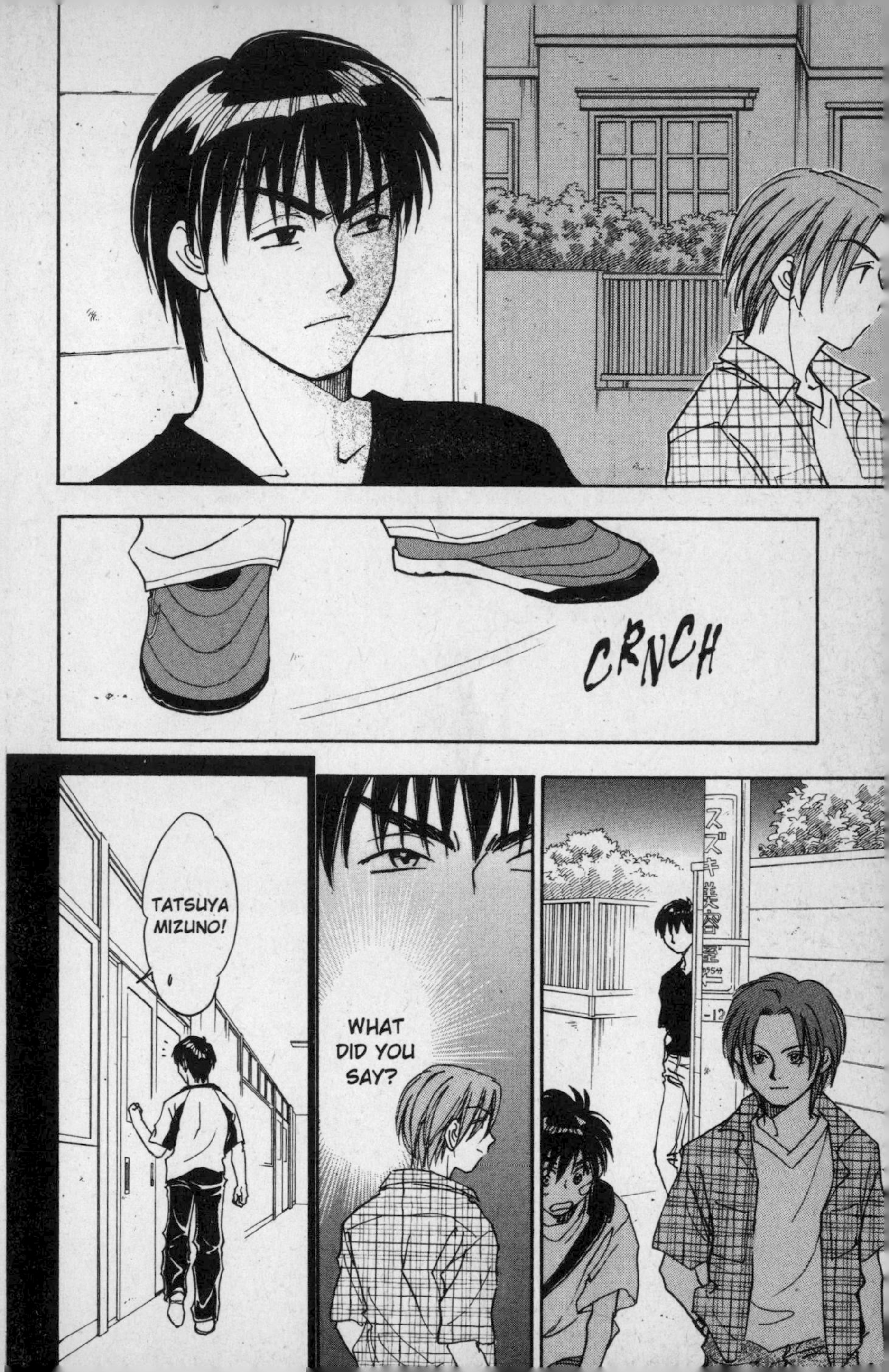
CRNCH
WHAT DID YOU SAY?
TATSUYA MIZUNO!

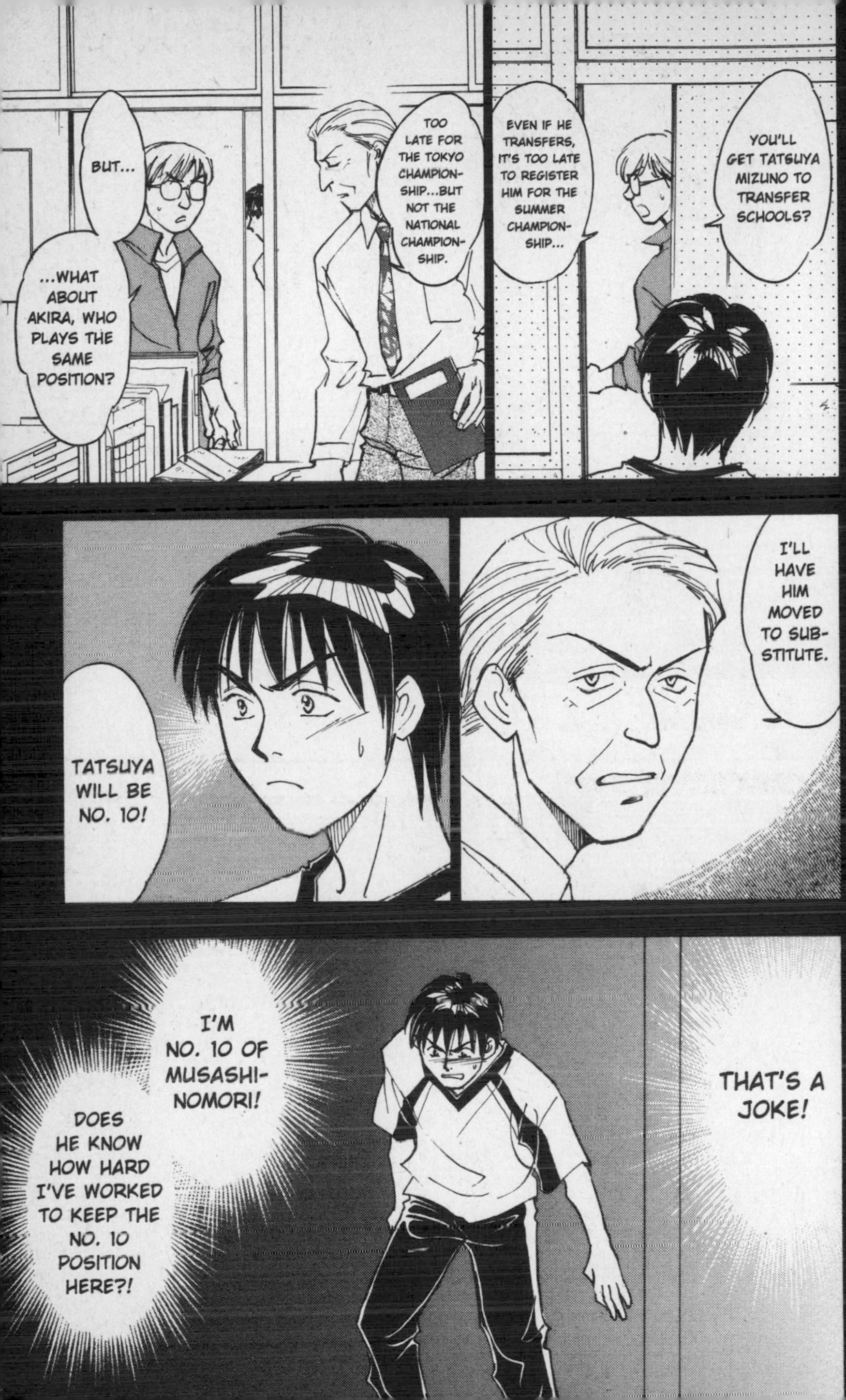
YOU'LL GET TATSUYA MIZUNO TO TRANSFER SCHOOLS?
EVEN IF HE TRANSFERS, IT'S TOO LATE TO REGISTER HIM FOR THE SUMMER CHAMPIONSHIP...
TOO LATE FOR THE TOKYO CHAMPIONSHIP...BUT NOT THE NATIONAL CHAMPIONSHIP.
BUT...
...WHAT ABOUT AKIRA, WHO PLAYS THE SAME POSITION?
I'LL HAVE HIM MOVED TO SUBSTITUTE.
TATSUYA WILL BE NO. 10!
THAT'S A JOKE!
I'M NO. 10 OF MUSASHI-NOMORI!
DOES HE KNOW HOW HARD I'VE WORKED TO KEEP THE NO. 10 POSITION HERE?!

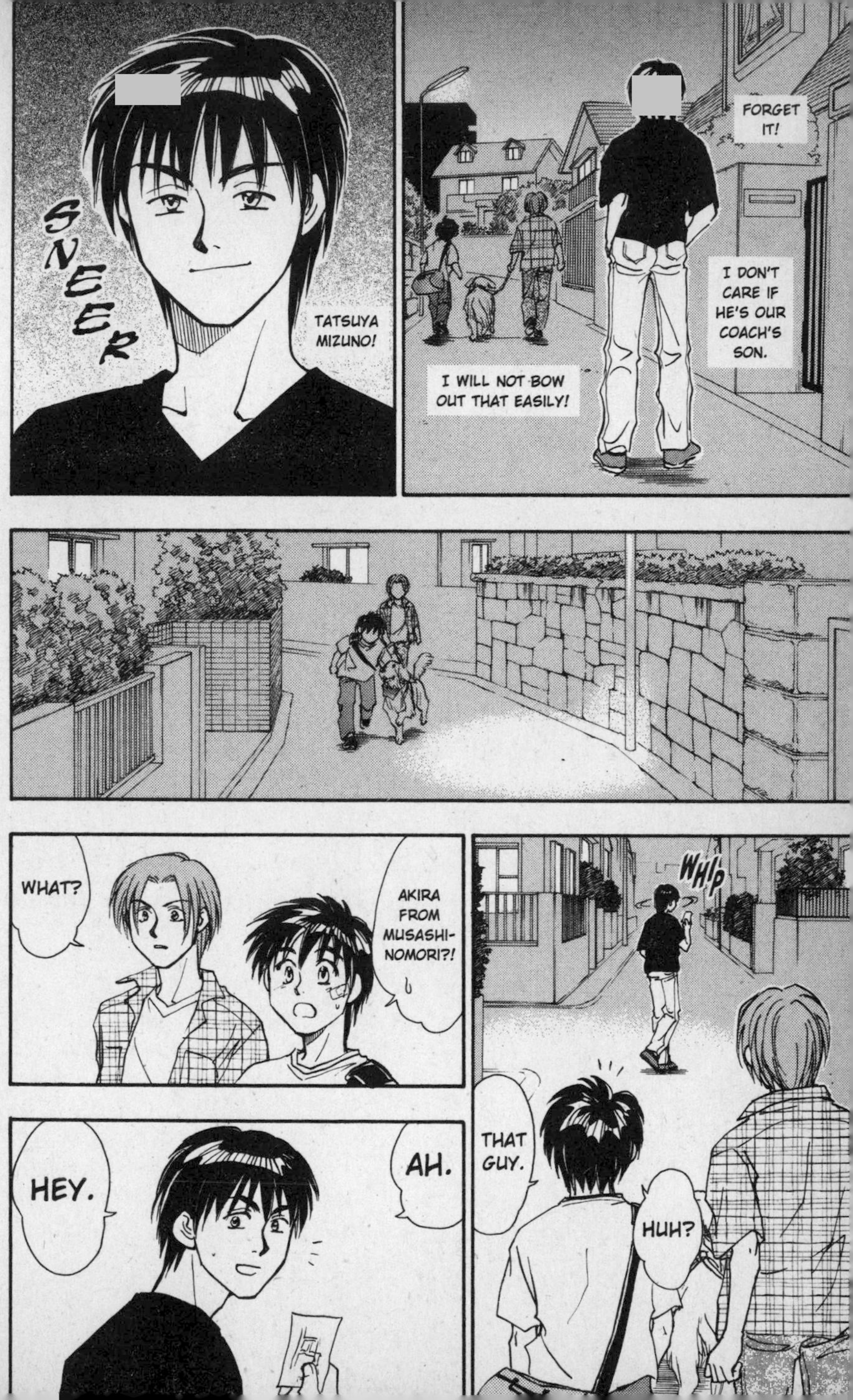
FORGET IT!
I DON'T CARE IF HE'S OUR COACH'S SON.
I WILL NOT BOW OUT THAT EASILY!
SNEER
TATSUYA MIZUNO!
WHIP
THAT GUY.
HUH?
AKIRA FROM MUSASHI-NOMORI?!
WHAT?
AH.
HEY.

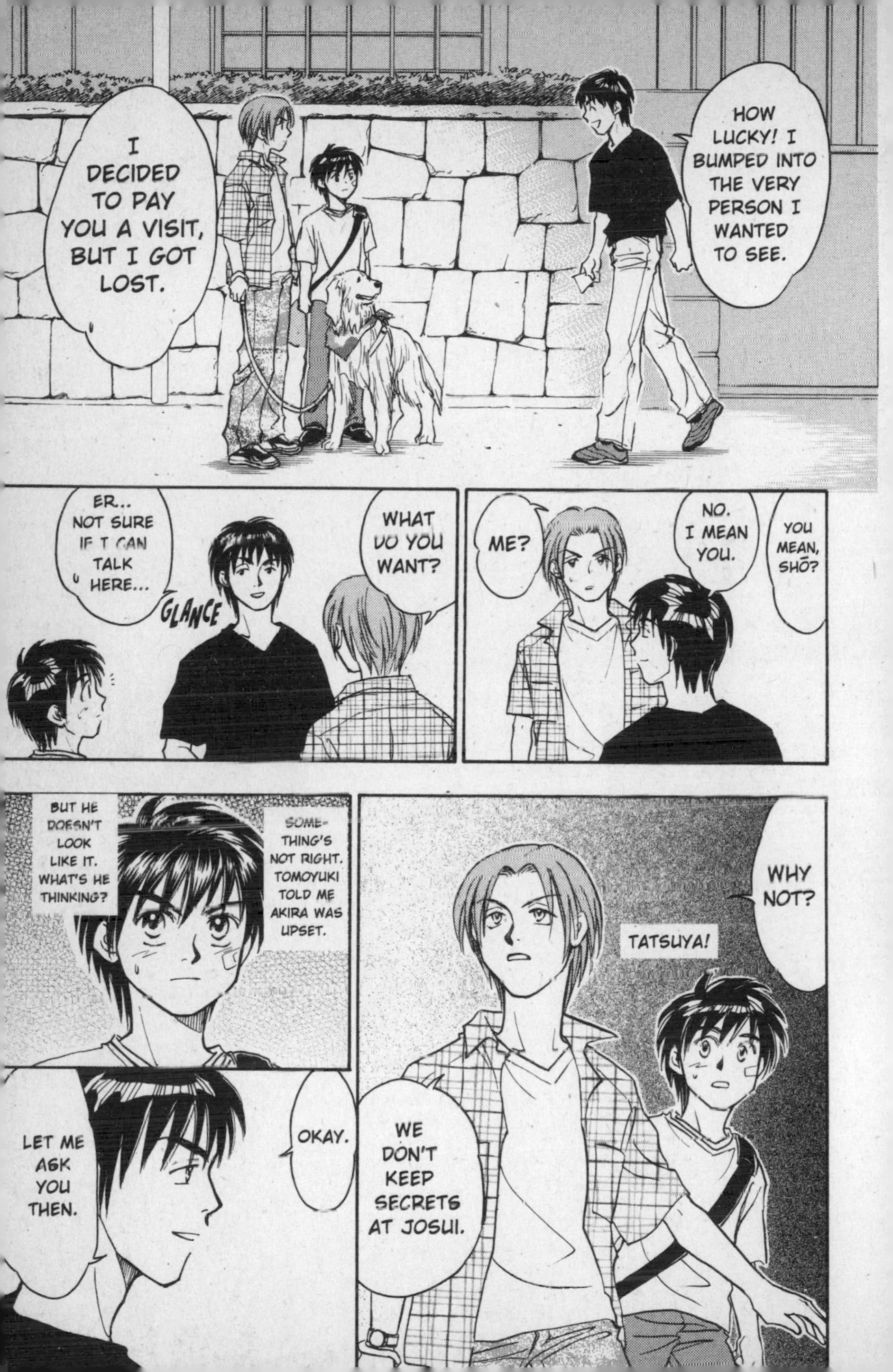
HOW LUCKY! I BUMPED INTO THE VERY PERSON I WANTED TO SEE.
I DECIDED TO PAY YOU A VISIT, BUT I GOT LOST.
YOU MEAN, SHŌ?
NO. I MEAN YOU.
ME?
WHAT DO YOU WANT?
ER... NOT SURE IF I CAN TALK HERE...
GLANCE
WHY NOT?
TATSUYA!
WE DON'T KEEP SECRETS AT JOSUI.
SOME-THING'S NOT RIGHT. TOMOYUKI TOLD ME AKIRA WAS UPSET.
BUT HE DOESN'T LOOK LIKE IT. WHAT'S HE THINKING?
OKAY.
LET ME ASK YOU THEN.

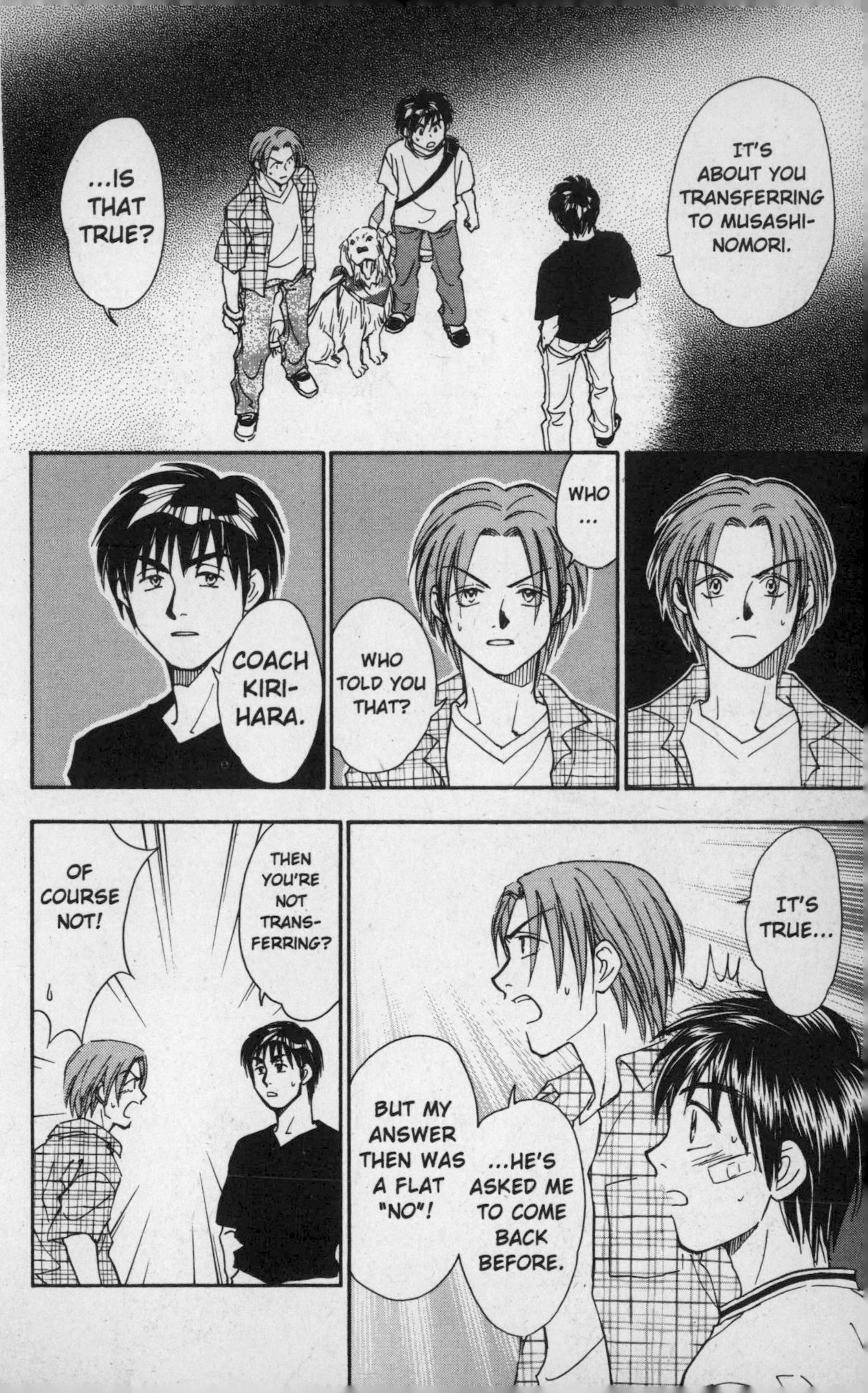
IT'S ABOUT YOU TRANSFERRING TO MUSASHI-NOMORI.
...IS THAT TRUE?
WHO ...
WHO TOLD YOU THAT?
COACH KIRI-HARA.
IT'S TRUE...
...HE'S ASKED ME TO COME BACK BEFORE.
BUT MY ANSWER THEN WAS A FLAT "NO"!
THEN YOU'RE NOT TRANS-FERRING?
OF COURSE NOT!

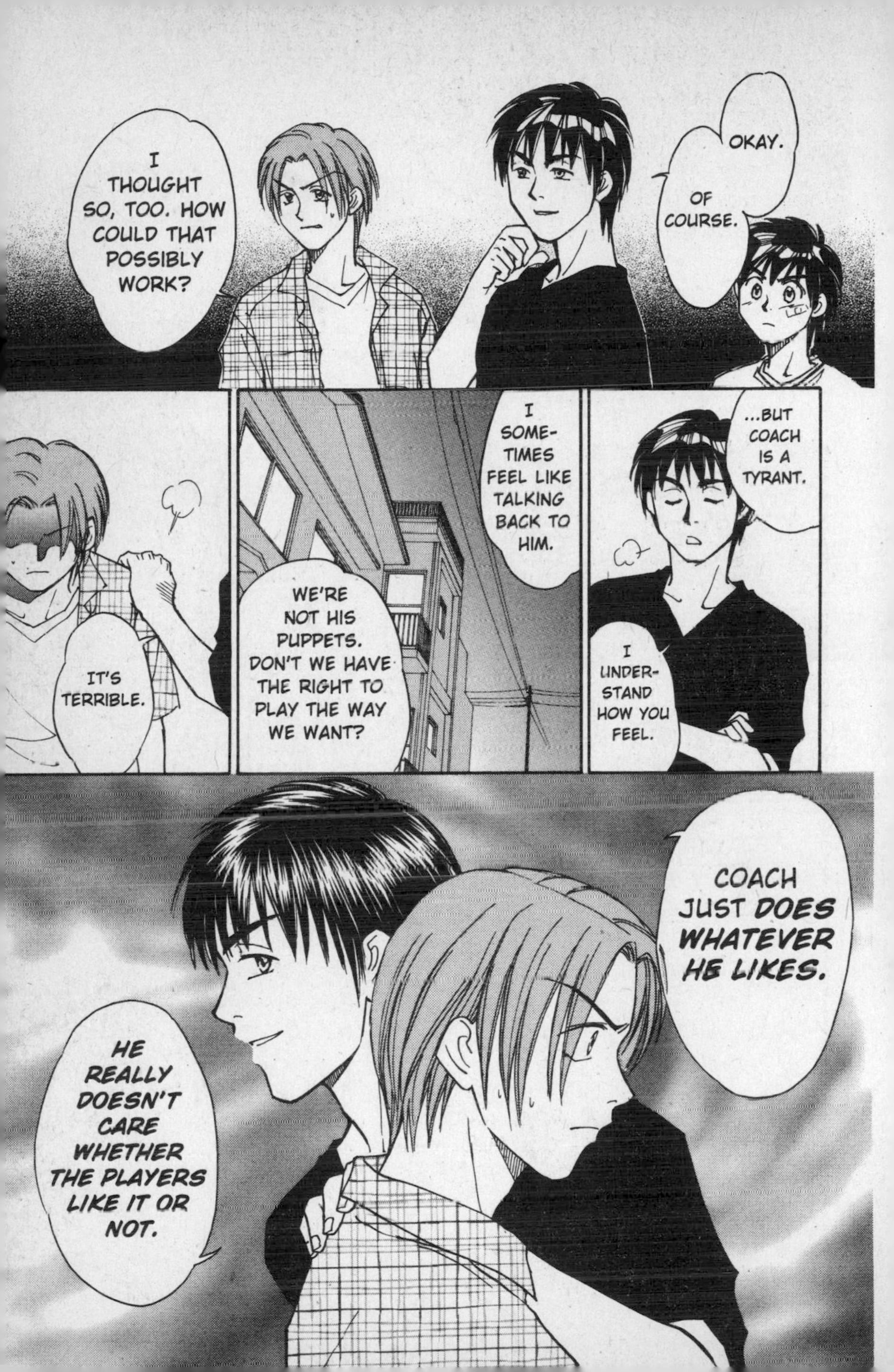
OKAY.
OF COURSE.
I THOUGHT SO, TOO. HOW COULD THAT POSSIBLY WORK?
...BUT COACH IS A TYRANT.
I UNDERSTAND HOW YOU FEEL.
I SOMETIMES FEEL LIKE TALKING BACK TO HIM.
WE'RE NOT HIS PUPPETS. DON'T WE HAVE THE RIGHT TO PLAY THE WAY WE WANT?
IT'S TERRIBLE.
COACH JUST **DOES WHATEVER HE LIKES.**
HE REALLY DOESN'T CARE WHETHER THE PLAYERS LIKE IT OR NOT.

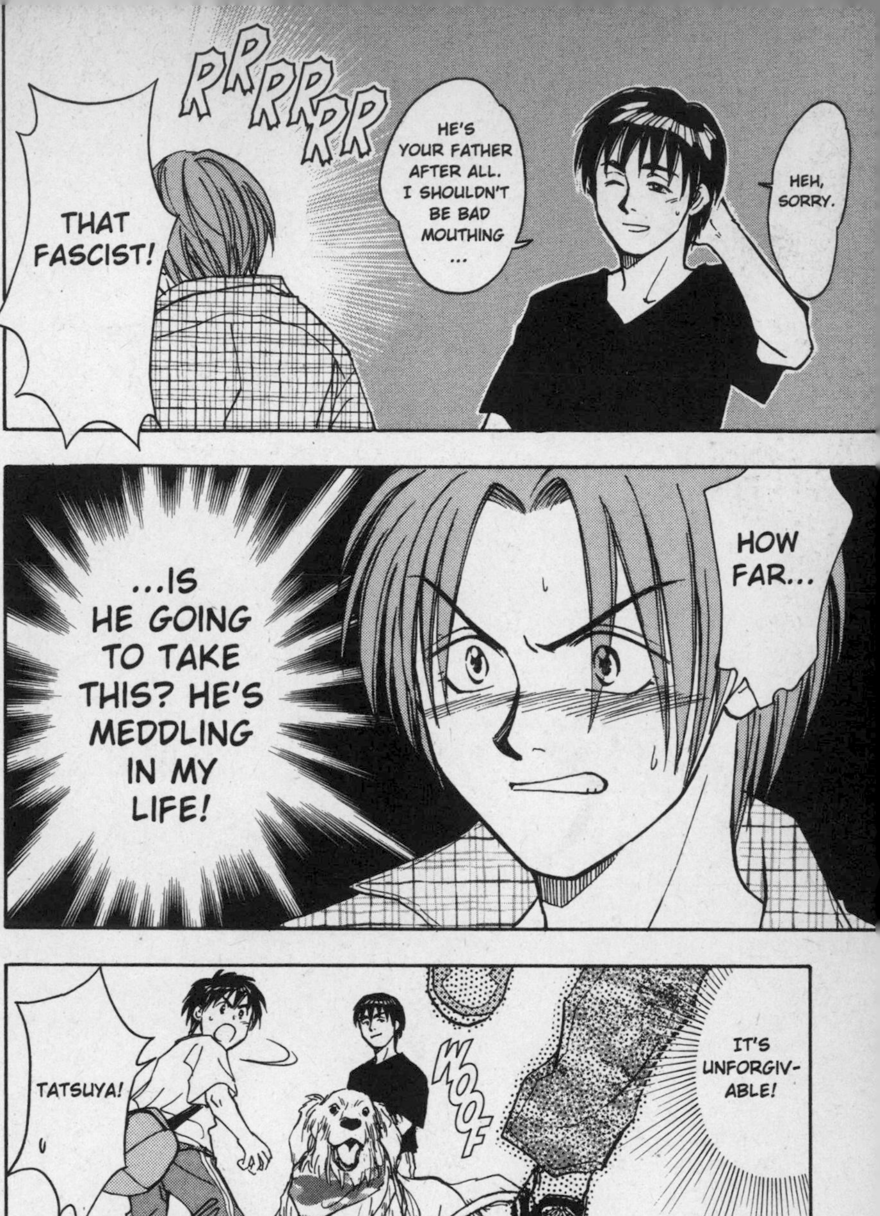
HEH, SORRY.
HE'S YOUR FATHER AFTER ALL. I SHOULDN'T BE BAD MOUTHING ...
RRRRRR
THAT FASCIST!
HOW FAR...
...IS HE GOING TO TAKE THIS? HE'S MEDDLING IN MY LIFE!
IT'S UNFORGIV-ABLE!
WOOF
TATSUYA!

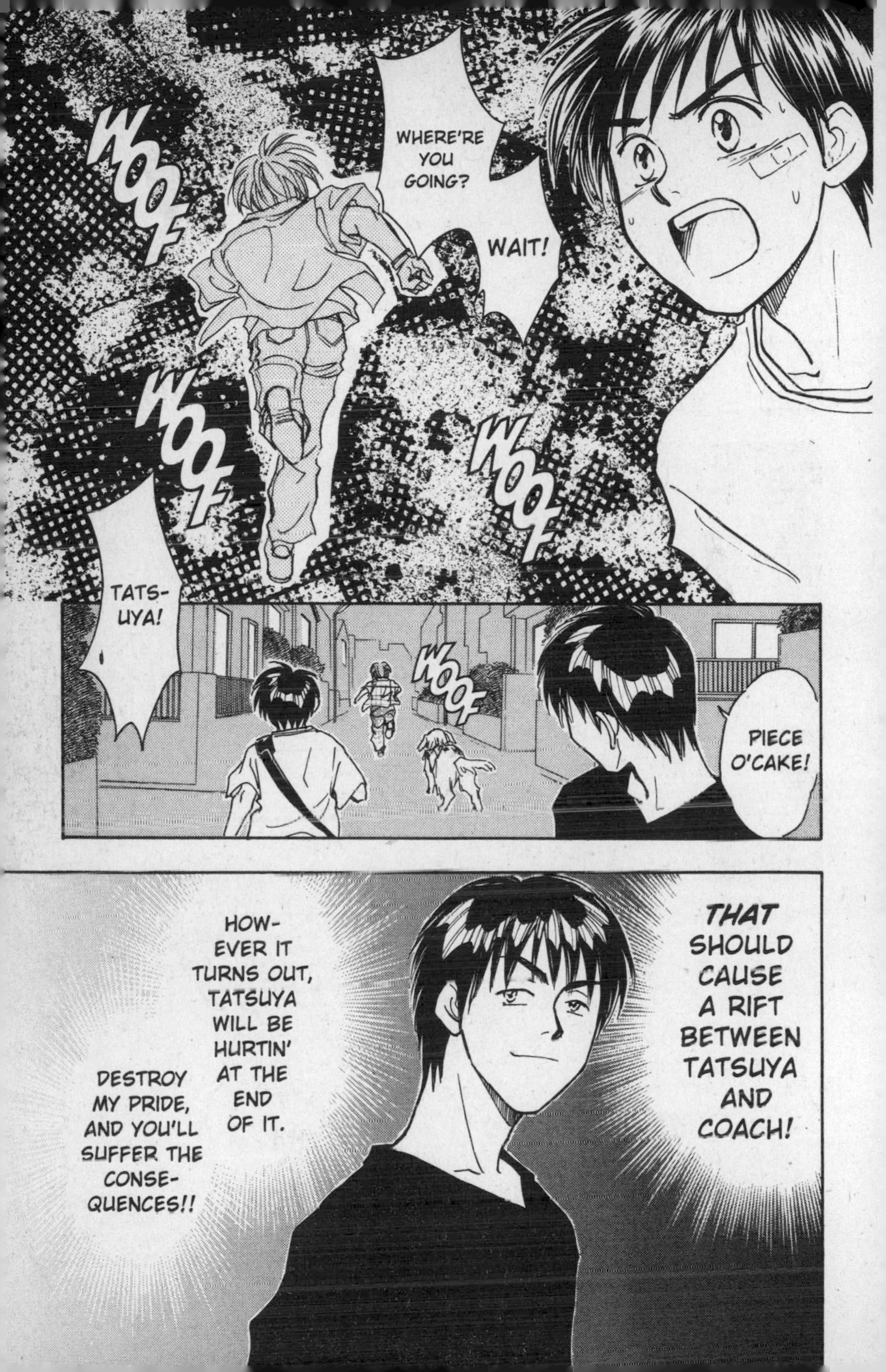
WHERE'RE YOU GOING?
WAIT!
WOOF
WOOF
WOOF
TATSU-UYA!
PIECE O'CAKE!
WOOF
THAT SHOULD CAUSE A RIFT BETWEEN TATSUYA AND COACH!
HOW-EVER IT TURNS OUT, TATSUYA WILL BE HURTIN' AT THE END OF IT.
DESTROY MY PRIDE, AND YOU'LL SUFFER THE CONSE-QUENCES!!

WHISTLE!

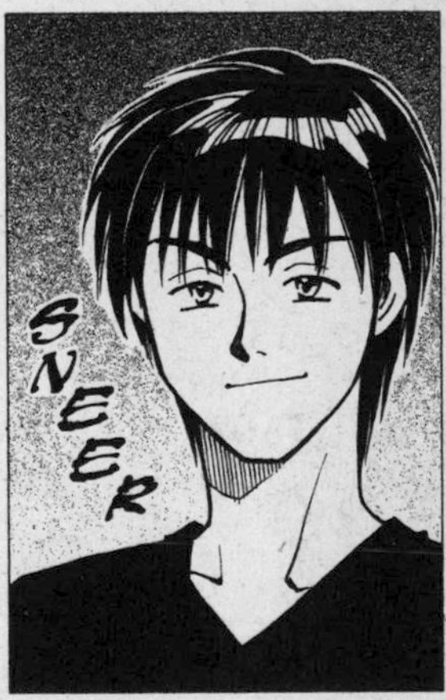
SNEER

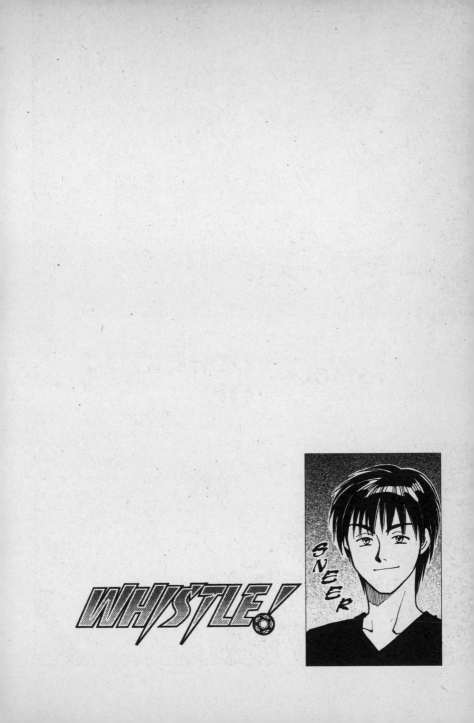

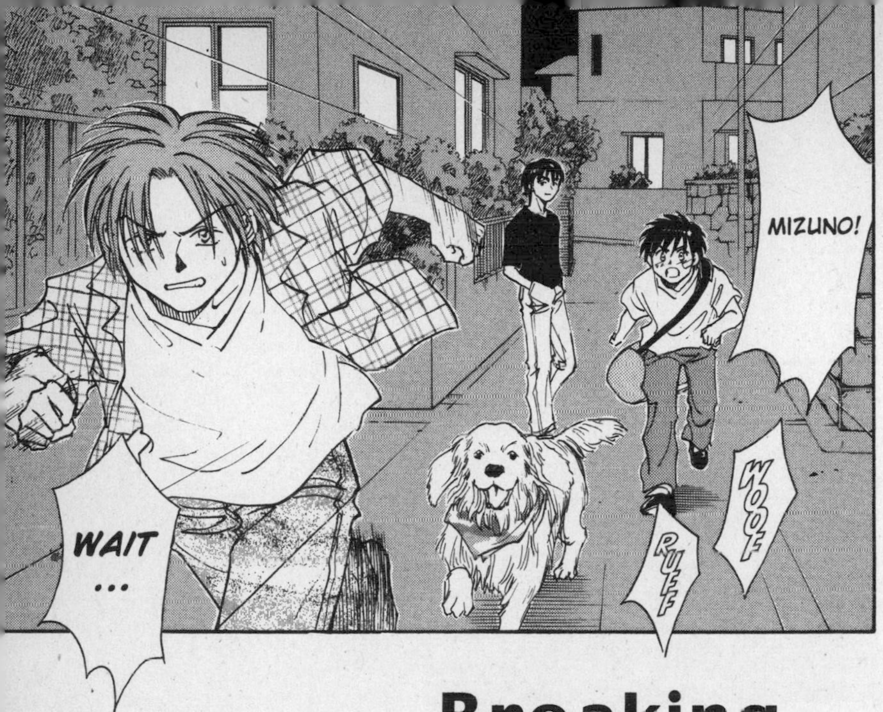
MIZUNO!
WOOF
RUFF
WAIT ...

STAGE.65 Breaking Off

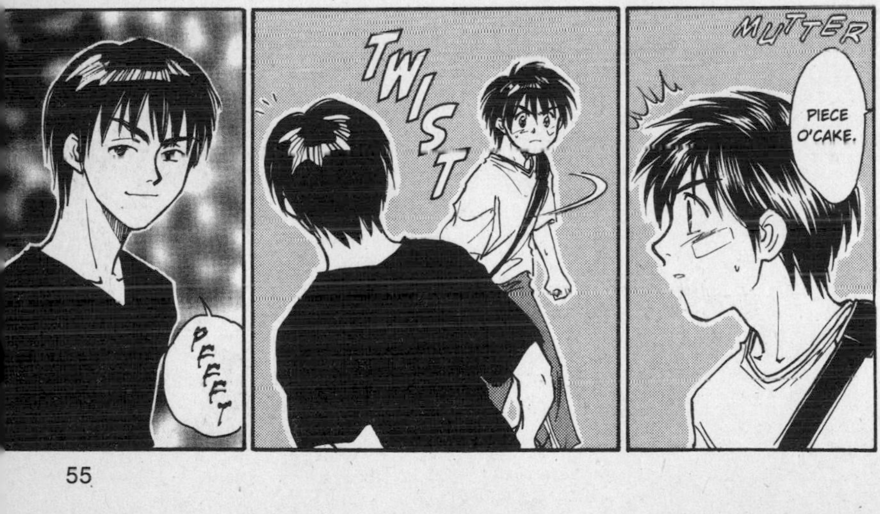
MUTTER
PIECE O'CAKE.
TWIST
PFFFT

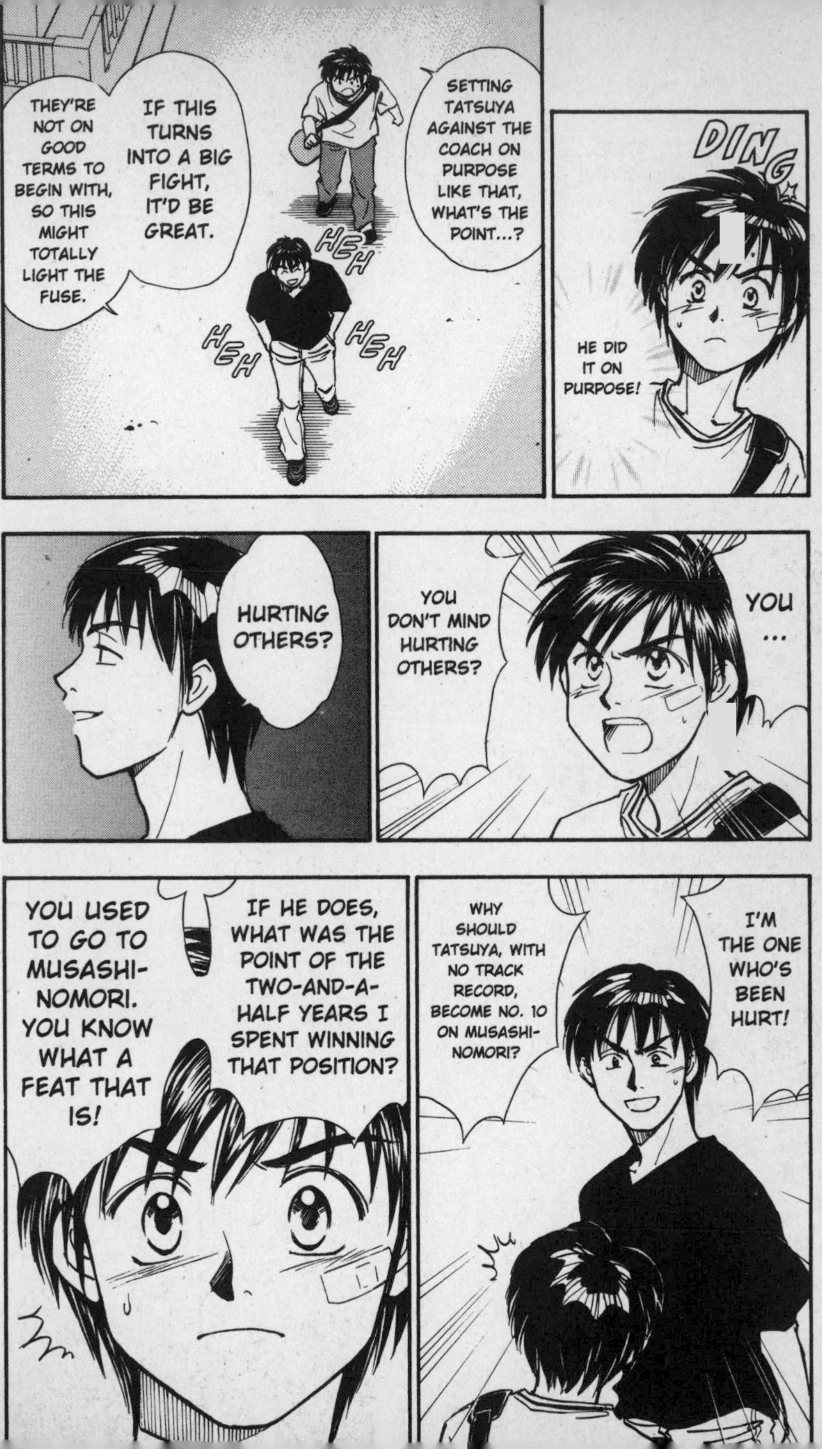
DING
HE DID IT ON PURPOSE!
SETTING TATSUYA AGAINST THE COACH ON PURPOSE LIKE THAT, WHAT'S THE POINT...?
IF THIS TURNS INTO A BIG FIGHT, IT'D BE GREAT.
THEY'RE NOT ON GOOD TERMS TO BEGIN WITH, SO THIS MIGHT TOTALLY LIGHT THE FUSE.
HEH
HEH
HEH
YOU ...
YOU DON'T MIND HURTING OTHERS?
HURTING OTHERS?
I'M THE ONE WHO'S BEEN HURT!
WHY SHOULD TATSUYA, WITH NO TRACK RECORD, BECOME NO. 10 ON MUSASHI-NOMORI?
IF HE DOES, WHAT WAS THE POINT OF THE TWO-AND-A-HALF YEARS I SPENT WINNING THAT POSITION?
YOU USED TO GO TO MUSASHI-NOMORI. YOU KNOW WHAT A FEAT THAT IS!

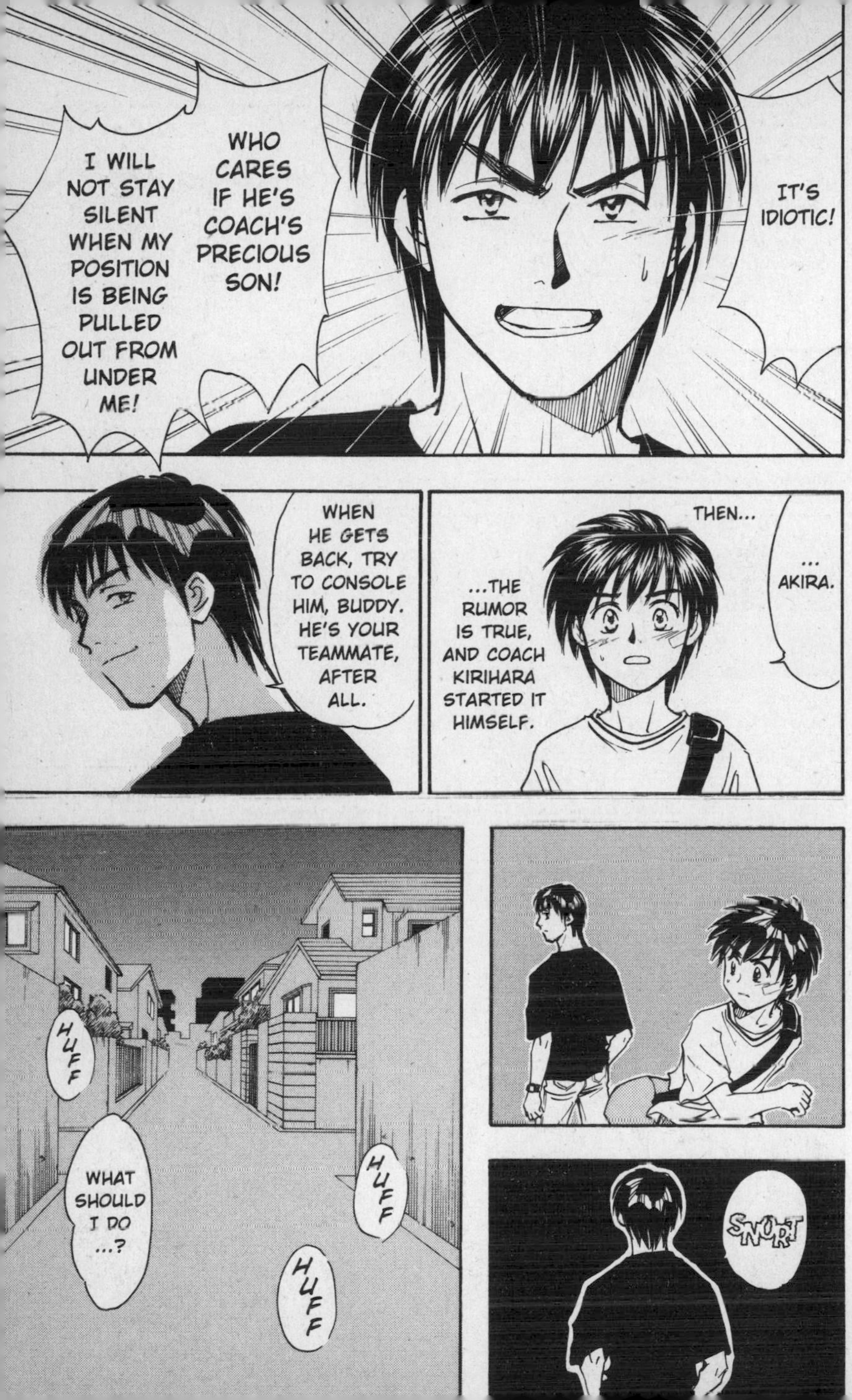
IT'S IDIOTIC!
WHO CARES IF HE'S COACH'S PRECIOUS SON!
I WILL NOT STAY SILENT WHEN MY POSITION IS BEING PULLED OUT FROM UNDER ME!
... AKIRA.
THEN...
...THE RUMOR IS TRUE, AND COACH KIRIHARA STARTED IT HIMSELF.
WHEN HE GETS BACK, TRY TO CONSOLE HIM, BUDDY. HE'S YOUR TEAMMATE, AFTER ALL.
SNORT
HUFF
WHAT SHOULD I DO ...?
HUFF
HUFF

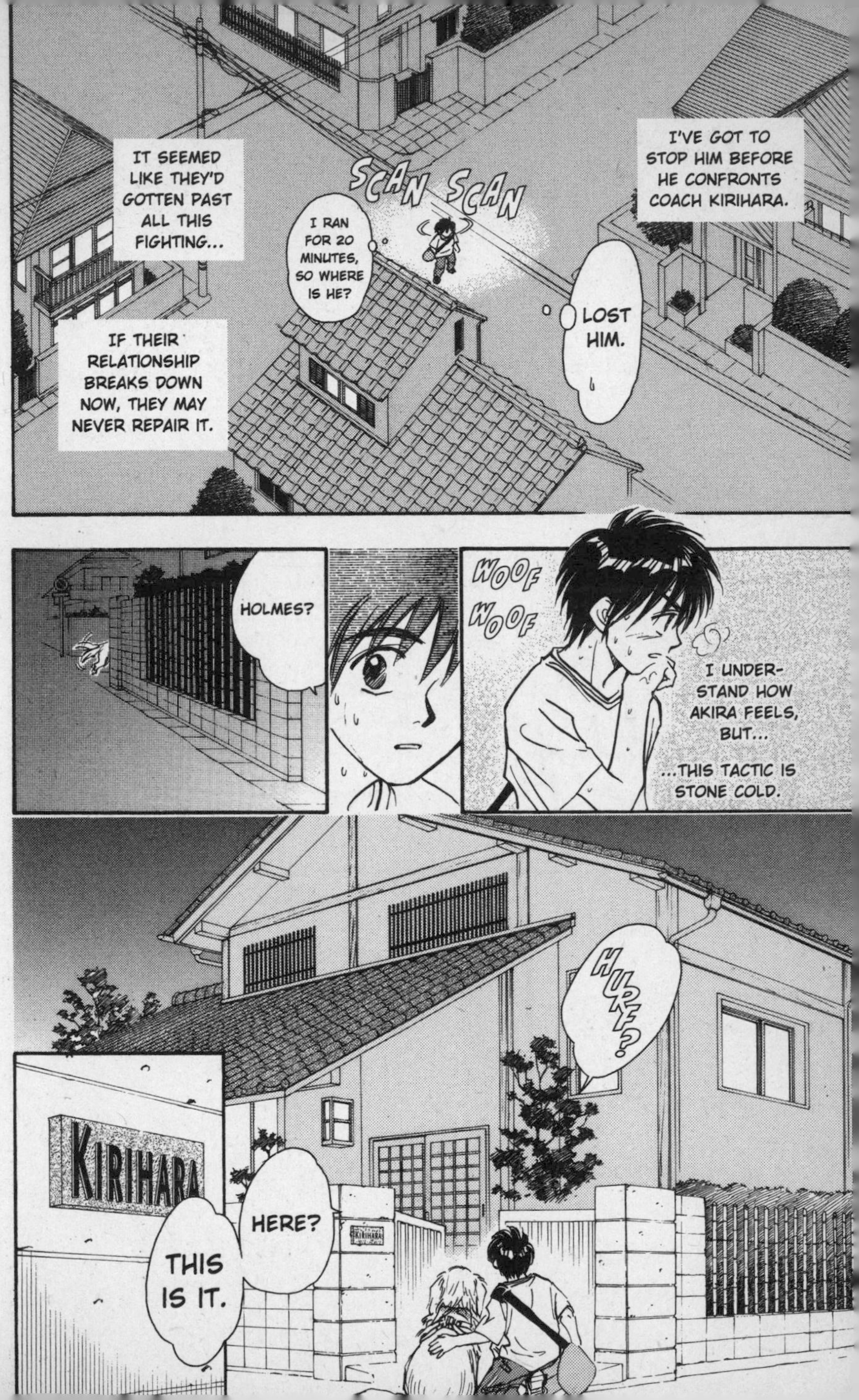
I'VE GOT TO STOP HIM BEFORE HE CONFRONTS COACH KIRIHARA.
LOST HIM.
SCAN SCAN
I RAN FOR 20 MINUTES, SO WHERE IS HE?
IT SEEMED LIKE THEY'D GOTTEN PAST ALL THIS FIGHTING...
IF THEIR RELATIONSHIP BREAKS DOWN NOW, THEY MAY NEVER REPAIR IT.
WOOF WOOF
I UNDER-STAND HOW AKIRA FEELS, BUT...
...THIS TACTIC IS STONE COLD.
HOLMES?
HUFF?
KIRIHARA
HERE?
THIS IS IT.

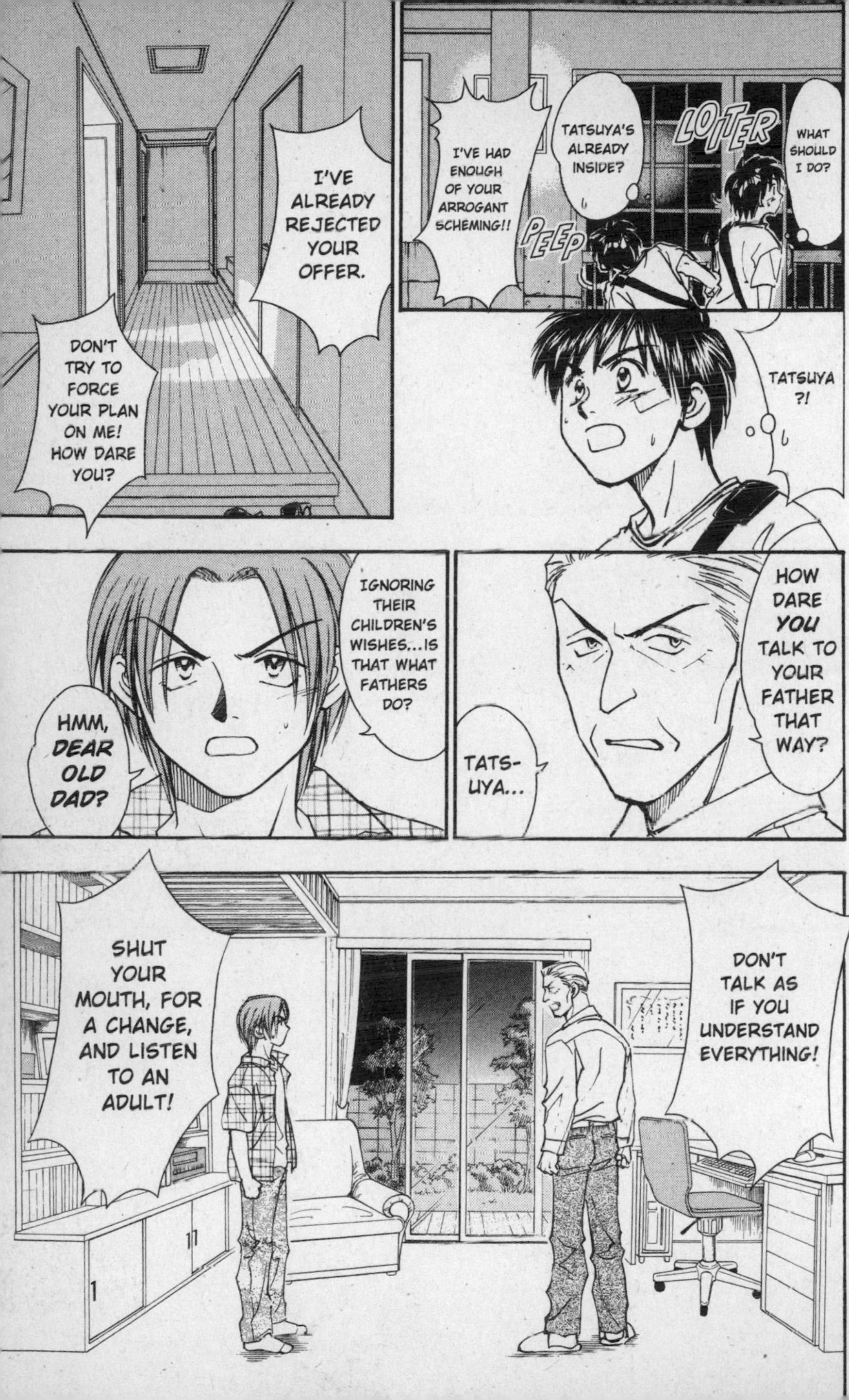
WHAT SHOULD I DO?
LOITER
TATSUYA'S ALREADY INSIDE?
PEEP
I'VE HAD ENOUGH OF YOUR ARROGANT SCHEMING!!
TATSUYA ?!
I'VE ALREADY REJECTED YOUR OFFER.
DON'T TRY TO FORCE YOUR PLAN ON ME! HOW DARE YOU?
HOW DARE *YOU* TALK TO YOUR FATHER THAT WAY?
TATS-UYA...
IGNORING THEIR CHILDREN'S WISHES...IS THAT WHAT FATHERS DO?
HMM, *DEAR OLD DAD?*
DON'T TALK AS IF YOU UNDERSTAND EVERYTHING!
SHUT YOUR MOUTH, FOR A CHANGE, AND LISTEN TO AN ADULT!

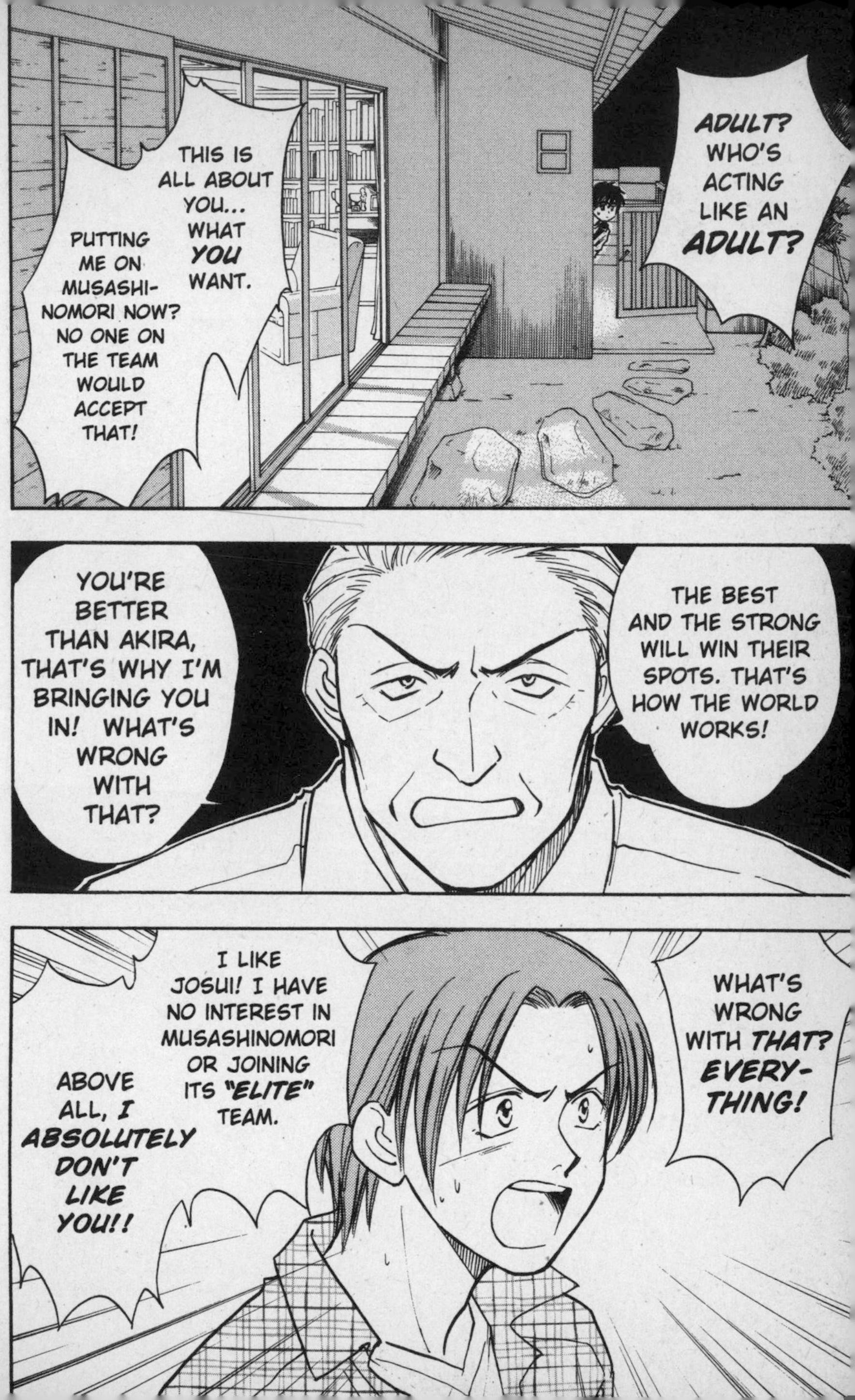
ADULT? WHO'S ACTING LIKE AN ADULT?
THIS IS ALL ABOUT YOU... WHAT YOU WANT.
PUTTING ME ON MUSASHI-NOMORI NOW? NO ONE ON THE TEAM WOULD ACCEPT THAT!
THE BEST AND THE STRONG WILL WIN THEIR SPOTS. THAT'S HOW THE WORLD WORKS!
YOU'RE BETTER THAN AKIRA, THAT'S WHY I'M BRINGING YOU IN! WHAT'S WRONG WITH THAT?
WHAT'S WRONG WITH THAT? EVERY-THING!
I LIKE JOSUI! I HAVE NO INTEREST IN MUSASHINOMORI OR JOINING ITS "ELITE" TEAM.
ABOVE ALL, I ABSOLUTELY DON'T LIKE YOU!!

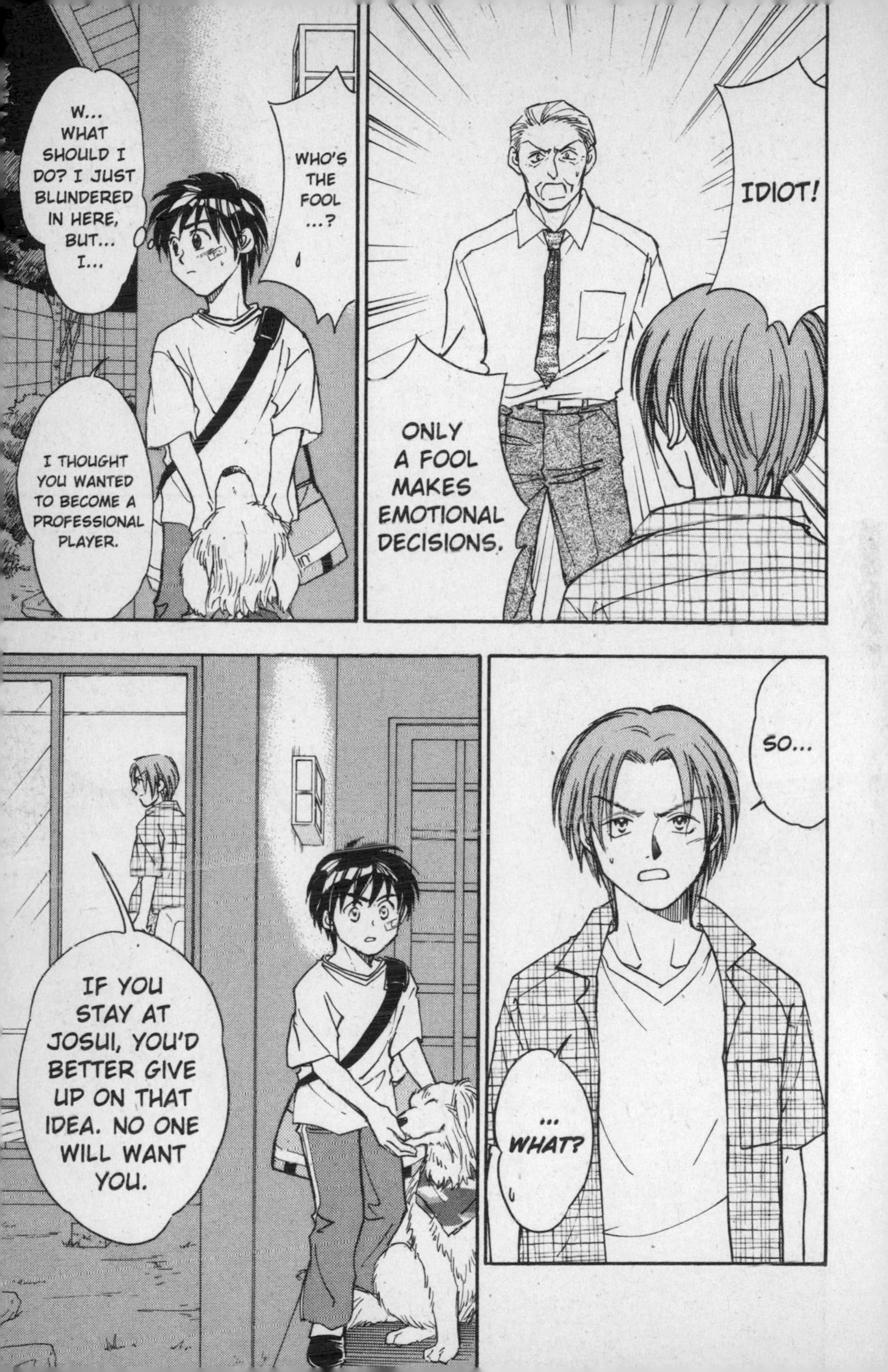
IDIOT!
ONLY A FOOL MAKES EMOTIONAL DECISIONS.
WHO'S THE FOOL ...?
W... WHAT SHOULD I DO? I JUST BLUNDERED IN HERE, BUT... I...
I THOUGHT YOU WANTED TO BECOME A PROFESSIONAL PLAYER.
SO...
... WHAT?
IF YOU STAY AT JOSUI, YOU'D BETTER GIVE UP ON THAT IDEA. NO ONE WILL WANT YOU.

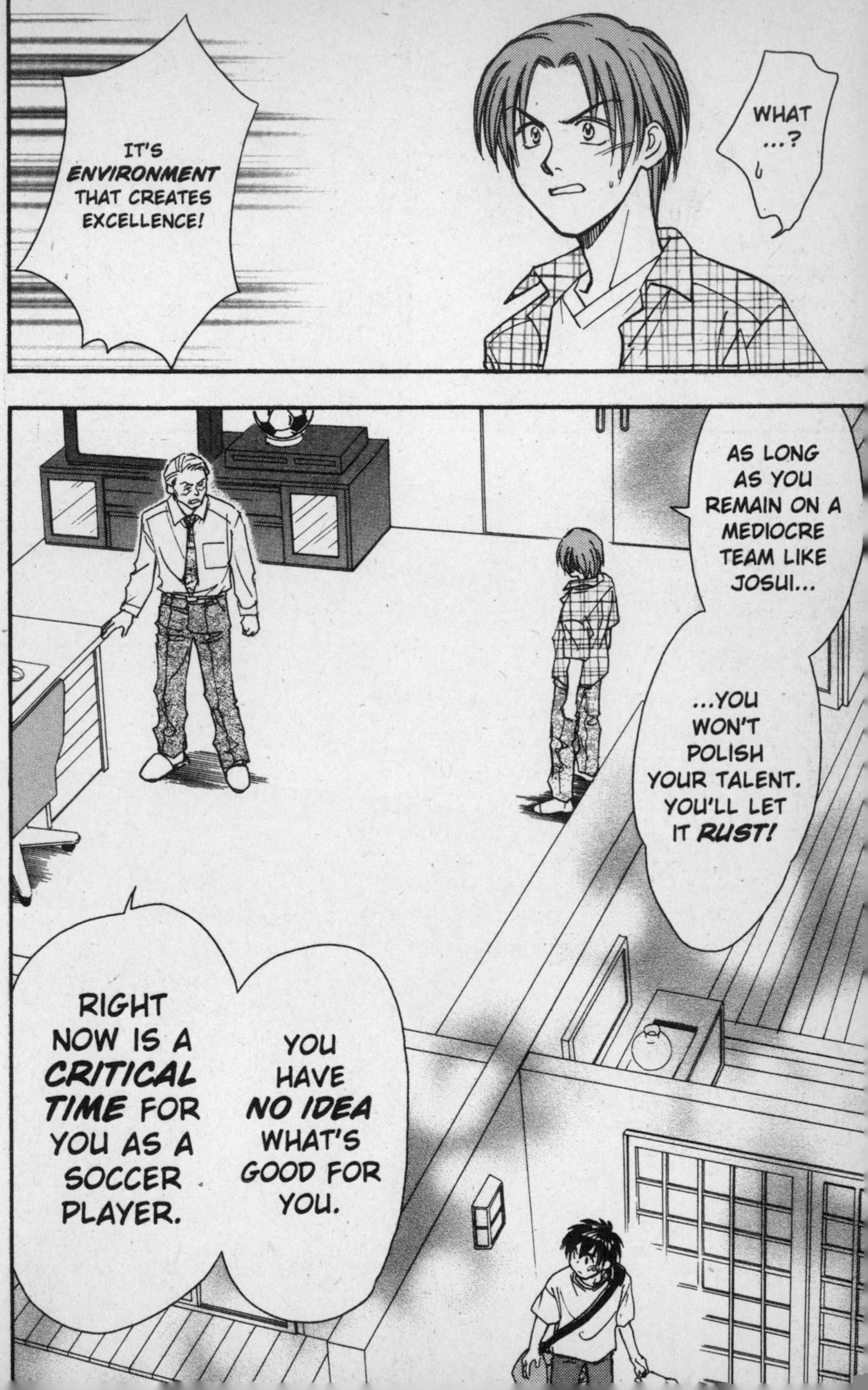
WHAT ...?
IT'S ENVIRONMENT THAT CREATES EXCELLENCE!
AS LONG AS YOU REMAIN ON A MEDIOCRE TEAM LIKE JOSUI...
...YOU WON'T POLISH YOUR TALENT. YOU'LL LET IT RUST!
YOU HAVE NO IDEA WHAT'S GOOD FOR YOU.
RIGHT NOW IS A CRITICAL TIME FOR YOU AS A SOCCER PLAYER.

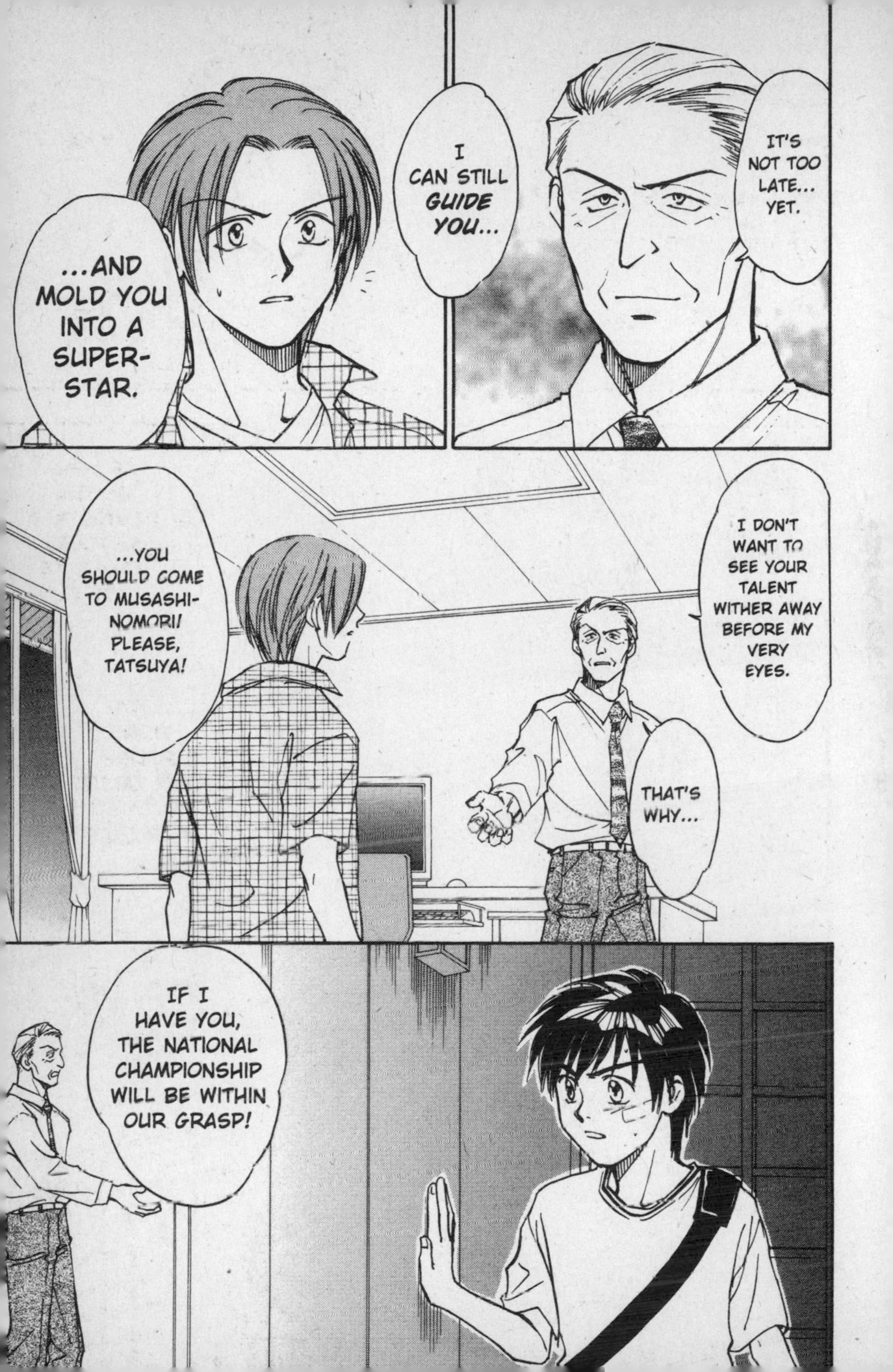
IT'S NOT TOO LATE... YET.
I CAN STILL *GUIDE* *YOU*...
...AND MOLD YOU INTO A SUPER-STAR.
I DON'T WANT TO SEE YOUR TALENT WITHER AWAY BEFORE MY VERY EYES.
THAT'S WHY...
...YOU SHOULD COME TO MUSASHI-NOMORI! PLEASE, TATSUYA!
IF I HAVE YOU, THE NATIONAL CHAMPIONSHIP WILL BE WITHIN OUR GRASP!

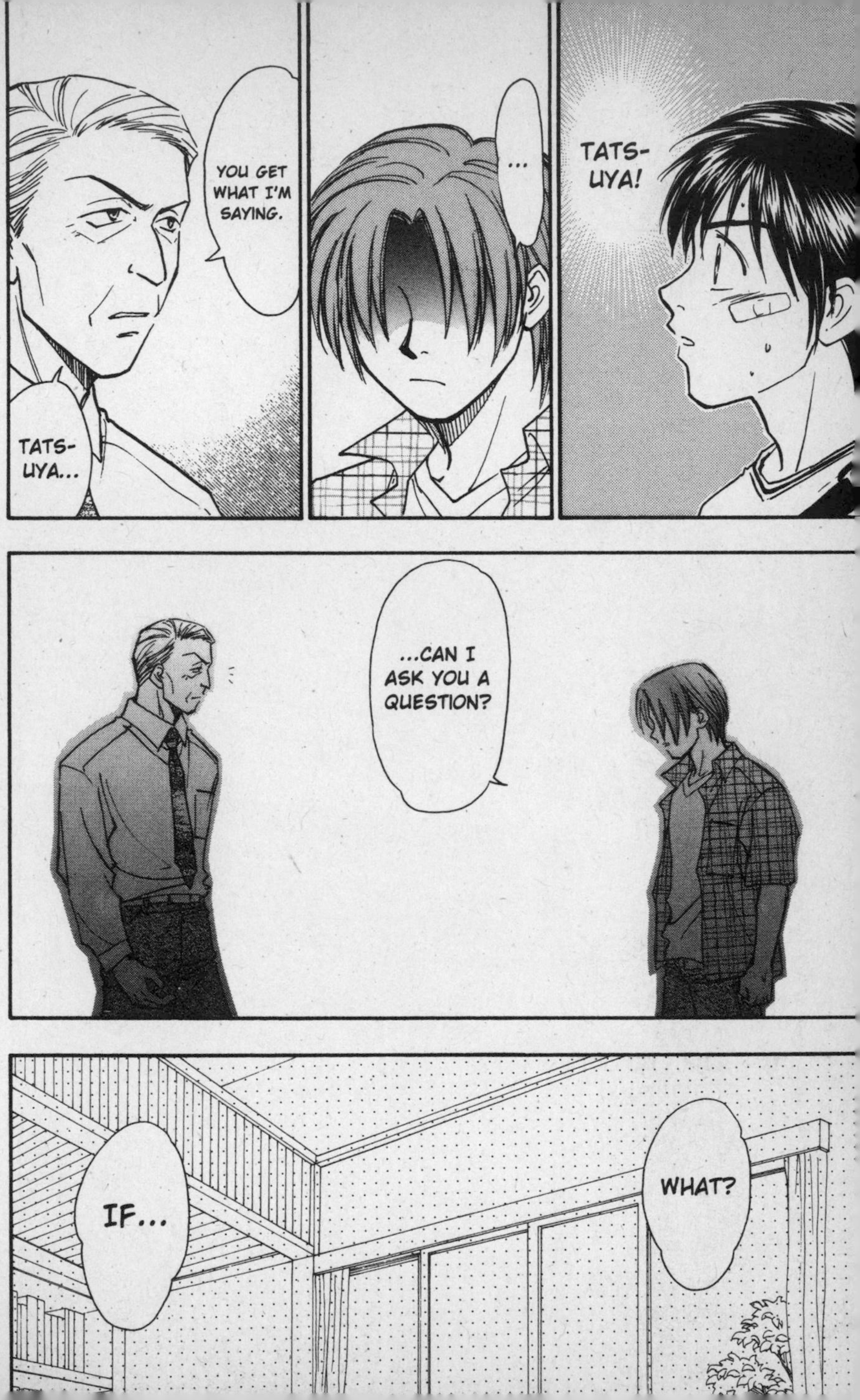
TATS-UYA!
...
YOU GET WHAT I'M SAYING.
TATS-UYA...
...CAN I ASK YOU A QUESTION?
WHAT?
IF...

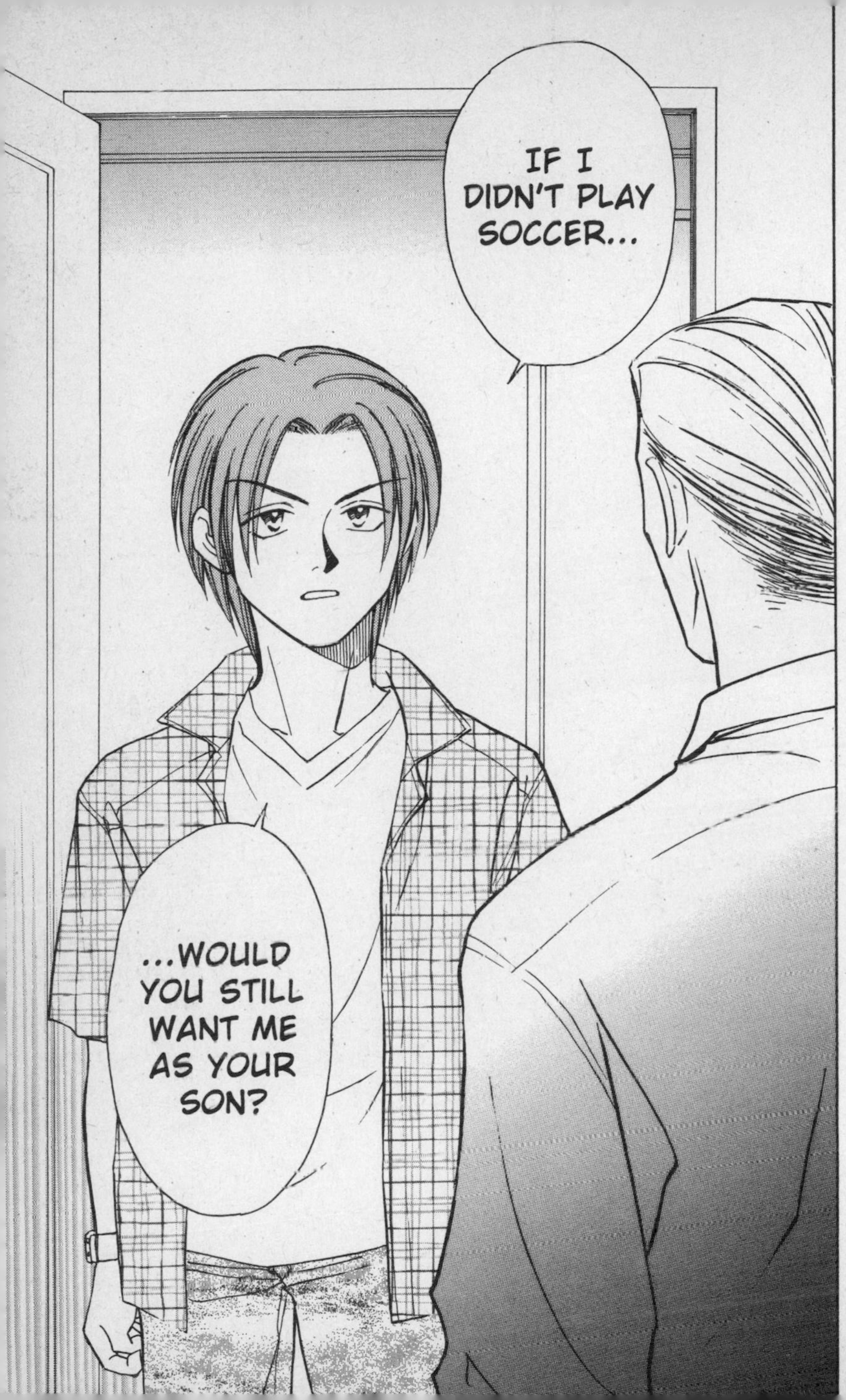
IF I DIDN'T PLAY SOCCER...
...WOULD YOU STILL WANT ME AS YOUR SON?

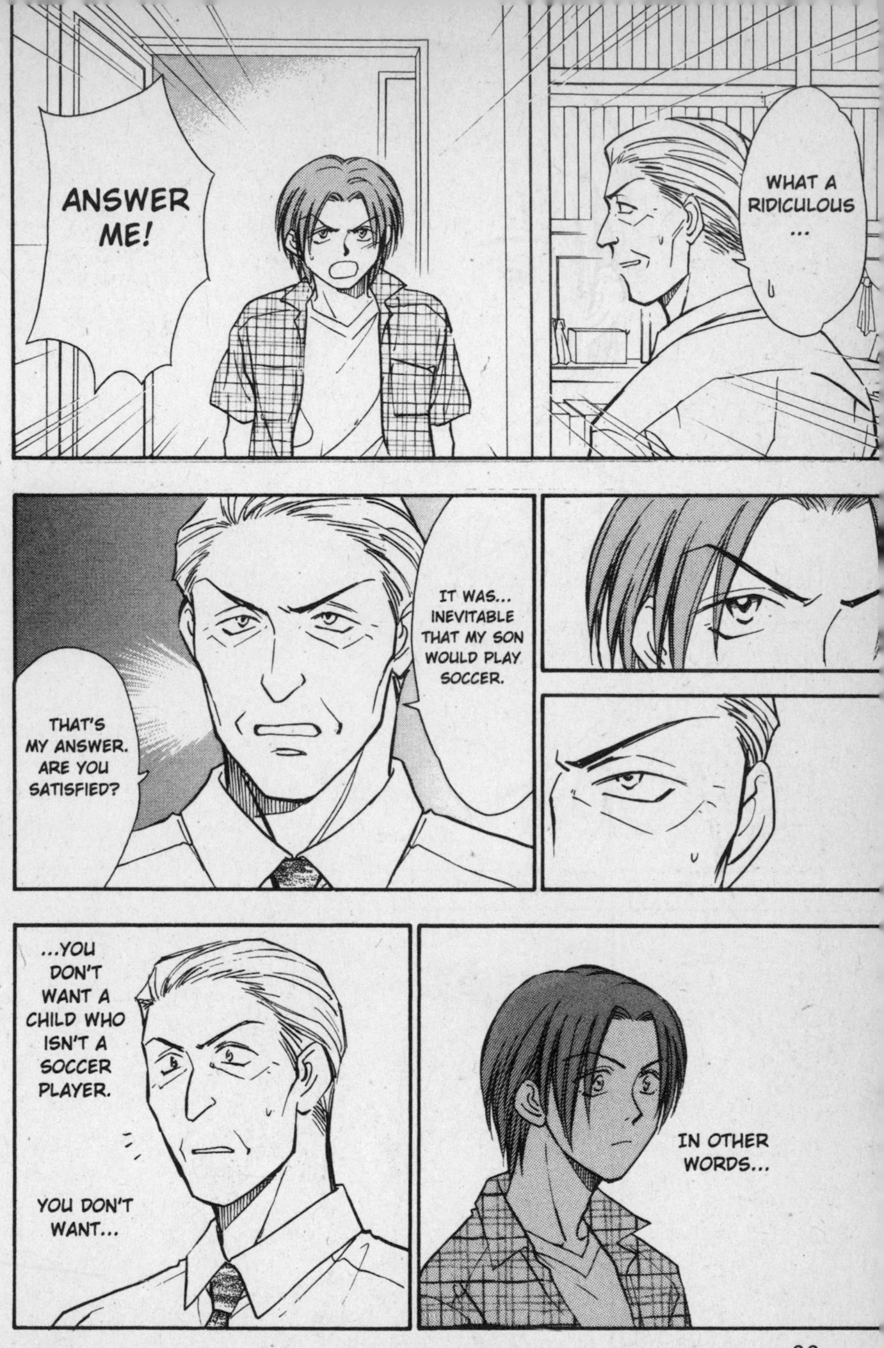
WHAT A RIDICULOUS ...
ANSWER ME!
IT WAS... INEVITABLE THAT MY SON WOULD PLAY SOCCER.
THAT'S MY ANSWER. ARE YOU SATISFIED?
IN OTHER WORDS...
...YOU DON'T WANT A CHILD WHO ISN'T A SOCCER PLAYER.
YOU DON'T WANT...

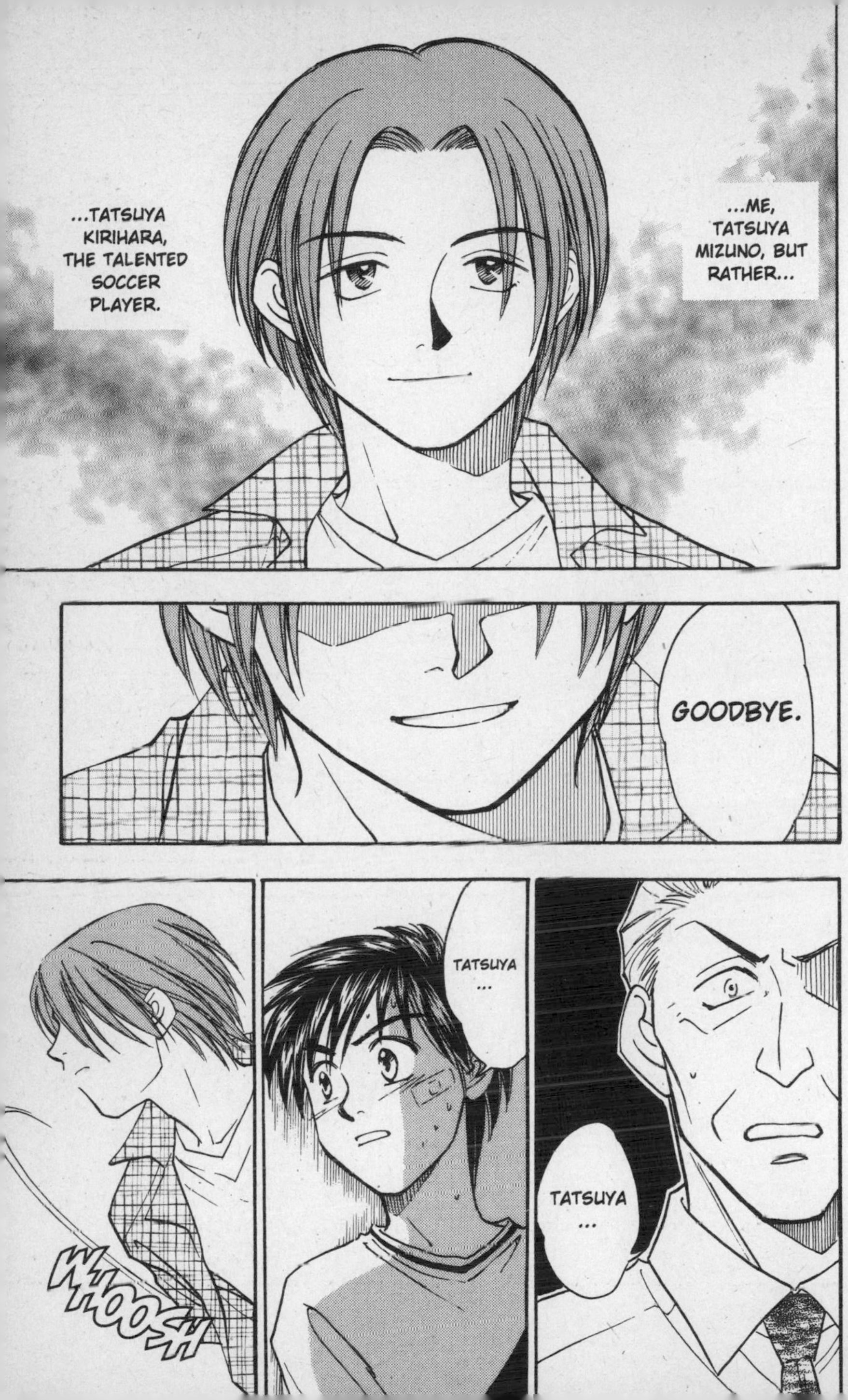
...ME, TATSUYA MIZUNO, BUT RATHER...
...TATSUYA KIRIHARA, THE TALENTED SOCCER PLAYER.
GOODBYE.
TATSUYA ...
TATSUYA ...
WHOOSH

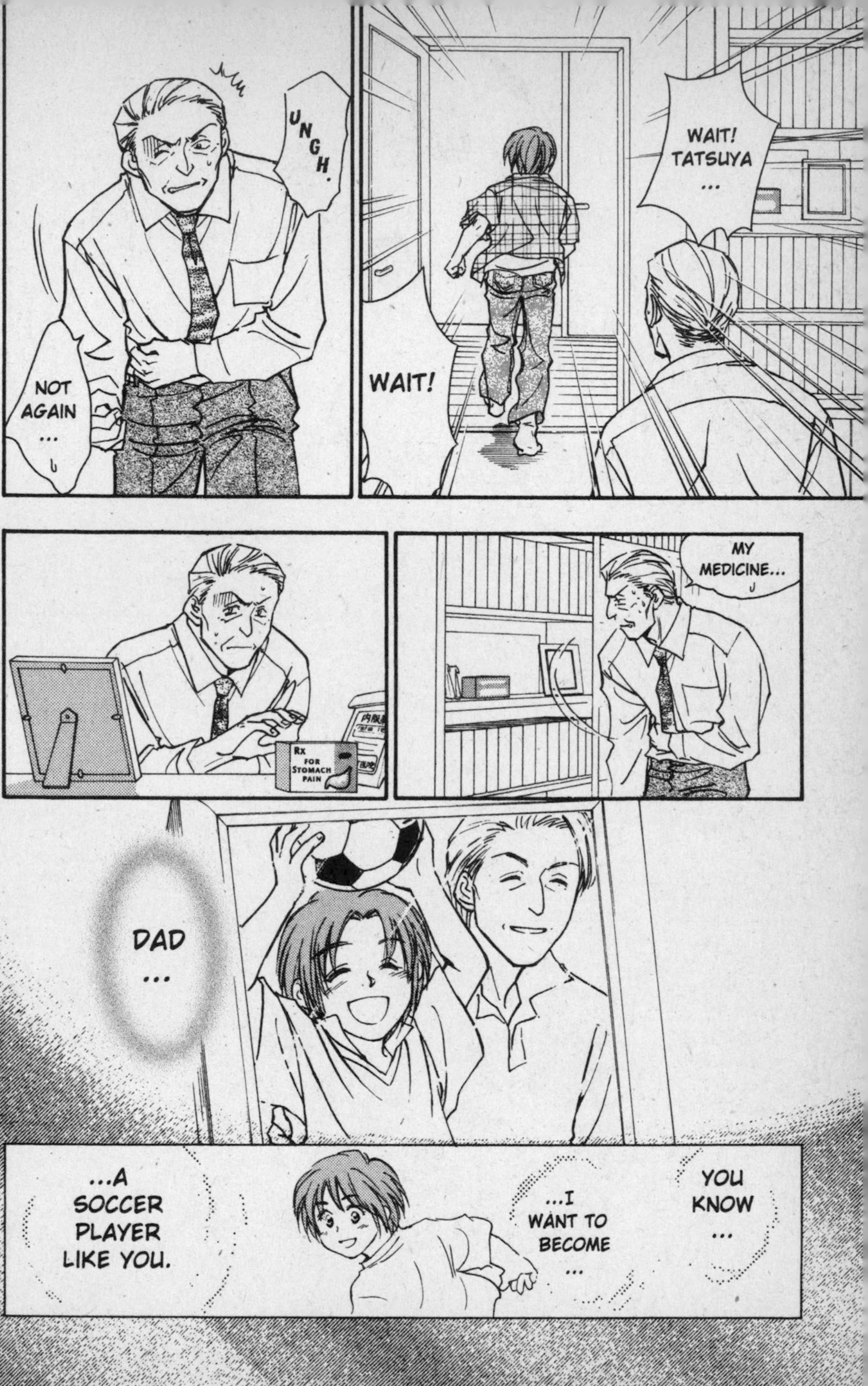
WAIT! TATSUYA ...
WAIT!
UNGH.
NOT AGAIN ...
MY MEDICINE...
RX FOR STOMACH PAIN
DAD ...
YOU KNOW ...
...I WANT TO BECOME ...
...A SOCCER PLAYER LIKE YOU.

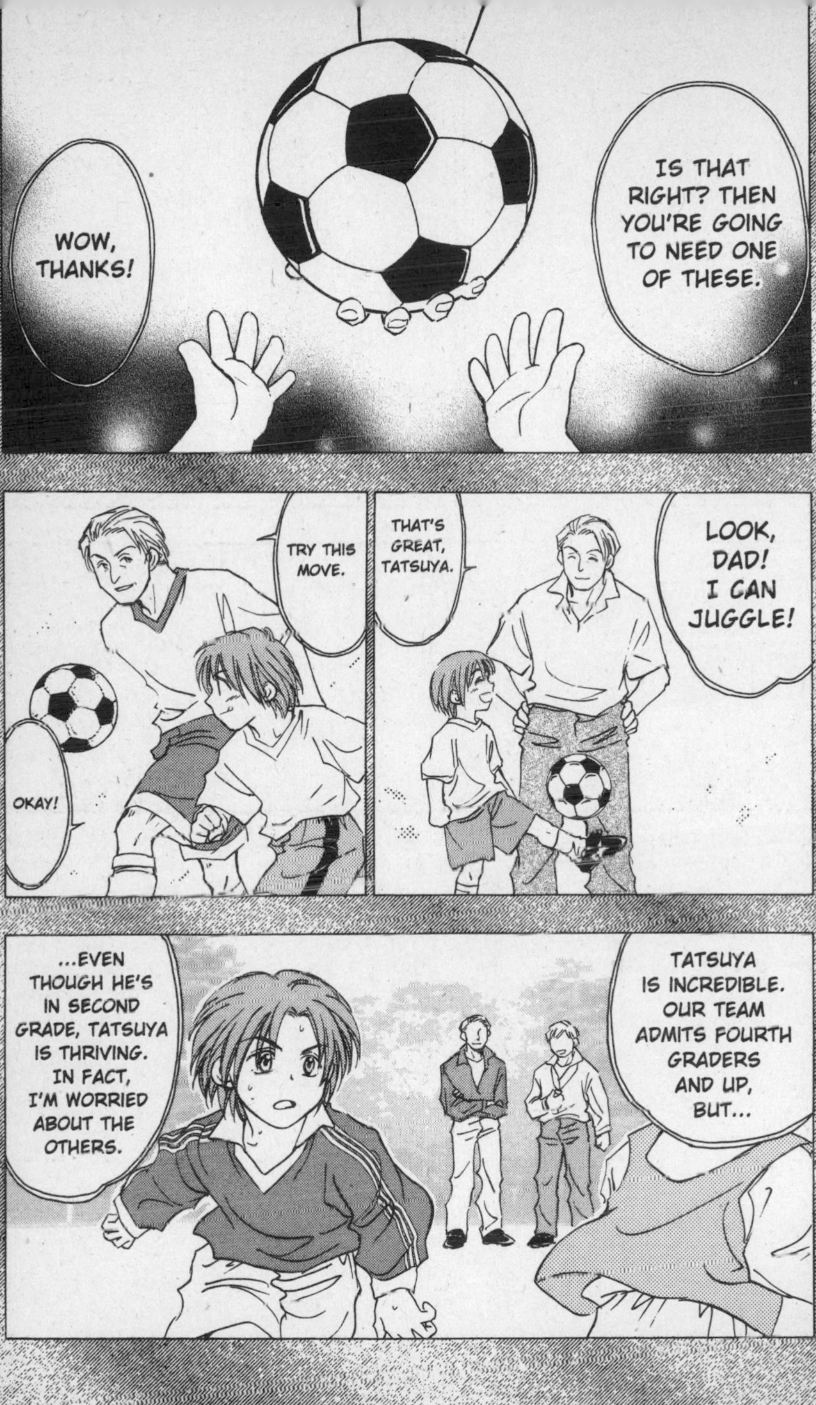
IS THAT RIGHT? THEN YOU'RE GOING TO NEED ONE OF THESE.
WOW, THANKS!
LOOK, DAD! I CAN JUGGLE!
THAT'S GREAT, TATSUYA.
TRY THIS MOVE.
OKAY!
TATSUYA IS INCREDIBLE. OUR TEAM ADMITS FOURTH GRADERS AND UP, BUT...
...EVEN THOUGH HE'S IN SECOND GRADE, TATSUYA IS THRIVING. IN FACT, I'M WORRIED ABOUT THE OTHERS.

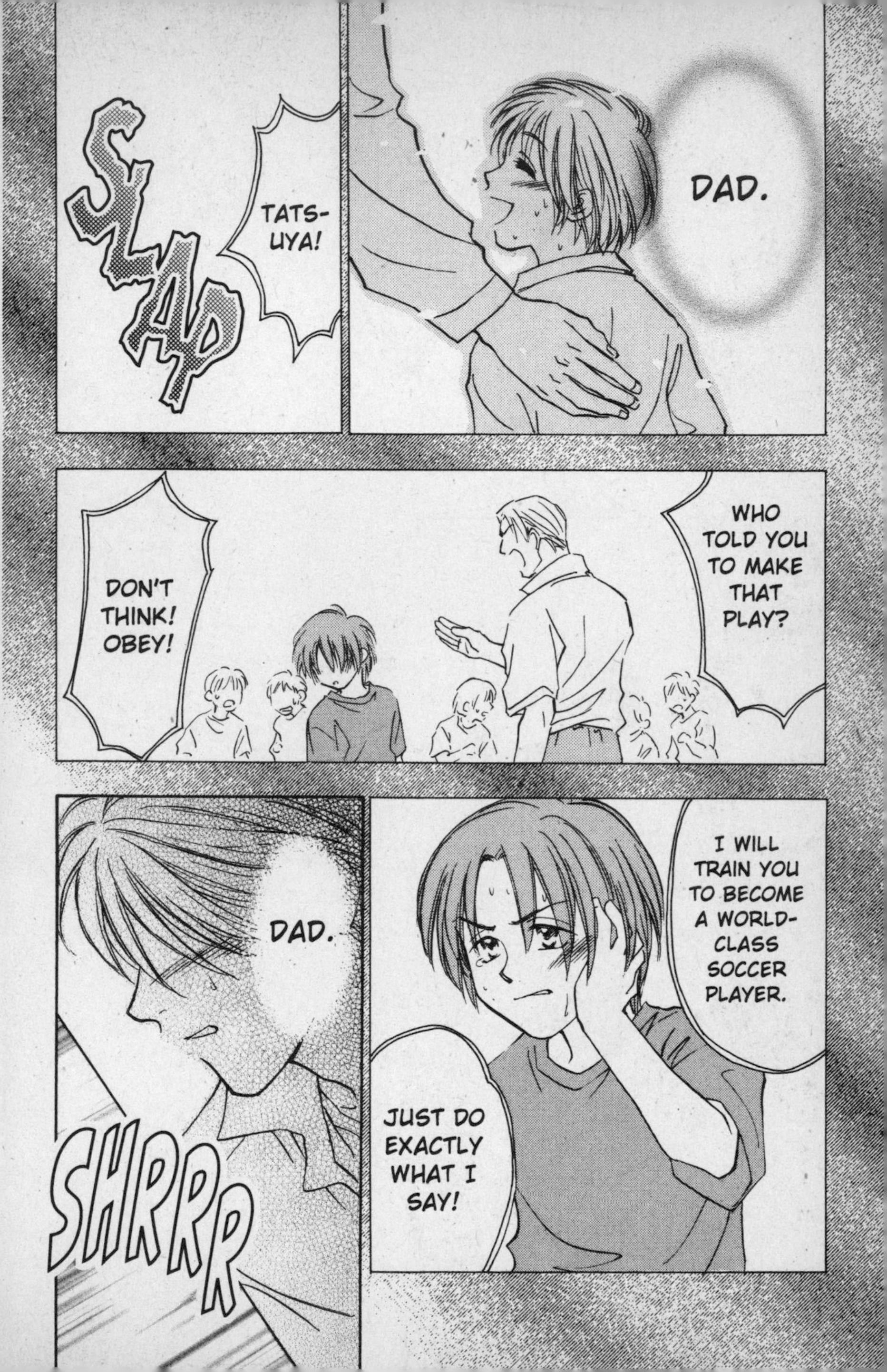
DAD.
TATS-UYA!
SLAP
WHO TOLD YOU TO MAKE THAT PLAY?
DON'T THINK! OBEY!
I WILL TRAIN YOU TO BECOME A WORLD-CLASS SOCCER PLAYER.
JUST DO EXACTLY WHAT I SAY!
DAD.
SHRRR

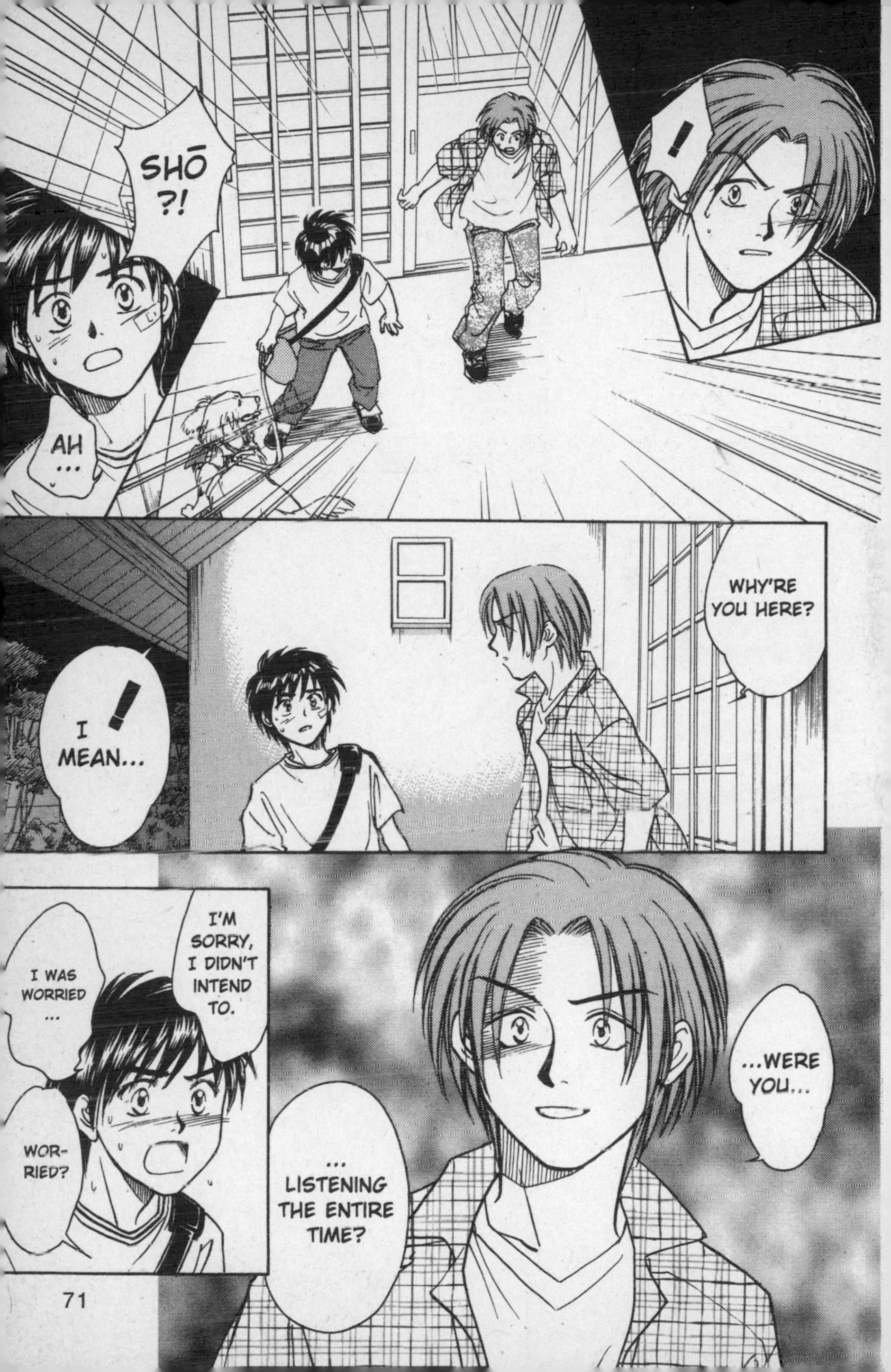

!
SHŌ ?!
AH ...
WHY'RE YOU HERE?
!
I MEAN...
...WERE YOU...
... LISTENING THE ENTIRE TIME?
I'M SORRY, I DIDN'T INTEND TO.
I WAS WORRIED ...
WOR-RIED?

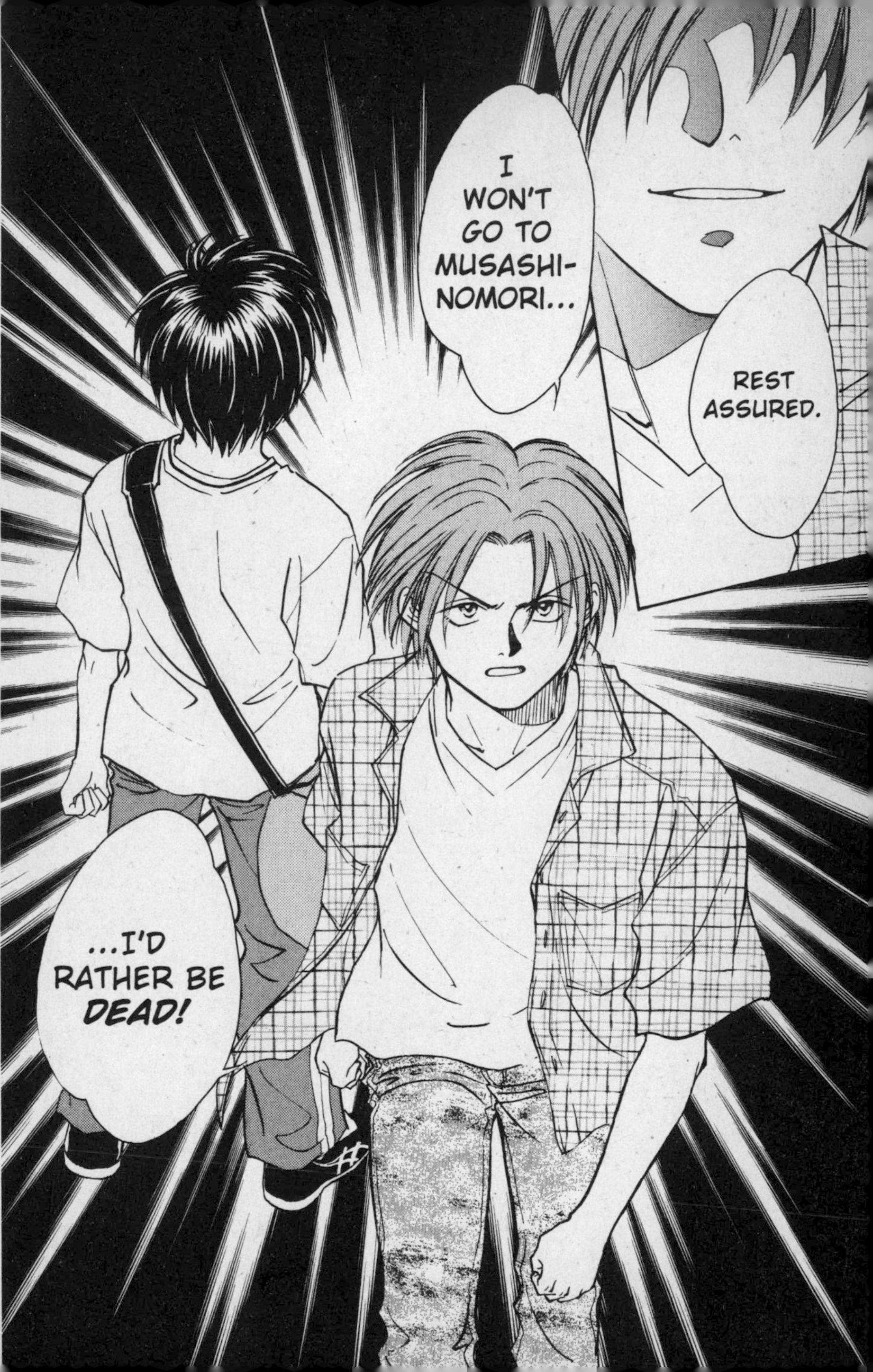
I WON'T GO TO MUSASHI-NOMORI...
REST ASSURED.
...I'D RATHER BE *DEAD!*

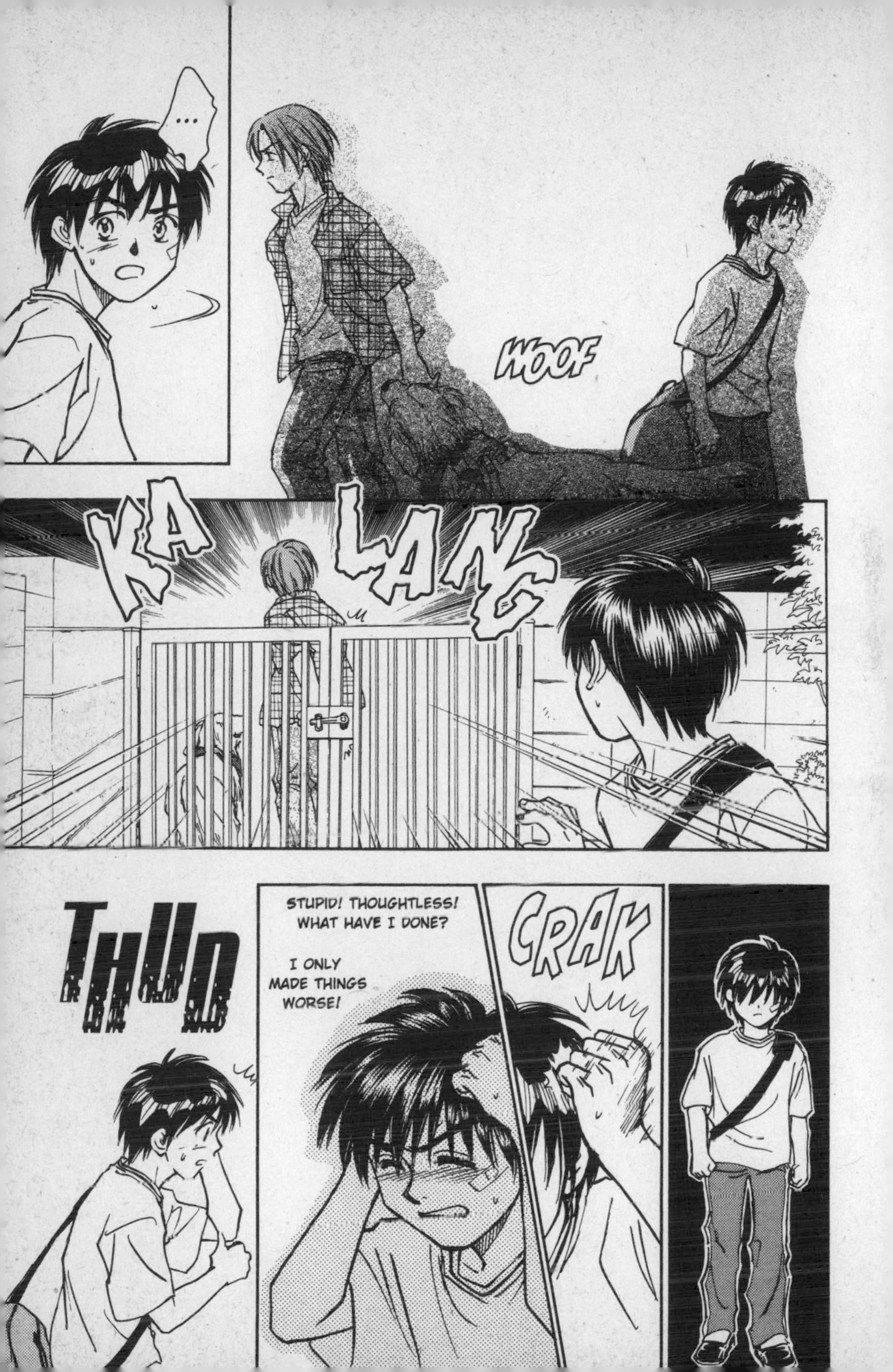
WOOF
...
KA LANG
CRAK
STUPID! THOUGHTLESS! WHAT HAVE I DONE?
I ONLY MADE THINGS WORSE!
THUD

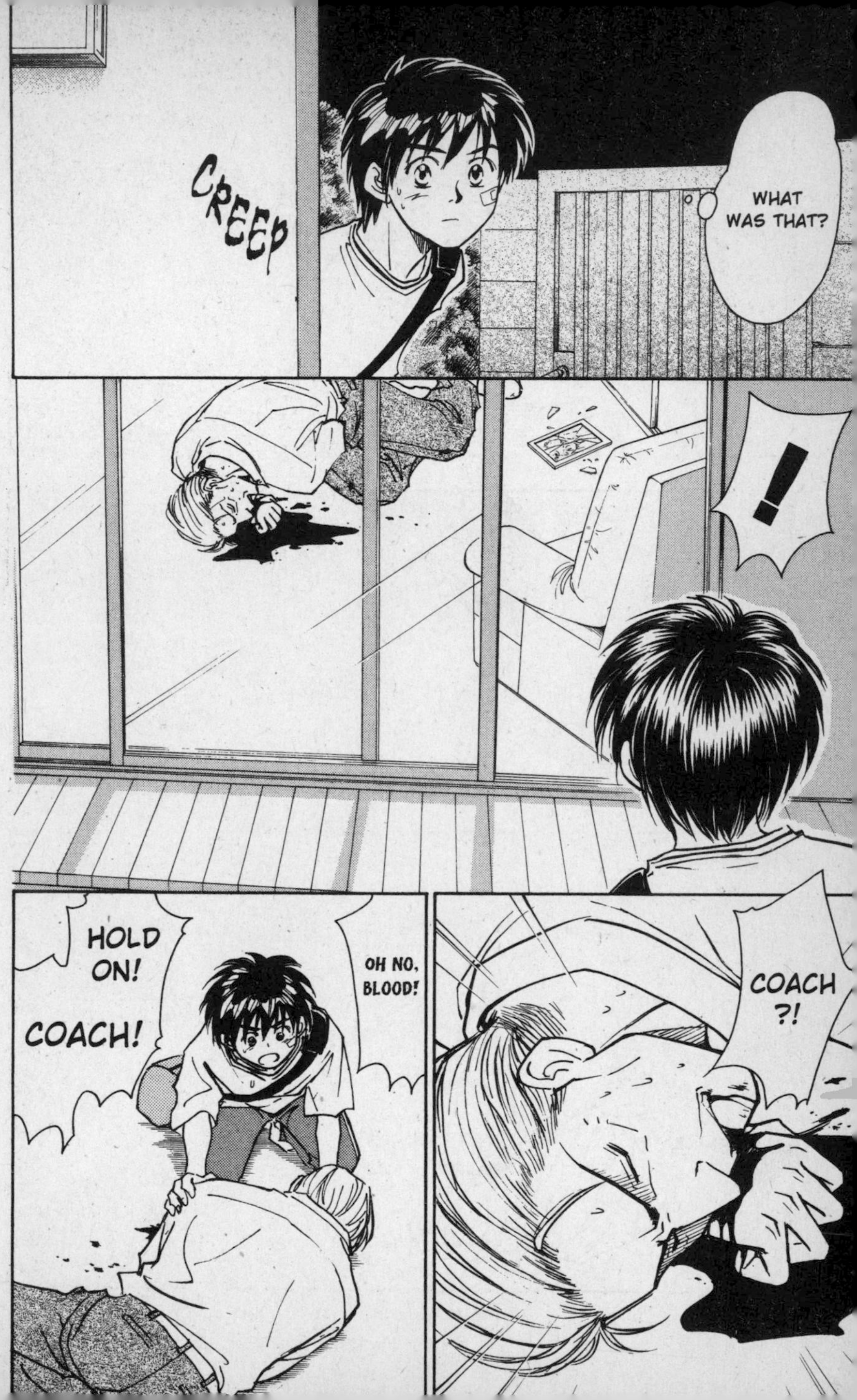
WHAT WAS THAT?
CREEP
!
COACH ?!
OH NO, BLOOD!
HOLD ON! COACH!

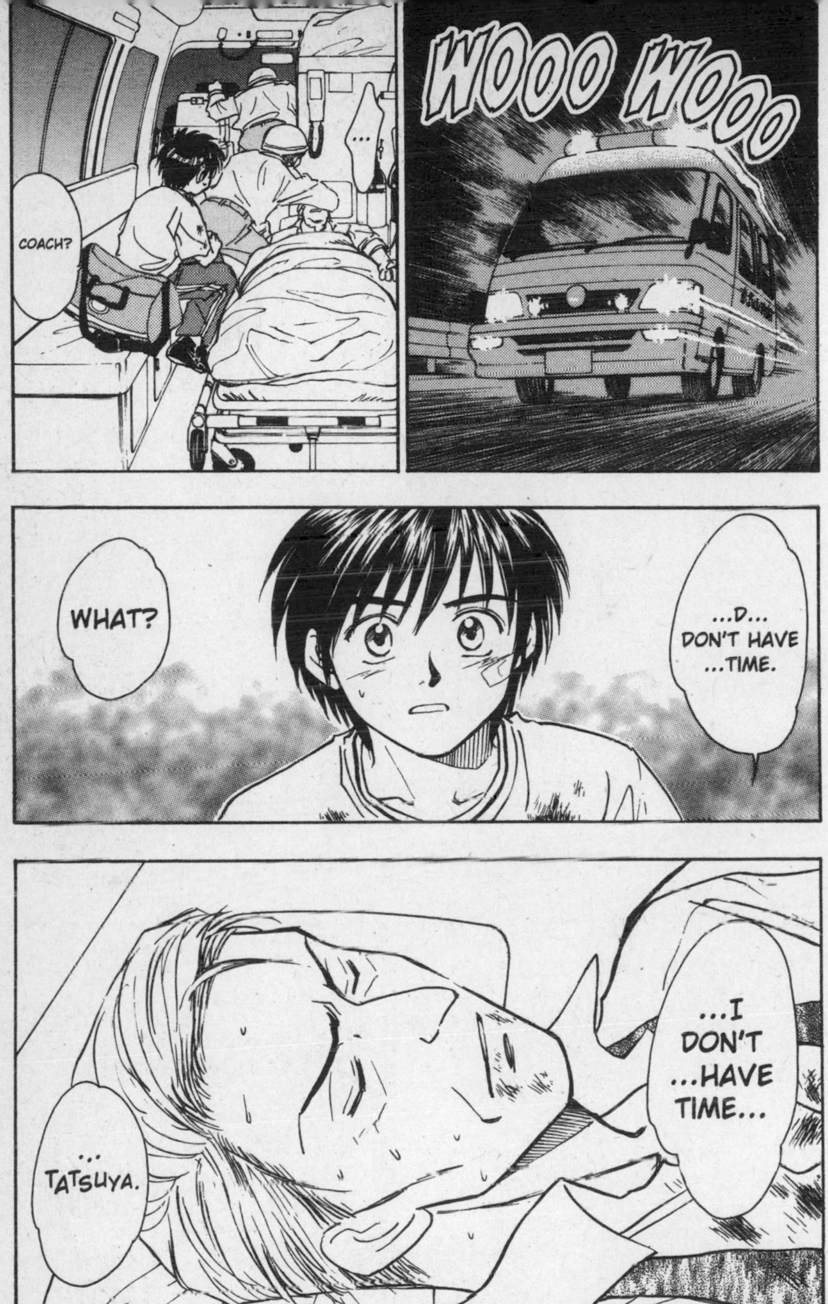
WOOO WOOO
...
COACH?
...D... DON'T HAVE ...TIME.
WHAT?
...I DON'T ...HAVE TIME...
... TATSUYA.

WHISTLE!

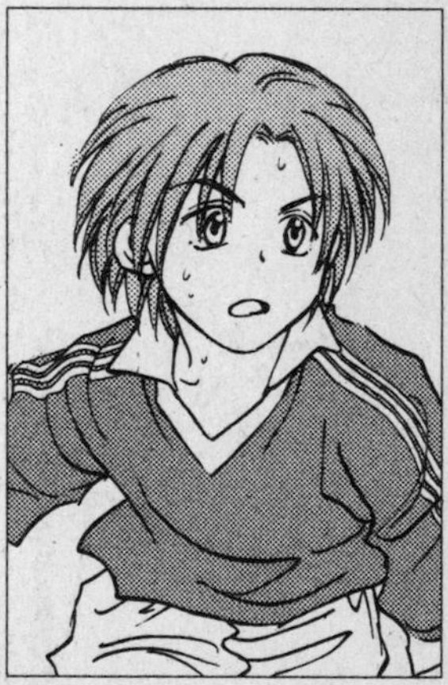

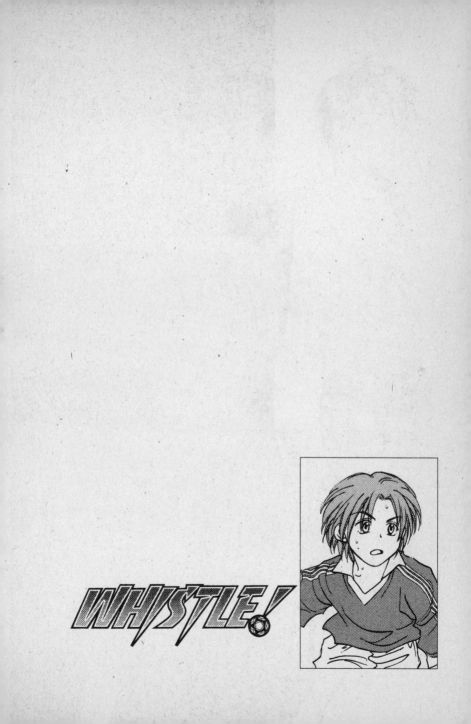

STAGE.66
Residue

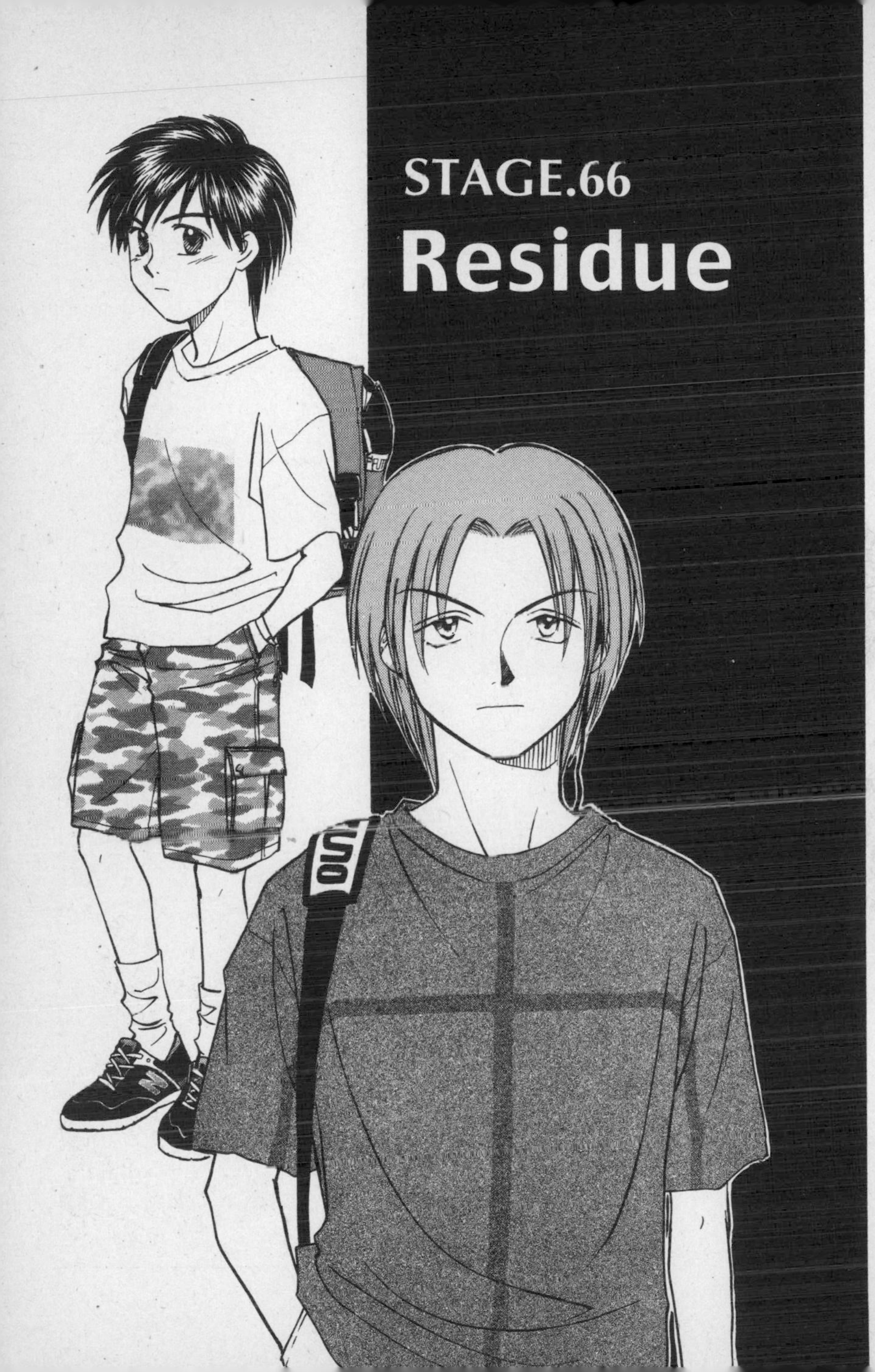

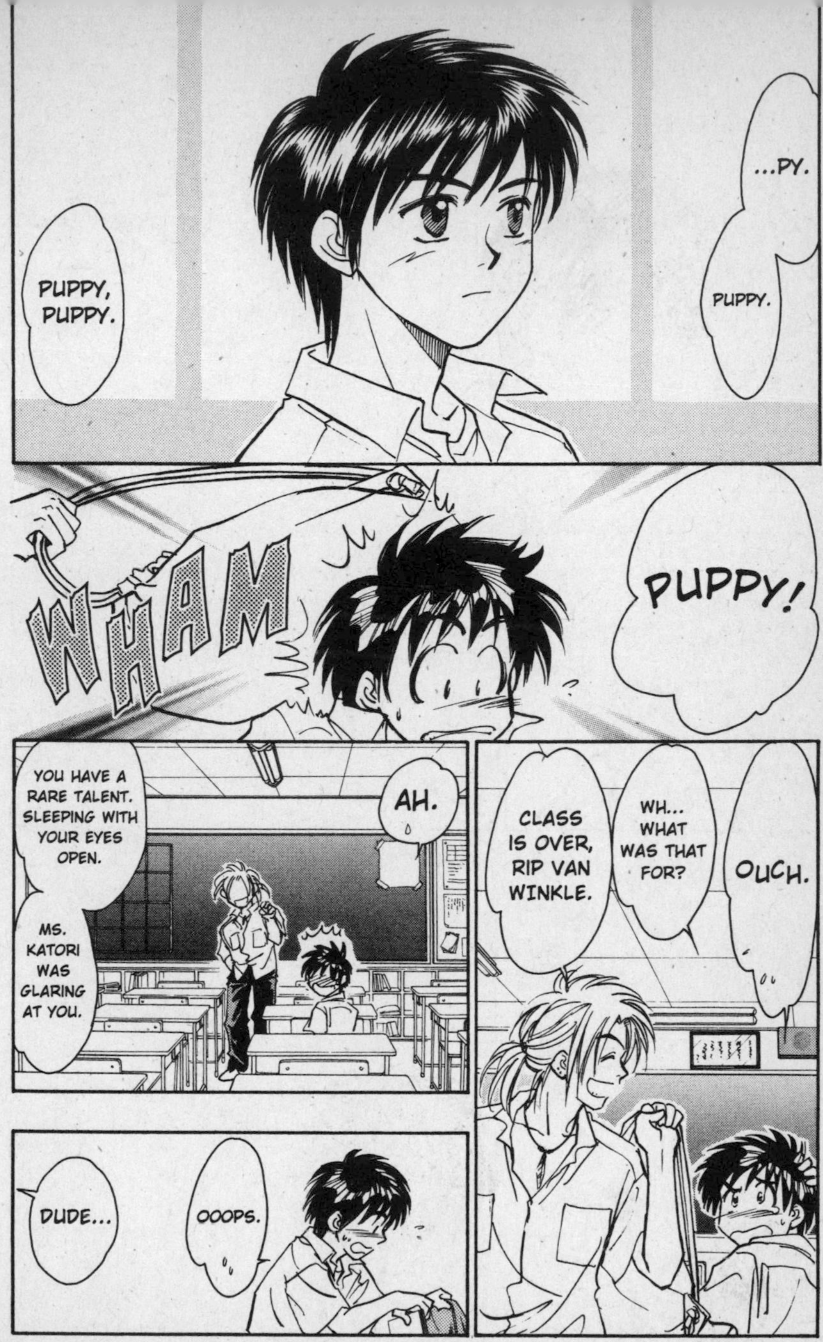
...PY.
PUPPY.
PUPPY, PUPPY.
PUPPY!
WHAM
OUCH.
WH... WHAT WAS THAT FOR?
CLASS IS OVER, RIP VAN WINKLE.
AH.
YOU HAVE A RARE TALENT. SLEEPING WITH YOUR EYES OPEN.
MS. KATORI WAS GLARING AT YOU.
OOOPS.
DUDE...

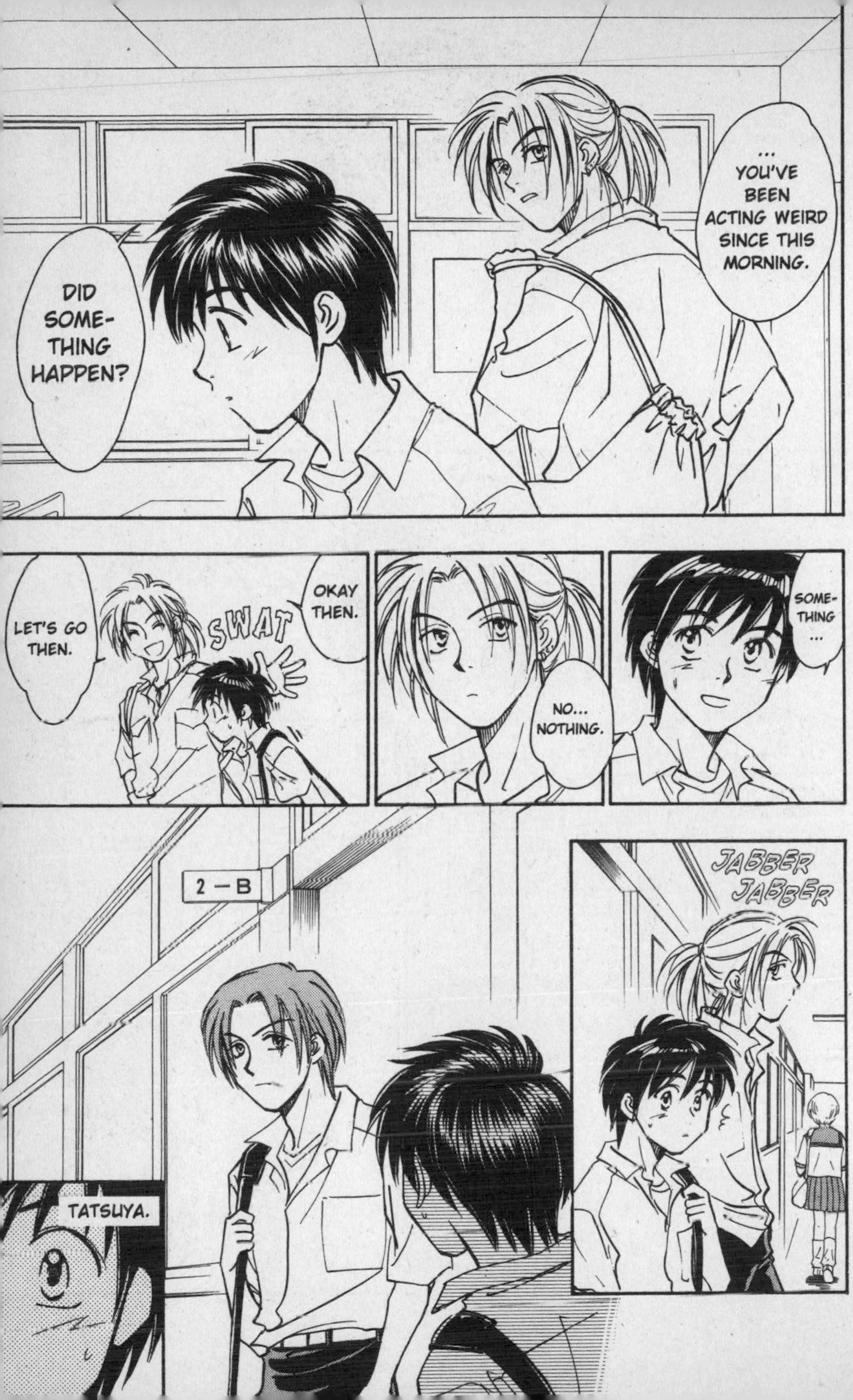
... YOU'VE BEEN ACTING WEIRD SINCE THIS MORNING.
DID SOME-THING HAPPEN?
SOME-THING ...
NO... NOTHING.
OKAY THEN.
SWAT
LET'S GO THEN.
JABBER JABBER
2 — B
TATSUYA.

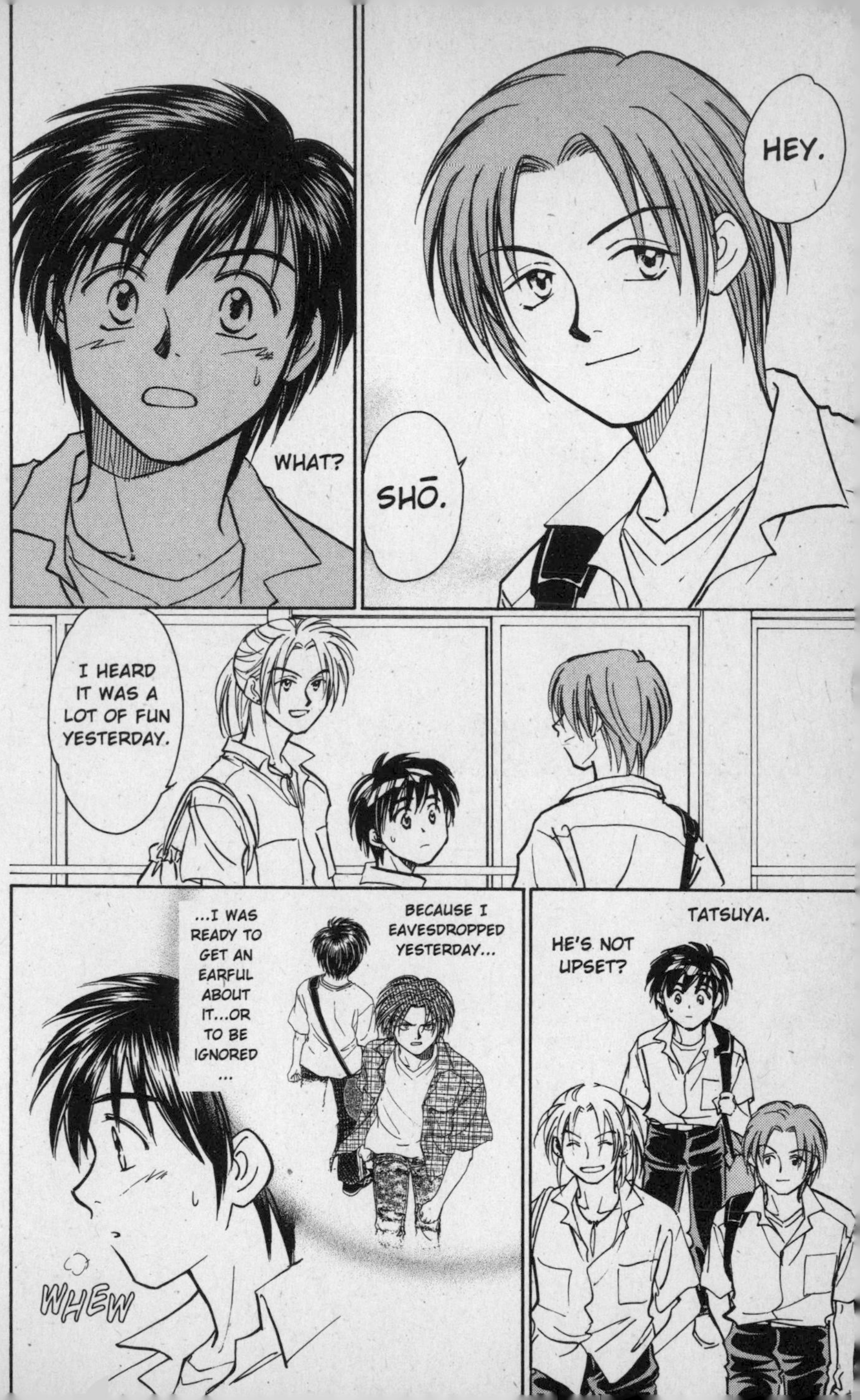
HEY.
SHŌ.
WHAT?
I HEARD IT WAS A LOT OF FUN YESTERDAY.
TATSUYA.
HE'S NOT UPSET?
BECAUSE I EAVESDROPPED YESTERDAY...
...I WAS READY TO GET AN EARFUL ABOUT IT...OR TO BE IGNORED ...
WHEW

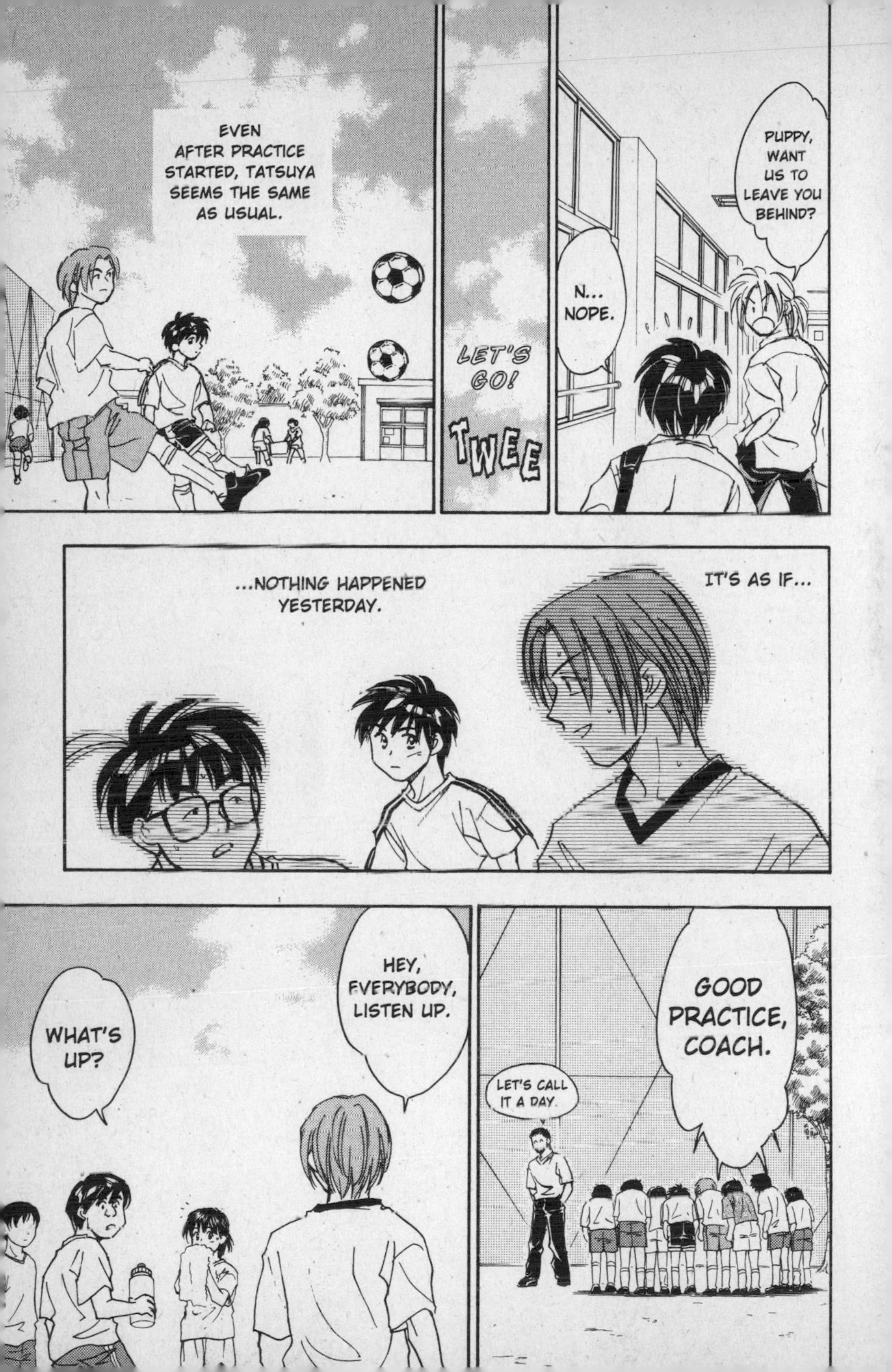
PUPPY, WANT US TO LEAVE YOU BEHIND?
N... NOPE.
LET'S GO!
TWEE
EVEN AFTER PRACTICE STARTED, TATSUYA SEEMS THE SAME AS USUAL.
IT'S AS IF...
...NOTHING HAPPENED YESTERDAY.
GOOD PRACTICE, COACH.
LET'S CALL IT A DAY.
HEY, EVERYBODY, LISTEN UP.
WHAT'S UP?

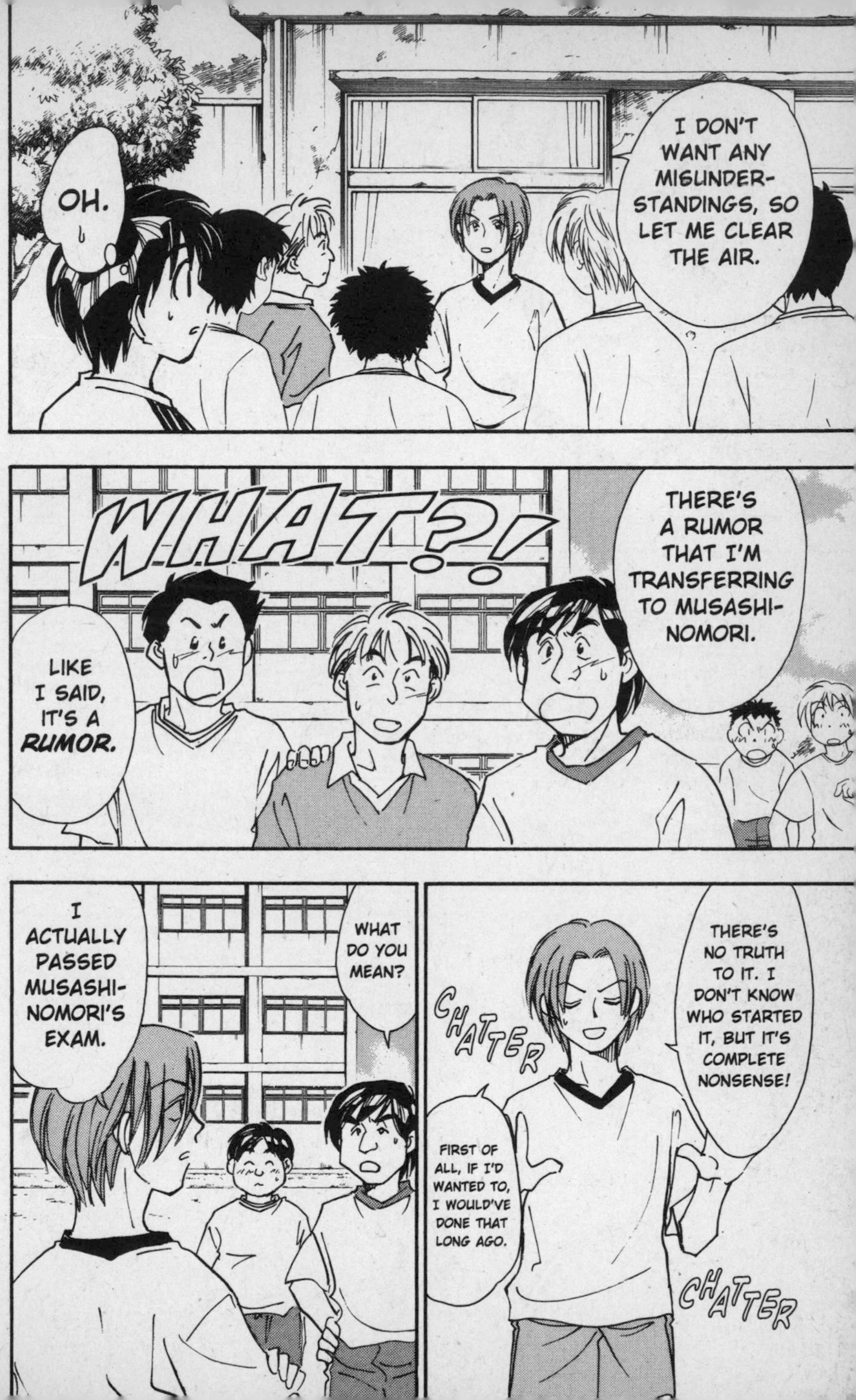

I DON'T WANT ANY MISUNDER-STANDINGS, SO LET ME CLEAR THE AIR.
OH.
THERE'S A RUMOR THAT I'M TRANSFERRING TO MUSASHI-NOMORI.
WHAT?!
LIKE I SAID, IT'S A *RUMOR.*
THERE'S NO TRUTH TO IT. I DON'T KNOW WHO STARTED IT, BUT IT'S COMPLETE NONSENSE!
CHATTER
FIRST OF ALL, IF I'D WANTED TO, I WOULD'VE DONE THAT LONG AGO.
CHATTER
WHAT DO YOU MEAN?
I ACTUALLY PASSED MUSASHI-NOMORI'S EXAM.

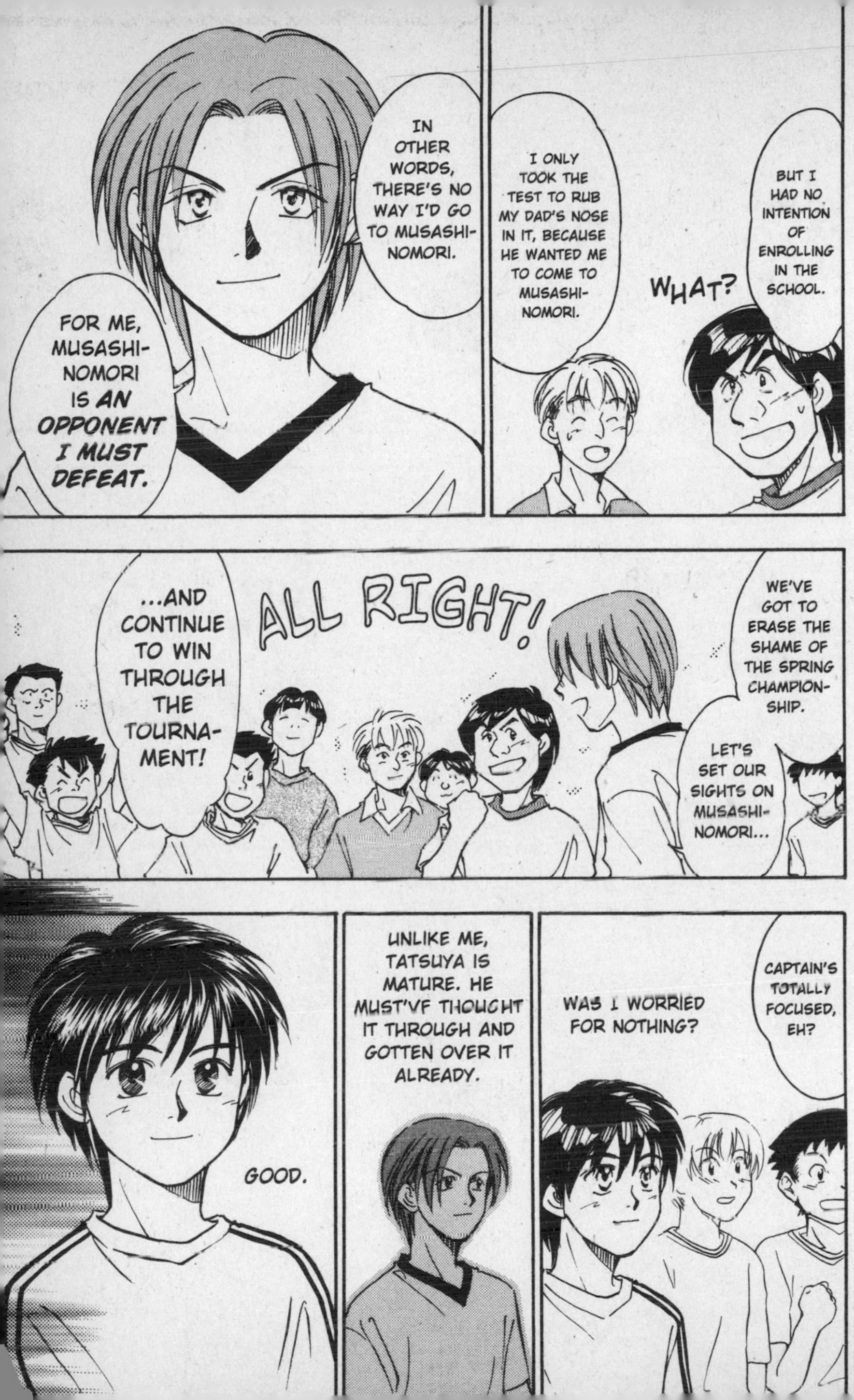
BUT I HAD NO INTENTION OF ENROLLING IN THE SCHOOL.
WHAT?
I ONLY TOOK THE TEST TO RUB MY DAD'S NOSE IN IT, BECAUSE HE WANTED ME TO COME TO MUSASHI-NOMORI.
IN OTHER WORDS, THERE'S NO WAY I'D GO TO MUSASHI-NOMORI.
FOR ME, MUSASHI-NOMORI IS AN OPPONENT I MUST DEFEAT.
WE'VE GOT TO ERASE THE SHAME OF THE SPRING CHAMPION-SHIP.
LET'S SET OUR SIGHTS ON MUSASHI-NOMORI...
...AND CONTINUE TO WIN THROUGH THE TOURNA-MENT!
ALL RIGHT!
CAPTAIN'S TOTALLY FOCUSED, EH?
WAS I WORRIED FOR NOTHING?
UNLIKE ME, TATSUYA IS MATURE. HE MUST'VE THOUGHT IT THROUGH AND GOTTEN OVER IT ALREADY.
GOOD.

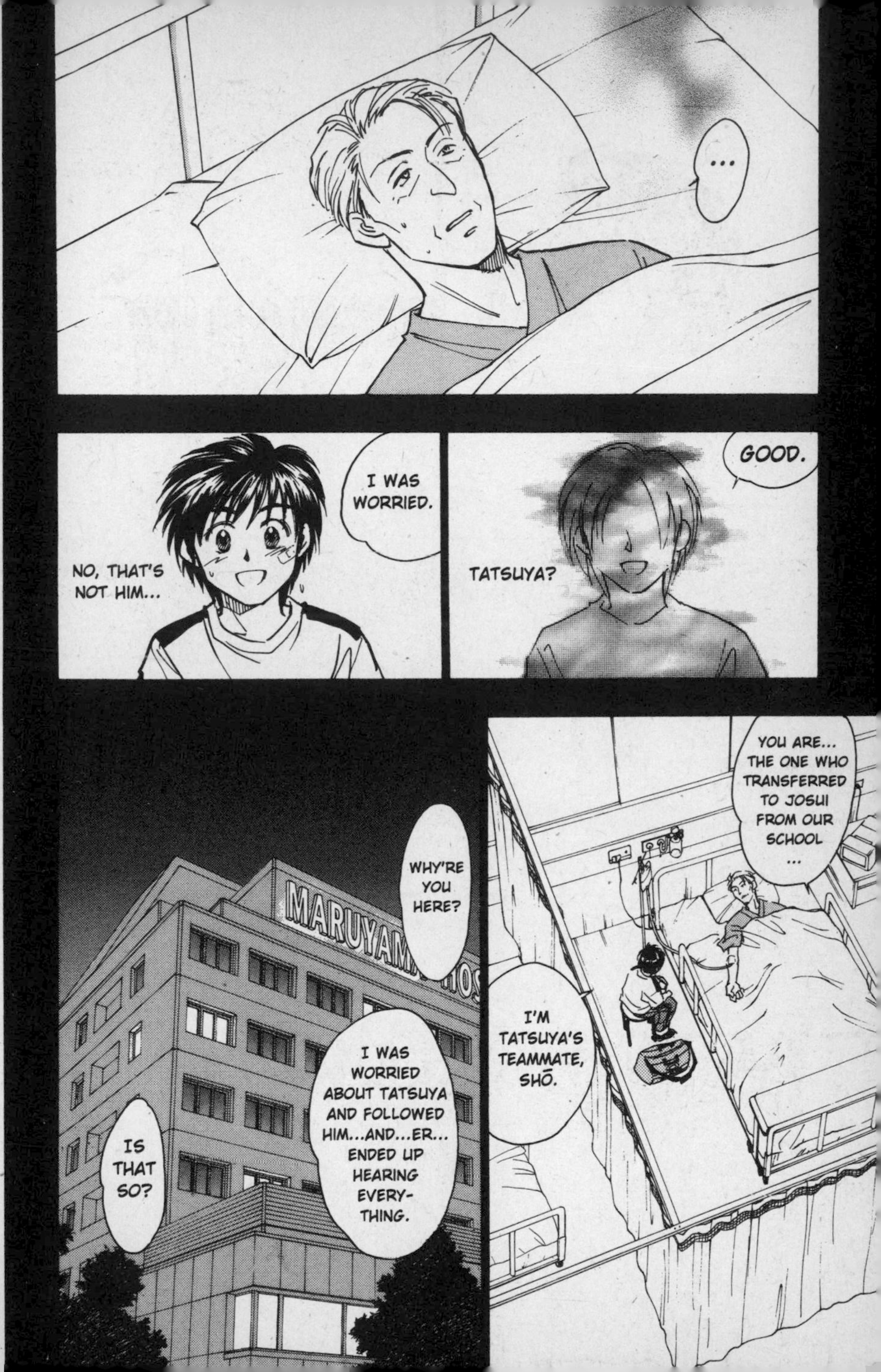
...
GOOD.
TATSUYA?
I WAS WORRIED.
NO, THAT'S NOT HIM...
YOU ARE... THE ONE WHO TRANSFERRED TO JOSUI FROM OUR SCHOOL ...
I'M TATSUYA'S TEAMMATE, SHŌ.
MARUYAMA
WHY'RE YOU HERE?
I WAS WORRIED ABOUT TATSUYA AND FOLLOWED HIM...AND...ER... ENDED UP HEARING EVERYTHING.
IS THAT SO?

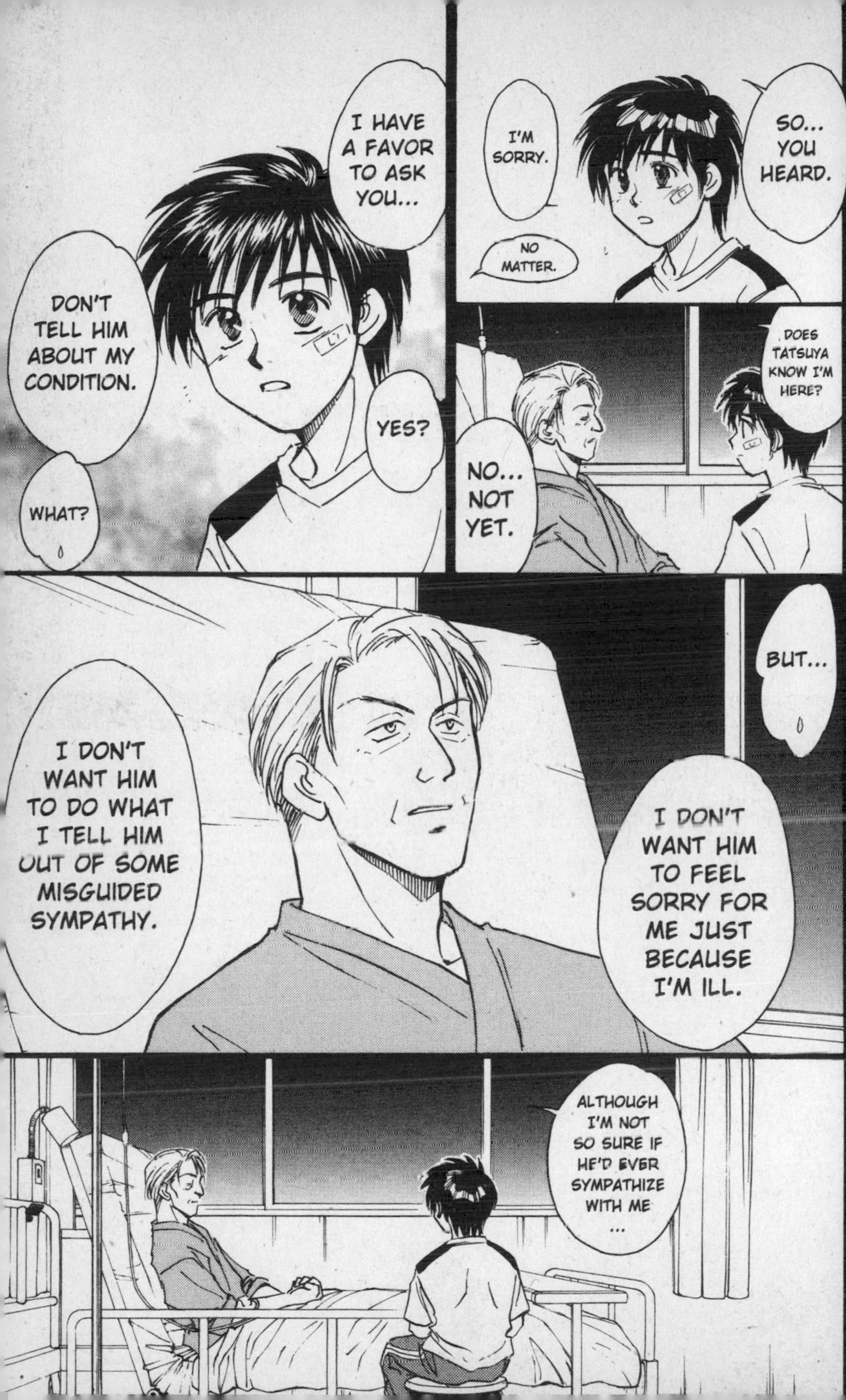
SO... YOU HEARD.
I'M SORRY.
NO MATTER.
DOES TATSUYA KNOW I'M HERE?
NO... NOT YET.
I HAVE A FAVOR TO ASK YOU...
YES?
DON'T TELL HIM ABOUT MY CONDITION.
WHAT?
BUT...
I DON'T WANT HIM TO FEEL SORRY FOR ME JUST BECAUSE I'M ILL.
I DON'T WANT HIM TO DO WHAT I TELL HIM OUT OF SOME MISGUIDED SYMPATHY.
ALTHOUGH I'M NOT SO SURE IF HE'D EVER SYMPATHIZE WITH ME ...

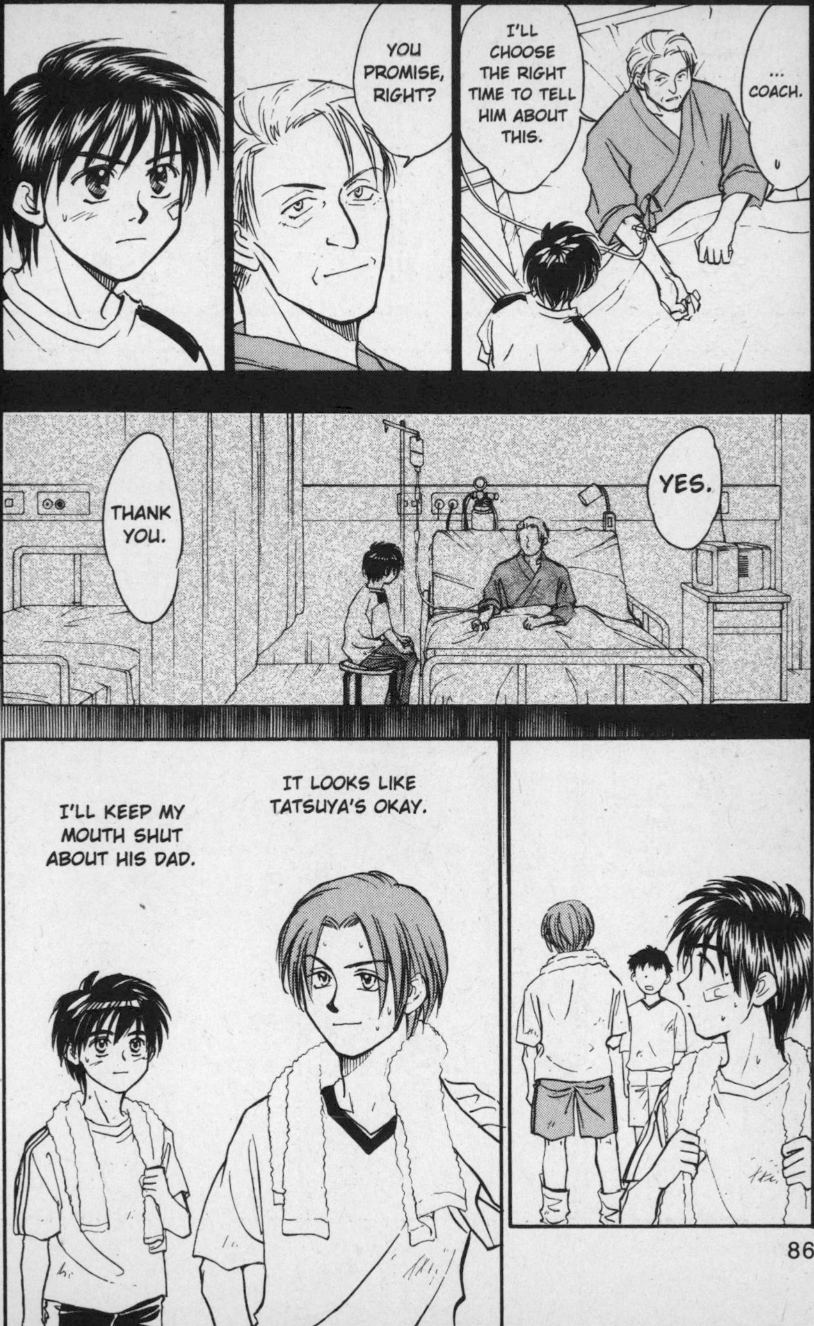
... COACH.
I'LL CHOOSE THE RIGHT TIME TO TELL HIM ABOUT THIS.
YOU PROMISE, RIGHT?
YES.
THANK YOU.
IT LOOKS LIKE TATSUYA'S OKAY.
I'LL KEEP MY MOUTH SHUT ABOUT HIS DAD.

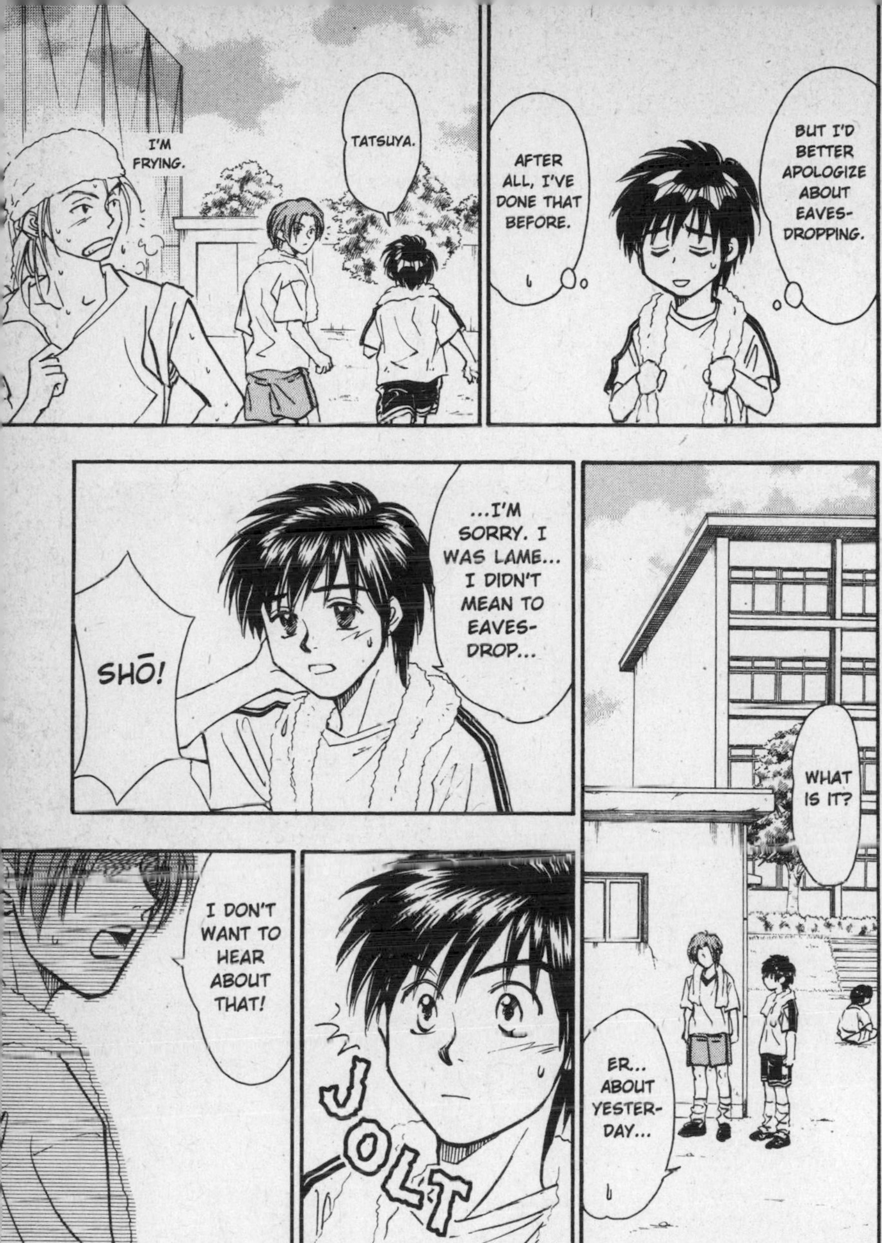
BUT I'D BETTER APOLOGIZE ABOUT EAVES-DROPPING.
AFTER ALL, I'VE DONE THAT BEFORE.
TATSUYA.
I'M FRYING.
WHAT IS IT?
ER... ABOUT YESTER-DAY...
...I'M SORRY. I WAS LAME... I DIDN'T MEAN TO EAVES-DROP...
SHŌ!
JOLT
I DON'T WANT TO HEAR ABOUT THAT!

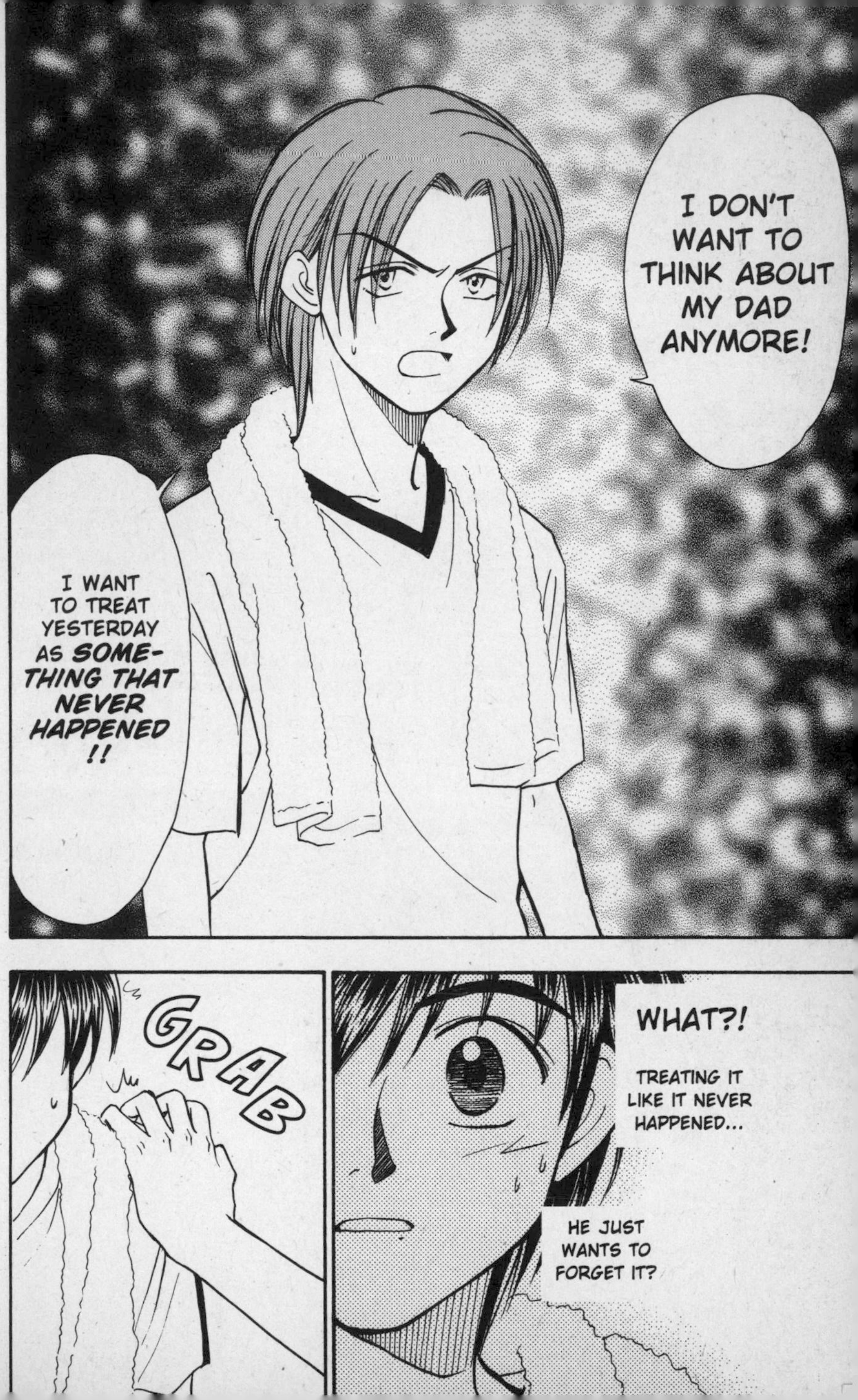
I DON'T WANT TO THINK ABOUT MY DAD ANYMORE!
I WANT TO TREAT YESTERDAY AS **SOMETHING THAT NEVER HAPPENED**!!
WHAT?!
TREATING IT LIKE IT NEVER HAPPENED...
HE JUST WANTS TO FORGET IT?
GRAB

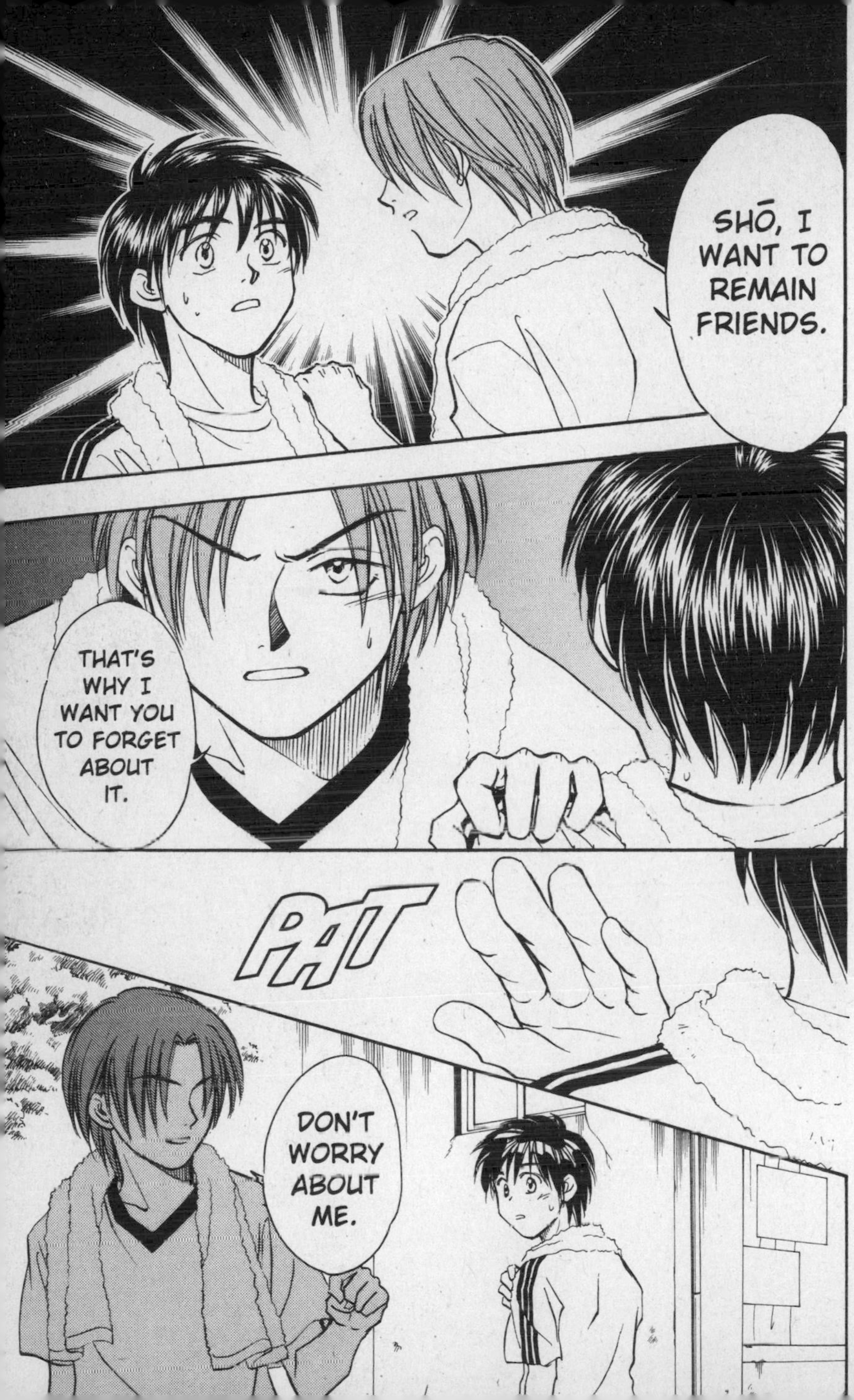
SHŌ, I WANT TO REMAIN FRIENDS.
THAT'S WHY I WANT YOU TO FORGET ABOUT IT.
PAT
DON'T WORRY ABOUT ME.

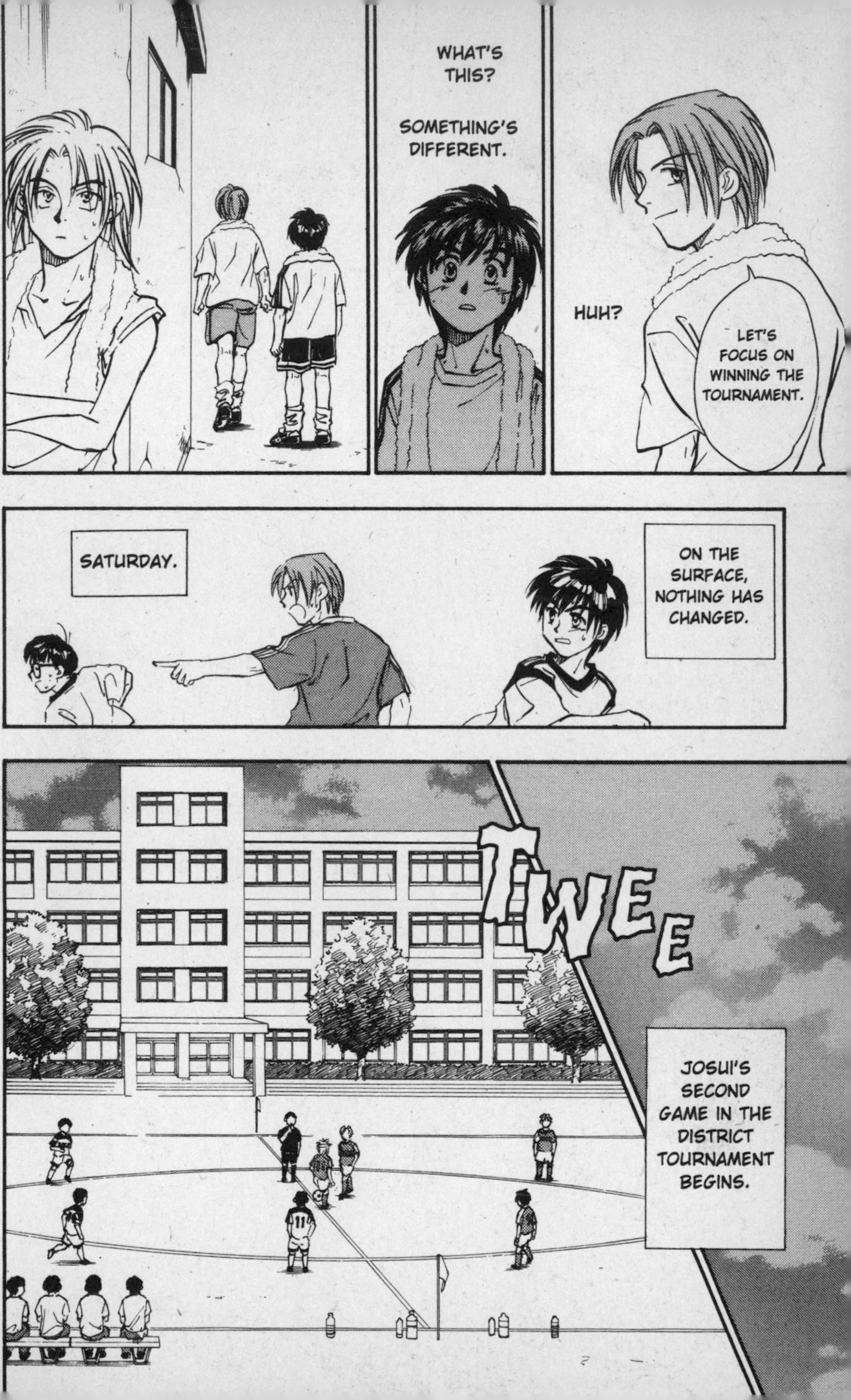
LET'S FOCUS ON WINNING THE TOURNAMENT.
HUH?
WHAT'S THIS?
SOMETHING'S DIFFERENT.
ON THE SURFACE, NOTHING HAS CHANGED.
SATURDAY.
TWEE
JOSUI'S SECOND GAME IN THE DISTRICT TOURNAMENT BEGINS.

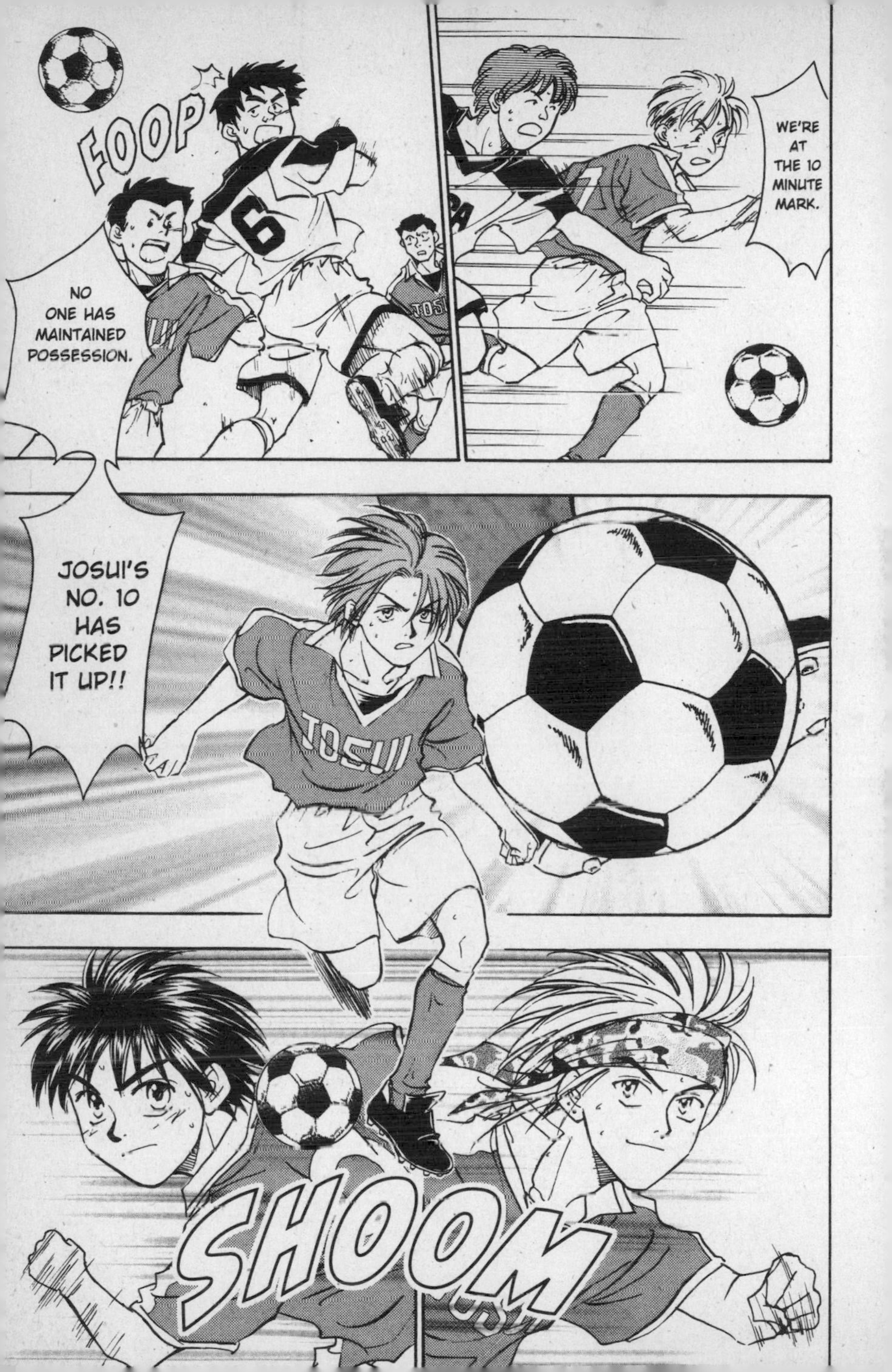
WE'RE AT THE 10 MINUTE MARK.
FOOP
NO ONE HAS MAINTAINED POSSESSION.
JOSUI'S NO. 10 HAS PICKED IT UP!!
JOSUI
SHOOM

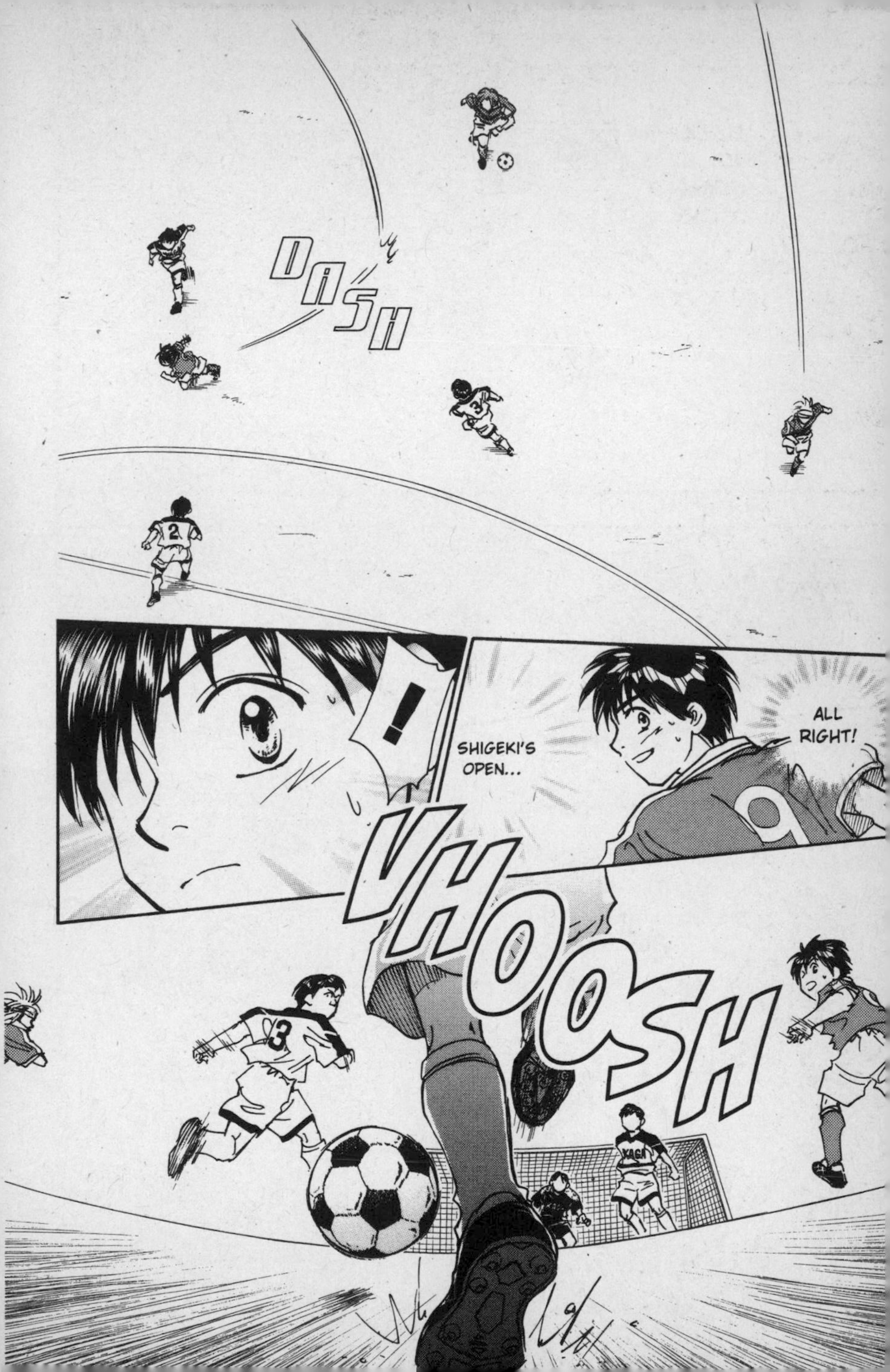
DASH
ALL RIGHT!
SHIGEKI'S OPEN...
!
VHOOSH

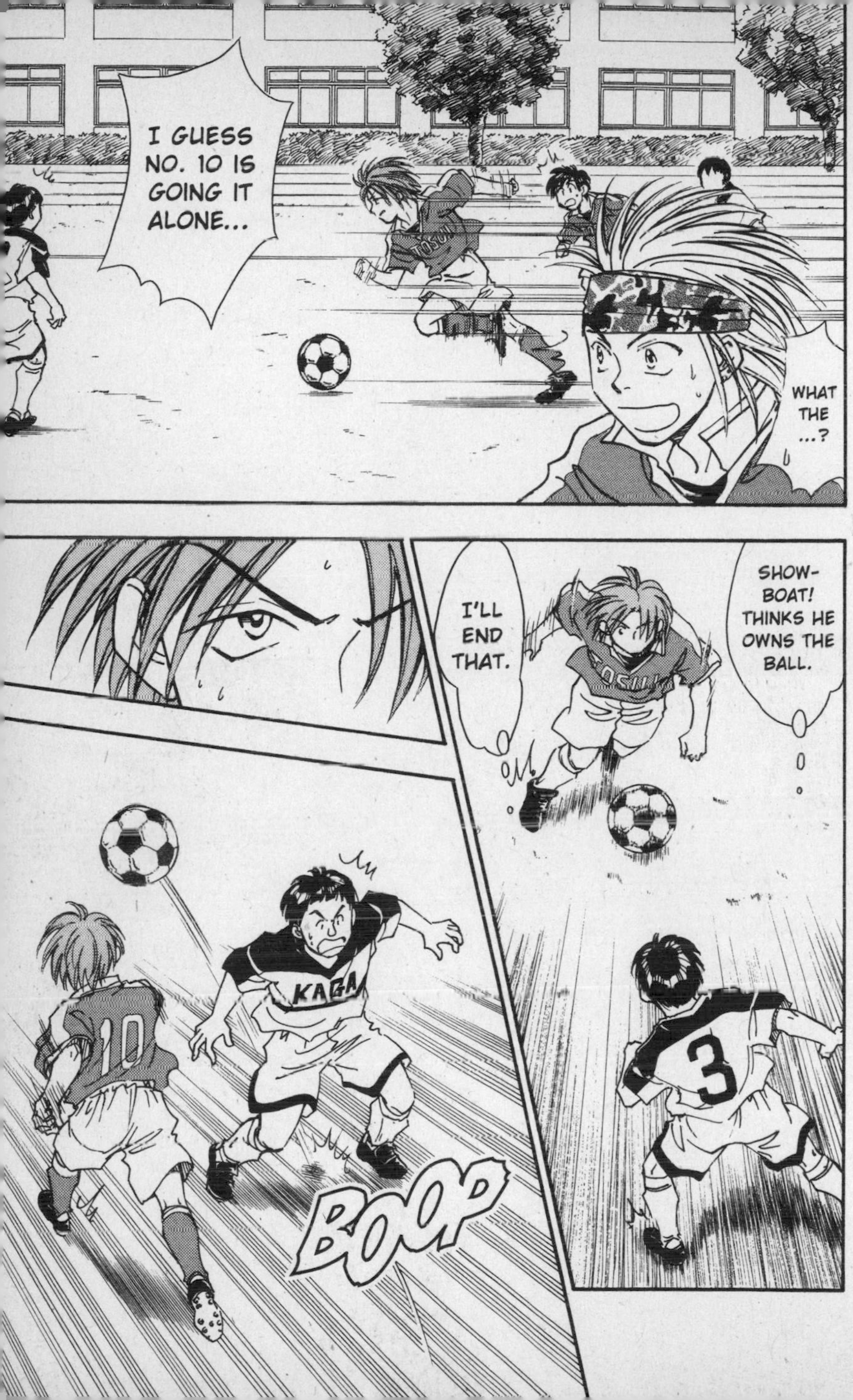

I GUESS NO. 10 IS GOING IT ALONE...
WHAT THE ...?
SHOW-BOAT! THINKS HE OWNS THE BALL.
I'LL END THAT.
BOOP

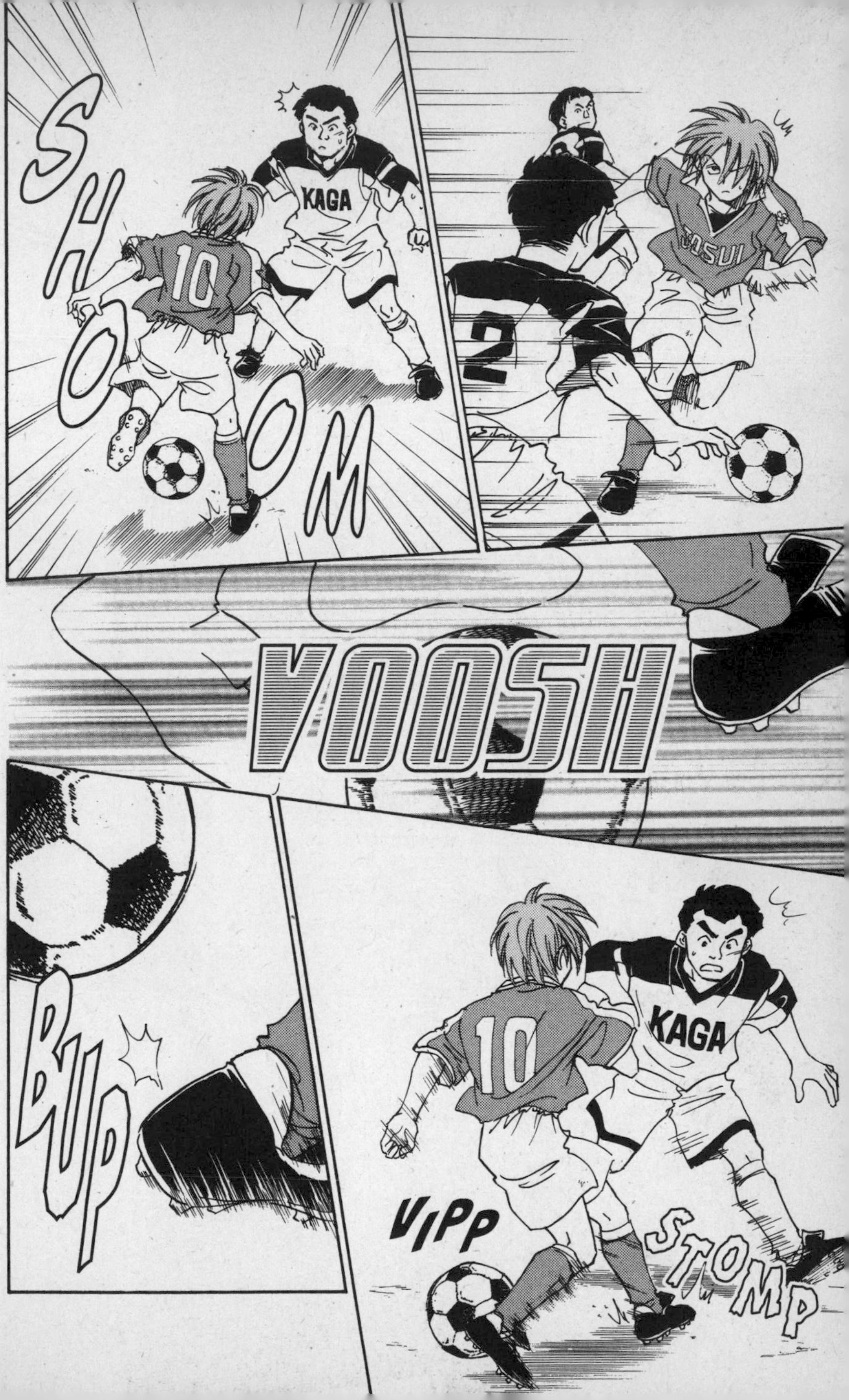
SHOOM
VOOSH
STOMP
VIPP
BUP

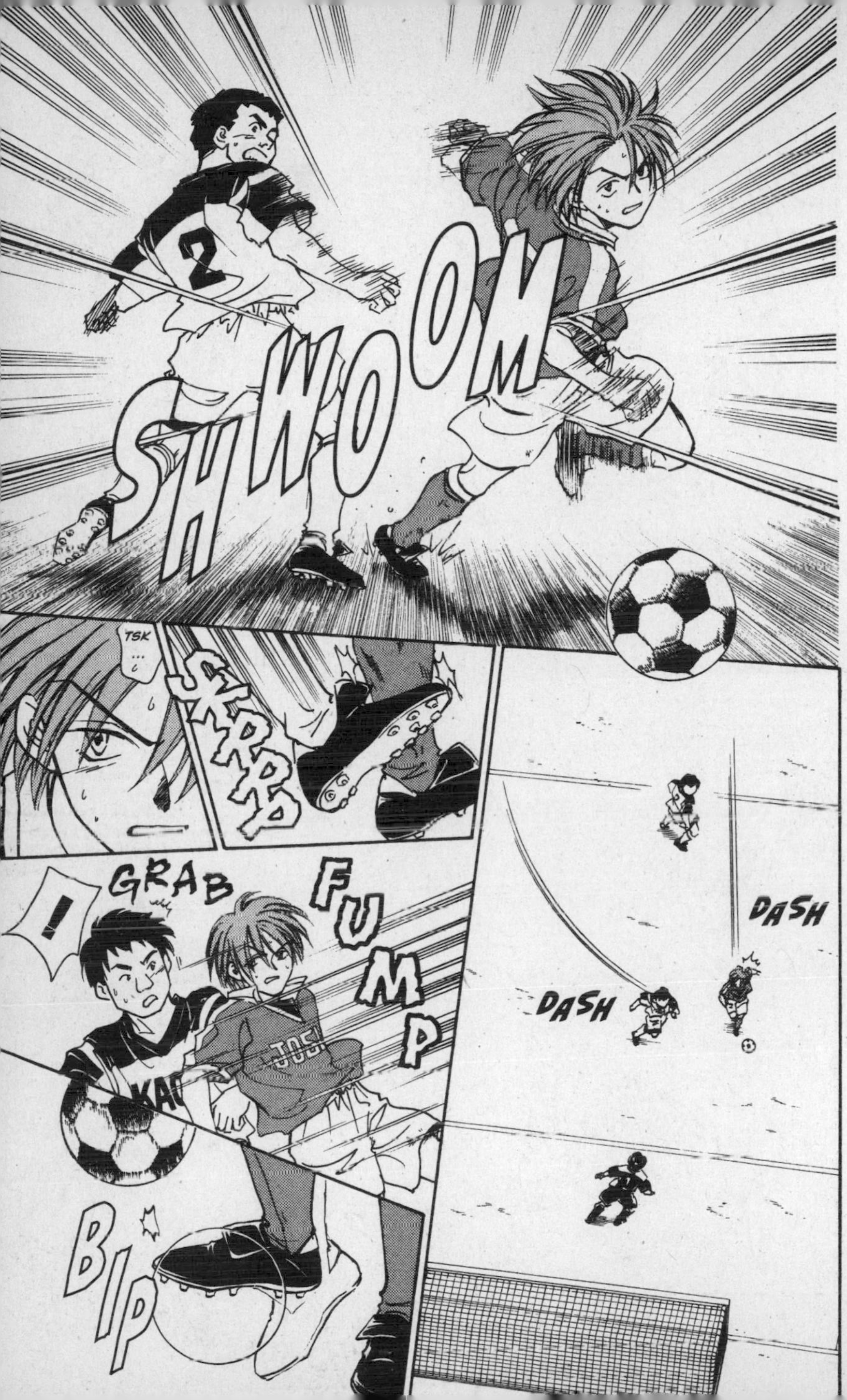

SHWOOM
DASH
DASH
SKRRP
TSK ...
FUMP
GRAB
!
BIP

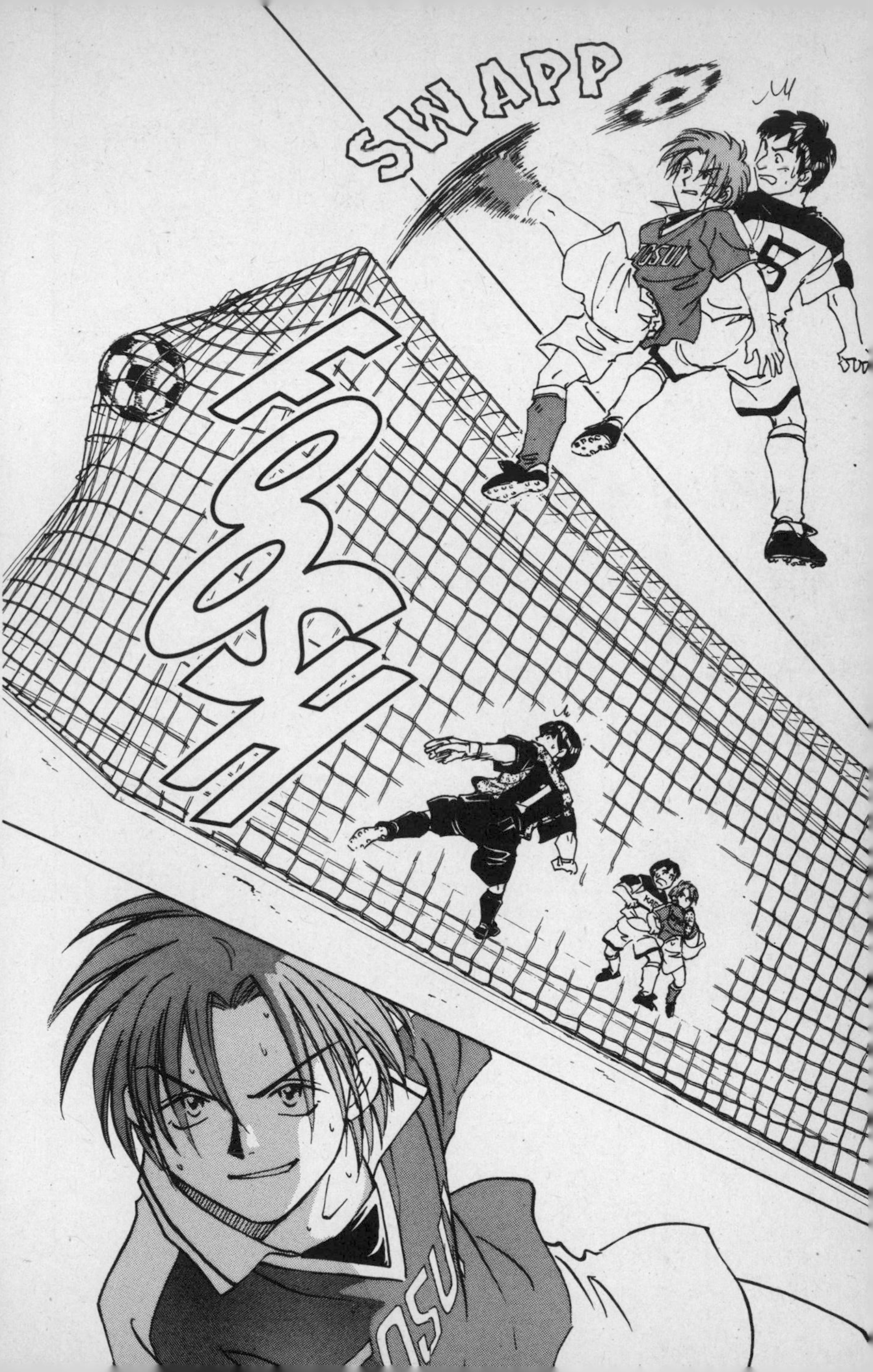
SWAPP
FOOSH

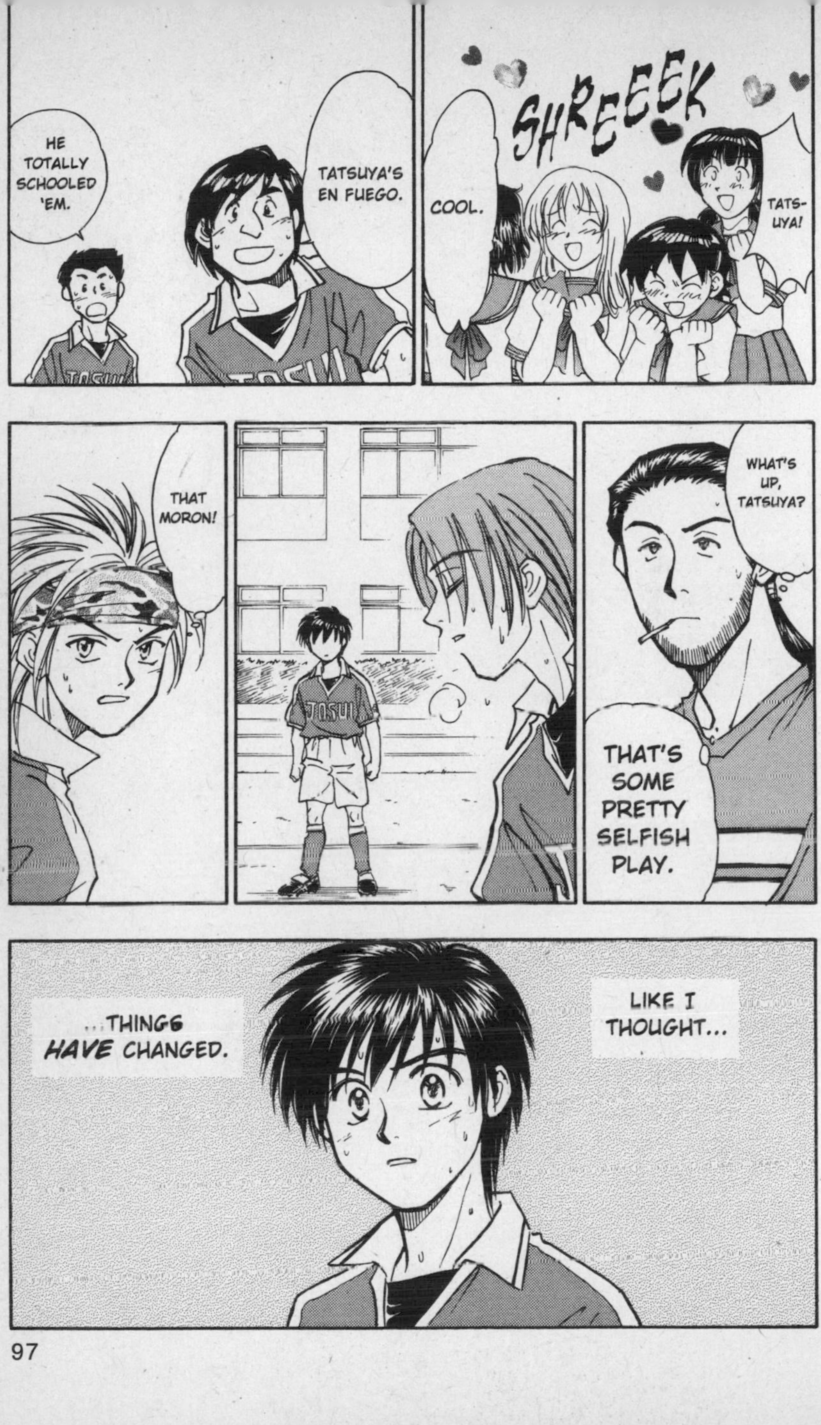
SHREEEK
TATS-UYA!
COOL.
TATSUYA'S EN FUEGO.
HE TOTALLY SCHOOLED 'EM.
WHAT'S UP, TATSUYA?
THAT'S SOME PRETTY SELFISH PLAY.
THAT MORON!
LIKE I THOUGHT...
...THINGS *HAVE* CHANGED.

WHISTLE!

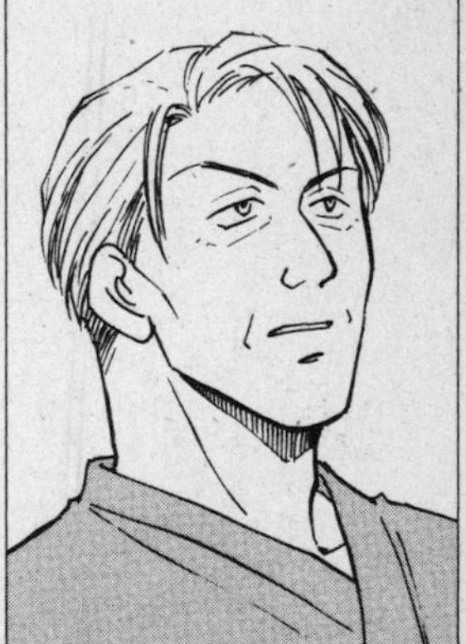

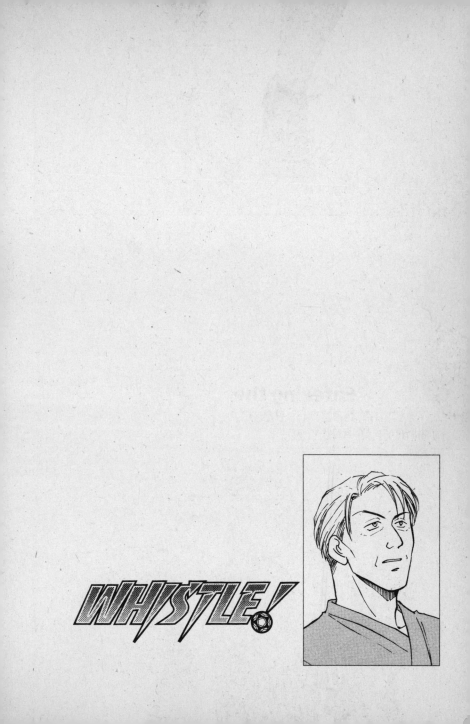

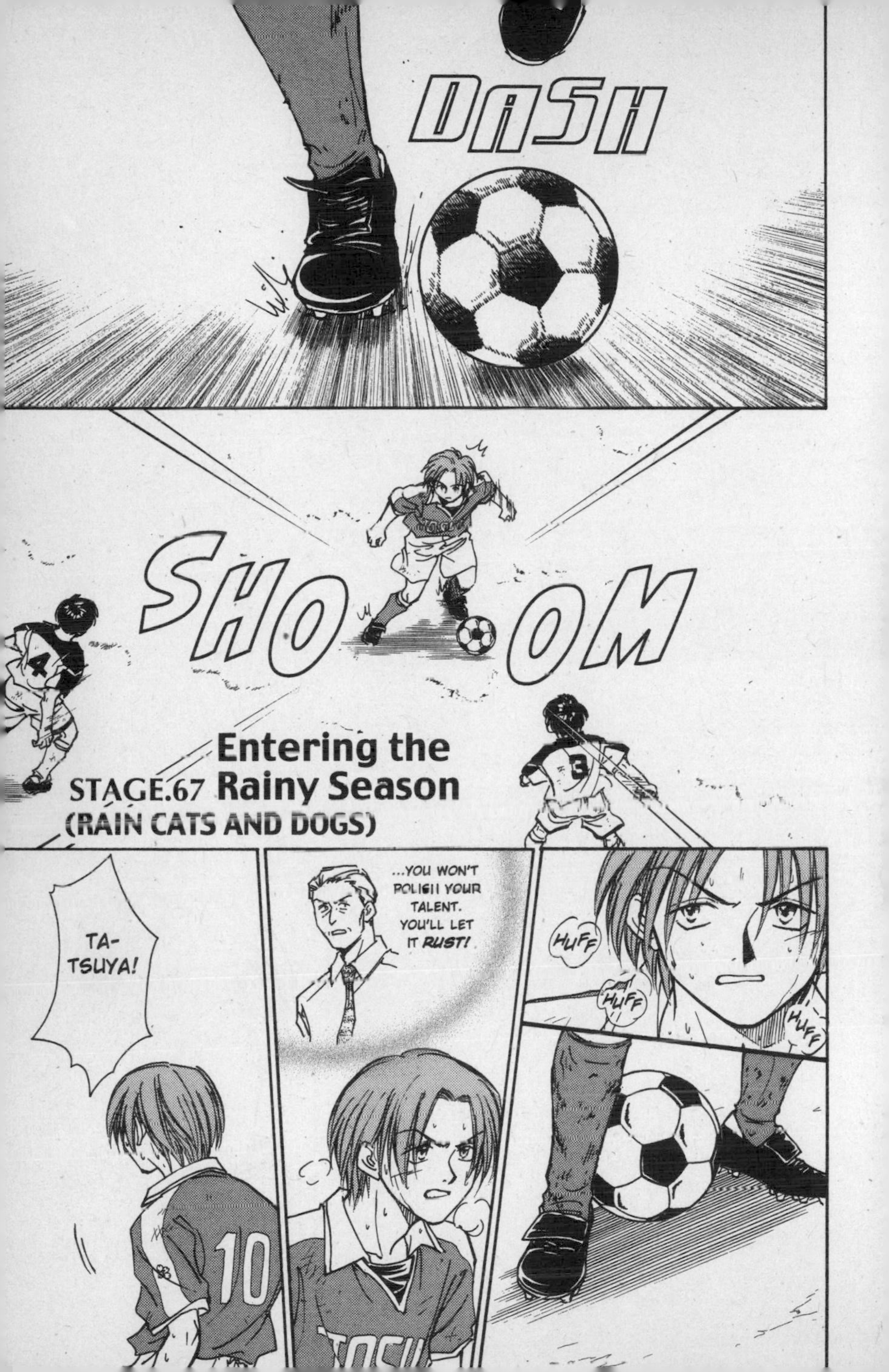
DASH
SHOOM
STAGE.67 Entering the Rainy Season
(RAIN CATS AND DOGS)
HUFF
HUFF
HUFF
...YOU WON'T POLISH YOUR TALENT. YOU'LL LET IT RUST!
TA-TSUYA!

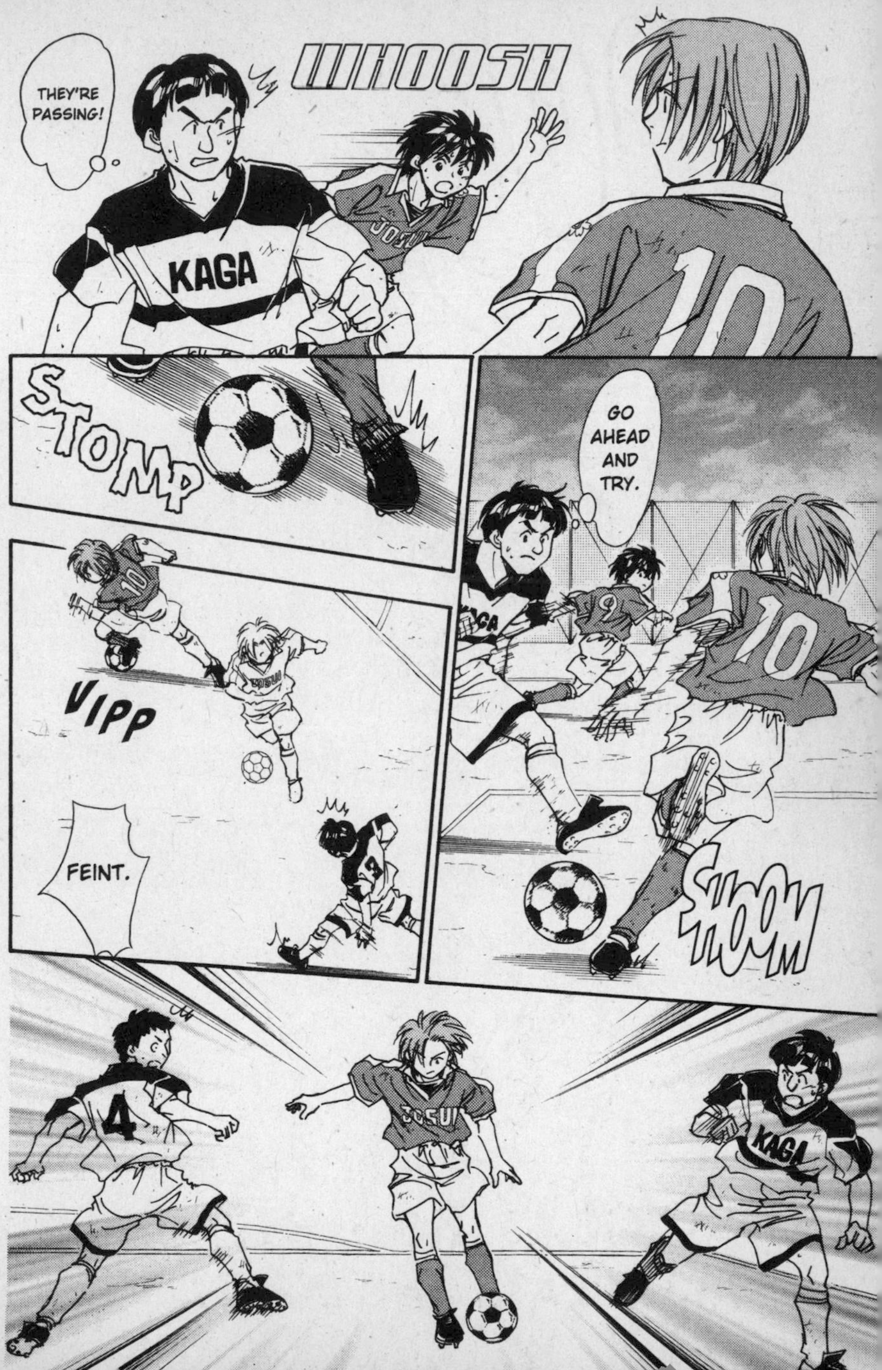
WHOOSH
THEY'RE PASSING!
GO AHEAD AND TRY.
STOMP
SHOOM
VIPP
FEINT.

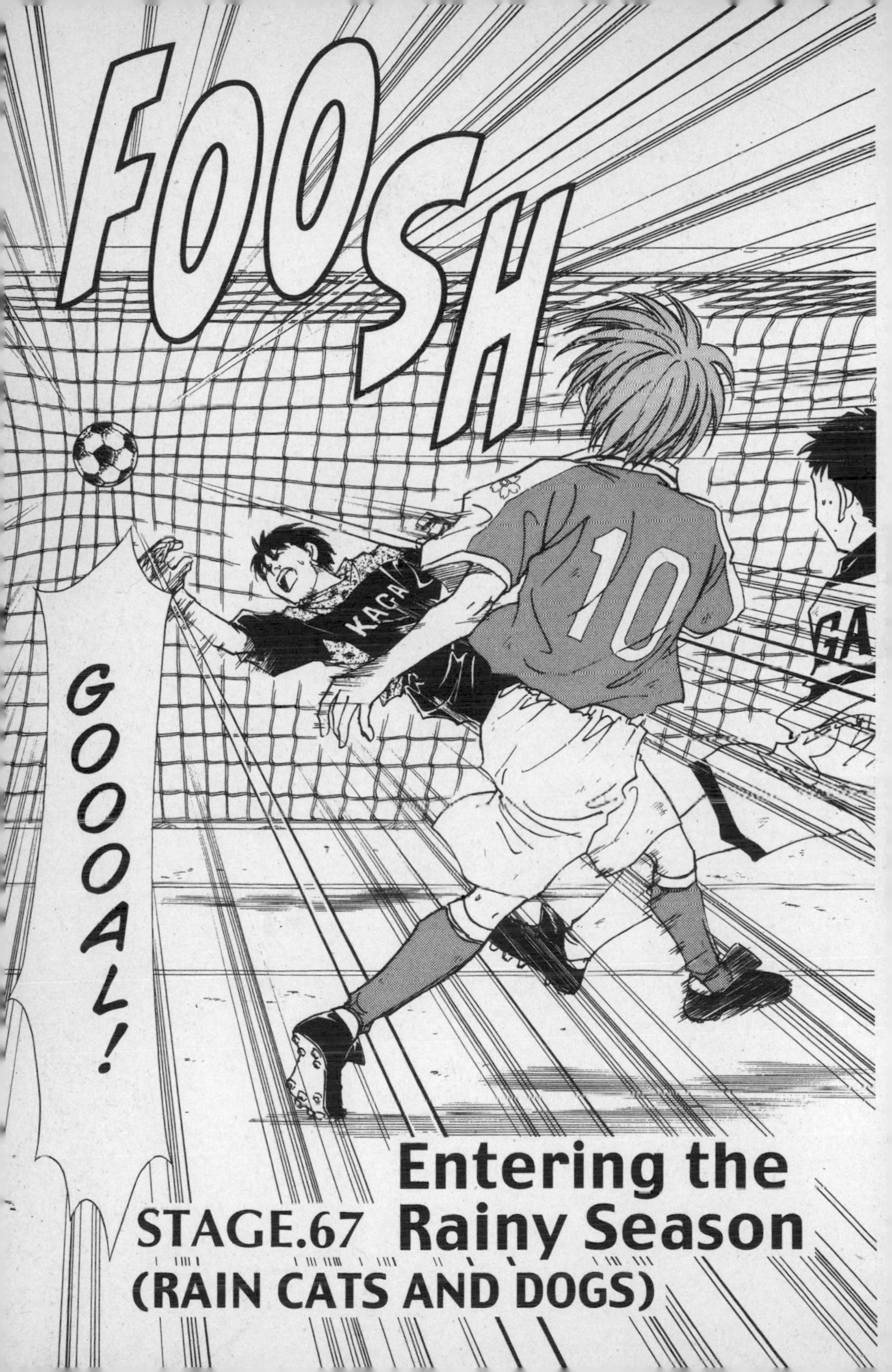
FOOSH
GOOOOAL!
KAGA
10
STAGE.67 Entering the Rainy Season
(RAIN CATS AND DOGS)

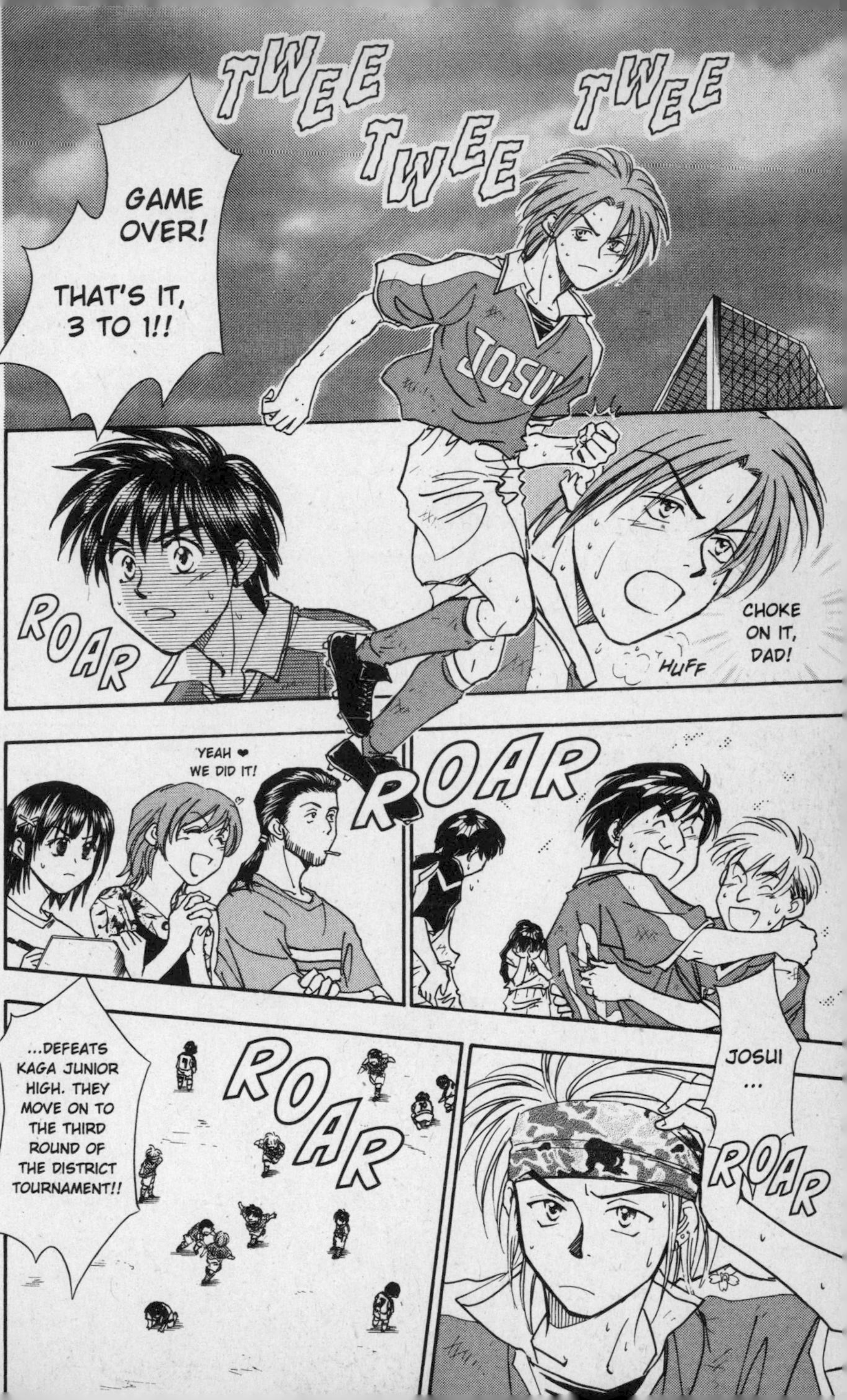
TWEE
TWEE
TWEE
GAME OVER!
THAT'S IT, 3 TO 1!!
CHOKE ON IT, DAD!
HUFF
ROAR
ROAR
YEAH ❤ WE DID IT!
JOSUI ...
ROAR
...DEFEATS KAGA JUNIOR HIGH. THEY MOVE ON TO THE THIRD ROUND OF THE DISTRICT TOURNAMENT!!
ROAR

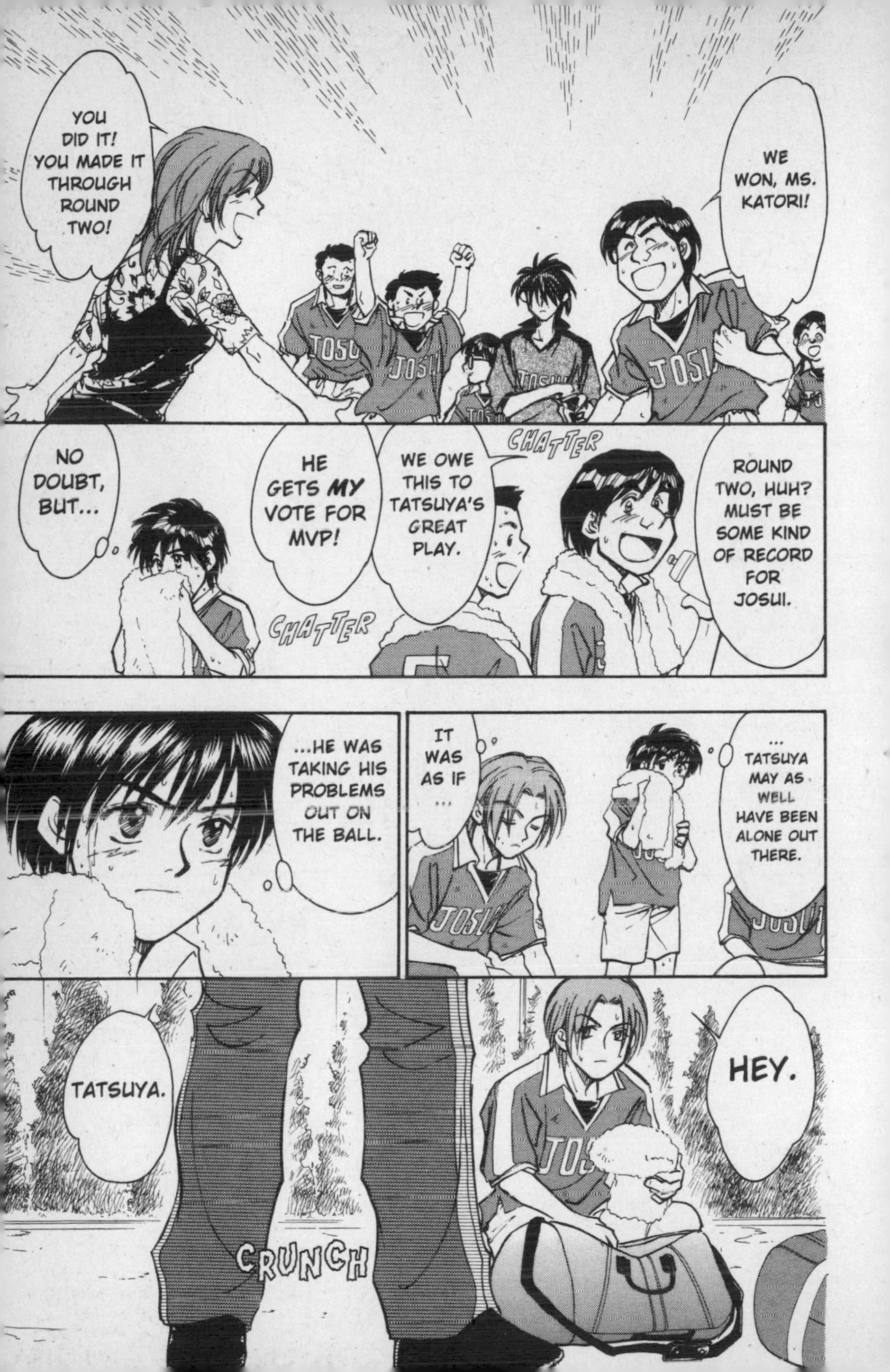
WE WON, MS. KATORI!
YOU DID IT! YOU MADE IT THROUGH ROUND TWO!
ROUND TWO, HUH? MUST BE SOME KIND OF RECORD FOR JOSUI.
CHATTER
WE OWE THIS TO TATSUYA'S GREAT PLAY.
HE GETS *MY* VOTE FOR MVP!
CHATTER
NO DOUBT, BUT...
... TATSUYA MAY AS WELL HAVE BEEN ALONE OUT THERE.
IT WAS AS IF ...
...HE WAS TAKING HIS PROBLEMS OUT ON THE BALL.
HEY.
TATSUYA.
CRUNCH

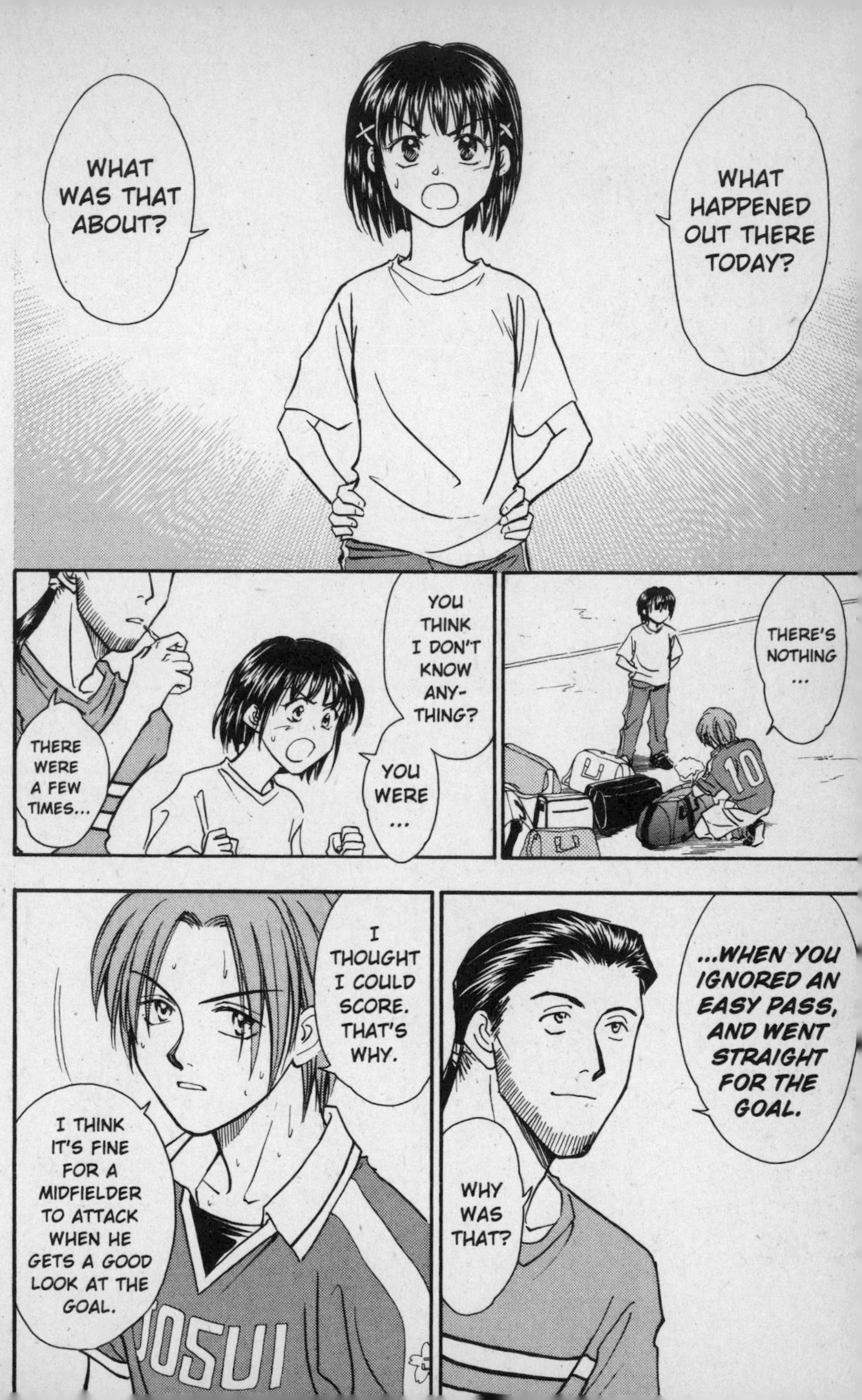
WHAT HAPPENED OUT THERE TODAY?
WHAT WAS THAT ABOUT?
THERE'S NOTHING ...
YOU THINK I DON'T KNOW ANY-THING?
YOU WERE ...
THERE WERE A FEW TIMES...
...WHEN YOU IGNORED AN EASY PASS, AND WENT STRAIGHT FOR THE GOAL.
WHY WAS THAT?
I THOUGHT I COULD SCORE. THAT'S WHY.
I THINK IT'S FINE FOR A MIDFIELDER TO ATTACK WHEN HE GETS A GOOD LOOK AT THE GOAL.

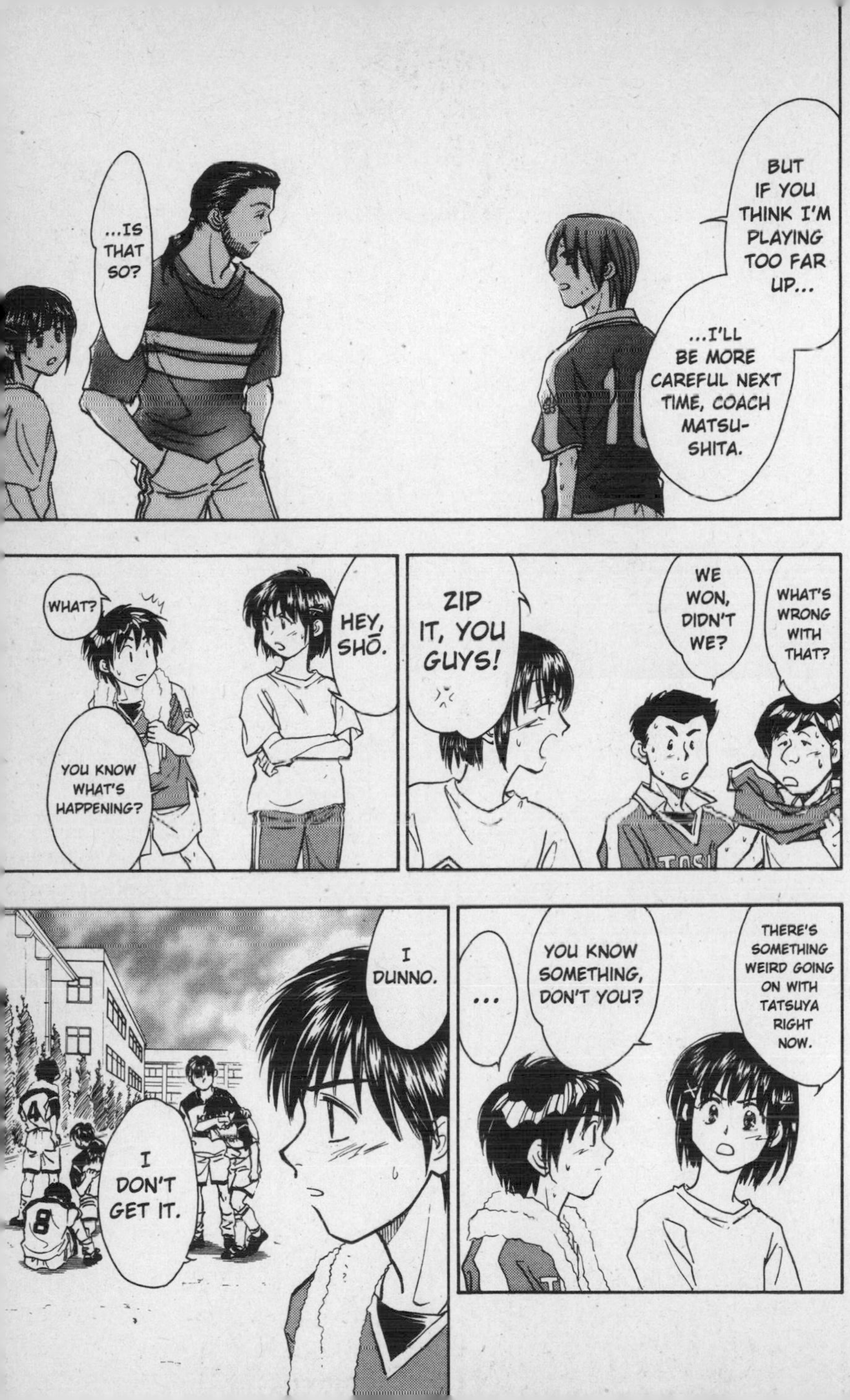
BUT IF YOU THINK I'M PLAYING TOO FAR UP...
...I'LL BE MORE CAREFUL NEXT TIME, COACH MATSU-SHITA.
...IS THAT SO?
WHAT'S WRONG WITH THAT?
WE WON, DIDN'T WE?
ZIP IT, YOU GUYS!
HEY, SHŌ.
WHAT?
YOU KNOW WHAT'S HAPPENING?
THERE'S SOMETHING WEIRD GOING ON WITH TATSUYA RIGHT NOW.
YOU KNOW SOMETHING, DON'T YOU?
...
I DUNNO.
I DON'T GET IT.

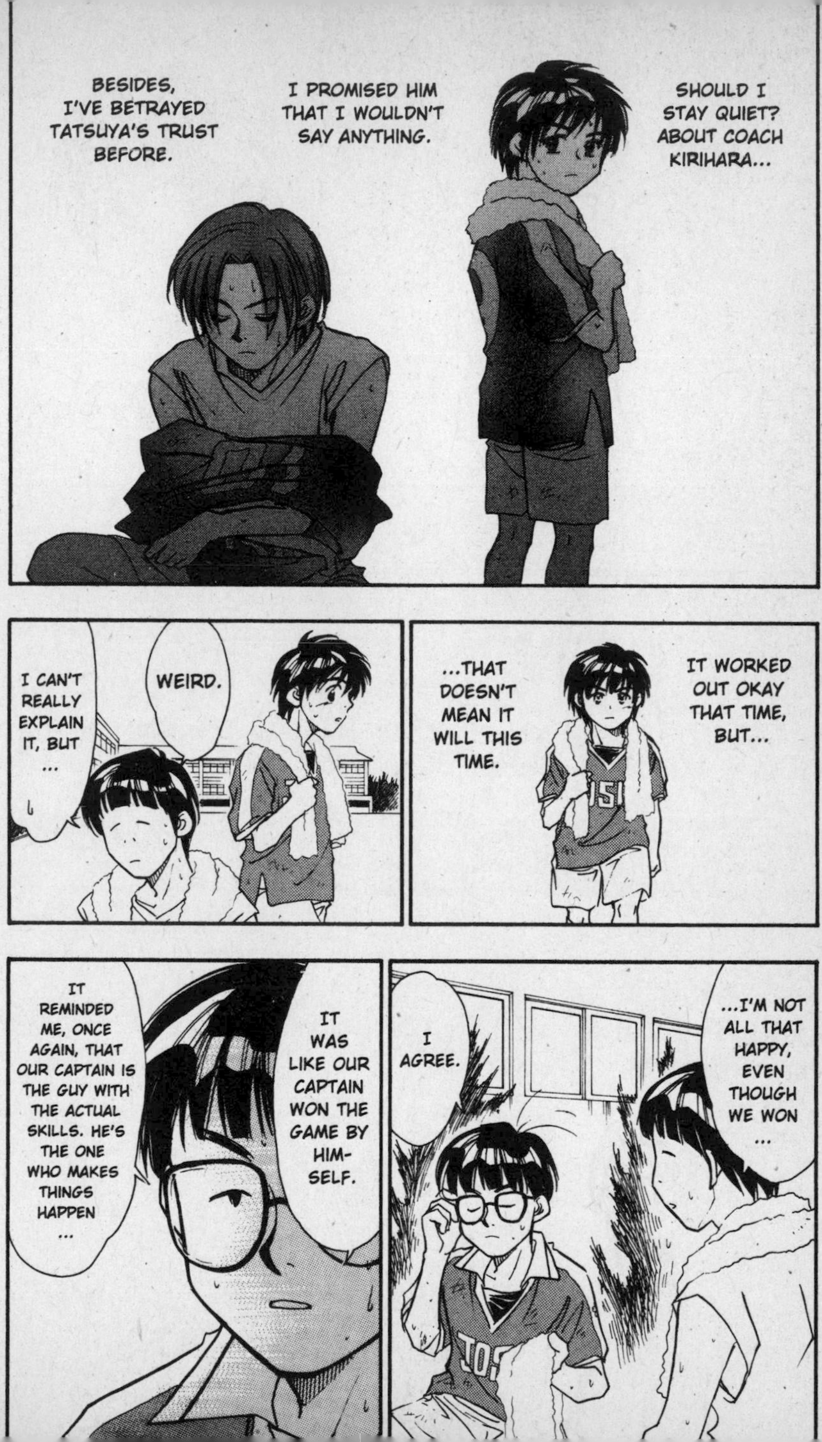
SHOULD I STAY QUIET? ABOUT COACH KIRIHARA...
I PROMISED HIM THAT I WOULDN'T SAY ANYTHING.
BESIDES, I'VE BETRAYED TATSUYA'S TRUST BEFORE.
IT WORKED OUT OKAY THAT TIME, BUT...
...THAT DOESN'T MEAN IT WILL THIS TIME.
WEIRD.
I CAN'T REALLY EXPLAIN IT, BUT ...
...I'M NOT ALL THAT HAPPY, EVEN THOUGH WE WON ...
I AGREE.
IT WAS LIKE OUR CAPTAIN WON THE GAME BY HIM-SELF.
IT REMINDED ME, ONCE AGAIN, THAT OUR CAPTAIN IS THE GUY WITH THE ACTUAL SKILLS. HE'S THE ONE WHO MAKES THINGS HAPPEN ...

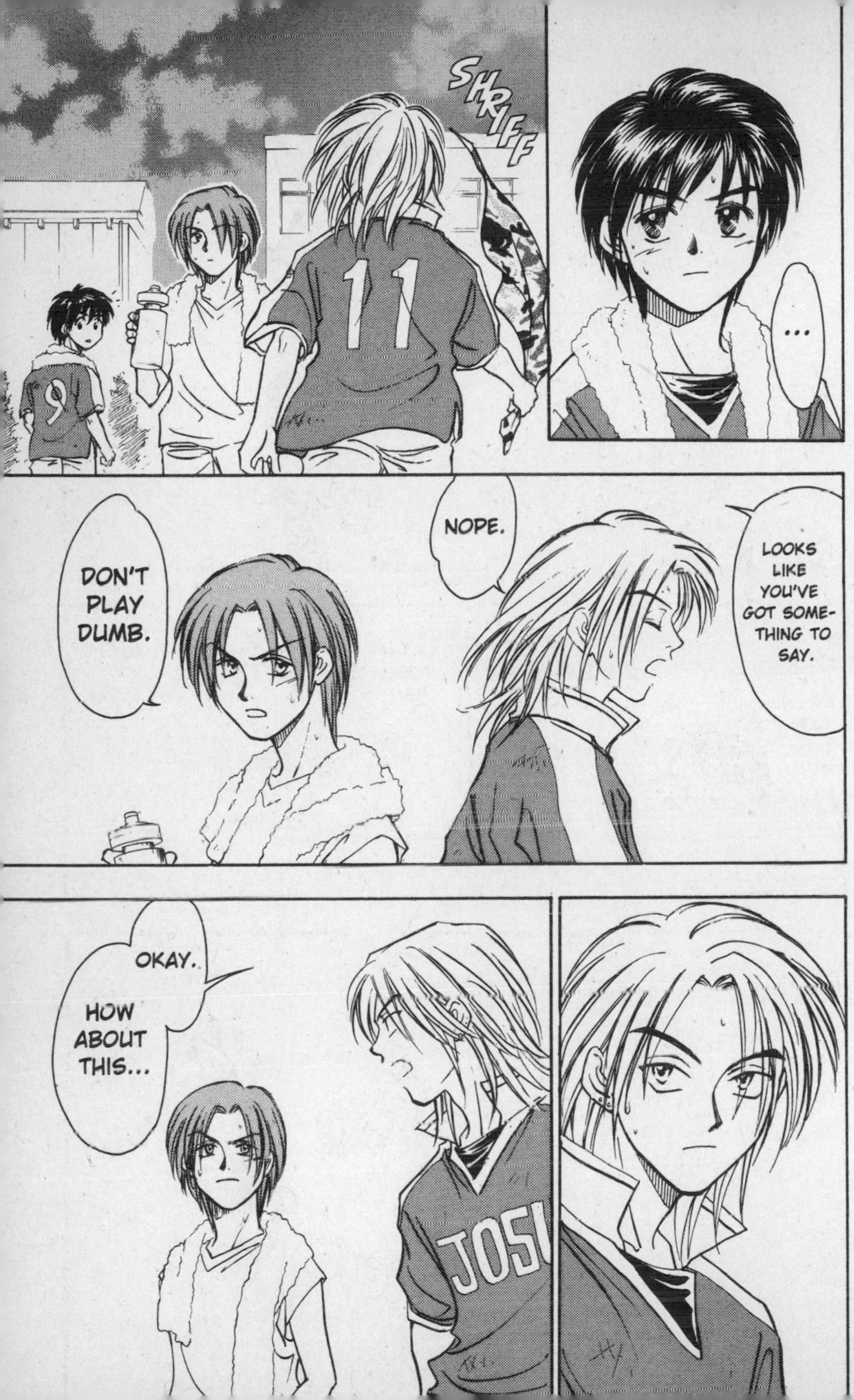
...
SHRIFF
LOOKS LIKE YOU'VE GOT SOME-THING TO SAY.
NOPE.
DON'T PLAY DUMB.
OKAY. HOW ABOUT THIS...

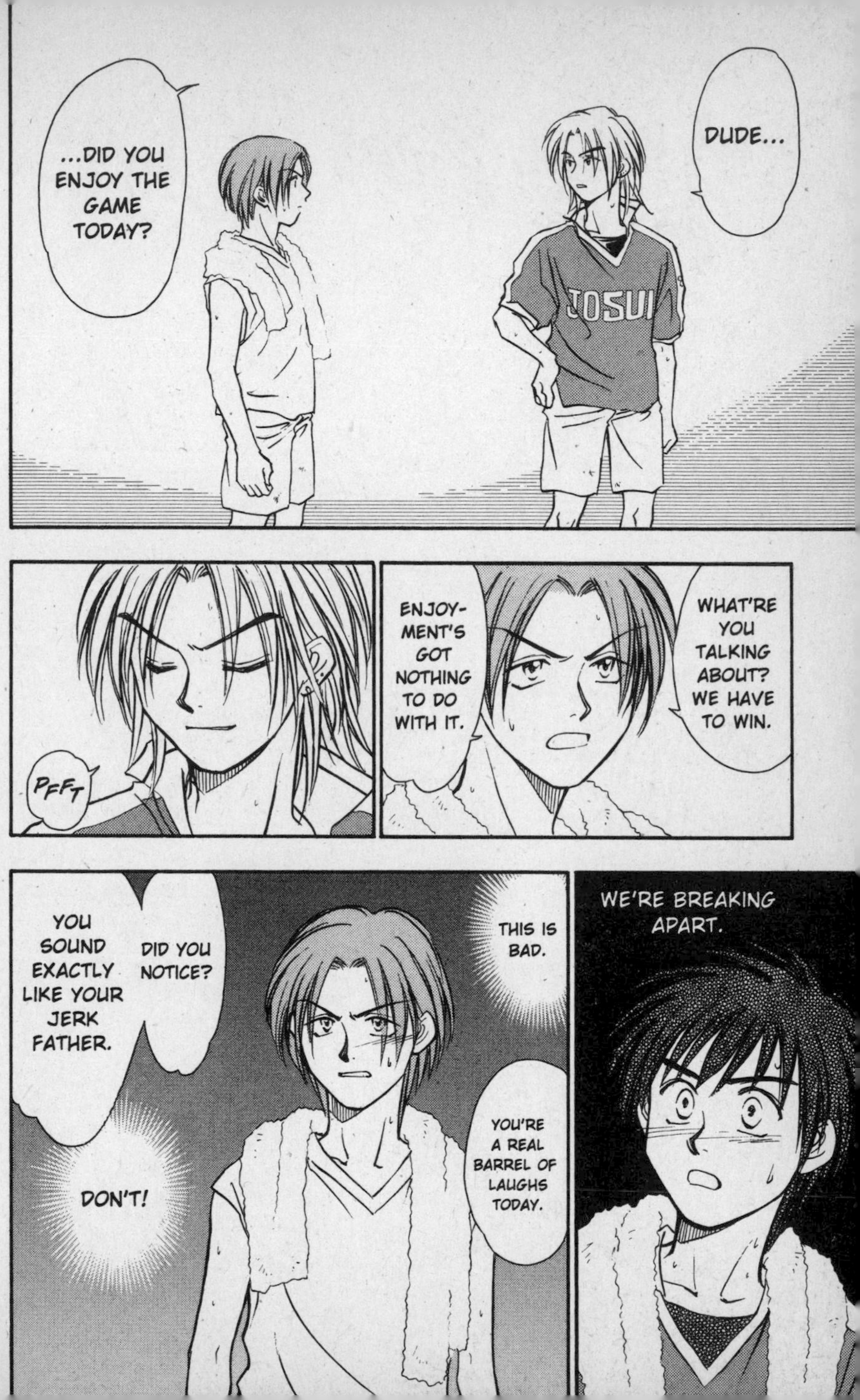
DUDE...
JOSUI
...DID YOU ENJOY THE GAME TODAY?
WHAT'RE YOU TALKING ABOUT? WE HAVE TO WIN.
ENJOY-MENT'S GOT NOTHING TO DO WITH IT.
PFFT
WE'RE BREAKING APART.
THIS IS BAD.
DID YOU NOTICE?
YOU SOUND EXACTLY LIKE YOUR JERK FATHER.
YOU'RE A REAL BARREL OF LAUGHS TODAY.
DON'T!

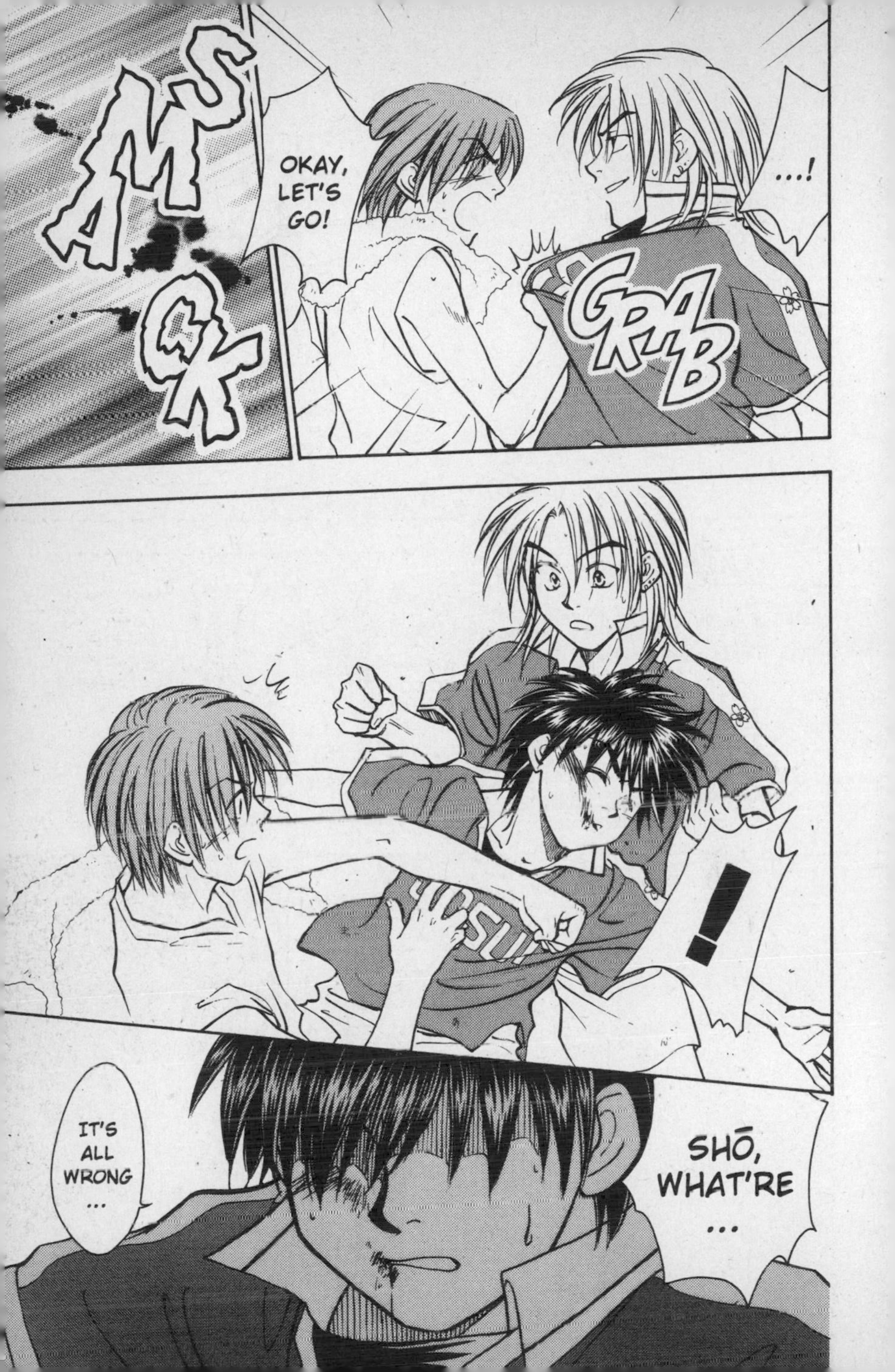
...!
OKAY, LET'S GO!
GRAB
SMACK
!
SHŌ, WHAT'RE ...
IT'S ALL WRONG ...

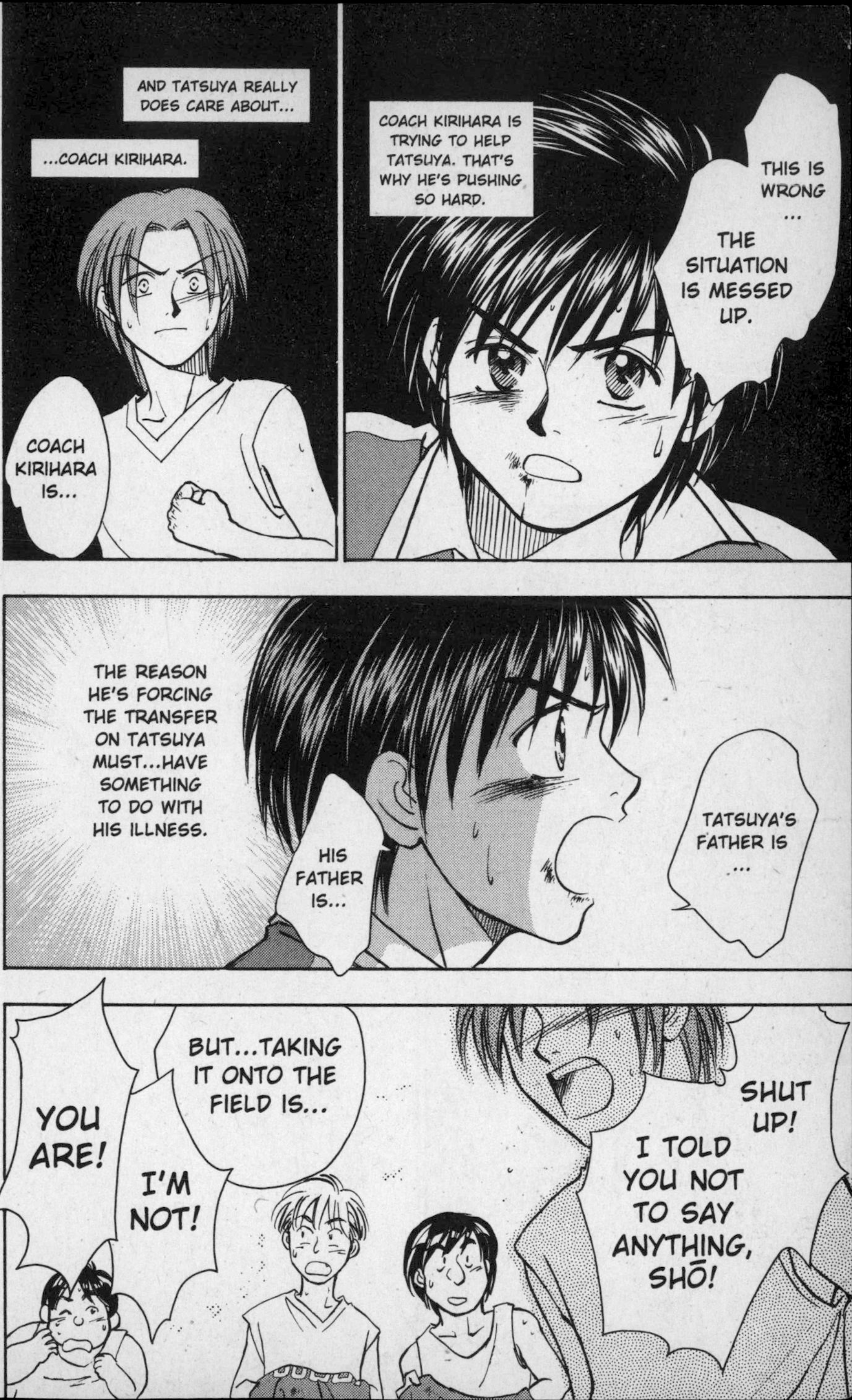
THIS IS WRONG ...
THE SITUATION IS MESSED UP.
COACH KIRIHARA IS TRYING TO HELP TATSUYA. THAT'S WHY HE'S PUSHING SO HARD.
AND TATSUYA REALLY DOES CARE ABOUT...
...COACH KIRIHARA.
COACH KIRIHARA IS...
THE REASON HE'S FORCING THE TRANSFER ON TATSUYA MUST...HAVE SOMETHING TO DO WITH HIS ILLNESS.
TATSUYA'S FATHER IS ...
HIS FATHER IS...
SHUT UP!
I TOLD YOU NOT TO SAY ANYTHING, SHŌ!
BUT...TAKING IT ONTO THE FIELD IS...
I'M NOT!
YOU ARE!

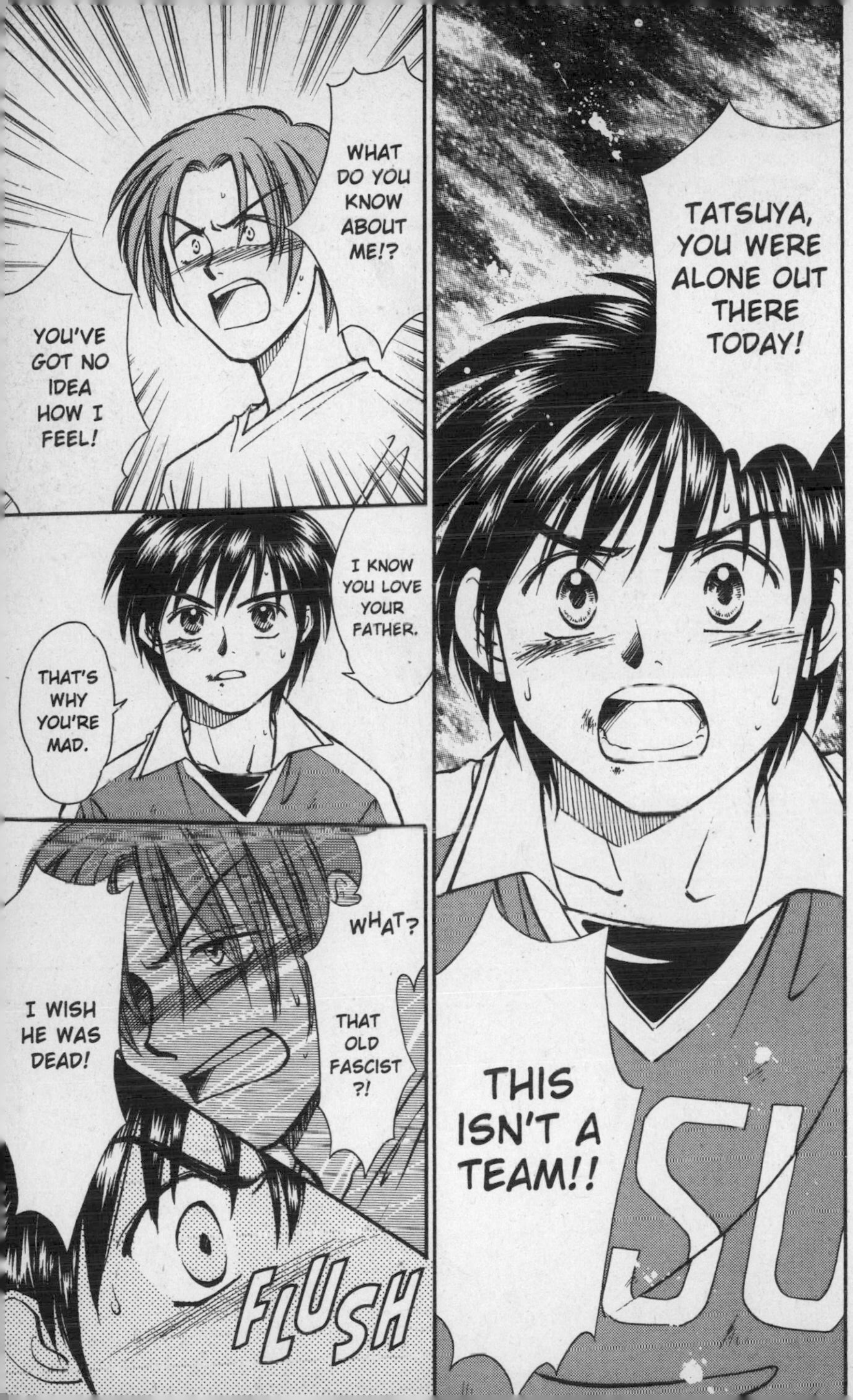
TATSUYA, YOU WERE ALONE OUT THERE TODAY!
THIS ISN'T A TEAM!!
WHAT DO YOU KNOW ABOUT ME!?
YOU'VE GOT NO IDEA HOW I FEEL!
I KNOW YOU LOVE YOUR FATHER.
THAT'S WHY YOU'RE MAD.
WHAT?
THAT OLD FASCIST?!
I WISH HE WAS DEAD!
FLUSH

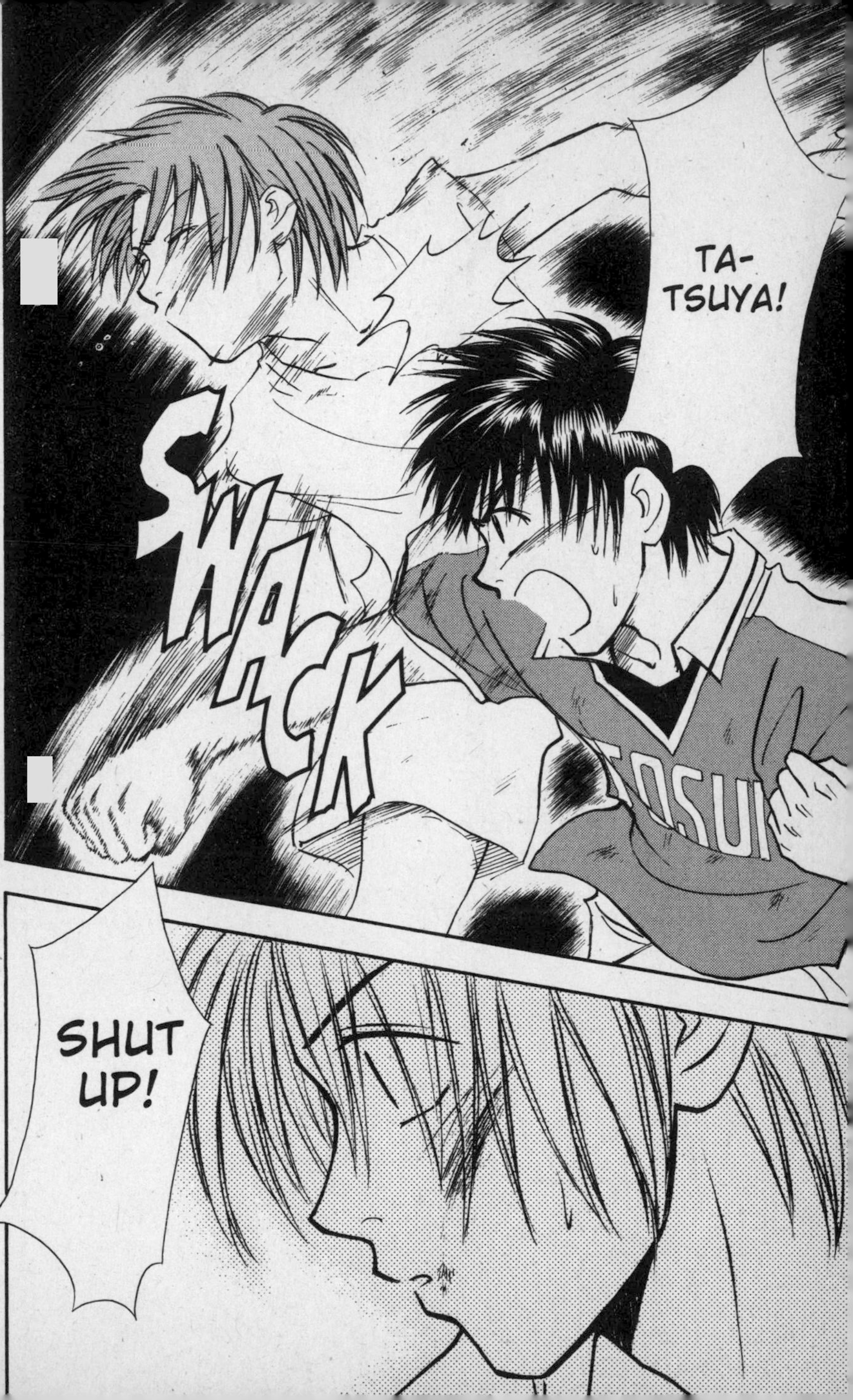
TA-
TSUYA!
SWACK
SHUT UP!

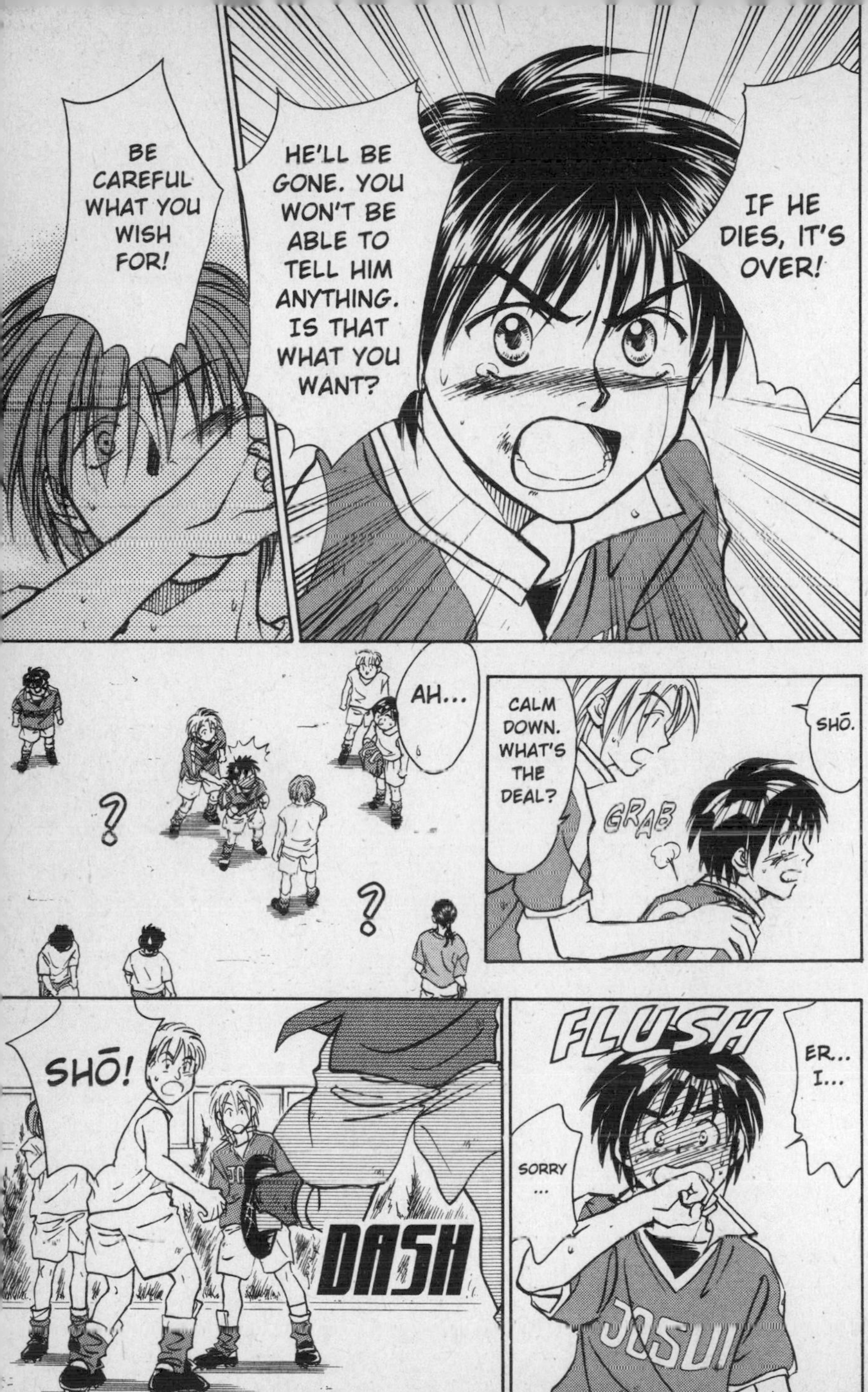
IF HE DIES, IT'S OVER!
HE'LL BE GONE. YOU WON'T BE ABLE TO TELL HIM ANYTHING. IS THAT WHAT YOU WANT?
BE CAREFUL WHAT YOU WISH FOR!
SHŌ.
GRAB
CALM DOWN. WHAT'S THE DEAL?
AH...
?
?
FLUSH
ER... I...
SORRY ...
SHŌ!
DASH

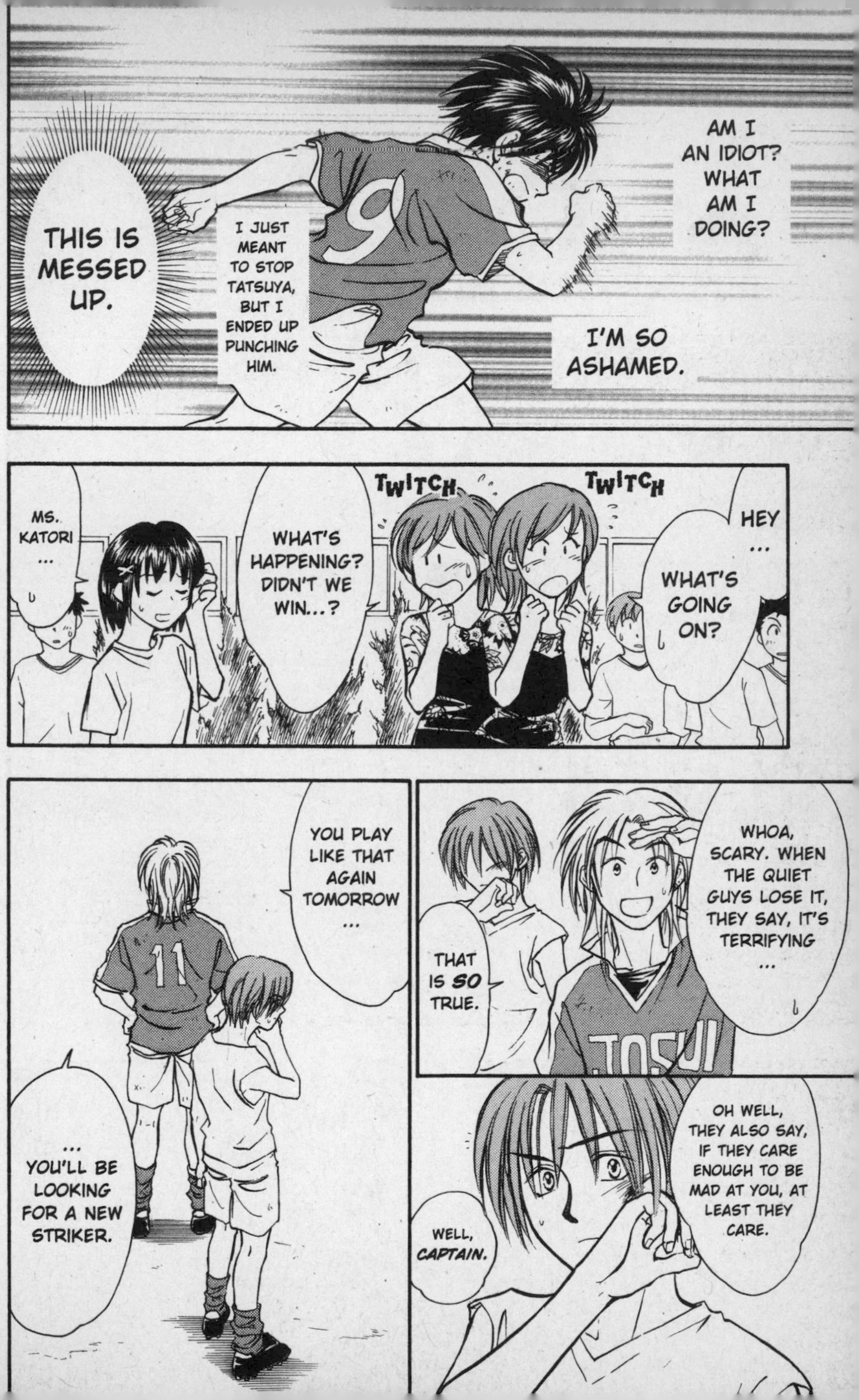
AM I AN IDIOT? WHAT AM I DOING?
I'M SO ASHAMED.
I JUST MEANT TO STOP TATSUYA, BUT I ENDED UP PUNCHING HIM.
THIS IS MESSED UP.
HEY ... WHAT'S GOING ON?
TWITCH
TWITCH
WHAT'S HAPPENING? DIDN'T WE WIN...?
MS. KATORI ...
WHOA, SCARY. WHEN THE QUIET GUYS LOSE IT, THEY SAY, IT'S TERRIFYING ...
THAT IS *SO* TRUE.
OH WELL, THEY ALSO SAY, IF THEY CARE ENOUGH TO BE MAD AT YOU, AT LEAST THEY CARE.
WELL, *CAPTAIN.*
YOU PLAY LIKE THAT AGAIN TOMORROW ...
... YOU'LL BE LOOKING FOR A NEW STRIKER.

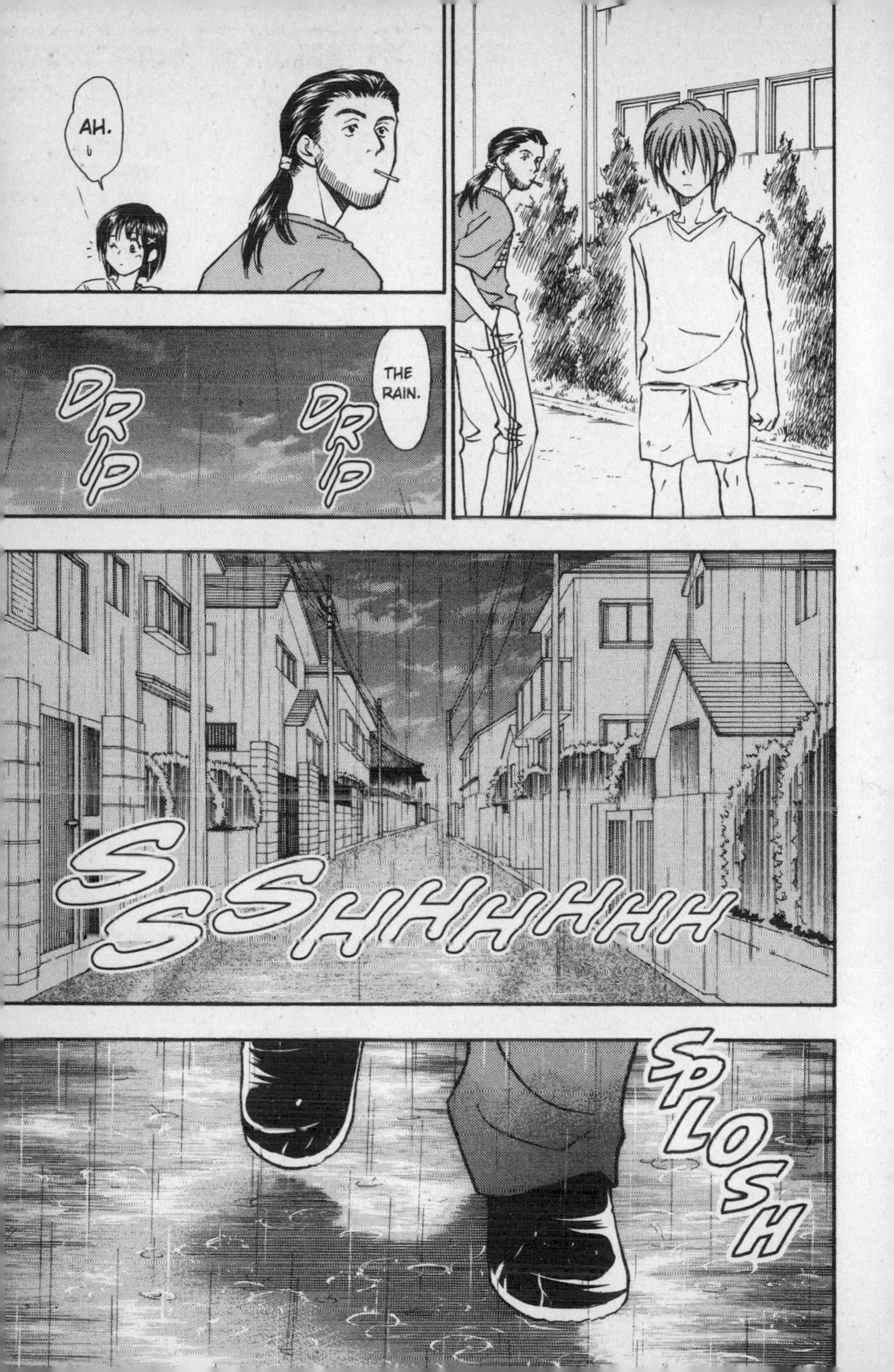
AH.
THE RAIN.
DRIP
DRIP
SSSHHHHHH
SPLOSH

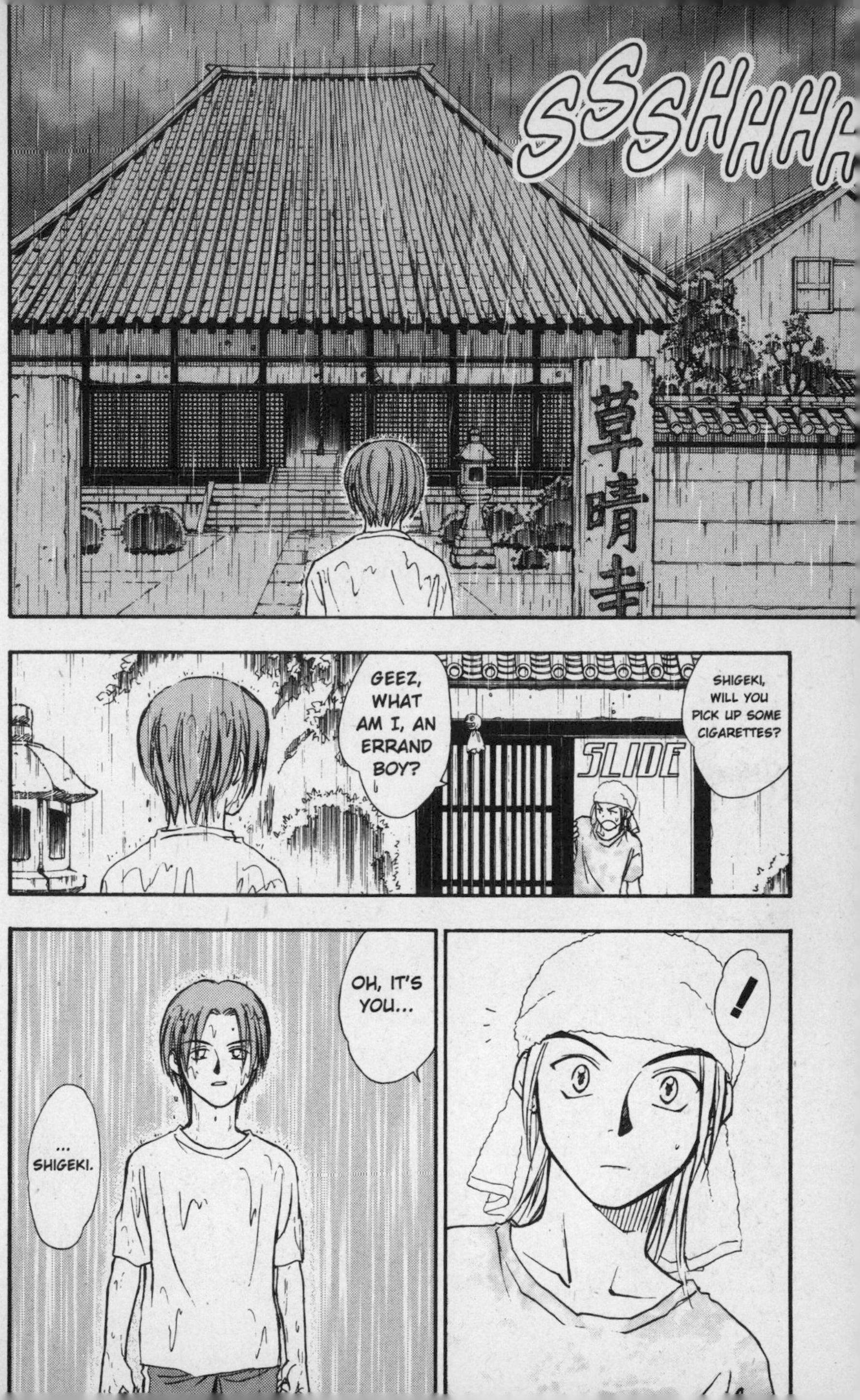
SSSHHH
草晴寺
SHIGEKI, WILL YOU PICK UP SOME CIGARETTES?
SLIDE
GEEZ, WHAT AM I, AN ERRAND BOY?
!
OH, IT'S YOU...
... SHIGEKI.

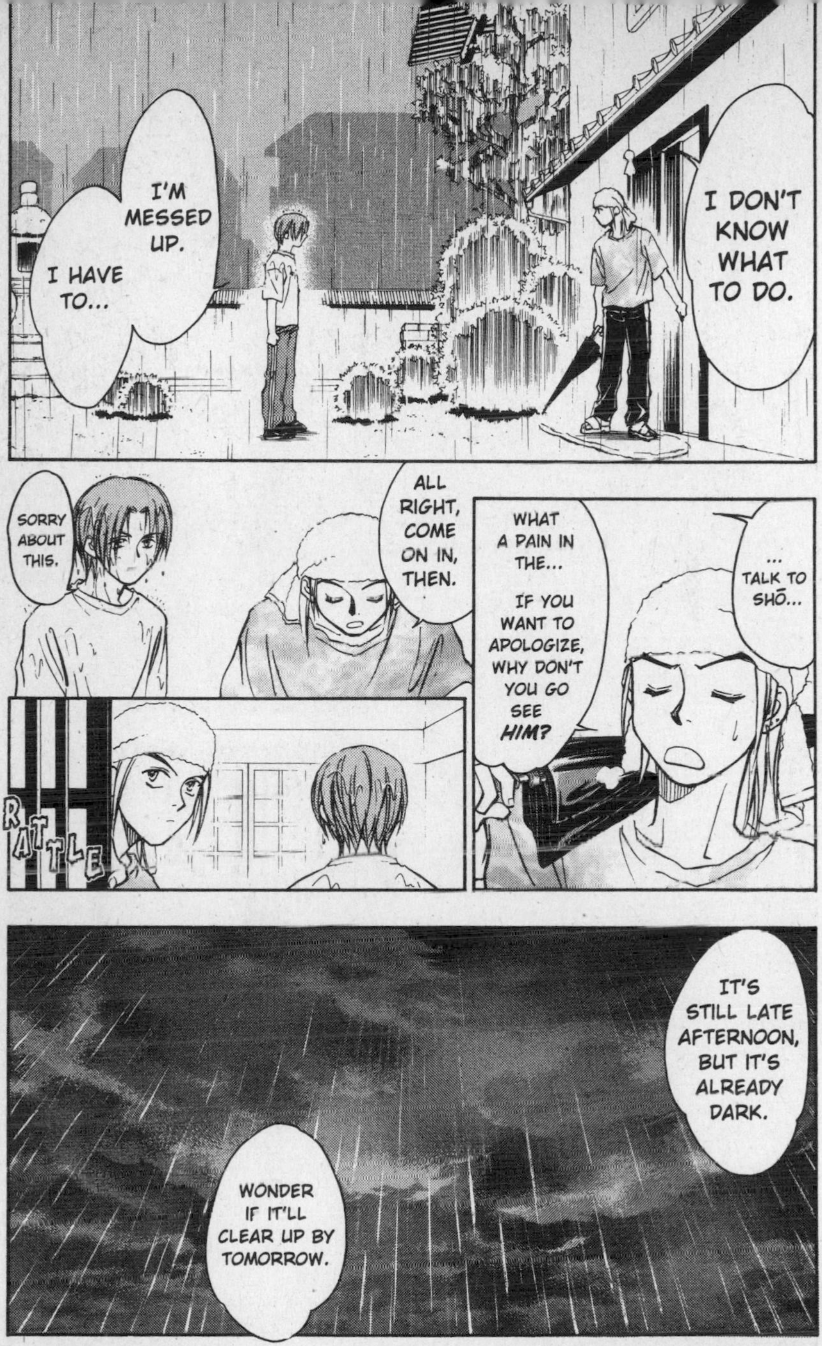
I DON'T KNOW WHAT TO DO.
I'M MESSED UP.
I HAVE TO...
... TALK TO SHŌ...
WHAT A PAIN IN THE...
IF YOU WANT TO APOLOGIZE, WHY DON'T YOU GO SEE *HIM?*
ALL RIGHT, COME ON IN, THEN.
SORRY ABOUT THIS.
RATTLE
IT'S STILL LATE AFTERNOON, BUT IT'S ALREADY DARK.
WONDER IF IT'LL CLEAR UP BY TOMORROW.

WHISTLE!

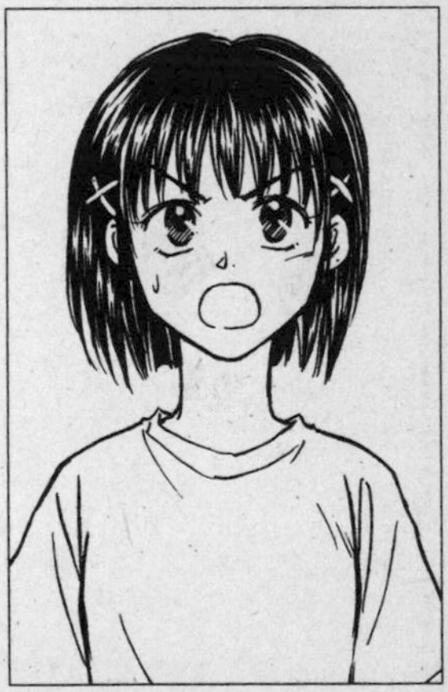

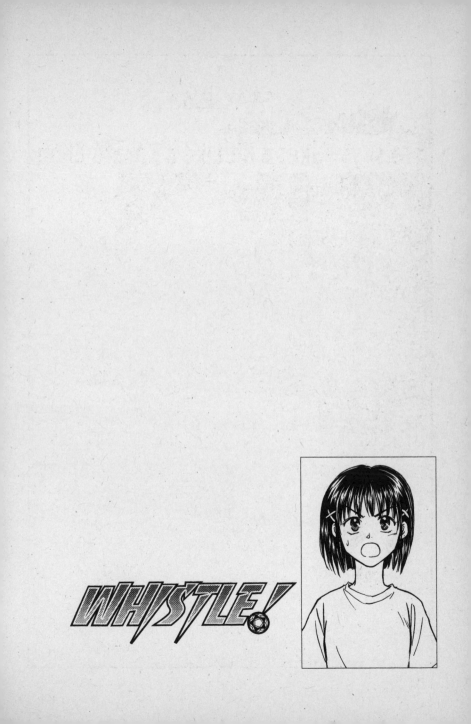

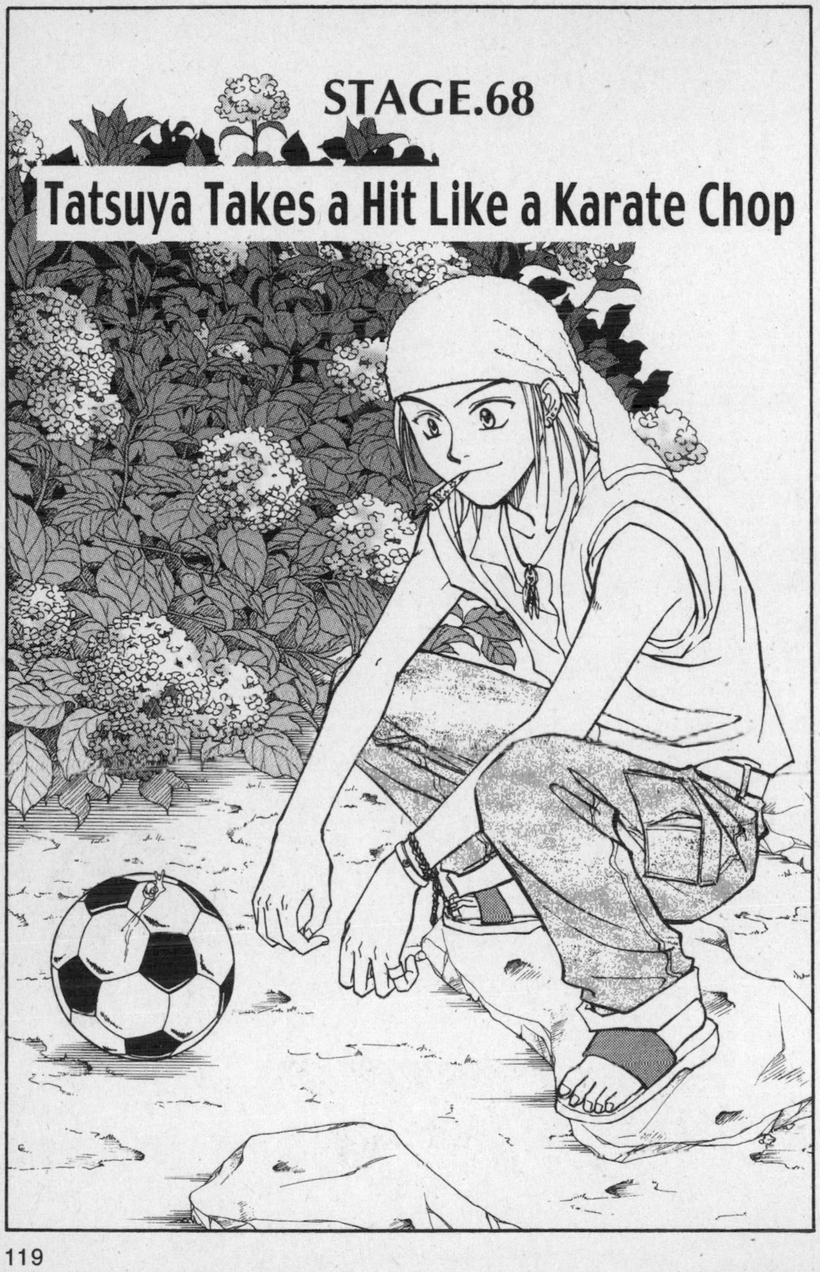
STAGE.68
Tatsuya Takes a Hit Like a Karate Chop

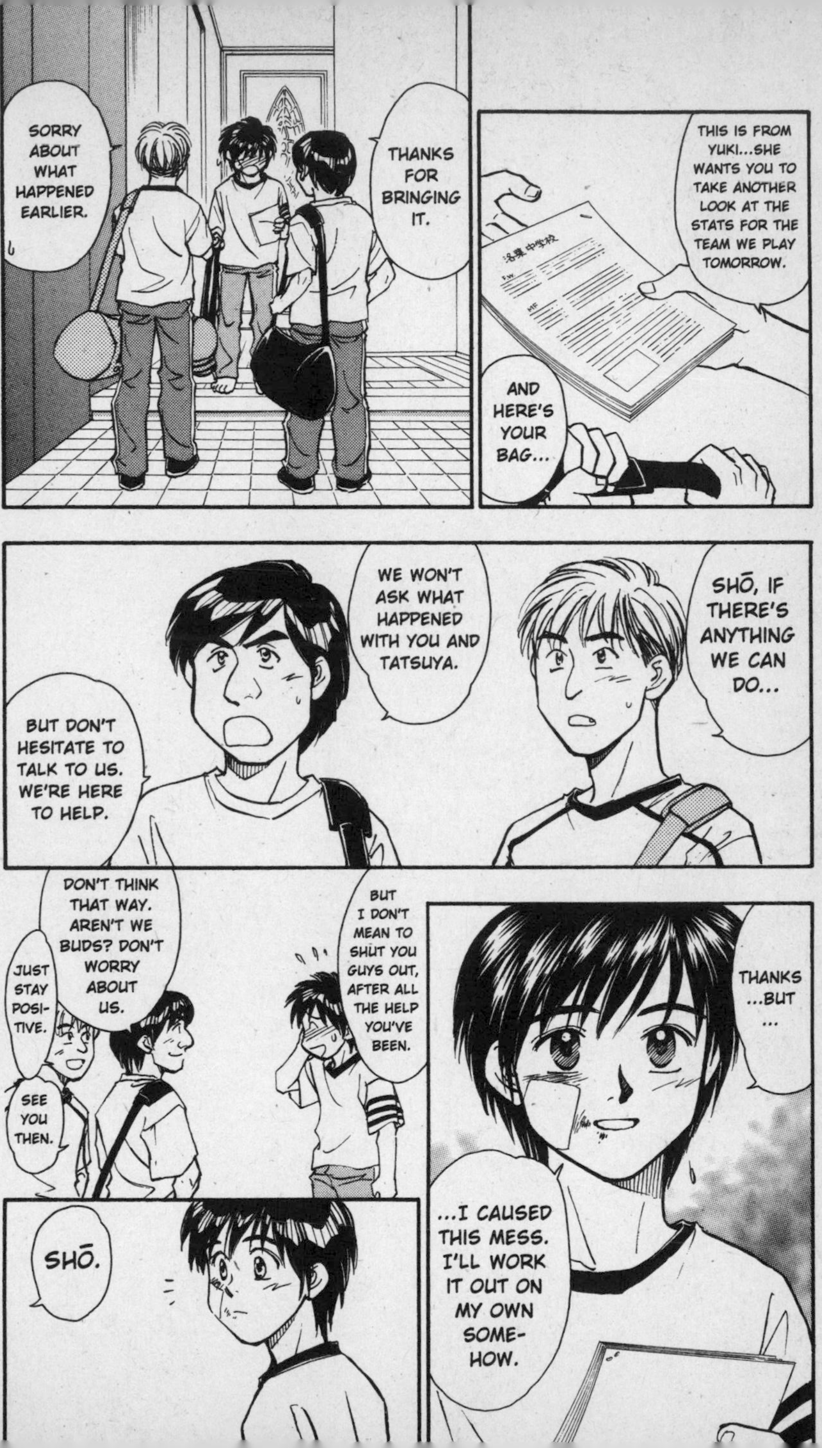
THIS IS FROM YUKI...SHE WANTS YOU TO TAKE ANOTHER LOOK AT THE STATS FOR THE TEAM WE PLAY TOMORROW.
AND HERE'S YOUR BAG...
THANKS FOR BRINGING IT.
SORRY ABOUT WHAT HAPPENED EARLIER.
SHŌ, IF THERE'S ANYTHING WE CAN DO...
WE WON'T ASK WHAT HAPPENED WITH YOU AND TATSUYA.
BUT DON'T HESITATE TO TALK TO US. WE'RE HERE TO HELP.
THANKS ...BUT ...
...I CAUSED THIS MESS. I'LL WORK IT OUT ON MY OWN SOME-HOW.
BUT I DON'T MEAN TO SHUT YOU GUYS OUT, AFTER ALL THE HELP YOU'VE BEEN.
DON'T THINK THAT WAY. AREN'T WE BUDS? DON'T WORRY ABOUT US.
JUST STAY POSI-TIVE.
SEE YOU THEN.
SHŌ.

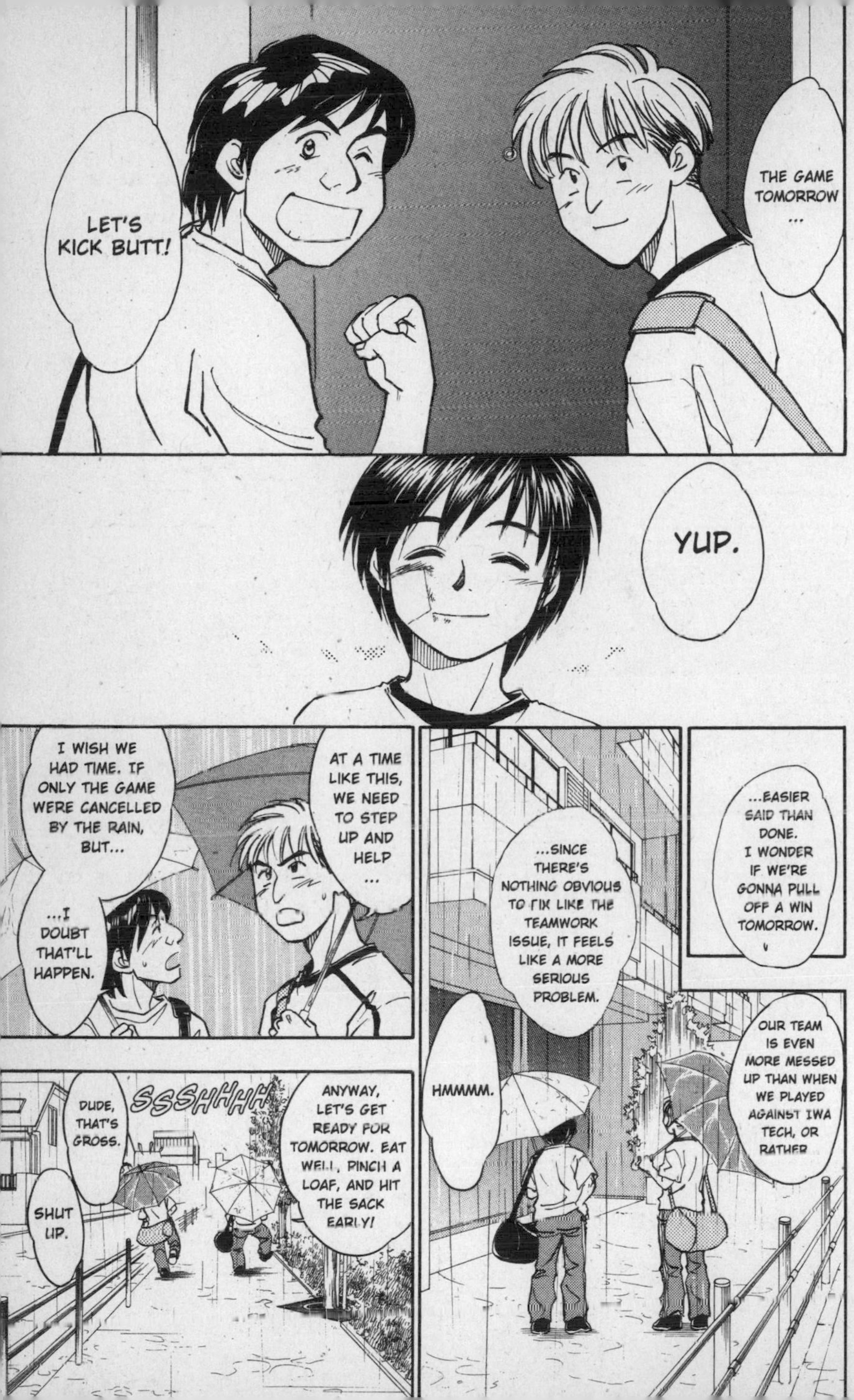
THE GAME TOMORROW ...
LET'S KICK BUTT!
YUP.
...EASIER SAID THAN DONE. I WONDER IF WE'RE GONNA PULL OFF A WIN TOMORROW.
OUR TEAM IS EVEN MORE MESSED UP THAN WHEN WE PLAYED AGAINST IWA TECH, OR RATHER
...SINCE THERE'S NOTHING OBVIOUS TO FIX LIKE THE TEAMWORK ISSUE, IT FEELS LIKE A MORE SERIOUS PROBLEM.
HMMMM.
AT A TIME LIKE THIS, WE NEED TO STEP UP AND HELP ...
I WISH WE HAD TIME. IF ONLY THE GAME WERE CANCELLED BY THE RAIN, BUT...
...I DOUBT THAT'LL HAPPEN.
ANYWAY, LET'S GET READY FOR TOMORROW. EAT WELL, PINCH A LOAF, AND HIT THE SACK EARLY!
SSSHHHH
DUDE, THAT'S GROSS.
SHUT UP.

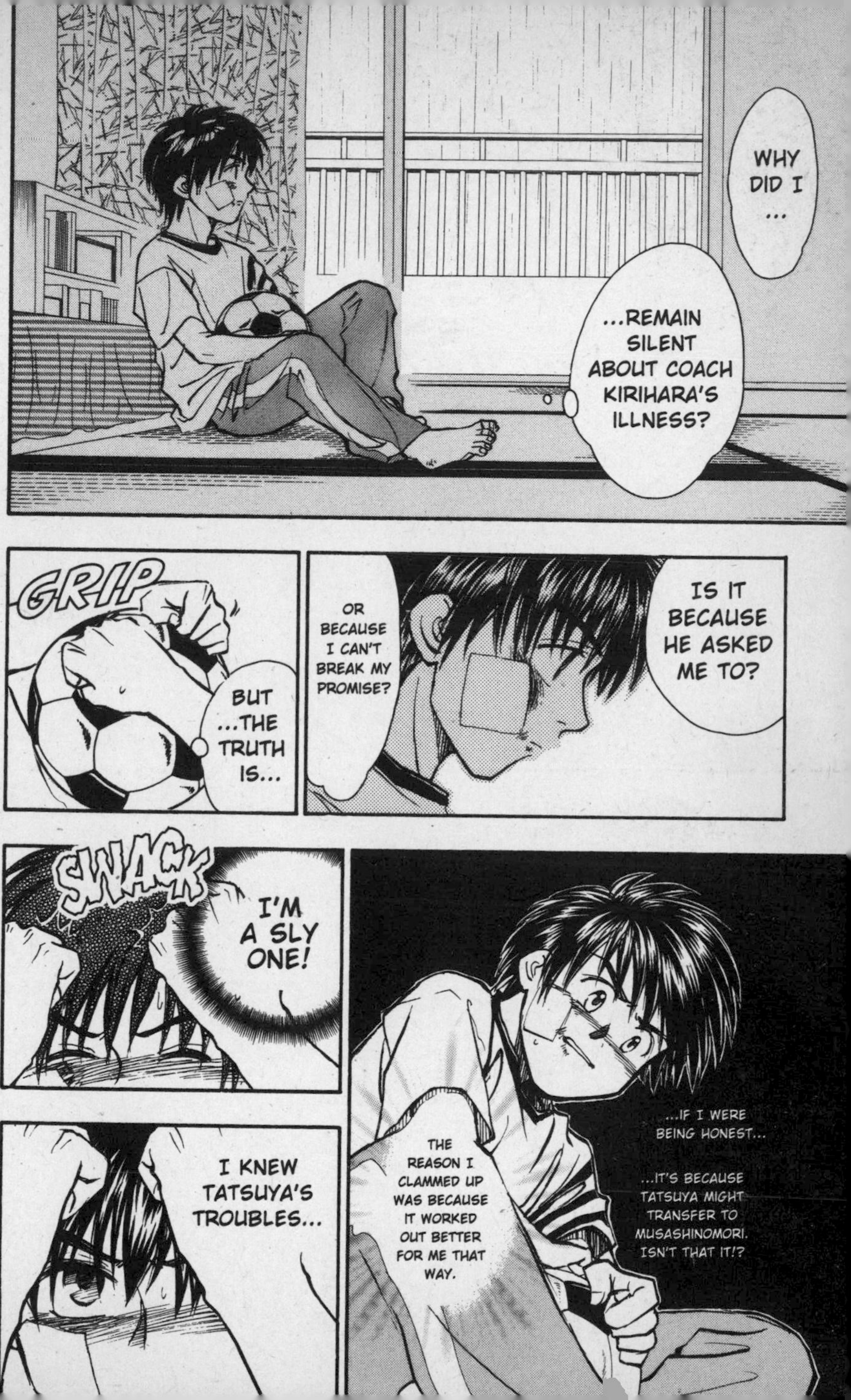
WHY DID I ...
...REMAIN SILENT ABOUT COACH KIRIHARA'S ILLNESS?
IS IT BECAUSE HE ASKED ME TO?
OR BECAUSE I CAN'T BREAK MY PROMISE?
GRIP
BUT ...THE TRUTH IS...
...IF I WERE BEING HONEST...
...IT'S BECAUSE TATSUYA MIGHT TRANSFER TO MUSASHINOMORI. ISN'T THAT IT!?
THE REASON I CLAMMED UP WAS BECAUSE IT WORKED OUT BETTER FOR ME THAT WAY.
SWACK
I'M A SLY ONE!
I KNEW TATSUYA'S TROUBLES...

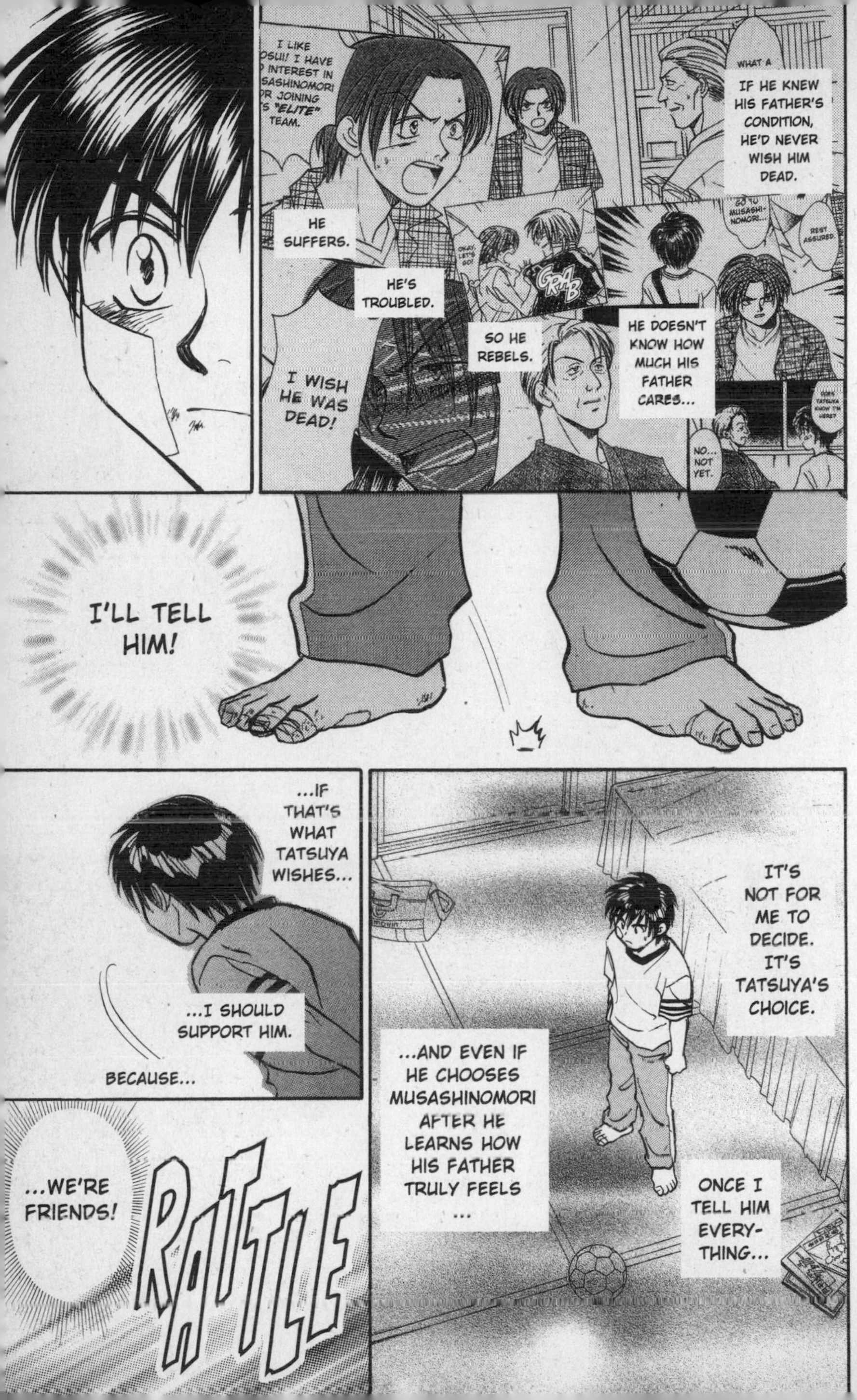
WHAT A
IF HE KNEW HIS FATHER'S CONDITION, HE'D NEVER WISH HIM DEAD.
REST ASSURED.
GO TO MUSASHINOMORI...
I LIKE OSUI! I HAVE INTEREST IN SASHINOMORI OR JOINING 'S "ELITE" TEAM.
HE SUFFERS.
OKAY, LET'S GO!
GRAB
HE'S TROUBLED.
DOES TATSUYA KNOW I'M HERE?
NO... NOT YET.
HE DOESN'T KNOW HOW MUCH HIS FATHER CARES...
SO HE REBELS.
I WISH HE WAS DEAD!
I'LL TELL HIM!
IT'S NOT FOR ME TO DECIDE. IT'S TATSUYA'S CHOICE.
ONCE I TELL HIM EVERYTHING...
...AND EVEN IF HE CHOOSES MUSASHINOMORI AFTER HE LEARNS HOW HIS FATHER TRULY FEELS ...
...IF THAT'S WHAT TATSUYA WISHES...
...I SHOULD SUPPORT HIM.
BECAUSE...
...WE'RE FRIENDS!
RATTLE

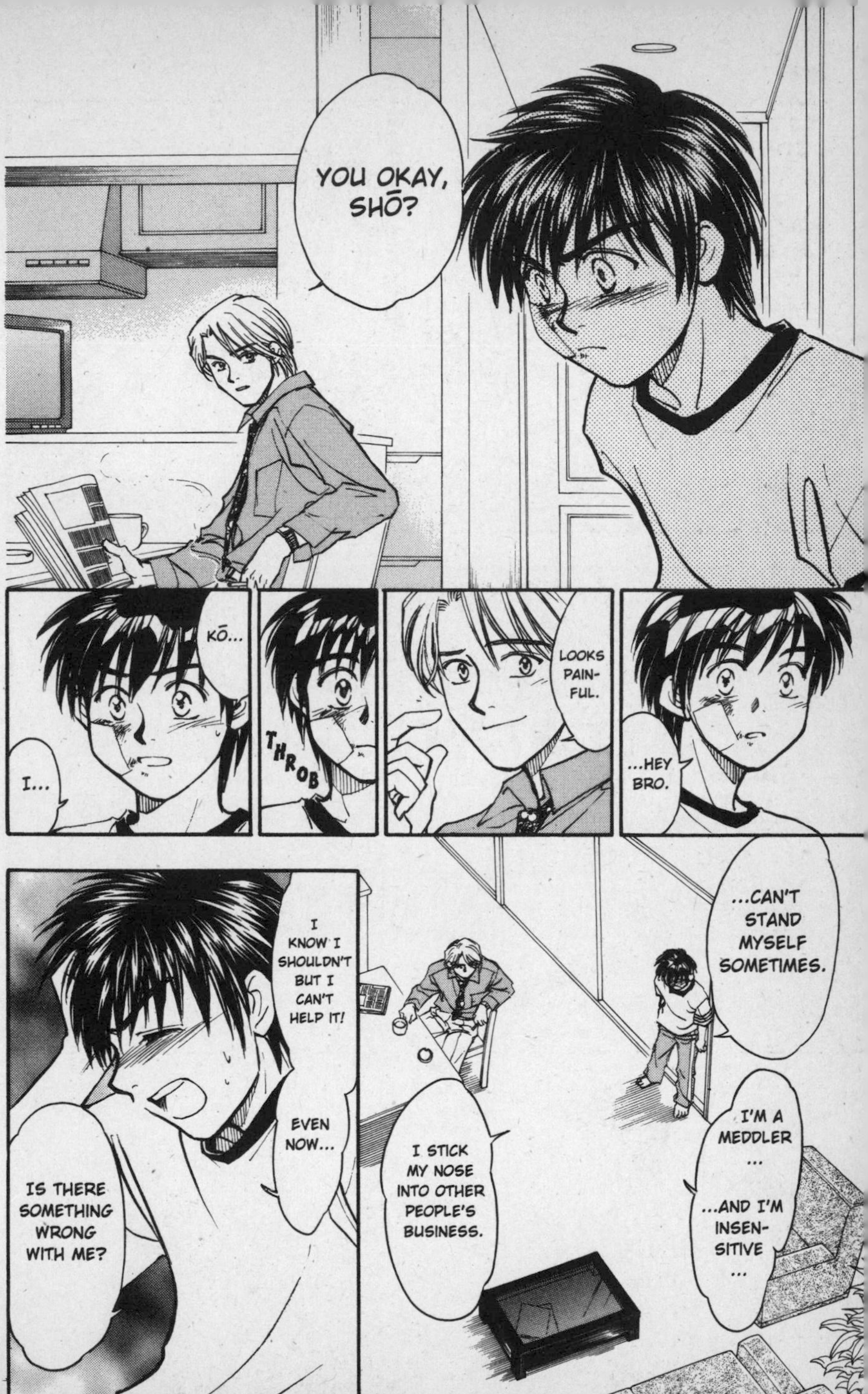
YOU OKAY, SHŌ?
...HEY BRO.
LOOKS PAIN-FUL.
THROB
KŌ...
I...
...CAN'T STAND MYSELF SOMETIMES.
I'M A MEDDLER ...
...AND I'M INSEN-SITIVE ...
I STICK MY NOSE INTO OTHER PEOPLE'S BUSINESS.
I KNOW I SHOULDN'T BUT I CAN'T HELP IT!
EVEN NOW...
IS THERE SOMETHING WRONG WITH ME?

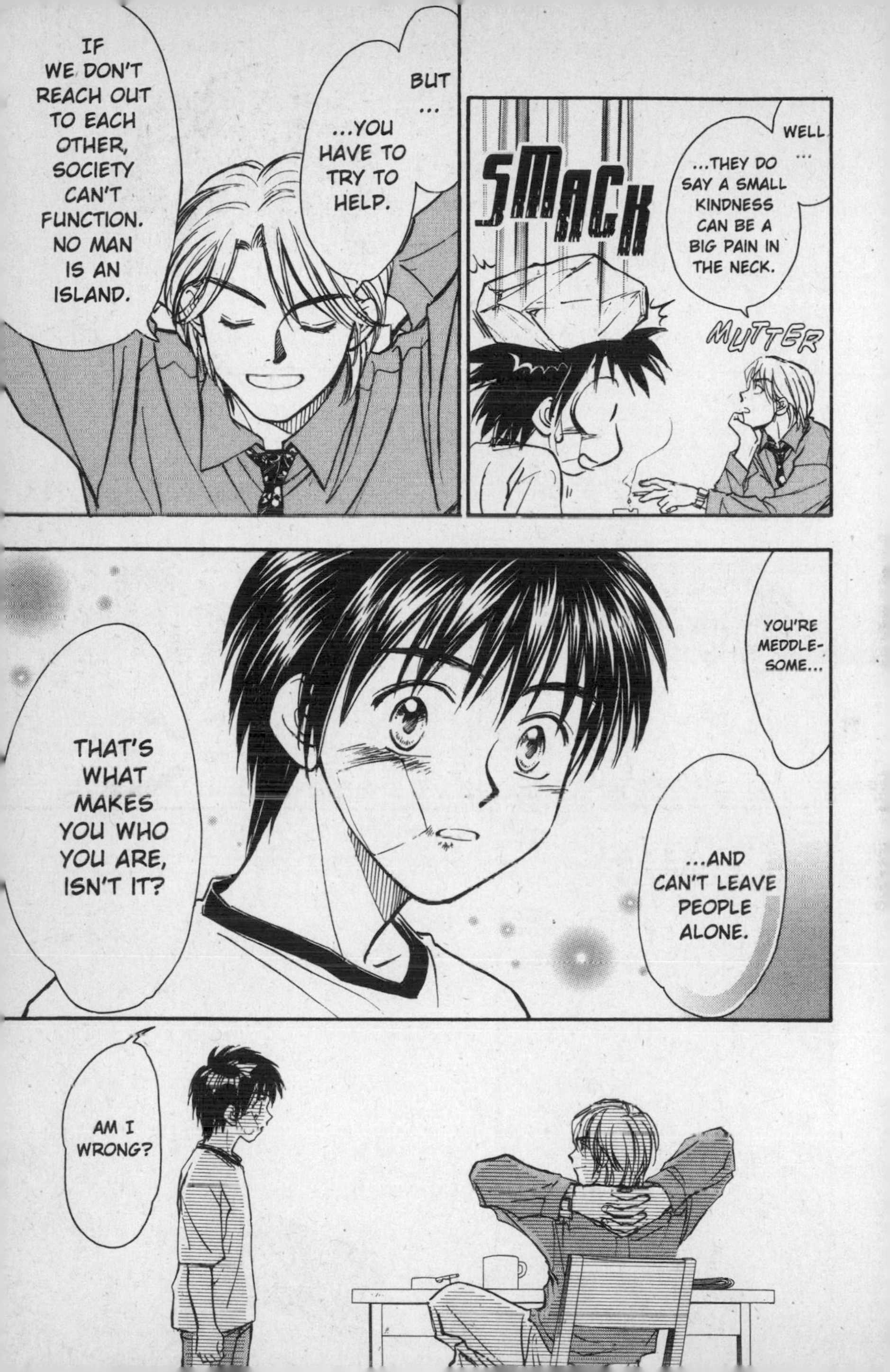
SMACK
WELL ... ...THEY DO SAY A SMALL KINDNESS CAN BE A BIG PAIN IN THE NECK.
MUTTER
BUT ...
...YOU HAVE TO TRY TO HELP.
IF WE DON'T REACH OUT TO EACH OTHER, SOCIETY CAN'T FUNCTION. NO MAN IS AN ISLAND.
YOU'RE MEDDLE-SOME...
...AND CAN'T LEAVE PEOPLE ALONE.
THAT'S WHAT MAKES YOU WHO YOU ARE, ISN'T IT?
AM I WRONG?

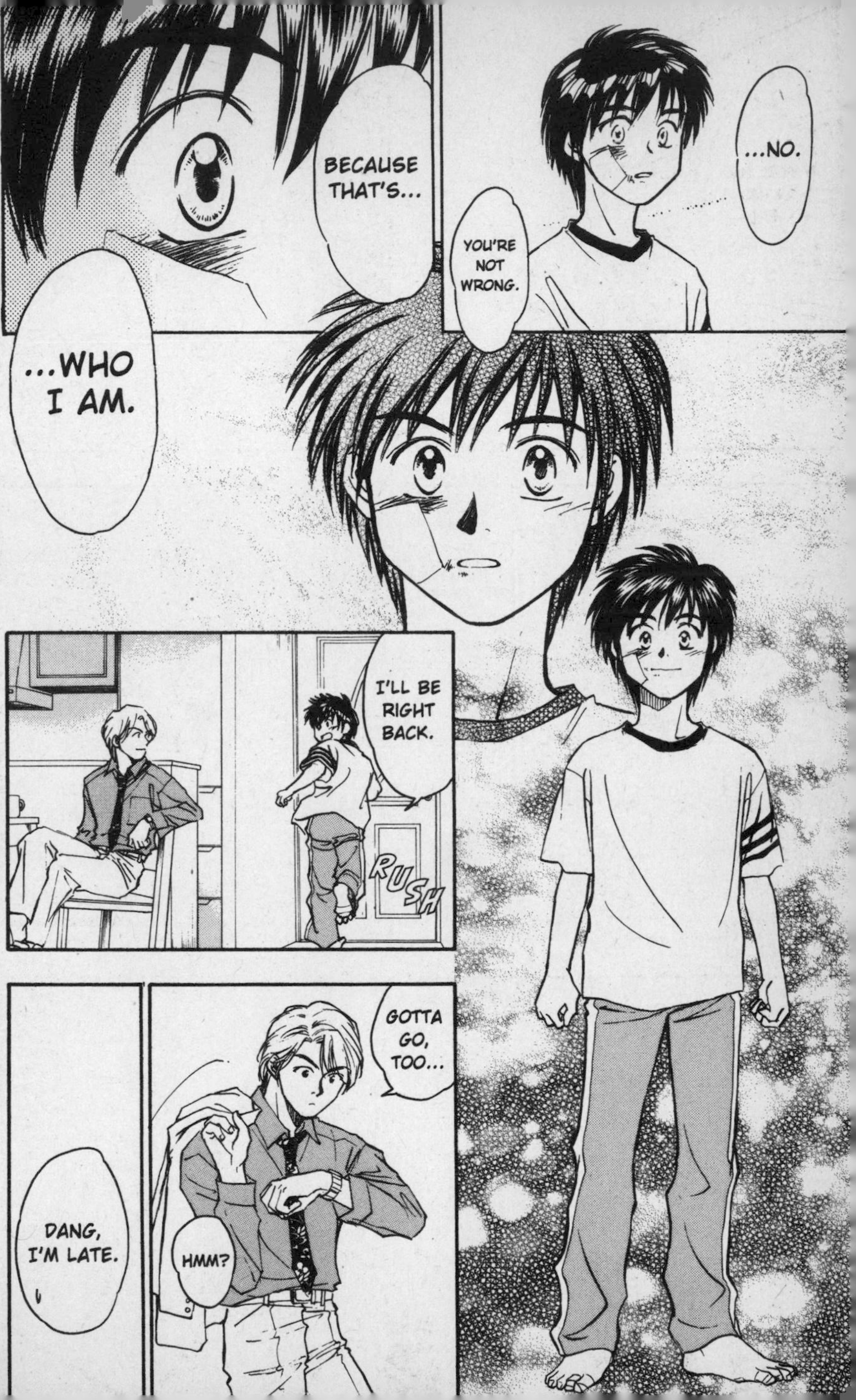

...NO.
YOU'RE NOT WRONG.
BECAUSE THAT'S...
...WHO I AM.
I'LL BE RIGHT BACK.
RUSH
GOTTA GO, TOO...
HMM?
DANG, I'M LATE.

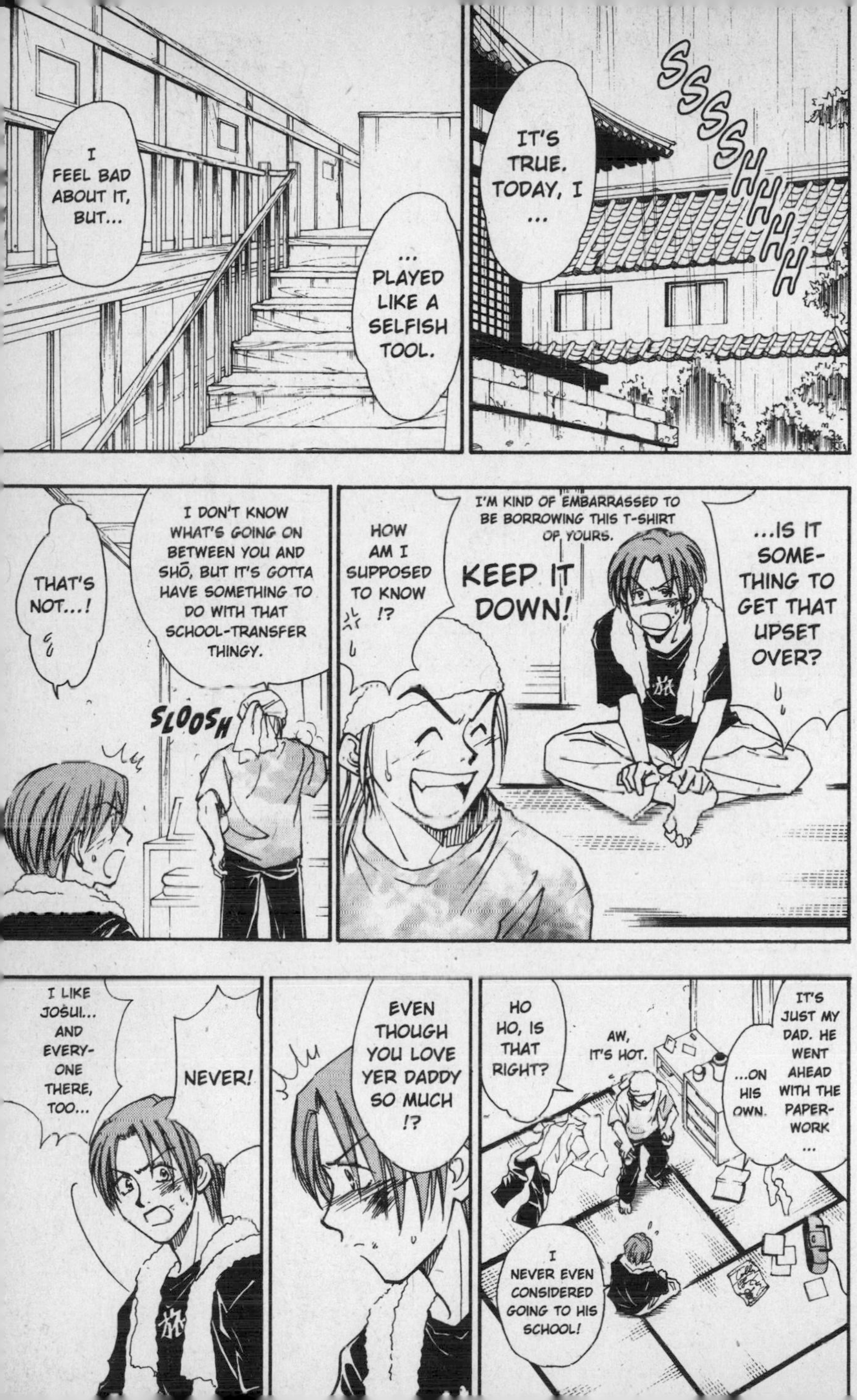
SSSSHHHHH
IT'S TRUE. TODAY, I ...
... PLAYED LIKE A SELFISH TOOL.
I FEEL BAD ABOUT IT, BUT...
...IS IT SOMETHING TO GET THAT UPSET OVER?
I'M KIND OF EMBARRASSED TO BE BORROWING THIS T-SHIRT OF YOURS.
KEEP IT DOWN!
HOW AM I SUPPOSED TO KNOW !?
I DON'T KNOW WHAT'S GOING ON BETWEEN YOU AND SHŌ, BUT IT'S GOTTA HAVE SOMETHING TO DO WITH THAT SCHOOL-TRANSFER THINGY.
SLOOSH
THAT'S NOT...!
IT'S JUST MY DAD. HE WENT AHEAD WITH THE PAPER-WORK...
...ON HIS OWN.
AW, IT'S HOT.
HO HO, IS THAT RIGHT?
I NEVER EVEN CONSIDERED GOING TO HIS SCHOOL!
EVEN THOUGH YOU LOVE YER DADDY SO MUCH !?
NEVER!
I LIKE JOSUI... AND EVERY-ONE THERE, TOO...

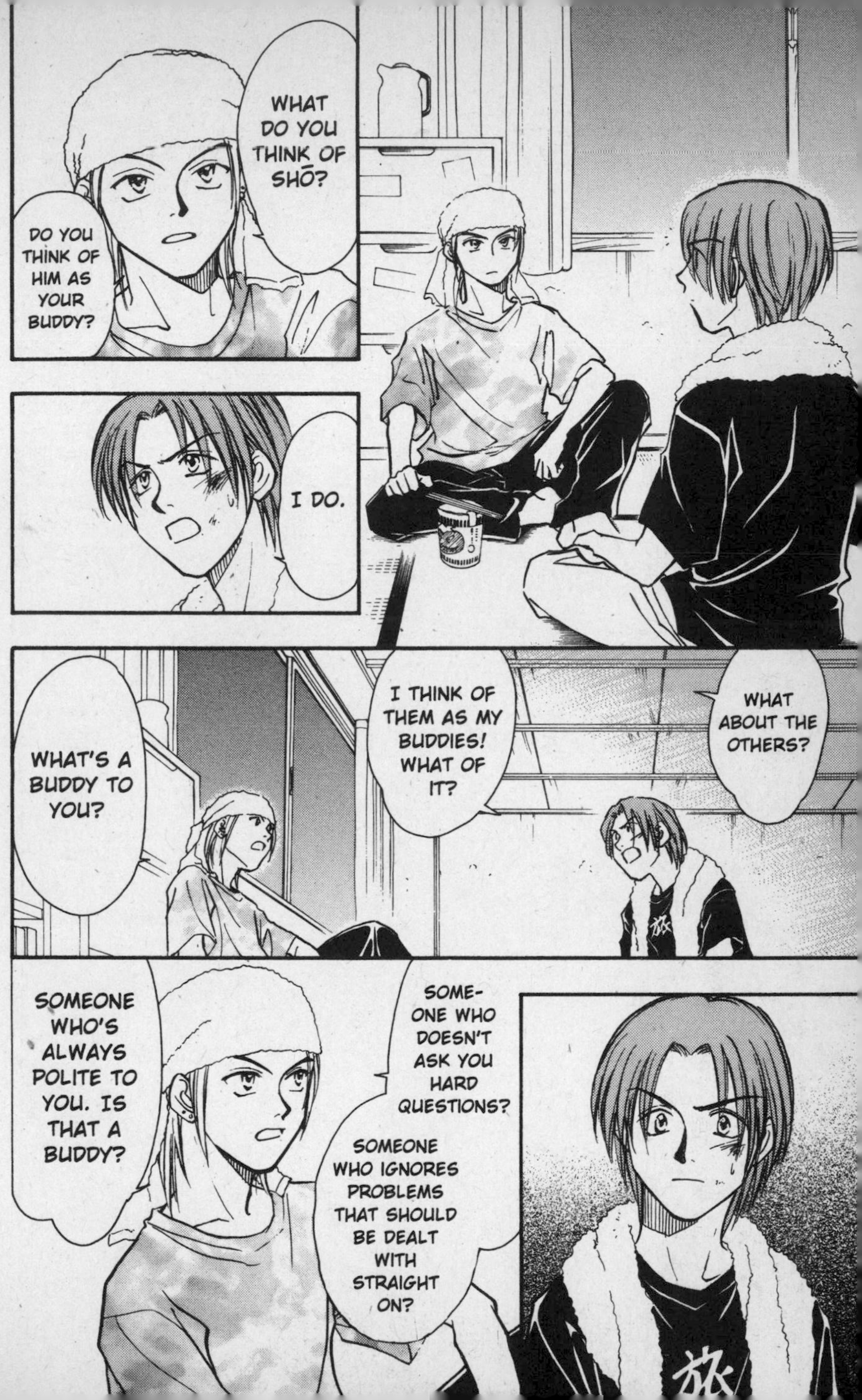
WHAT DO YOU THINK OF SHŌ?
DO YOU THINK OF HIM AS YOUR BUDDY?
I DO.
WHAT ABOUT THE OTHERS?
I THINK OF THEM AS MY BUDDIES! WHAT OF IT?
WHAT'S A BUDDY TO YOU?
SOME-ONE WHO DOESN'T ASK YOU HARD QUESTIONS?
SOMEONE WHO'S ALWAYS POLITE TO YOU. IS THAT A BUDDY?
SOMEONE WHO IGNORES PROBLEMS THAT SHOULD BE DEALT WITH STRAIGHT ON?

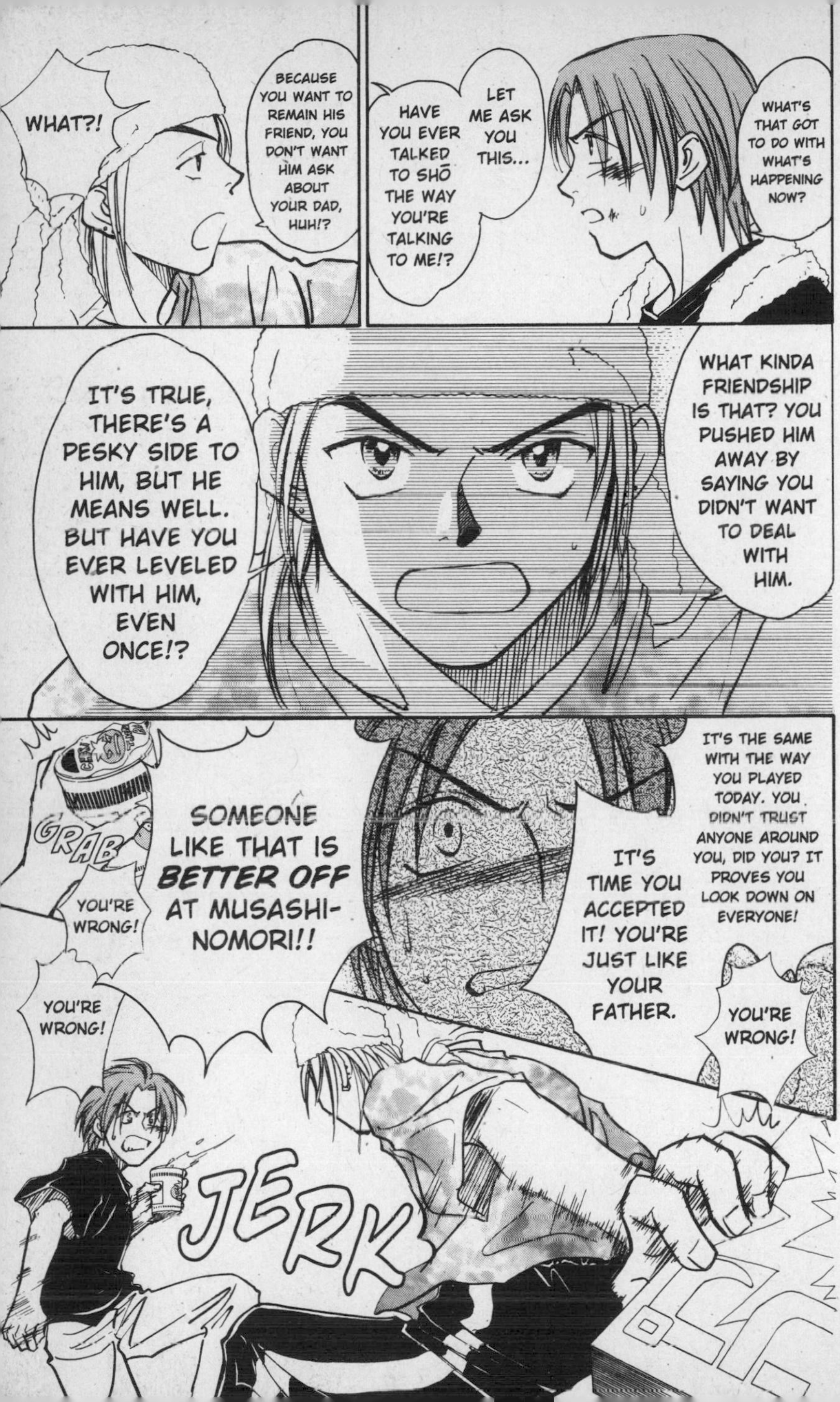
WHAT'S THAT GOT TO DO WITH WHAT'S HAPPENING NOW?
LET ME ASK YOU THIS...
HAVE YOU EVER TALKED TO SHŌ THE WAY YOU'RE TALKING TO ME!?
BECAUSE YOU WANT TO REMAIN HIS FRIEND, YOU DON'T WANT HIM ASK ABOUT YOUR DAD, HUH!?
WHAT?!
WHAT KINDA FRIENDSHIP IS THAT? YOU PUSHED HIM AWAY BY SAYING YOU DIDN'T WANT TO DEAL WITH HIM.
IT'S TRUE, THERE'S A PESKY SIDE TO HIM, BUT HE MEANS WELL. BUT HAVE YOU EVER LEVELED WITH HIM, EVEN ONCE!?
IT'S THE SAME WITH THE WAY YOU PLAYED TODAY. YOU DIDN'T TRUST ANYONE AROUND YOU, DID YOU? IT PROVES YOU LOOK DOWN ON EVERYONE!
IT'S TIME YOU ACCEPTED IT! YOU'RE JUST LIKE YOUR FATHER.
SOMEONE LIKE THAT IS ***BETTER OFF*** AT MUSASHI-NOMORI!!
YOU'RE WRONG!
GRAB
YOU'RE WRONG!
YOU'RE WRONG!
JERK

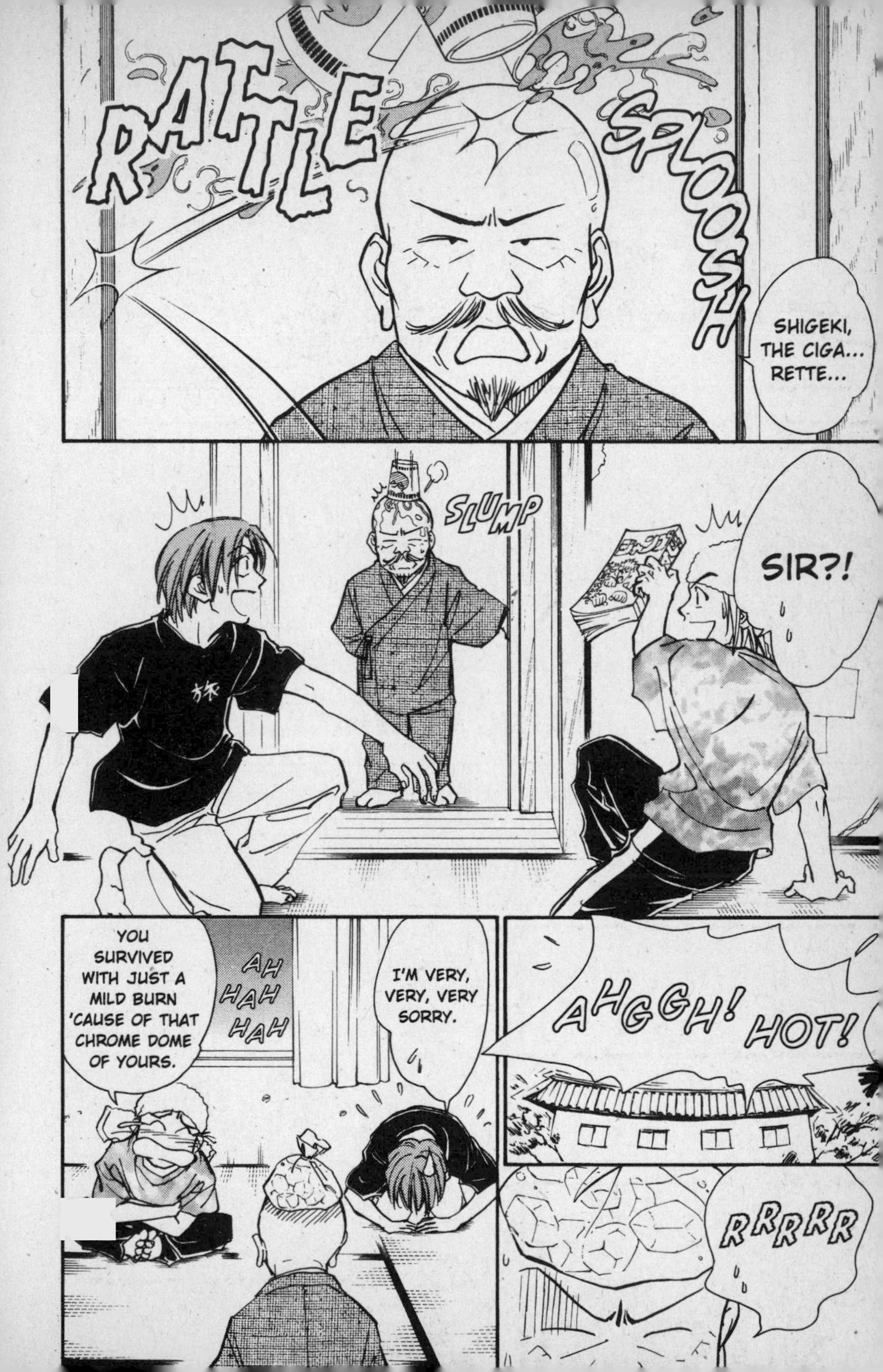
SPLOOSH
RATTLE
SHIGEKI, THE CIGA... RETTE...
SIR?!
SLUMP
AHGGH! HOT!
I'M VERY, VERY, VERY SORRY.
AH HAH HAH
YOU SURVIVED WITH JUST A MILD BURN 'CAUSE OF THAT CHROME DOME OF YOURS.
RRRRR

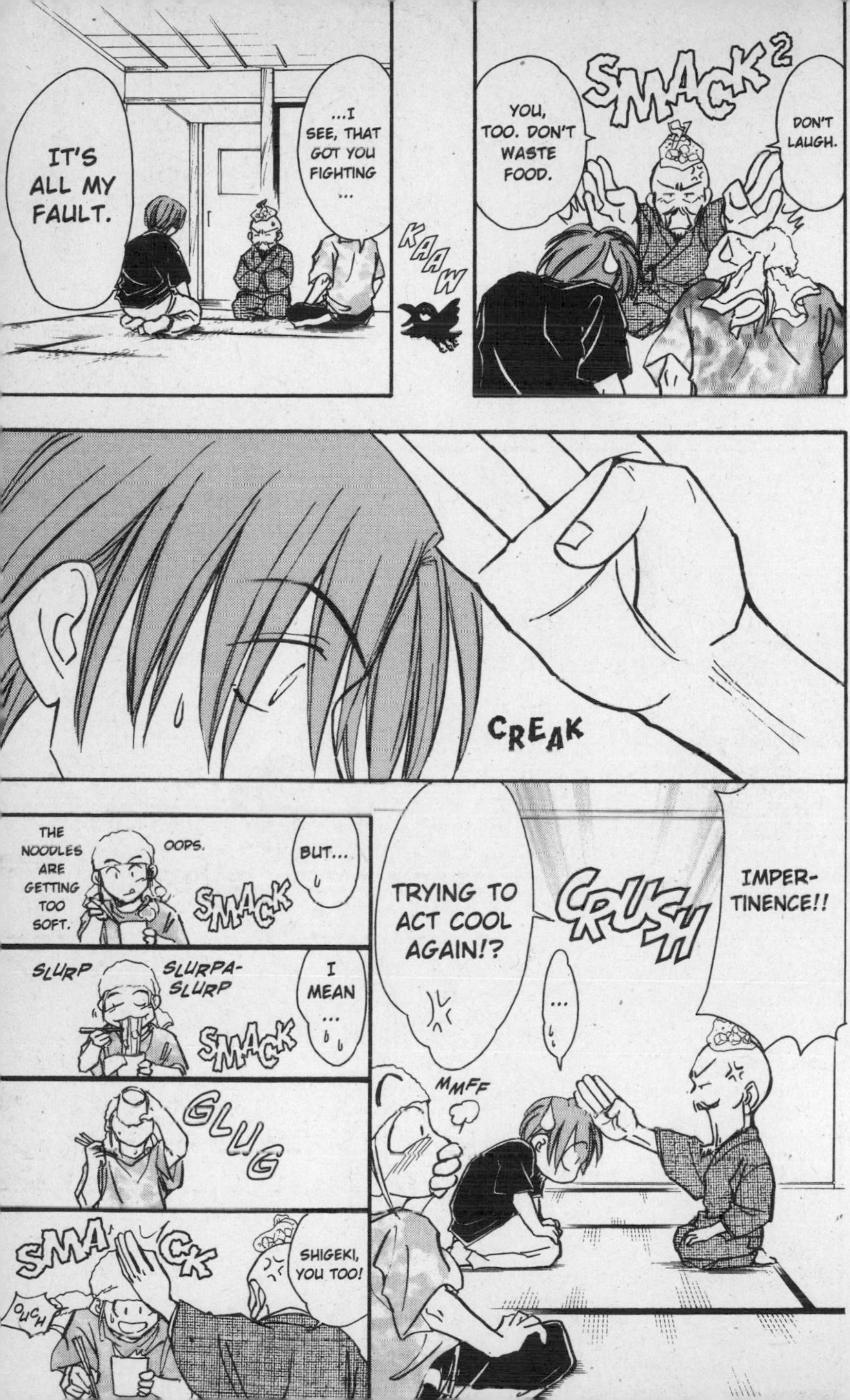
DON'T LAUGH.
SMACK 2
YOU, TOO. DON'T WASTE FOOD.
KAAW
...I SEE, THAT GOT YOU FIGHTING ...
IT'S ALL MY FAULT.
CREAK
IMPER-TINENCE!!
CRUSH
TRYING TO ACT COOL AGAIN!?
...
MMFF
BUT...
OOPS.
SMACK
THE NOODLES ARE GETTING TOO SOFT.
I MEAN ...
SLURPA-SLURP
SMACK
SLURP
GLUG
SHIGEKI, YOU TOO!
SMACK
OUCH

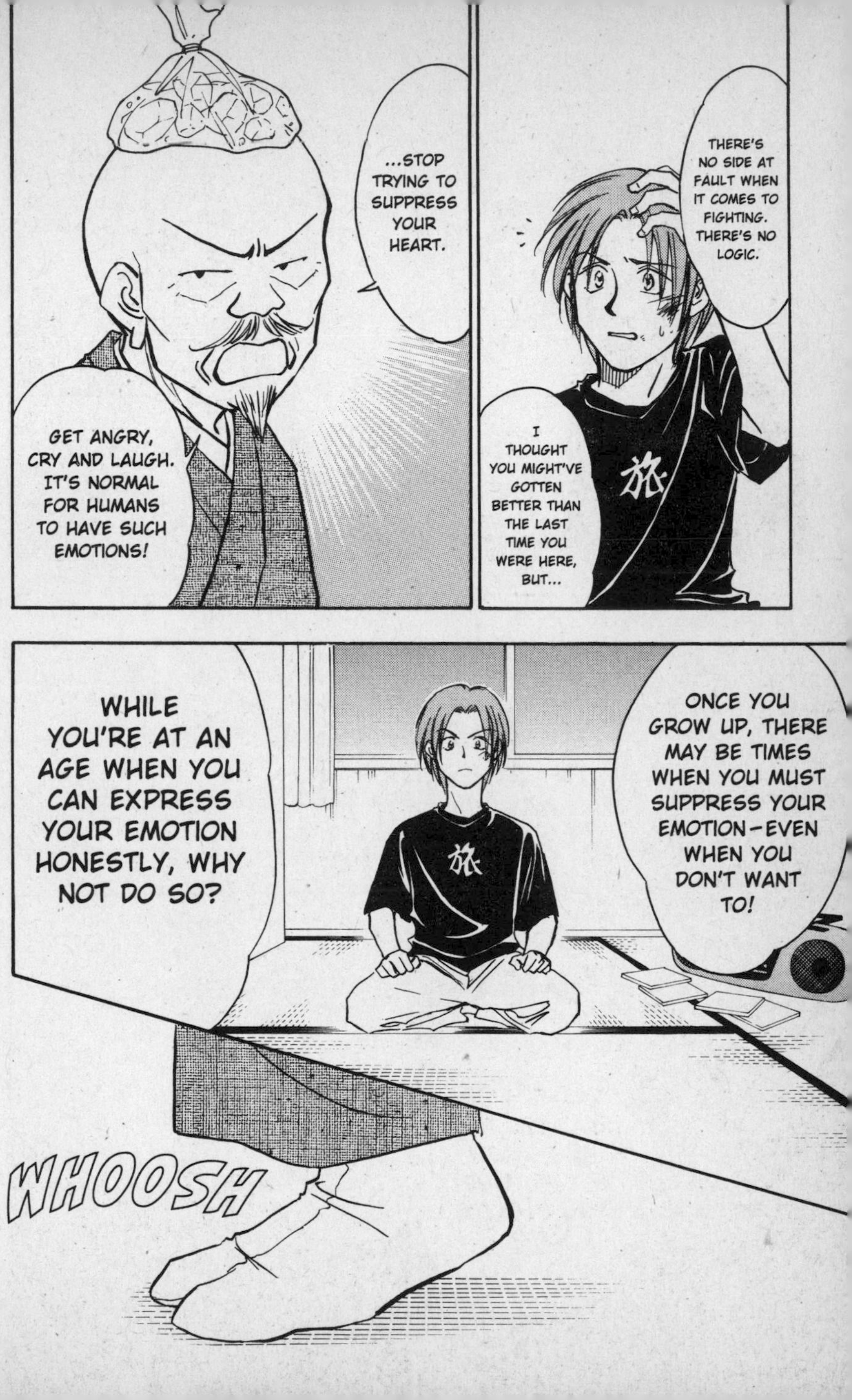
THERE'S NO SIDE AT FAULT WHEN IT COMES TO FIGHTING. THERE'S NO LOGIC.
I THOUGHT YOU MIGHT'VE GOTTEN BETTER THAN THE LAST TIME YOU WERE HERE, BUT...
...STOP TRYING TO SUPPRESS YOUR HEART.
GET ANGRY, CRY AND LAUGH. IT'S NORMAL FOR HUMANS TO HAVE SUCH EMOTIONS!
ONCE YOU GROW UP, THERE MAY BE TIMES WHEN YOU MUST SUPPRESS YOUR EMOTION—EVEN WHEN YOU DON'T WANT TO!
WHILE YOU'RE AT AN AGE WHEN YOU CAN EXPRESS YOUR EMOTION HONESTLY, WHY NOT DO SO?
WHOOSH

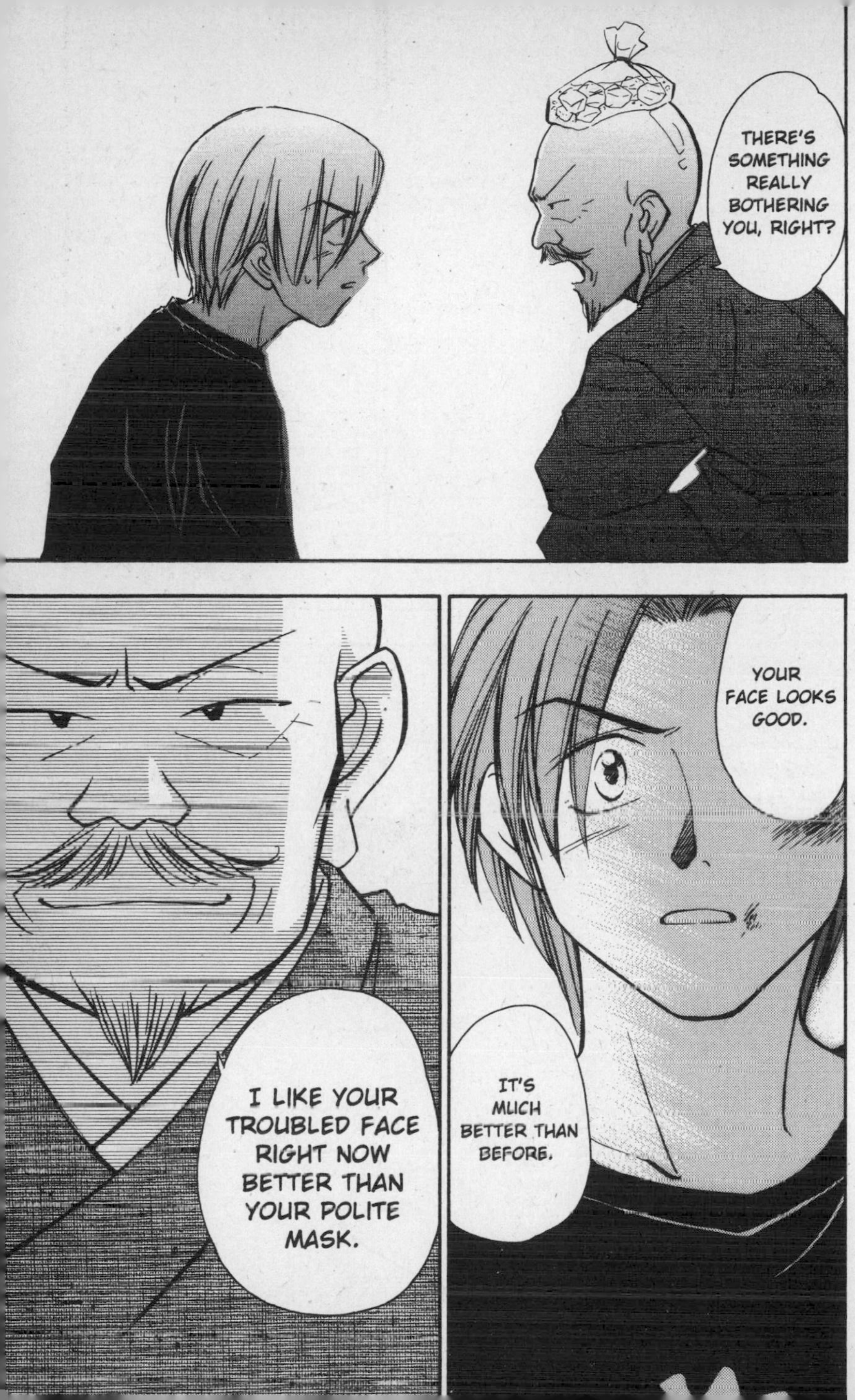
THERE'S SOMETHING REALLY BOTHERING YOU, RIGHT?
YOUR FACE LOOKS GOOD.
IT'S MUCH BETTER THAN BEFORE.
I LIKE YOUR TROUBLED FACE RIGHT NOW BETTER THAN YOUR POLITE MASK.

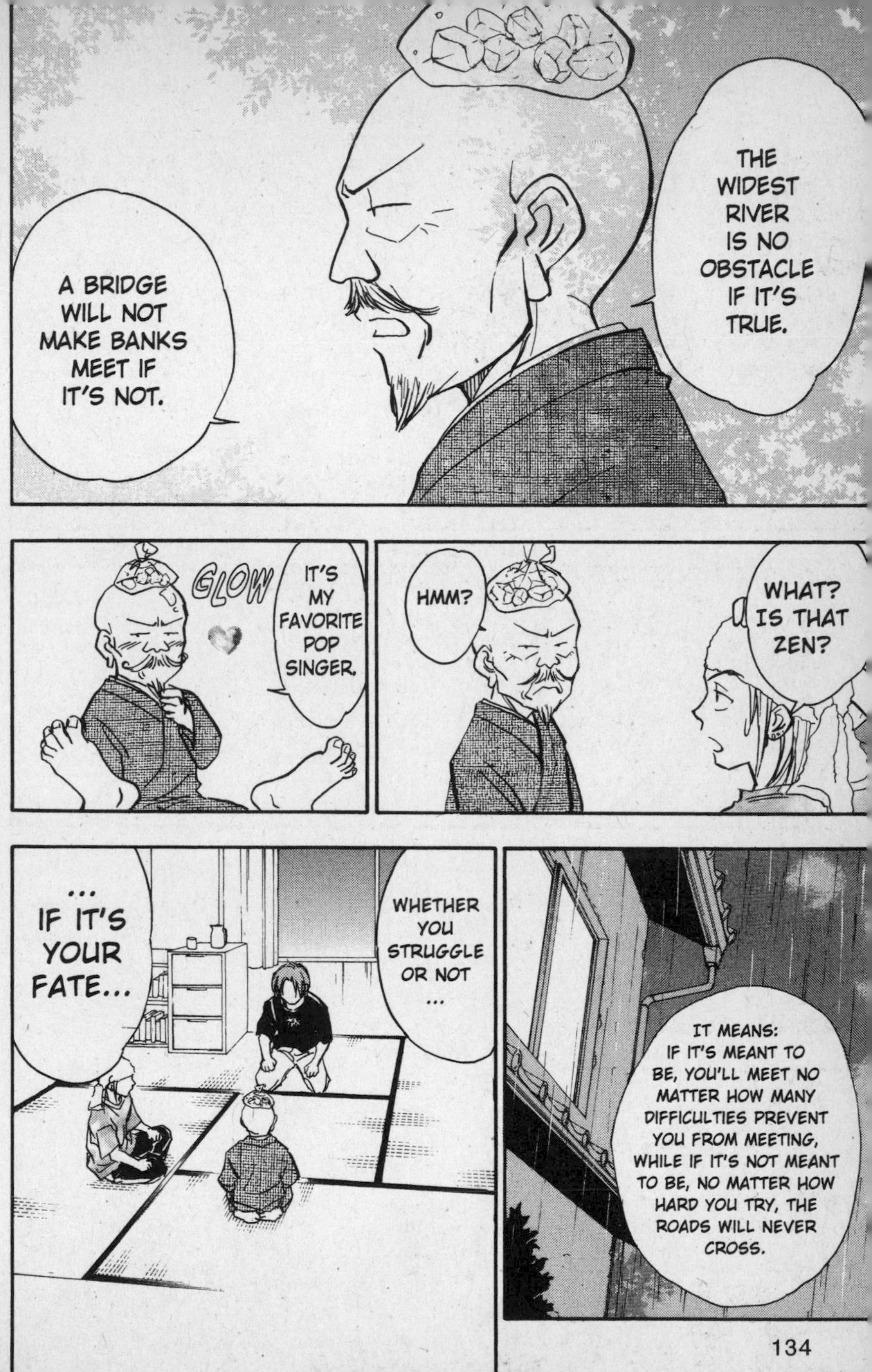
THE WIDEST RIVER IS NO OBSTACLE IF IT'S TRUE.
A BRIDGE WILL NOT MAKE BANKS MEET IF IT'S NOT.
WHAT? IS THAT ZEN?
HMM?
IT'S MY FAVORITE POP SINGER.
GLOW
IT MEANS: IF IT'S MEANT TO BE, YOU'LL MEET NO MATTER HOW MANY DIFFICULTIES PREVENT YOU FROM MEETING, WHILE IF IT'S NOT MEANT TO BE, NO MATTER HOW HARD YOU TRY, THE ROADS WILL NEVER CROSS.
WHETHER YOU STRUGGLE OR NOT ...
... IF IT'S YOUR FATE...

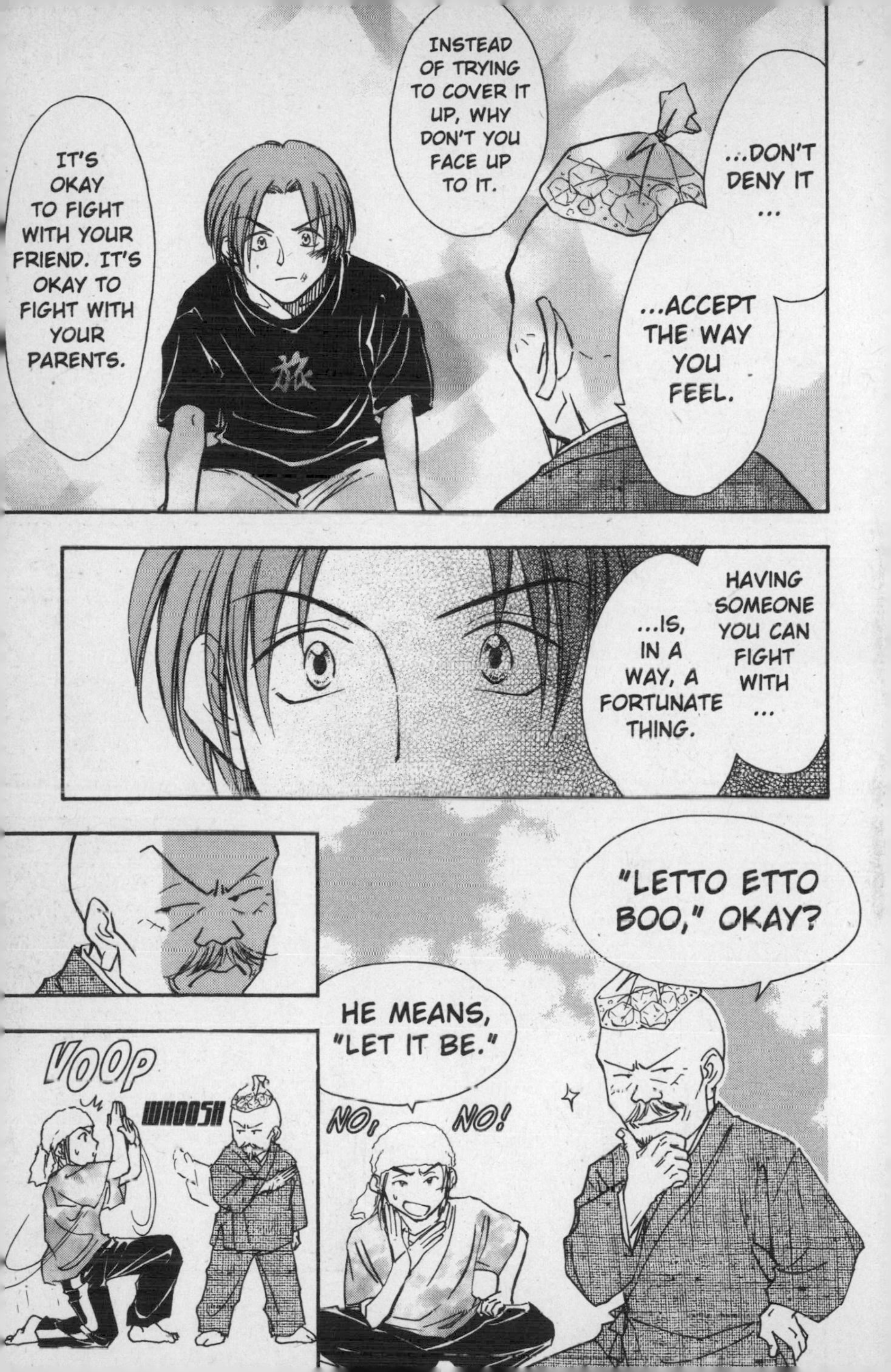
...DON'T DENY IT ...
...ACCEPT THE WAY YOU FEEL.
INSTEAD OF TRYING TO COVER IT UP, WHY DON'T YOU FACE UP TO IT.
IT'S OKAY TO FIGHT WITH YOUR FRIEND. IT'S OKAY TO FIGHT WITH YOUR PARENTS.
HAVING SOMEONE YOU CAN FIGHT WITH ...
...IS, IN A WAY, A FORTUNATE THING.
"LETTO ETTO BOO," OKAY?
HE MEANS, "LET IT BE."
NO! NO!
VOOP
WHOOSH

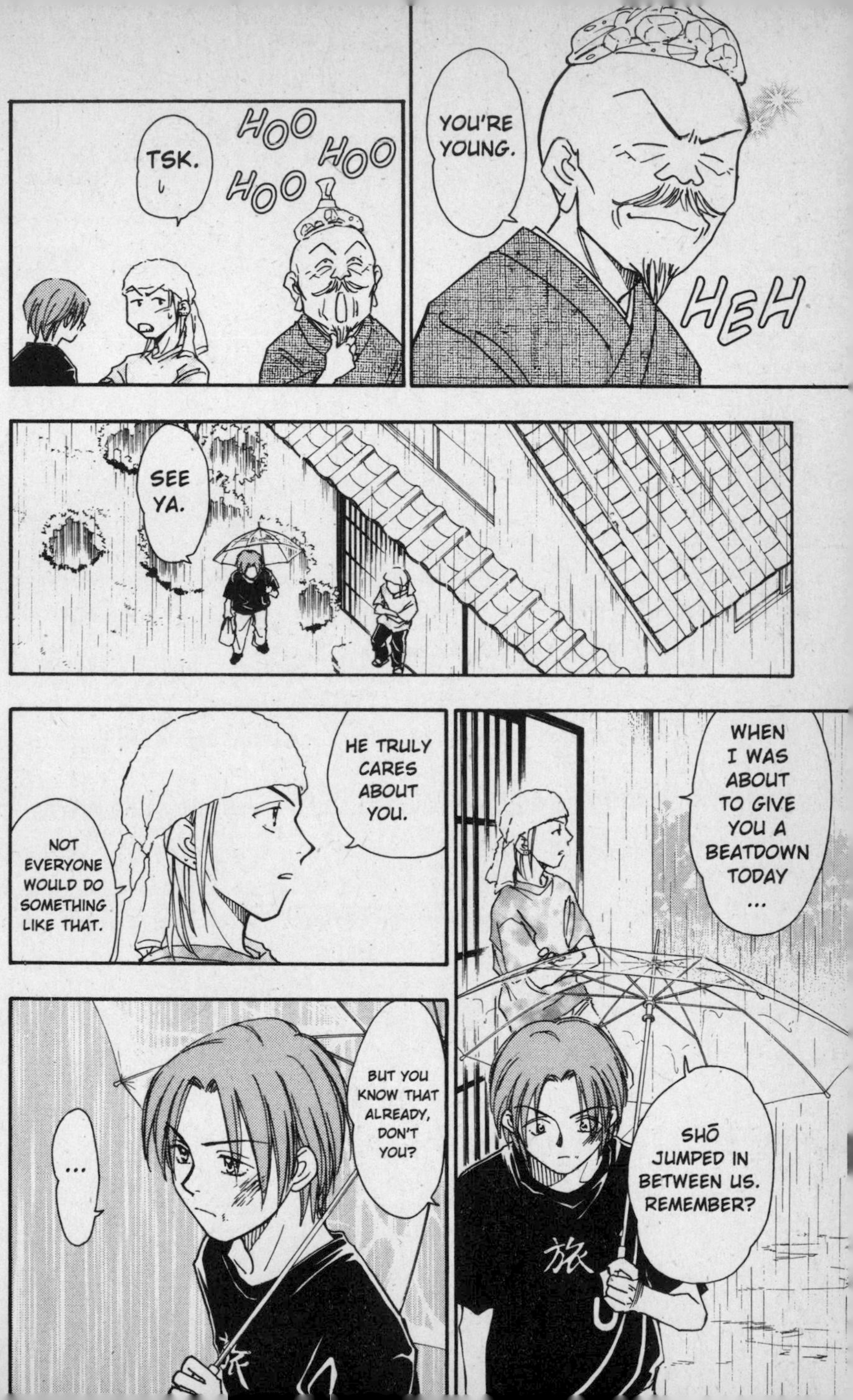
YOU'RE YOUNG.
HEH
HOO HOO HOO
TSK.
SEE YA.
WHEN I WAS ABOUT TO GIVE YOU A BEATDOWN TODAY ...
SHŌ JUMPED IN BETWEEN US. REMEMBER?
HE TRULY CARES ABOUT YOU.
NOT EVERYONE WOULD DO SOMETHING LIKE THAT.
BUT YOU KNOW THAT ALREADY, DON'T YOU?
...

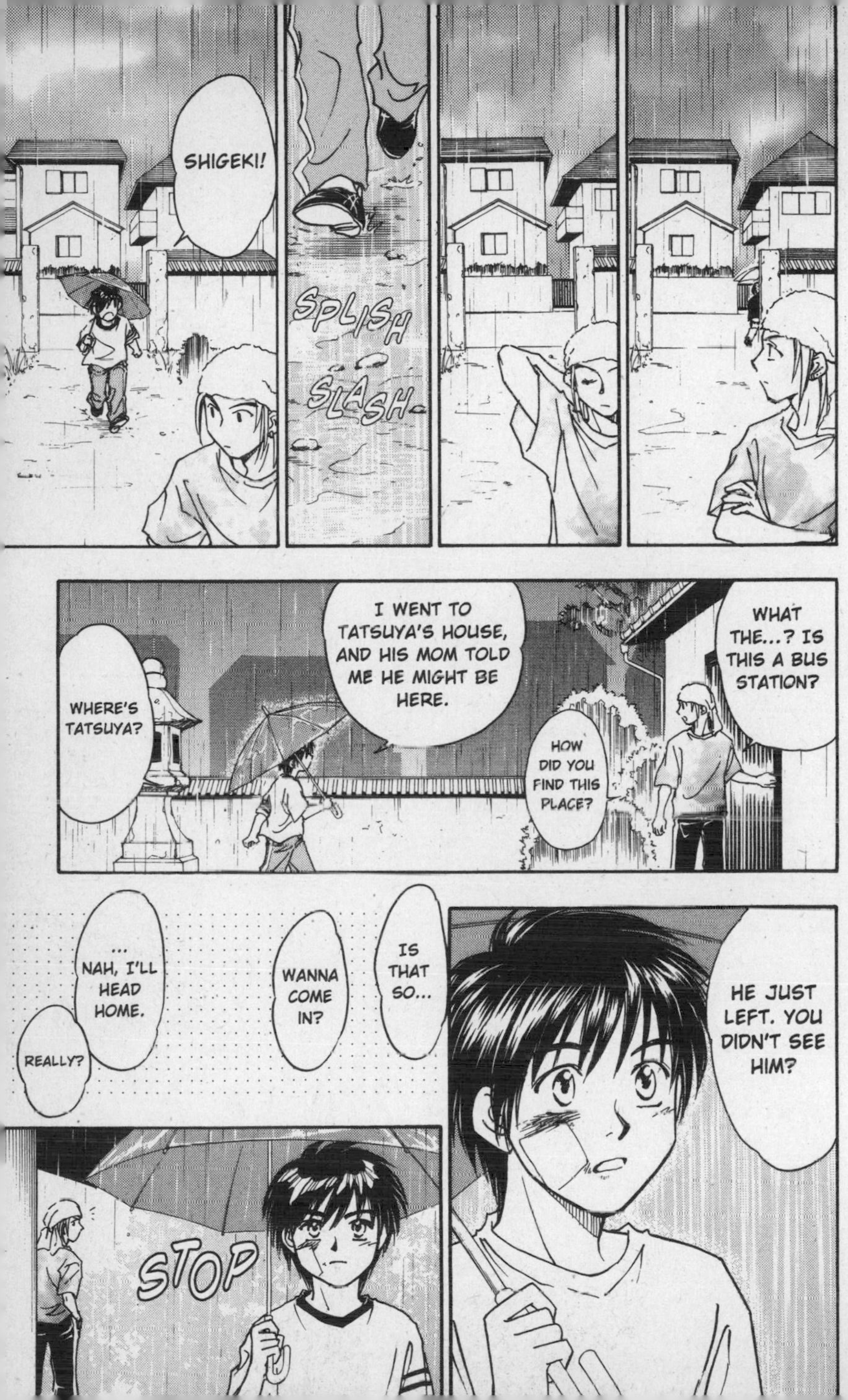

SPLISH
SLASH
SHIGEKI!
WHAT THE...? IS THIS A BUS STATION?
HOW DID YOU FIND THIS PLACE?
I WENT TO TATSUYA'S HOUSE, AND HIS MOM TOLD ME HE MIGHT BE HERE.
WHERE'S TATSUYA?
HE JUST LEFT. YOU DIDN'T SEE HIM?
IS THAT SO...
WANNA COME IN?
... NAH, I'LL HEAD HOME.
REALLY?
STOP

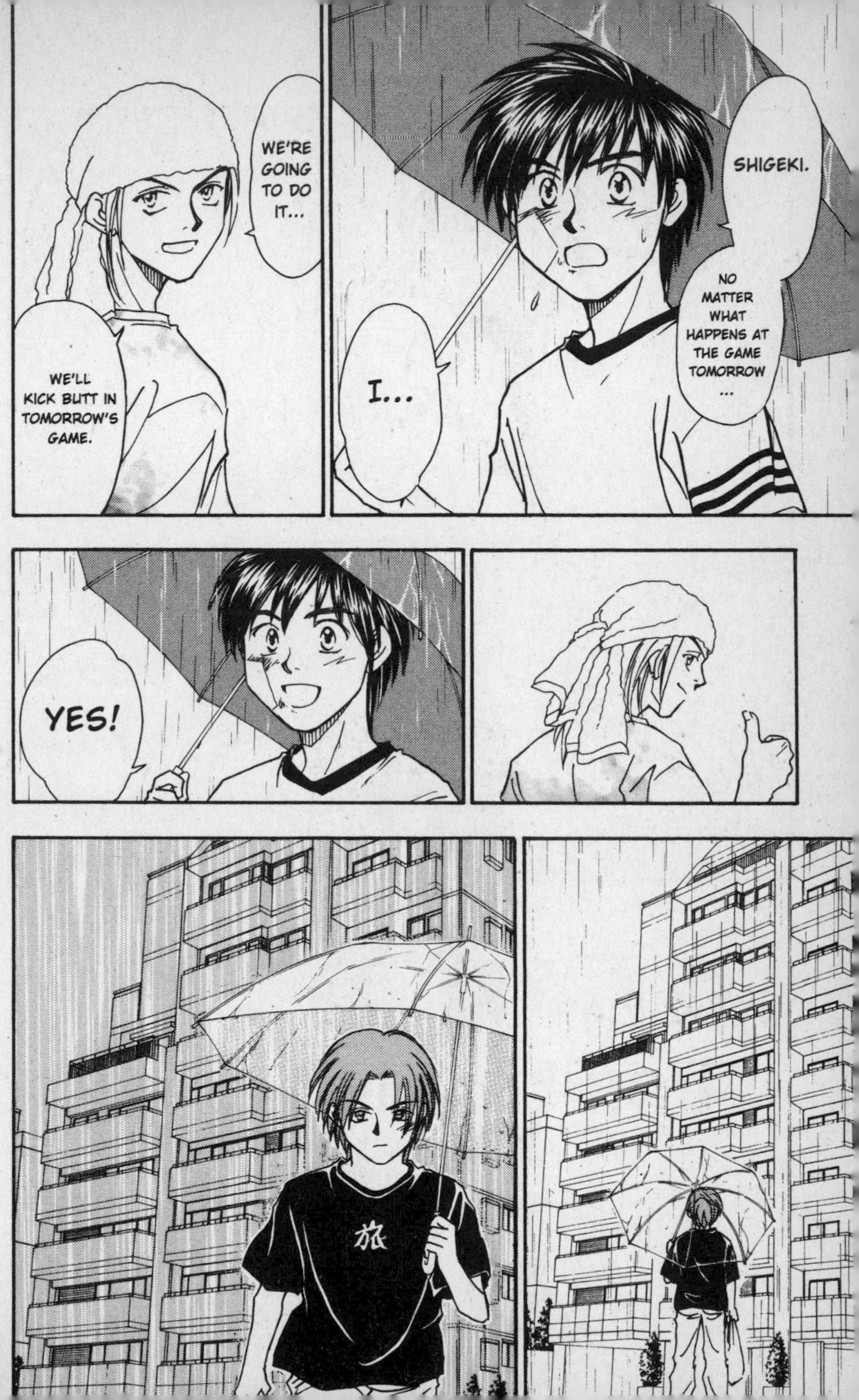
SHIGEKI.
NO MATTER WHAT HAPPENS AT THE GAME TOMORROW ...
I...
WE'RE GOING TO DO IT...
WE'LL KICK BUTT IN TOMORROW'S GAME.
YES!

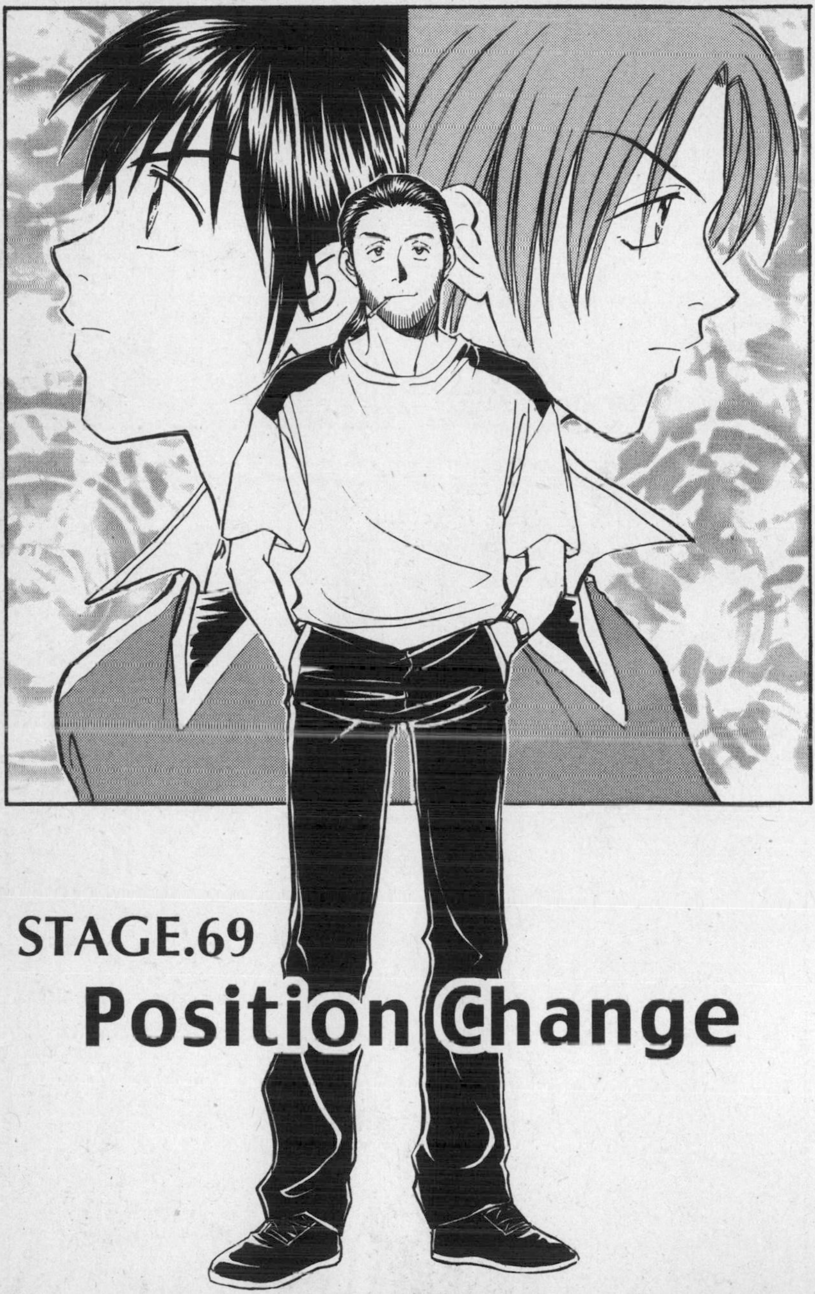

STAGE.69

Position Change

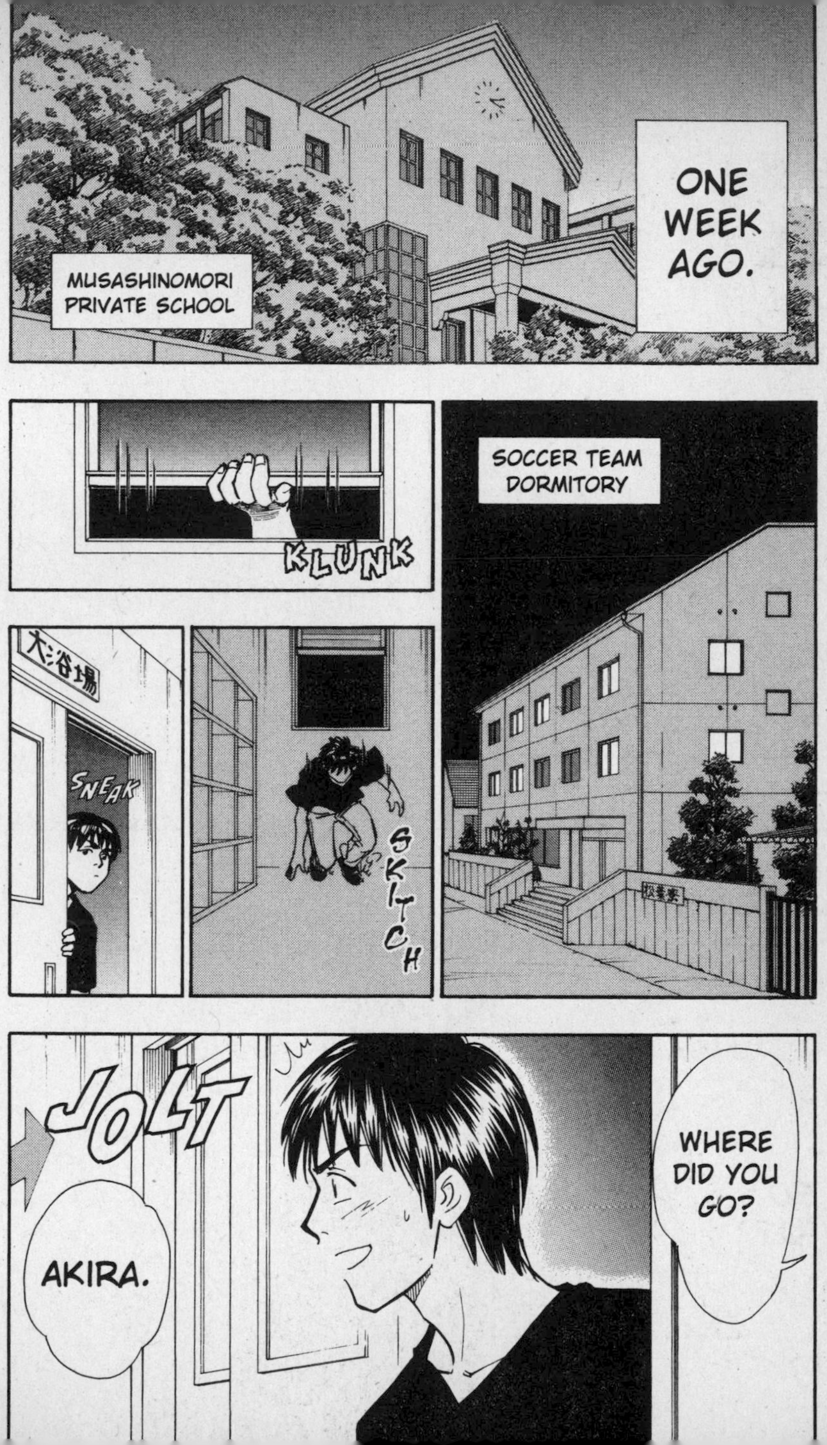

ONE WEEK AGO.
MUSASHINOMORI PRIVATE SCHOOL
SOCCER TEAM DORMITORY
KLUNK
SKITCH
大浴場
SNEAK
WHERE DID YOU GO?
JOLT
AKIRA.

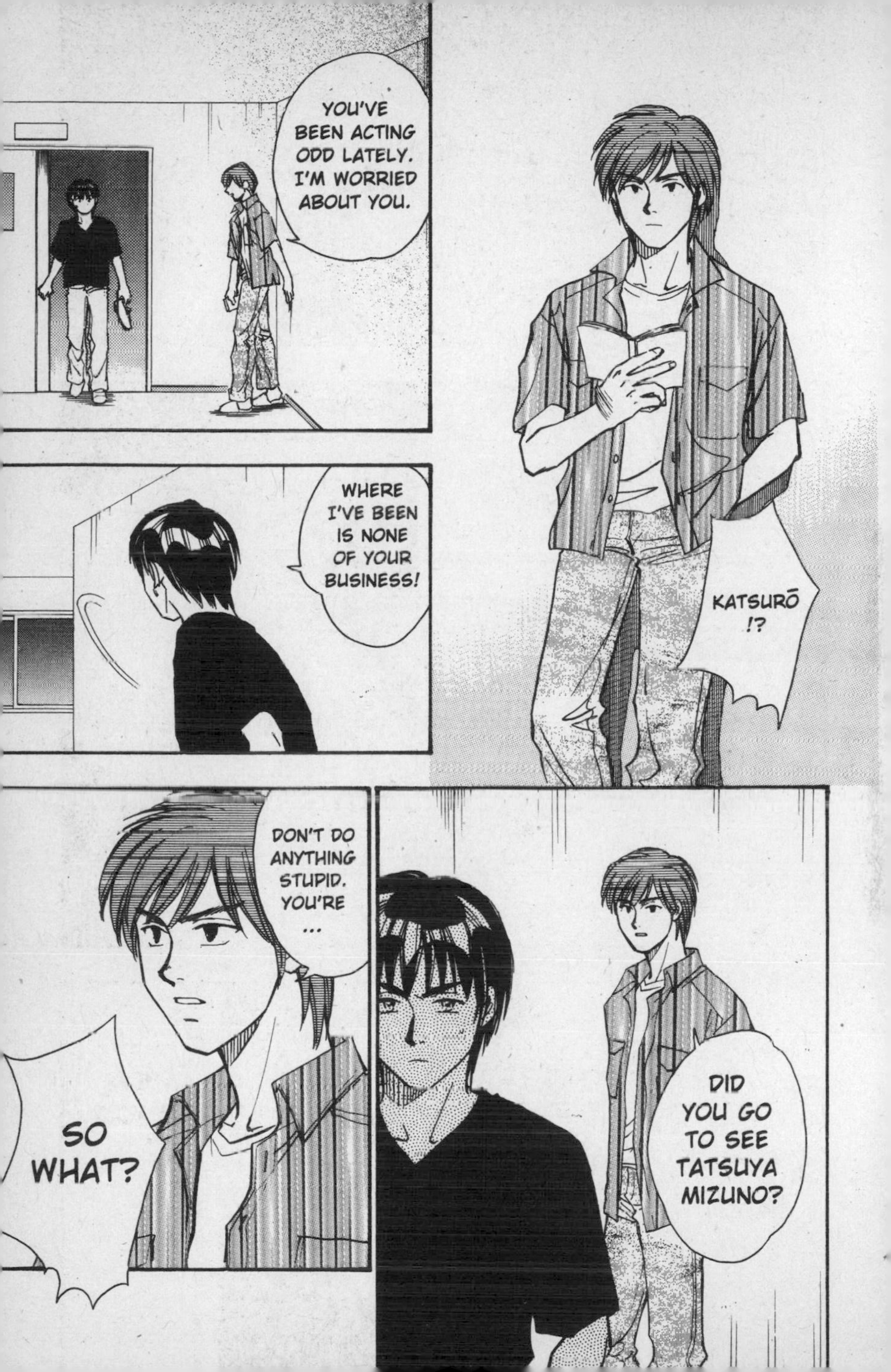
KATSURŌ!?
YOU'VE BEEN ACTING ODD LATELY. I'M WORRIED ABOUT YOU.
WHERE I'VE BEEN IS NONE OF YOUR BUSINESS!
DID YOU GO TO SEE TATSUYA MIZUNO?
DON'T DO ANYTHING STUPID. YOU'RE ...
SO WHAT?

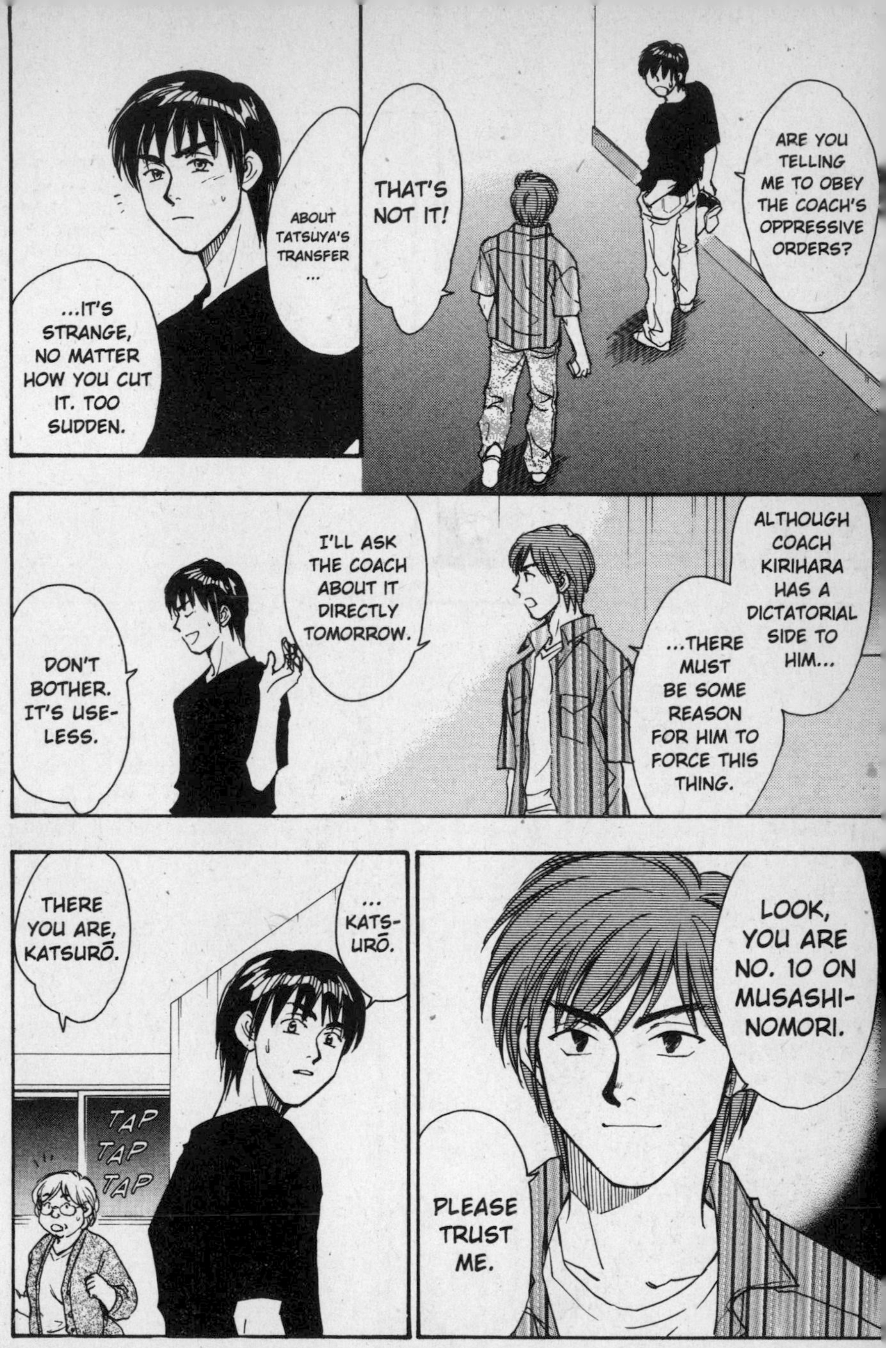
ARE YOU TELLING ME TO OBEY THE COACH'S OPPRESSIVE ORDERS?
THAT'S NOT IT!
ABOUT TATSUYA'S TRANSFER ...
...IT'S STRANGE, NO MATTER HOW YOU CUT IT. TOO SUDDEN.
ALTHOUGH COACH KIRIHARA HAS A DICTATORIAL SIDE TO HIM...
...THERE MUST BE SOME REASON FOR HIM TO FORCE THIS THING.
I'LL ASK THE COACH ABOUT IT DIRECTLY TOMORROW.
DON'T BOTHER. IT'S USE-LESS.
LOOK, YOU ARE NO. 10 ON MUSASHI-NOMORI.
PLEASE TRUST ME.
... KATS-URŌ.
THERE YOU ARE, KATSURŌ.
TAP TAP TAP

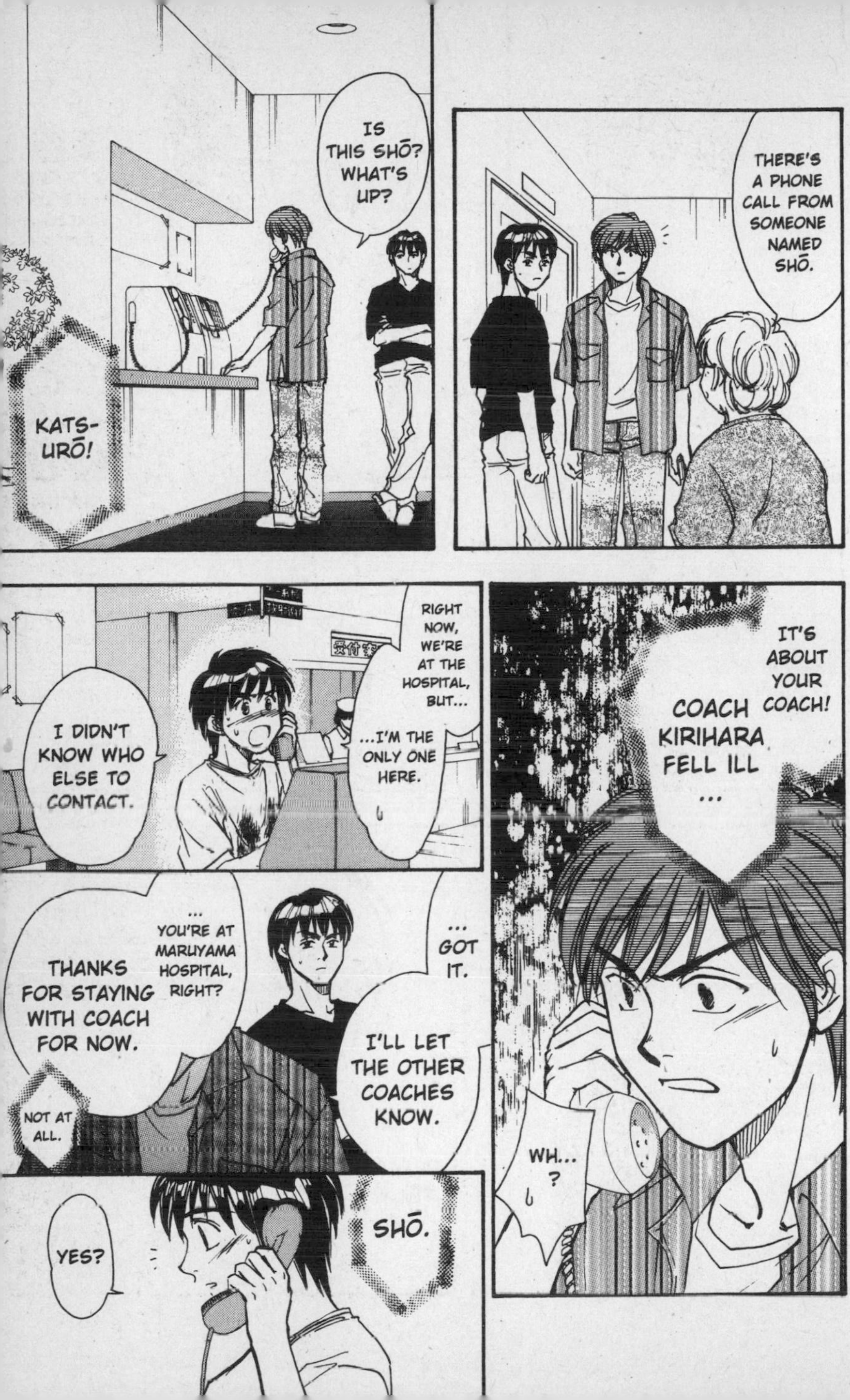
THERE'S A PHONE CALL FROM SOMEONE NAMED SHŌ.
IS THIS SHŌ? WHAT'S UP?
KATSU-URŌ!
IT'S ABOUT YOUR COACH!
COACH KIRIHARA FELL ILL ...
WH... ?
RIGHT NOW, WE'RE AT THE HOSPITAL, BUT...
...I'M THE ONLY ONE HERE.
I DIDN'T KNOW WHO ELSE TO CONTACT.
... GOT IT.
... YOU'RE AT MARUYAMA HOSPITAL, RIGHT?
I'LL LET THE OTHER COACHES KNOW.
THANKS FOR STAYING WITH COACH FOR NOW.
NOT AT ALL.
SHŌ.
YES?

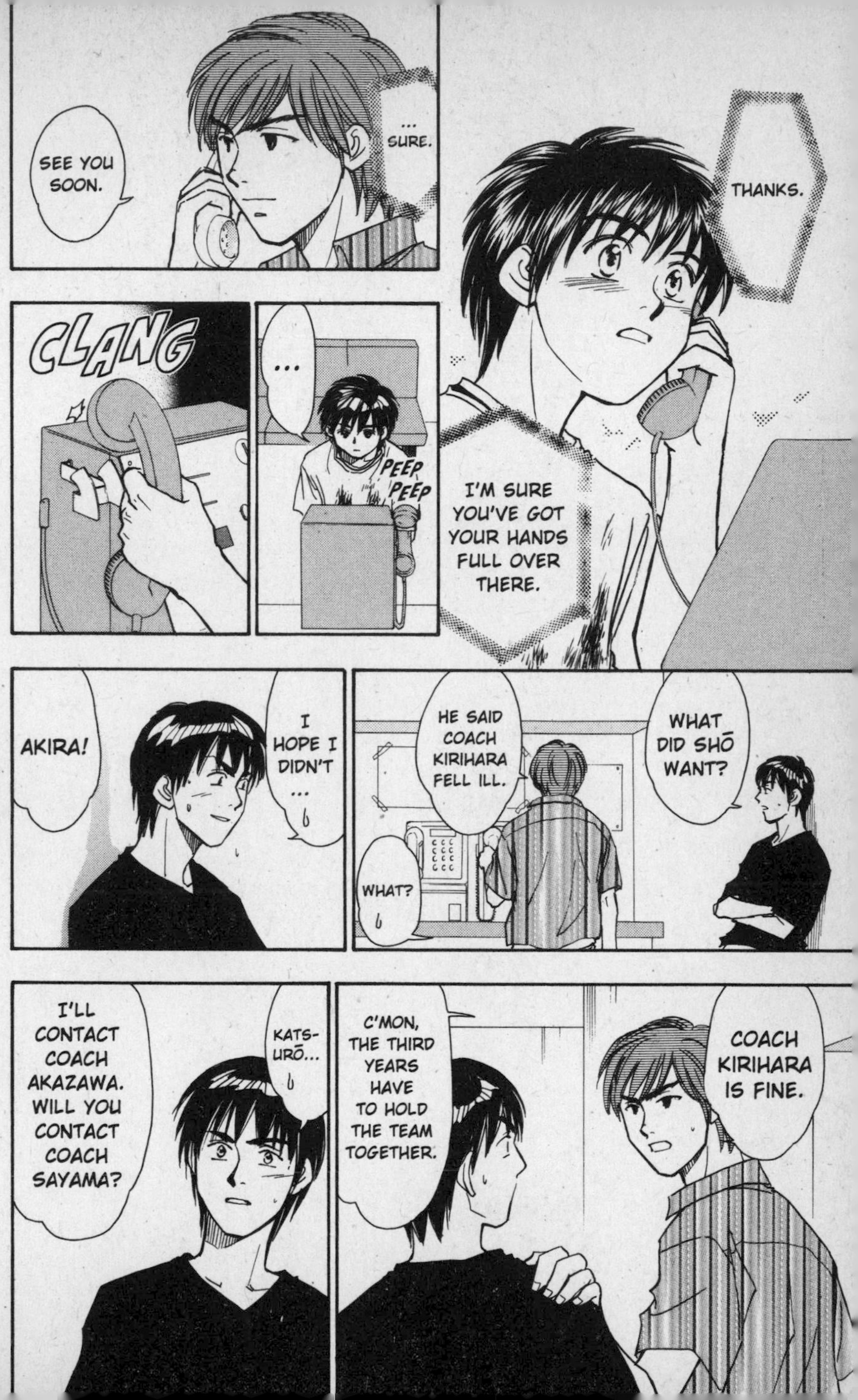
THANKS.
I'M SURE YOU'VE GOT YOUR HANDS FULL OVER THERE.
... SURE.
SEE YOU SOON.
...
PEEP PEEP
CLANG
WHAT DID SHŌ WANT?
HE SAID COACH KIRIHARA FELL ILL.
WHAT?
I HOPE I DIDN'T ...
AKIRA!
COACH KIRIHARA IS FINE.
C'MON, THE THIRD YEARS HAVE TO HOLD THE TEAM TOGETHER.
KATSURŌ...
I'LL CONTACT COACH AKAZAWA. WILL YOU CONTACT COACH SAYAMA?

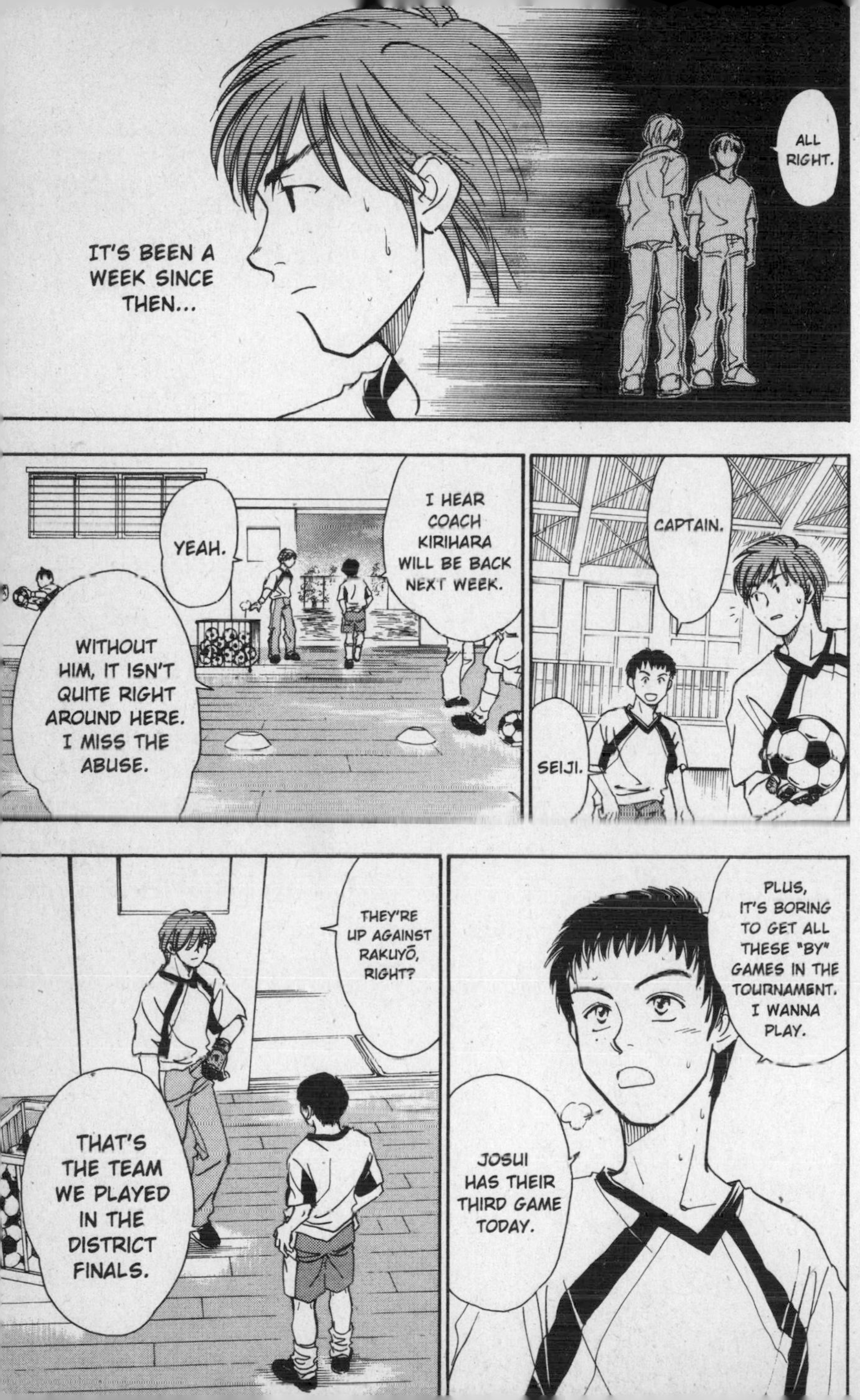
ALL RIGHT.
IT'S BEEN A WEEK SINCE THEN...
CAPTAIN.
SEIJI.
I HEAR COACH KIRIHARA WILL BE BACK NEXT WEEK.
YEAH.
WITHOUT HIM, IT ISN'T QUITE RIGHT AROUND HERE. I MISS THE ABUSE.
PLUS, IT'S BORING TO GET ALL THESE "BY" GAMES IN THE TOURNAMENT. I WANNA PLAY.
JOSUI HAS THEIR THIRD GAME TODAY.
THEY'RE UP AGAINST RAKUYŌ, RIGHT?
THAT'S THE TEAM WE PLAYED IN THE DISTRICT FINALS.

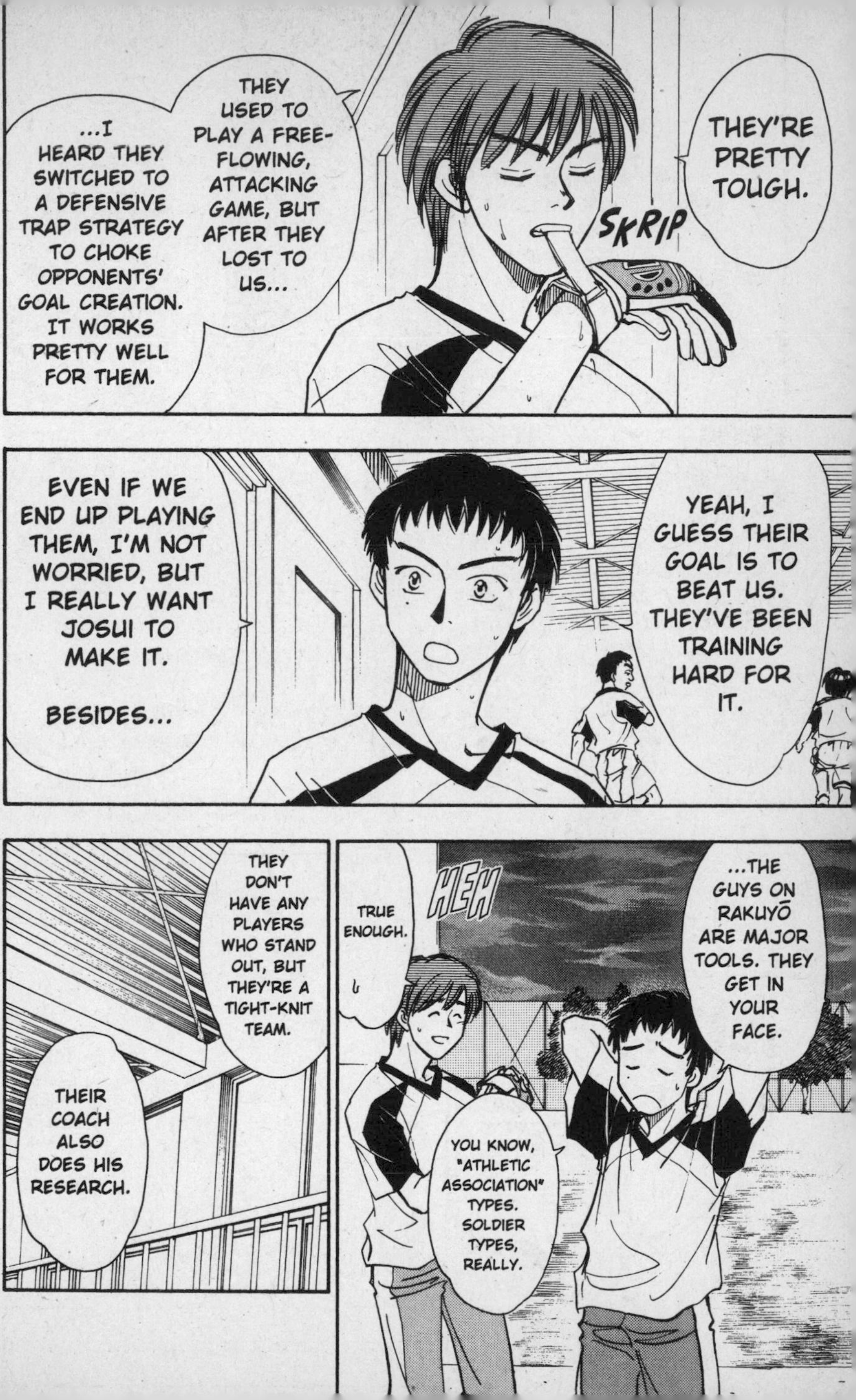
THEY'RE PRETTY TOUGH.
SKRIP
THEY USED TO PLAY A FREE-FLOWING, ATTACKING GAME, BUT AFTER THEY LOST TO US...
...I HEARD THEY SWITCHED TO A DEFENSIVE TRAP STRATEGY TO CHOKE OPPONENTS' GOAL CREATION. IT WORKS PRETTY WELL FOR THEM.
YEAH, I GUESS THEIR GOAL IS TO BEAT US. THEY'VE BEEN TRAINING HARD FOR IT.
EVEN IF WE END UP PLAYING THEM, I'M NOT WORRIED, BUT I REALLY WANT JOSUI TO MAKE IT.
BESIDES...
...THE GUYS ON RAKUYŌ ARE MAJOR TOOLS. THEY GET IN YOUR FACE.
HEH
TRUE ENOUGH.
YOU KNOW, "ATHLETIC ASSOCIATION" TYPES. SOLDIER TYPES, REALLY.
THEY DON'T HAVE ANY PLAYERS WHO STAND OUT, BUT THEY'RE A TIGHT-KNIT TEAM.
THEIR COACH ALSO DOES HIS RESEARCH.

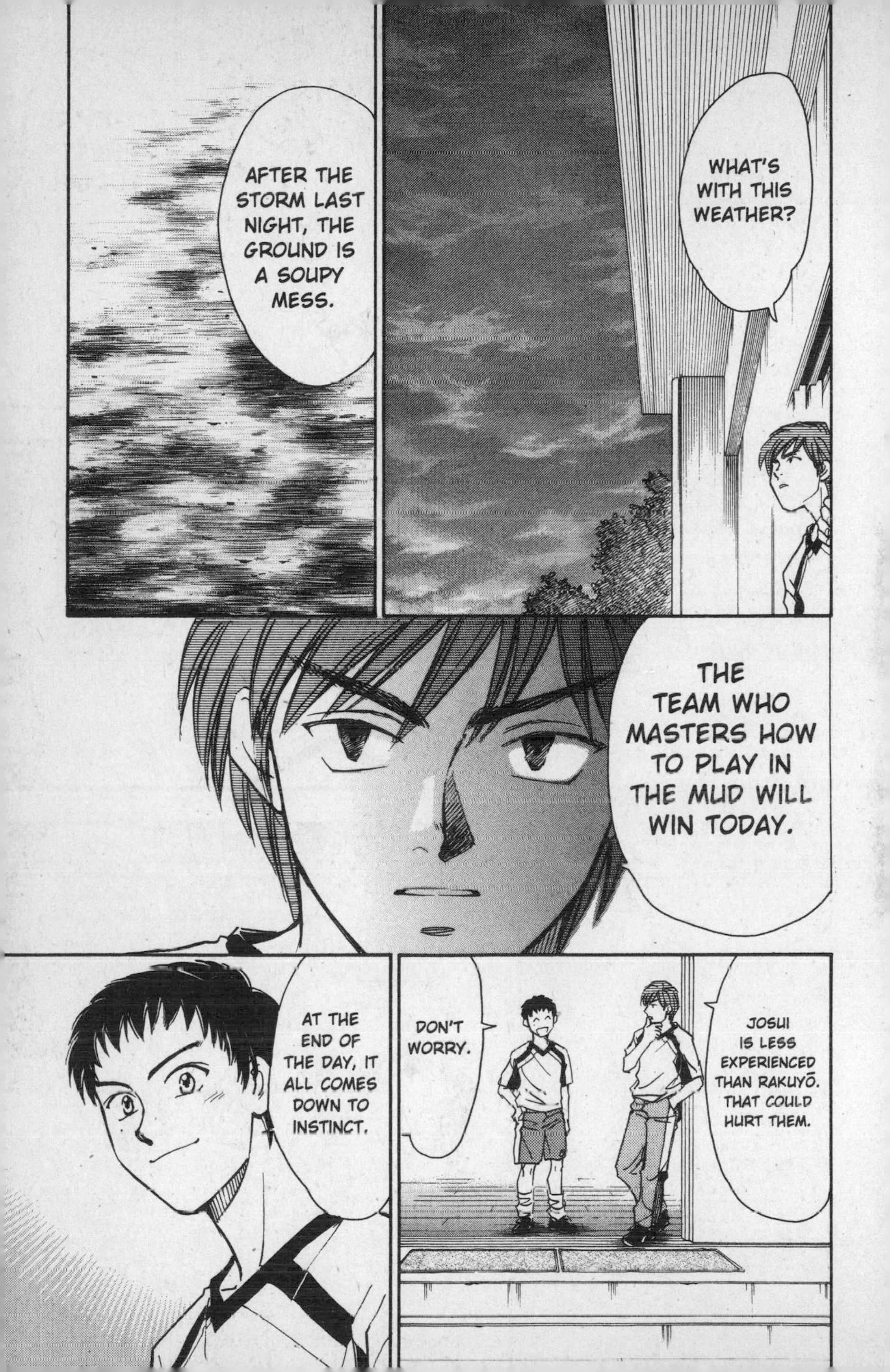
WHAT'S WITH THIS WEATHER?
AFTER THE STORM LAST NIGHT, THE GROUND IS A SOUPY MESS.
THE TEAM WHO MASTERS HOW TO PLAY IN THE MUD WILL WIN TODAY.
JOSUI IS LESS EXPERIENCED THAN RAKUYŌ. THAT COULD HURT THEM.
DON'T WORRY.
AT THE END OF THE DAY, IT ALL COMES DOWN TO INSTINCT.

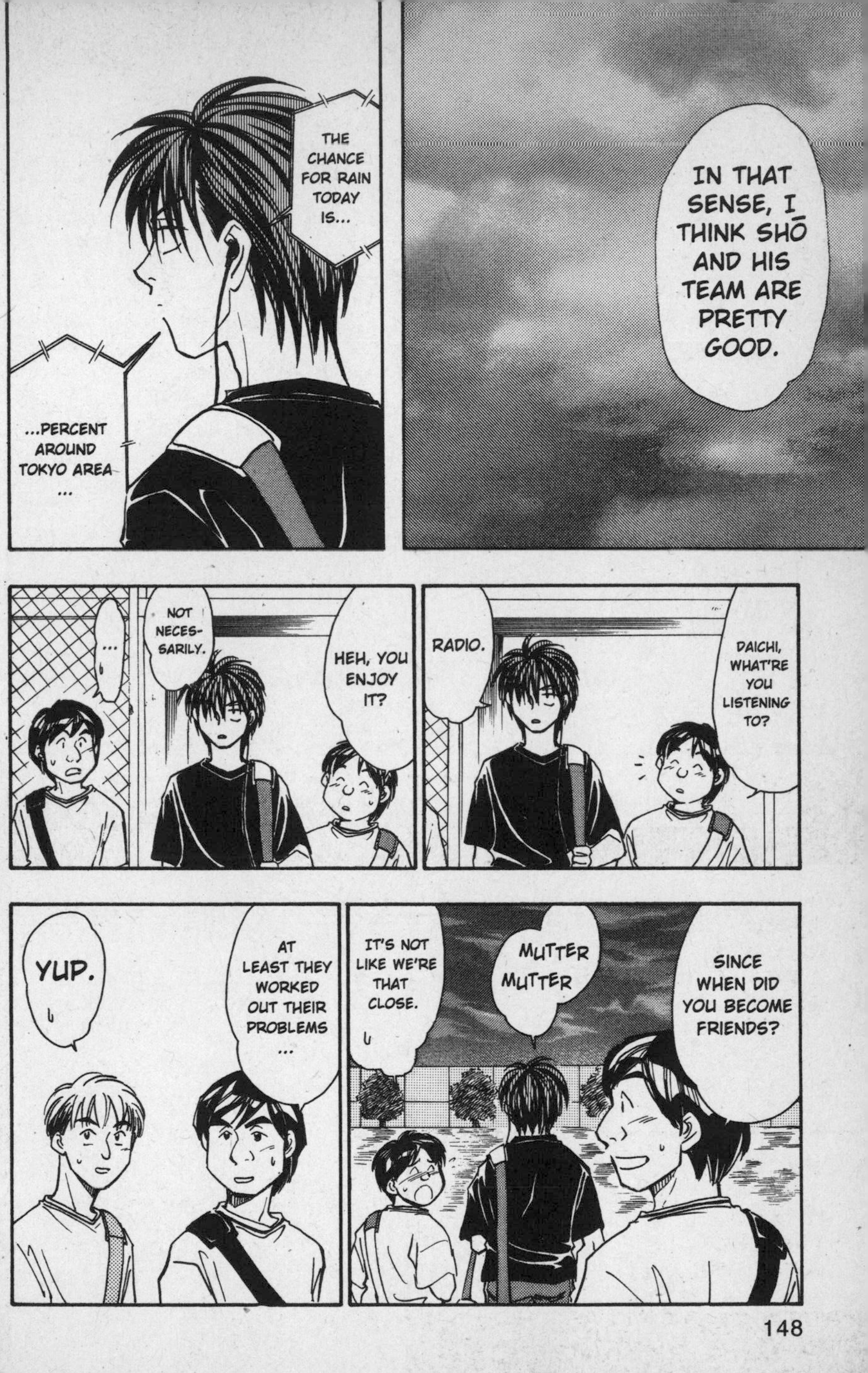
IN THAT SENSE, I THINK SHŌ AND HIS TEAM ARE PRETTY GOOD.
THE CHANCE FOR RAIN TODAY IS...
...PERCENT AROUND TOKYO AREA ...
DAICHI, WHAT'RE YOU LISTENING TO?
RADIO.
HEH, YOU ENJOY IT?
NOT NECES-SARILY.
...
SINCE WHEN DID YOU BECOME FRIENDS?
MUTTER MUTTER
IT'S NOT LIKE WE'RE THAT CLOSE.
AT LEAST THEY WORKED OUT THEIR PROBLEMS ...
YUP.

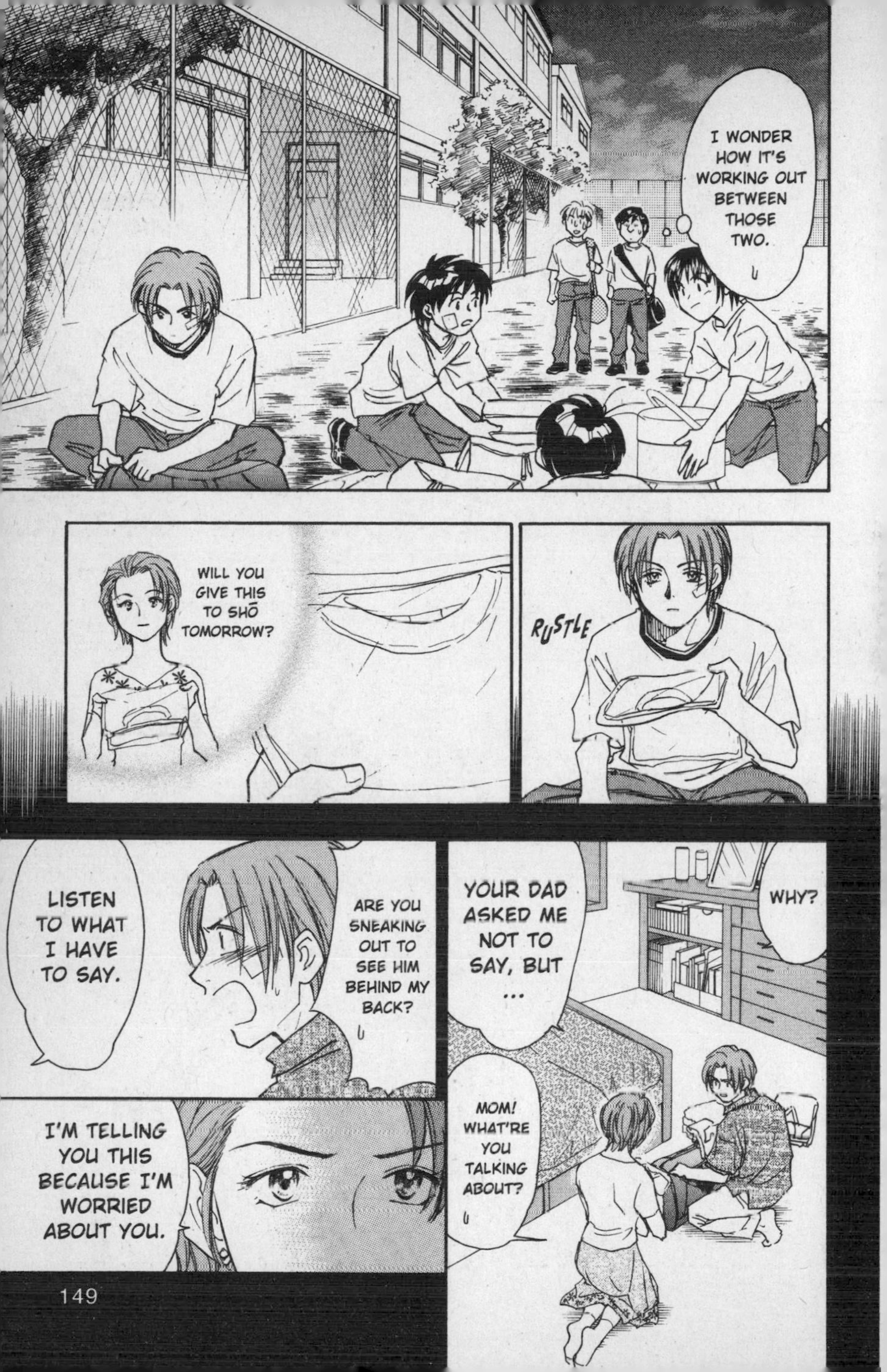
I WONDER HOW IT'S WORKING OUT BETWEEN THOSE TWO.
RUSTLE
WILL YOU GIVE THIS TO SHŌ TOMORROW?
WHY?
YOUR DAD ASKED ME NOT TO SAY, BUT ...
MOM! WHAT'RE YOU TALKING ABOUT?
ARE YOU SNEAKING OUT TO SEE HIM BEHIND MY BACK?
LISTEN TO WHAT I HAVE TO SAY.
I'M TELLING YOU THIS BECAUSE I'M WORRIED ABOUT YOU.

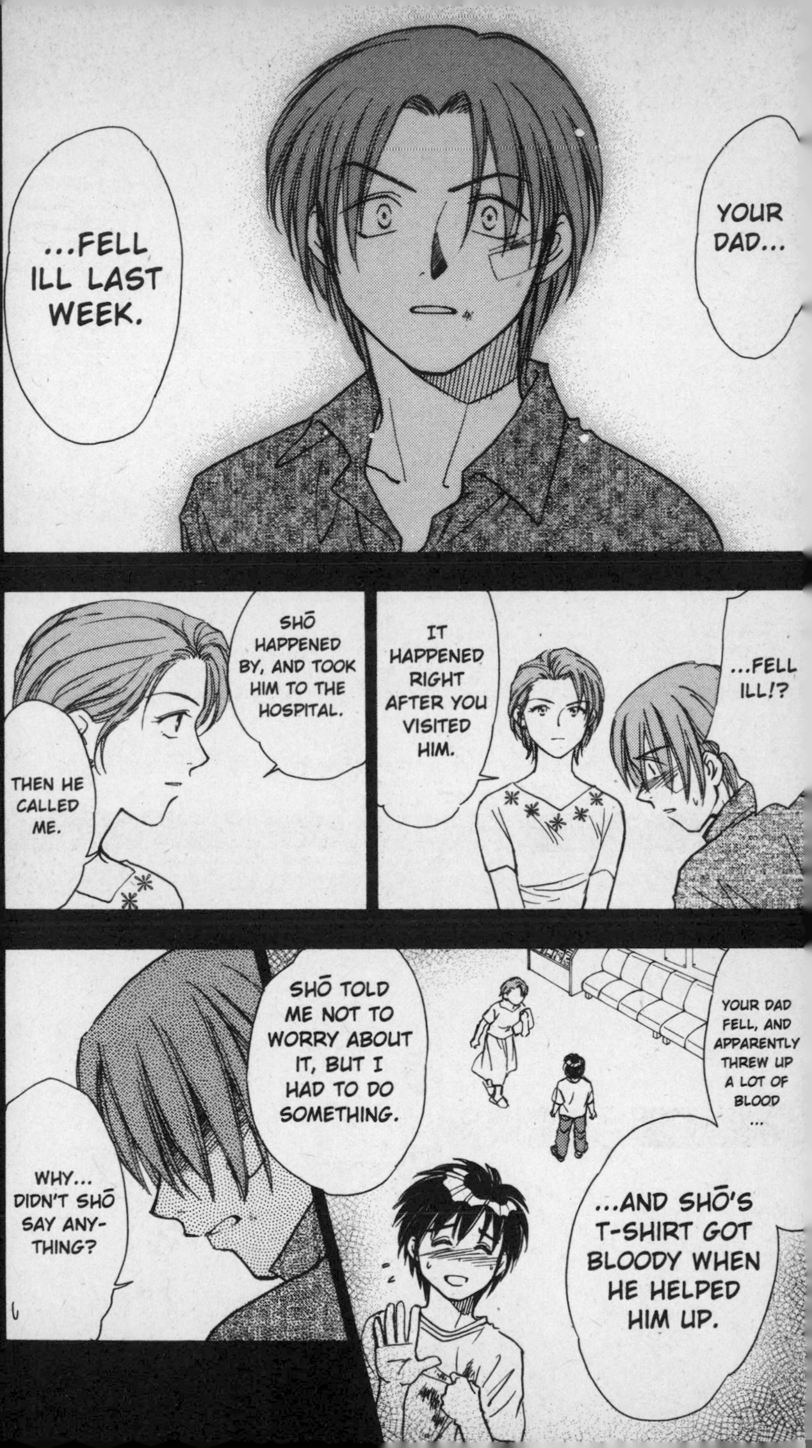
YOUR DAD...
...FELL ILL LAST WEEK.
...FELL ILL!?
IT HAPPENED RIGHT AFTER YOU VISITED HIM.
SHŌ HAPPENED BY, AND TOOK HIM TO THE HOSPITAL.
THEN HE CALLED ME.
YOUR DAD FELL, AND APPARENTLY THREW UP A LOT OF BLOOD ...
...AND SHŌ'S T-SHIRT GOT BLOODY WHEN HE HELPED HIM UP.
SHŌ TOLD ME NOT TO WORRY ABOUT IT, BUT I HAD TO DO SOMETHING.
WHY... DIDN'T SHŌ SAY ANY-THING?

READ THIS WAY

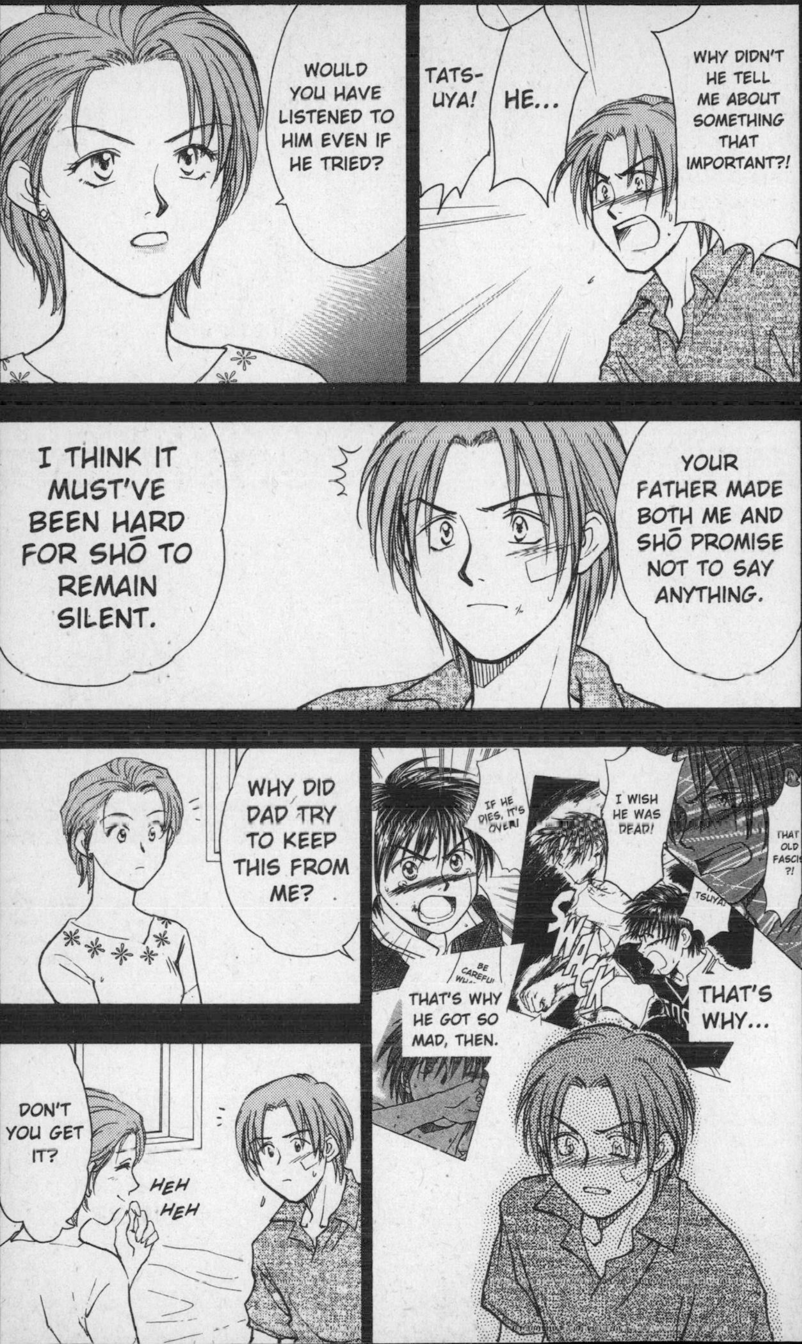

WHY DIDN'T HE TELL ME ABOUT SOMETHING THAT IMPORTANT?!
HE...
TATS-UYA!
WOULD YOU HAVE LISTENED TO HIM EVEN IF HE TRIED?
YOUR FATHER MADE BOTH ME AND SHŌ PROMISE NOT TO SAY ANYTHING.
I THINK IT MUST'VE BEEN HARD FOR SHŌ TO REMAIN SILENT.
THAT OLD FASCIS ?!
I WISH HE WAS DEAD!
IF HE DIES, IT'S OVER!
TSUYA!
SWACK
BE CAREFUL
THAT'S WHY...
THAT'S WHY HE GOT SO MAD, THEN.
WHY DID DAD TRY TO KEEP THIS FROM ME?
DON'T YOU GET IT?
HEH HEH

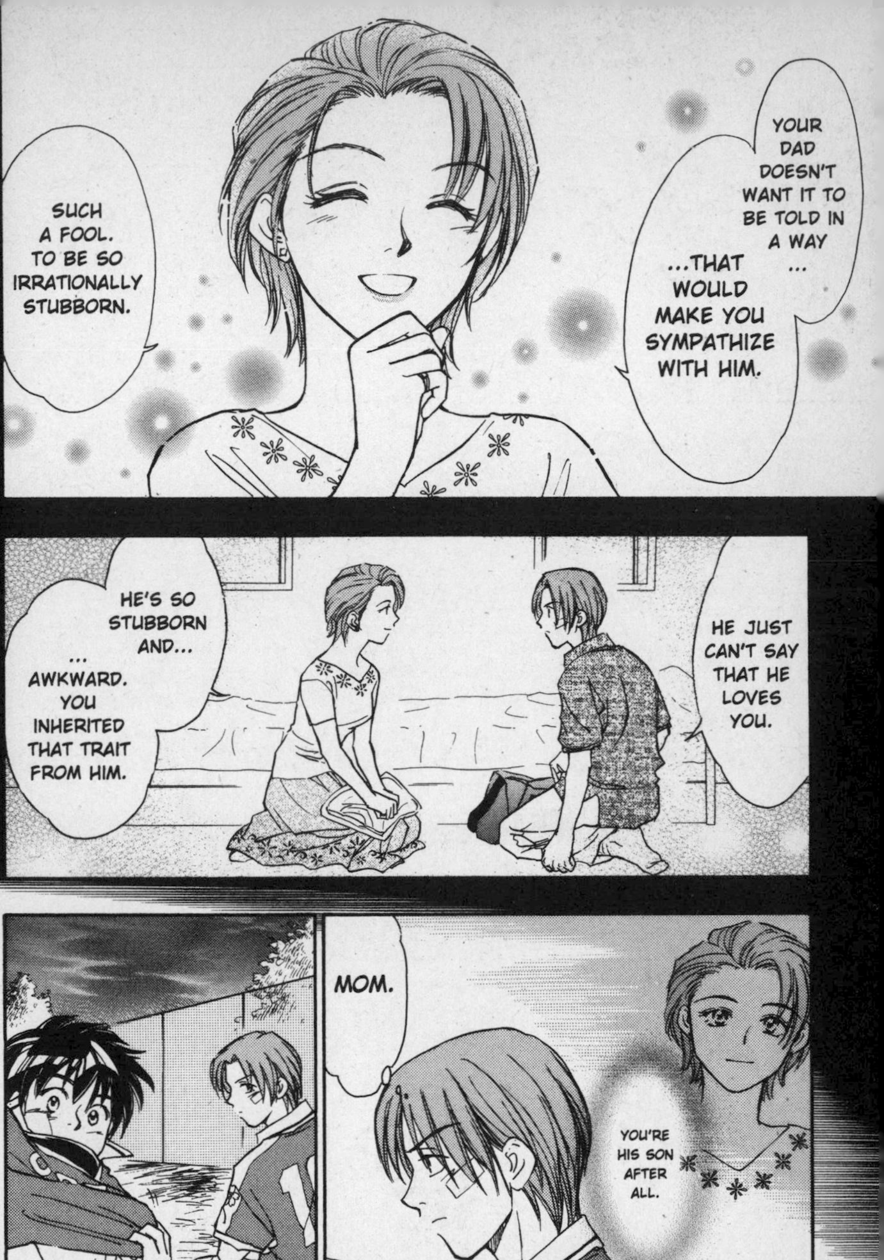
YOUR DAD DOESN'T WANT IT TO BE TOLD IN A WAY ... ...THAT WOULD MAKE YOU SYMPATHIZE WITH HIM.
SUCH A FOOL. TO BE SO IRRATIONALLY STUBBORN.
HE JUST CAN'T SAY THAT HE LOVES YOU.
HE'S SO STUBBORN AND... ... AWKWARD. YOU INHERITED THAT TRAIT FROM HIM.
YOU'RE HIS SON AFTER ALL.
MOM.

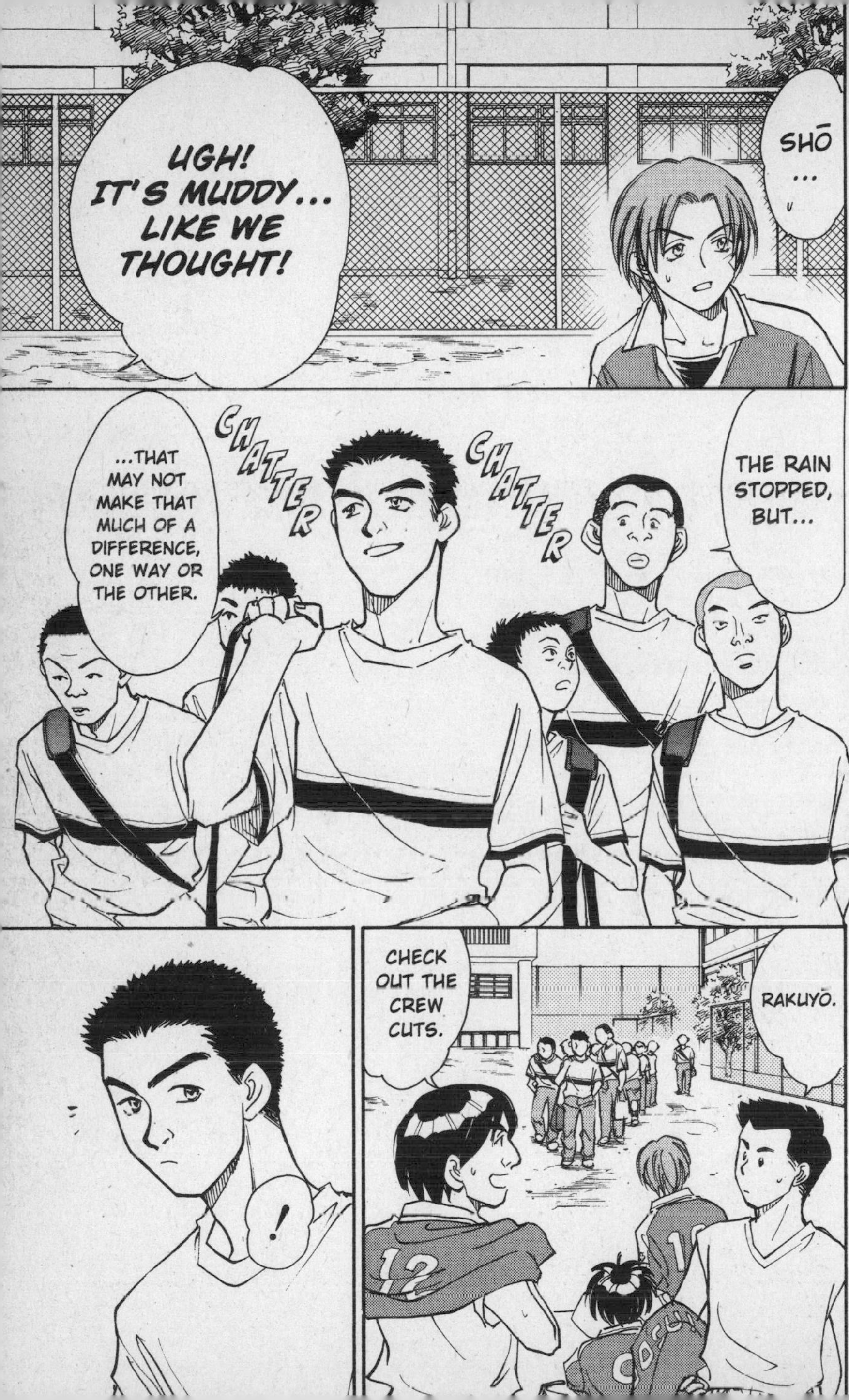
SHŌ ...
UGH! IT'S MUDDY... LIKE WE THOUGHT!
THE RAIN STOPPED, BUT...
CHATTER
CHATTER
...THAT MAY NOT MAKE THAT MUCH OF A DIFFERENCE, ONE WAY OR THE OTHER.
RAKUYŌ.
CHECK OUT THE CREW CUTS.
!

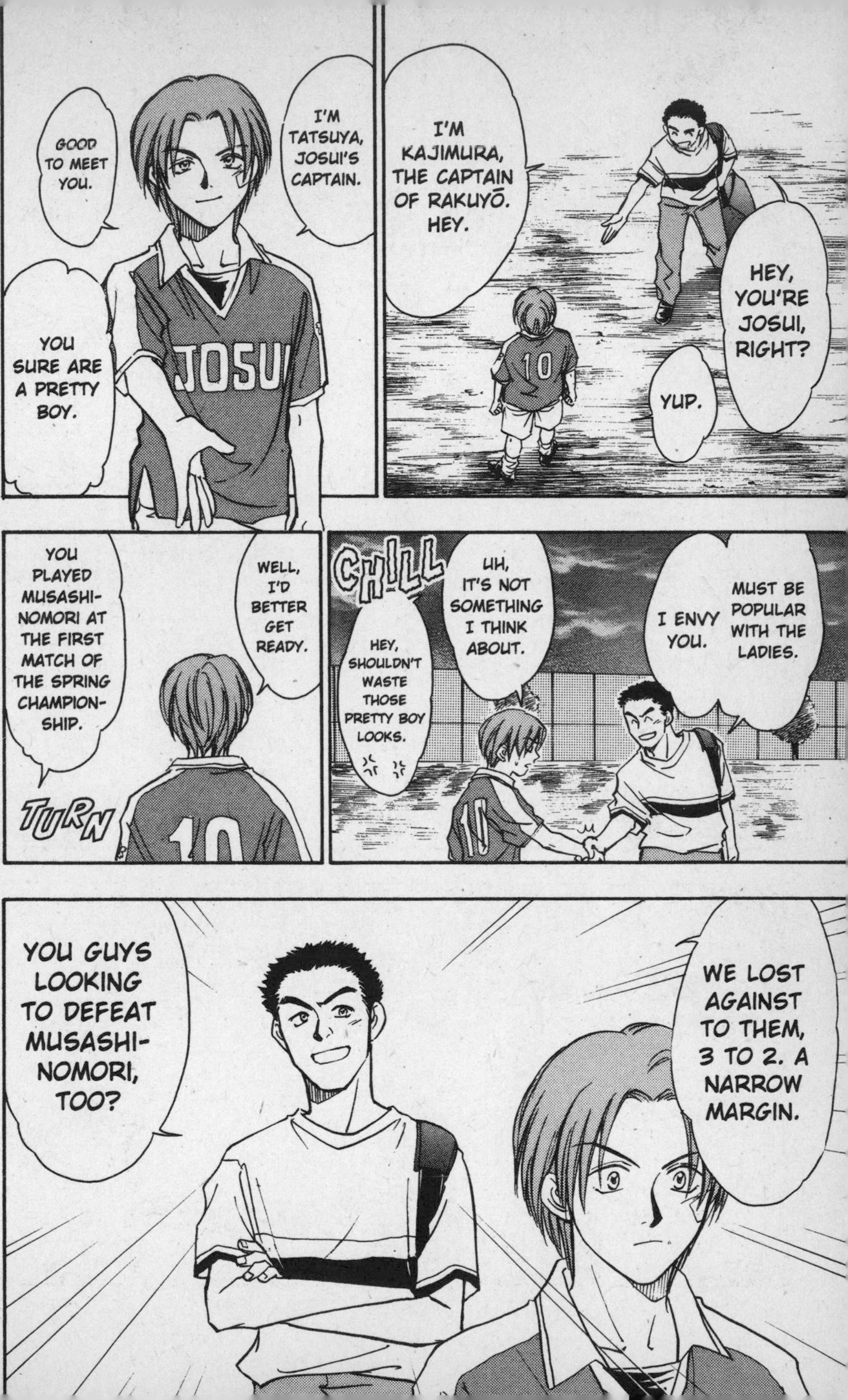
HEY, YOU'RE JOSUI, RIGHT?
YUP.
I'M KAJIMURA, THE CAPTAIN OF RAKUYŌ. HEY.
I'M TATSUYA, JOSUI'S CAPTAIN.
GOOD TO MEET YOU.
YOU SURE ARE A PRETTY BOY.
MUST BE POPULAR WITH THE LADIES.
I ENVY YOU.
UH, IT'S NOT SOMETHING I THINK ABOUT.
CHILL
HEY, SHOULDN'T WASTE THOSE PRETTY BOY LOOKS.
WELL, I'D BETTER GET READY.
YOU PLAYED MUSASHI-NOMORI AT THE FIRST MATCH OF THE SPRING CHAMPIONSHIP.
TURN
WE LOST AGAINST TO THEM, 3 TO 2. A NARROW MARGIN.
YOU GUYS LOOKING TO DEFEAT MUSASHI-NOMORI, TOO?

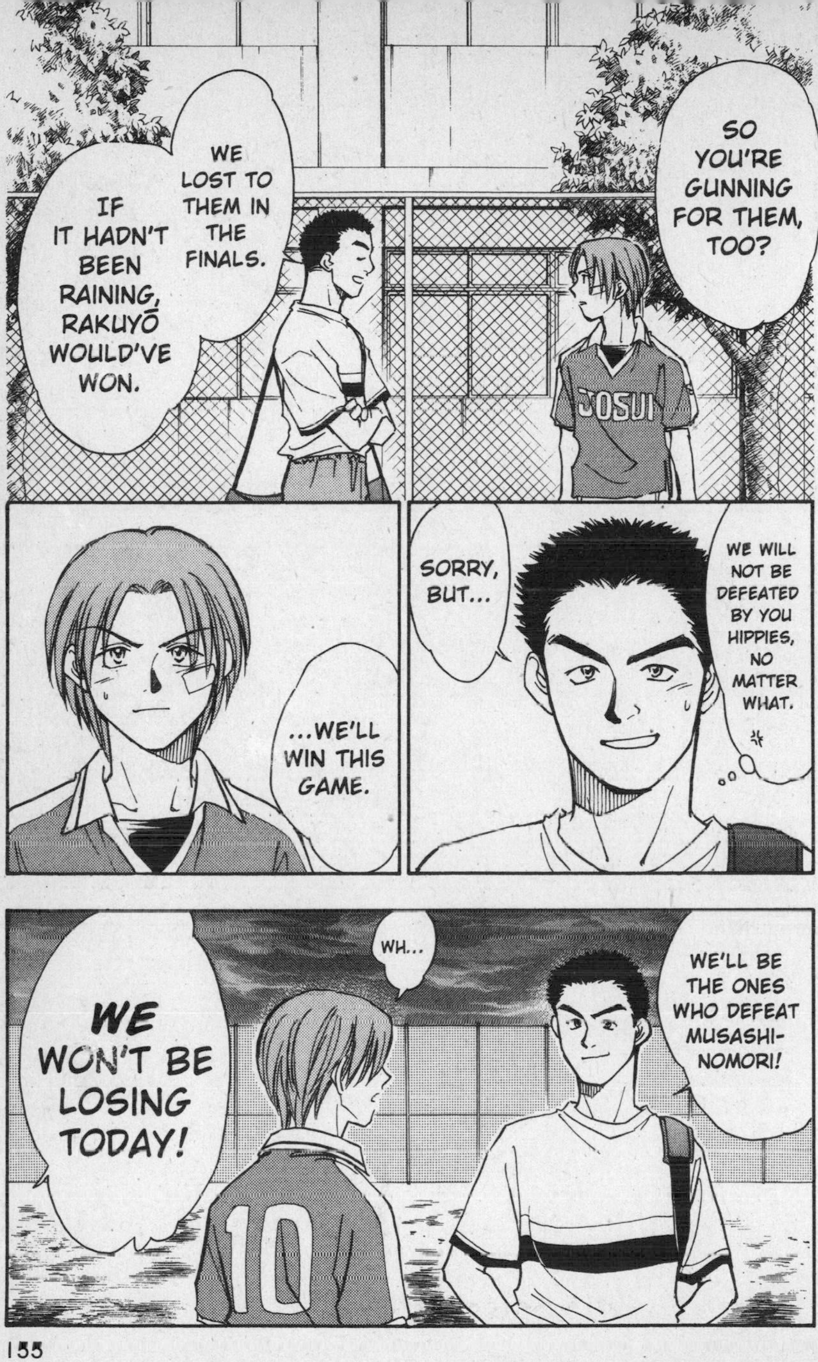
SO YOU'RE GUNNING FOR THEM, TOO?
WE LOST TO THEM IN THE FINALS.
IF IT HADN'T BEEN RAINING, RAKUYŌ WOULD'VE WON.
WE WILL NOT BE DEFEATED BY YOU HIPPIES, NO MATTER WHAT.
SORRY, BUT...
...WE'LL WIN THIS GAME.
WE'LL BE THE ONES WHO DEFEAT MUSASHI-NOMORI!
WH...
WE WON'T BE LOSING TODAY!

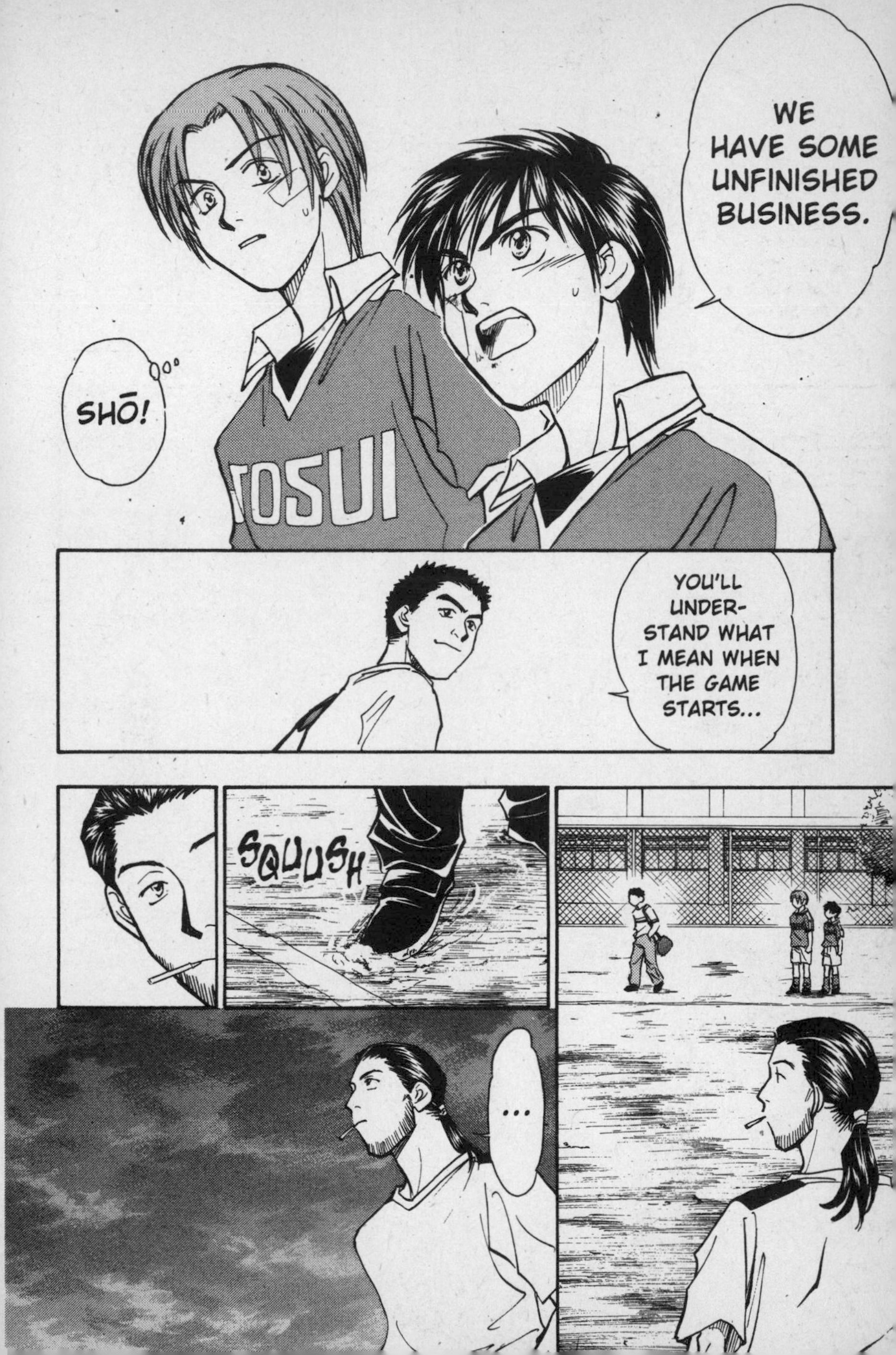
WE HAVE SOME UNFINISHED BUSINESS.
SHŌ!
YOU'LL UNDER-STAND WHAT I MEAN WHEN THE GAME STARTS...
SQUUSH
...

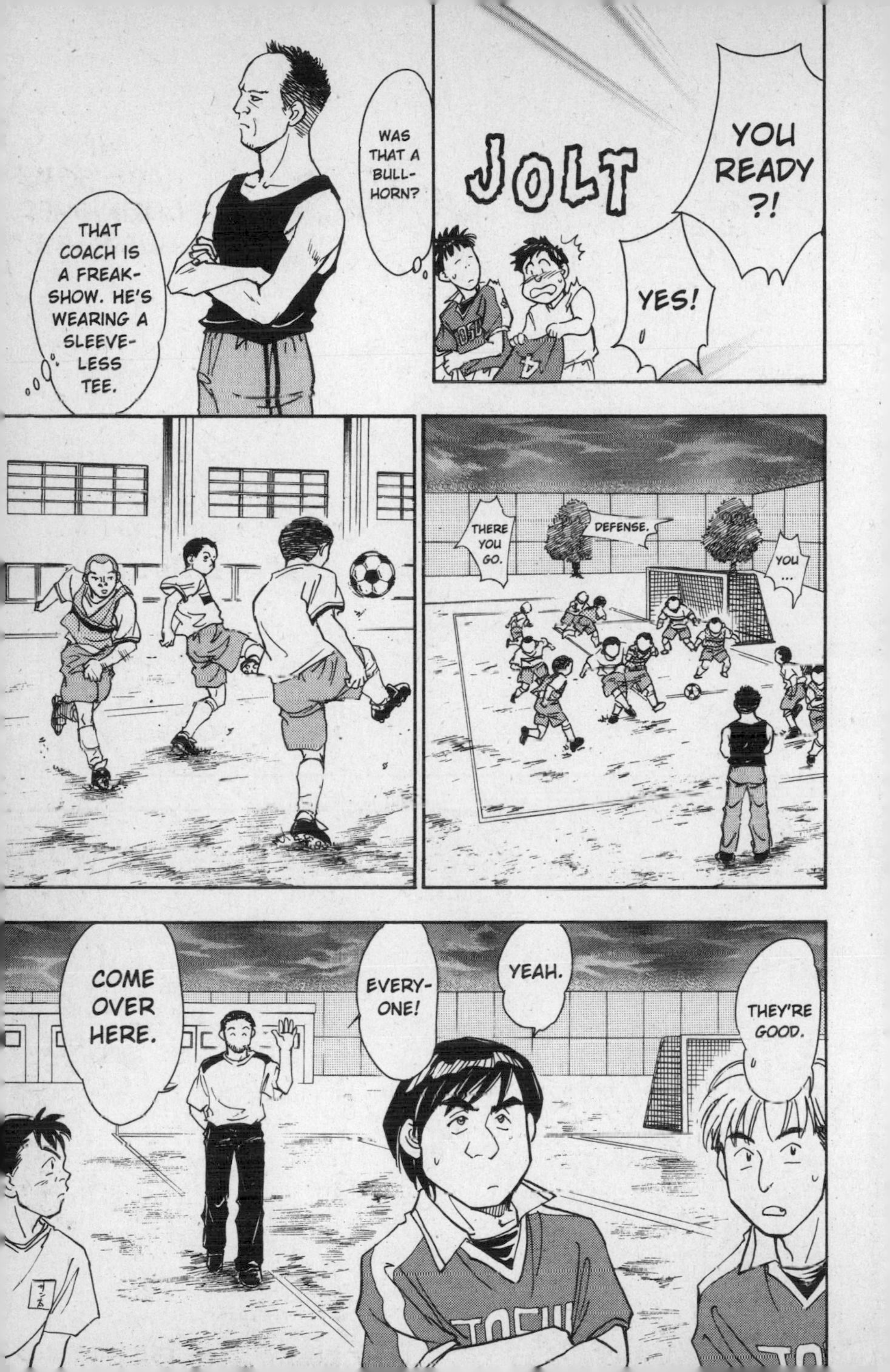
YOU READY ?!
YES!
JOLT
WAS THAT A BULL-HORN?
THAT COACH IS A FREAK-SHOW. HE'S WEARING A SLEEVE-LESS TEE.
YOU ...
DEFENSE.
THERE YOU GO.
THEY'RE GOOD.
YEAH.
EVERY-ONE!
COME OVER HERE.

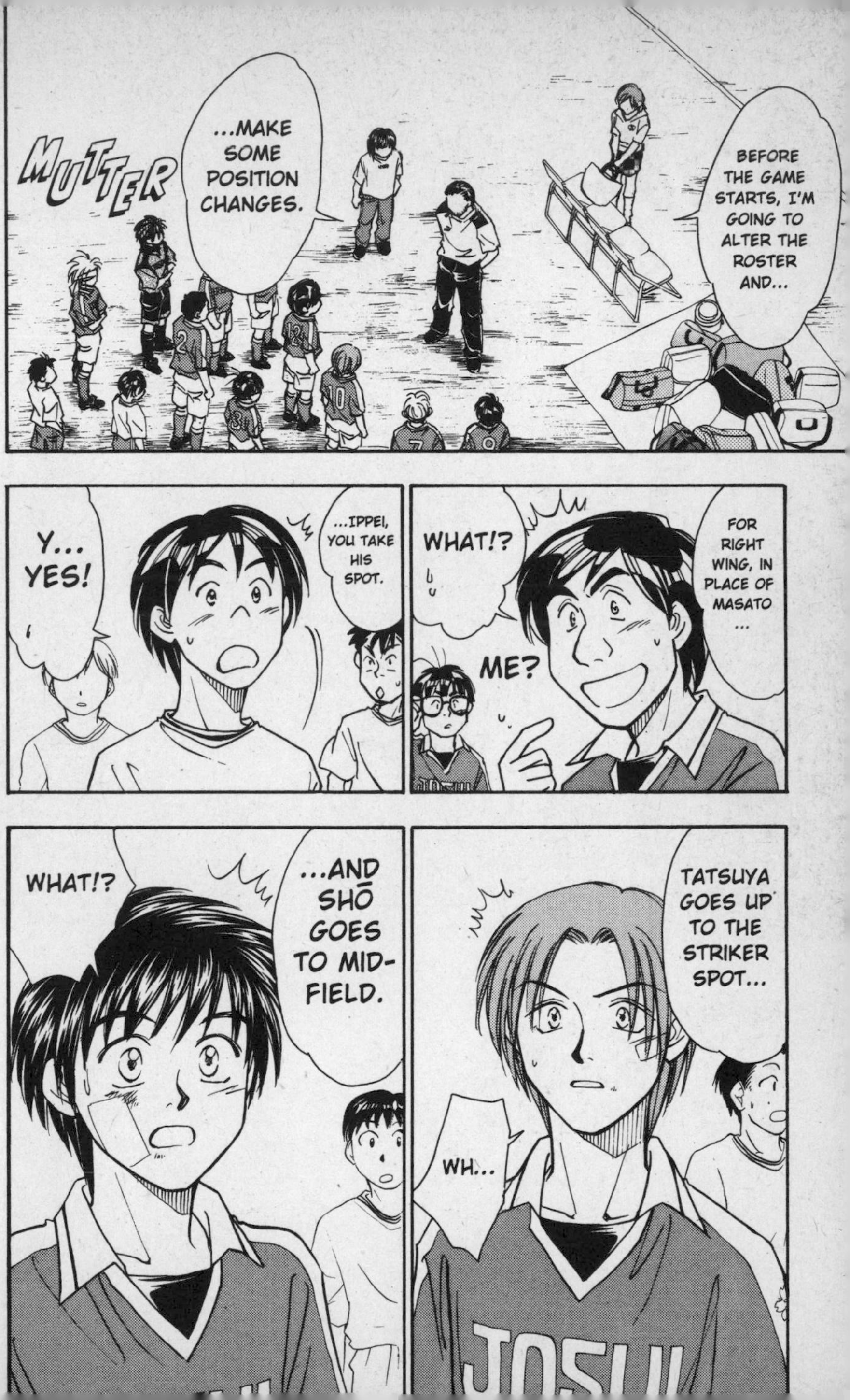
BEFORE THE GAME STARTS, I'M GOING TO ALTER THE ROSTER AND...
...MAKE SOME POSITION CHANGES.
MUTTER
FOR RIGHT WING, IN PLACE OF MASATO ...
WHAT!?
ME?
...IPPEI, YOU TAKE HIS SPOT.
Y... YES!
TATSUYA GOES UP TO THE STRIKER SPOT...
WH...
...AND SHŌ GOES TO MID-FIELD.
WHAT!?

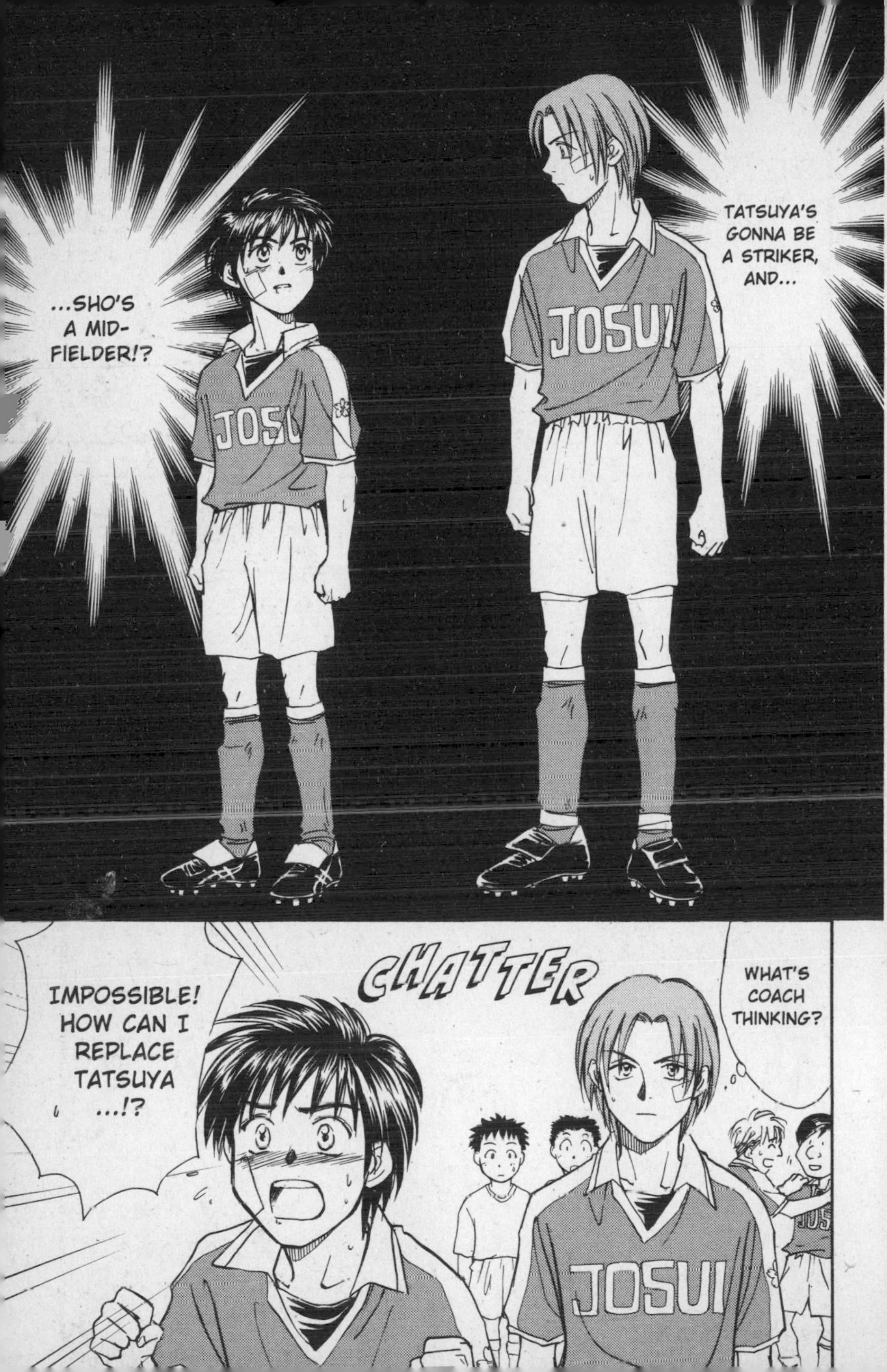
TATSUYA'S GONNA BE A STRIKER, AND...
...SHO'S A MID-FIELDER!?
WHAT'S COACH THINKING?
CHATTER
IMPOSSIBLE! HOW CAN I REPLACE TATSUYA ...!?

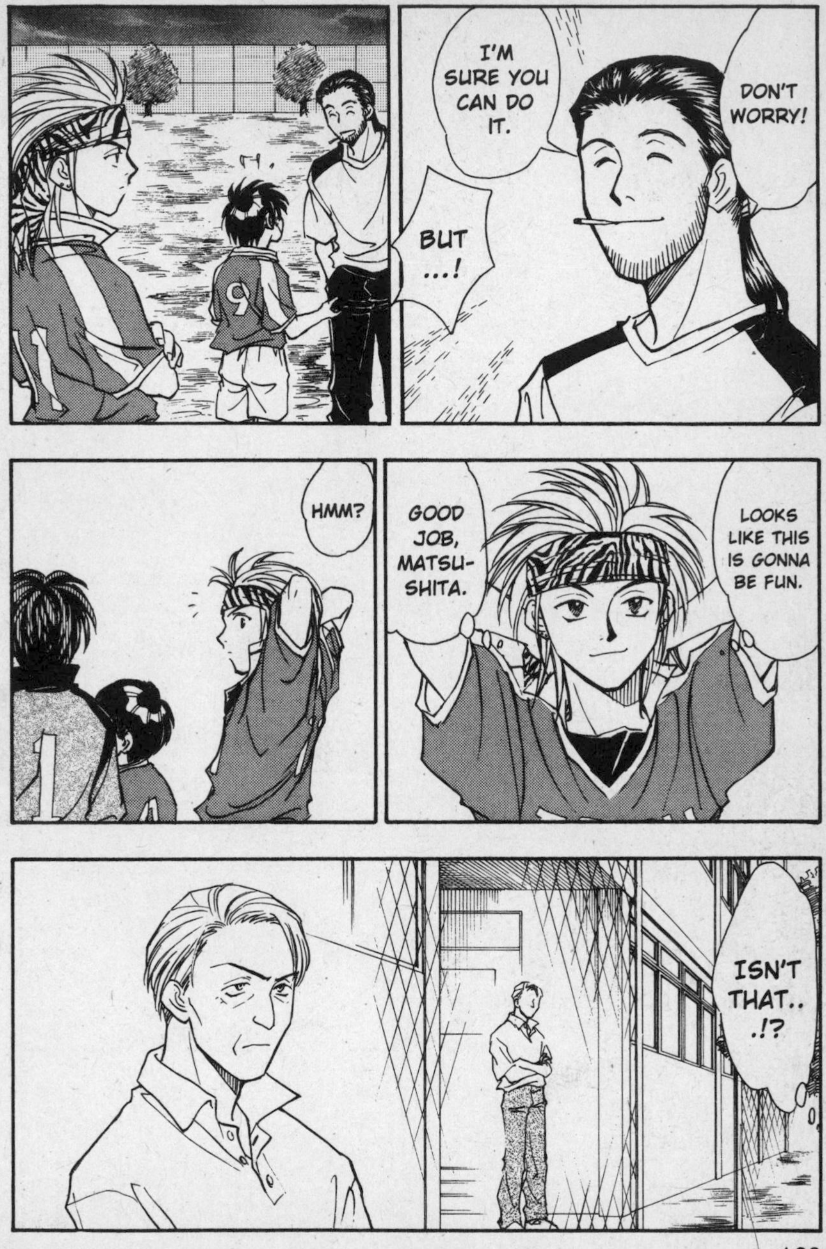
DON'T WORRY!
I'M SURE YOU CAN DO IT.
BUT ...!
LOOKS LIKE THIS IS GONNA BE FUN.
GOOD JOB, MATSUSHITA.
HMM?
ISN'T THAT.. .!?

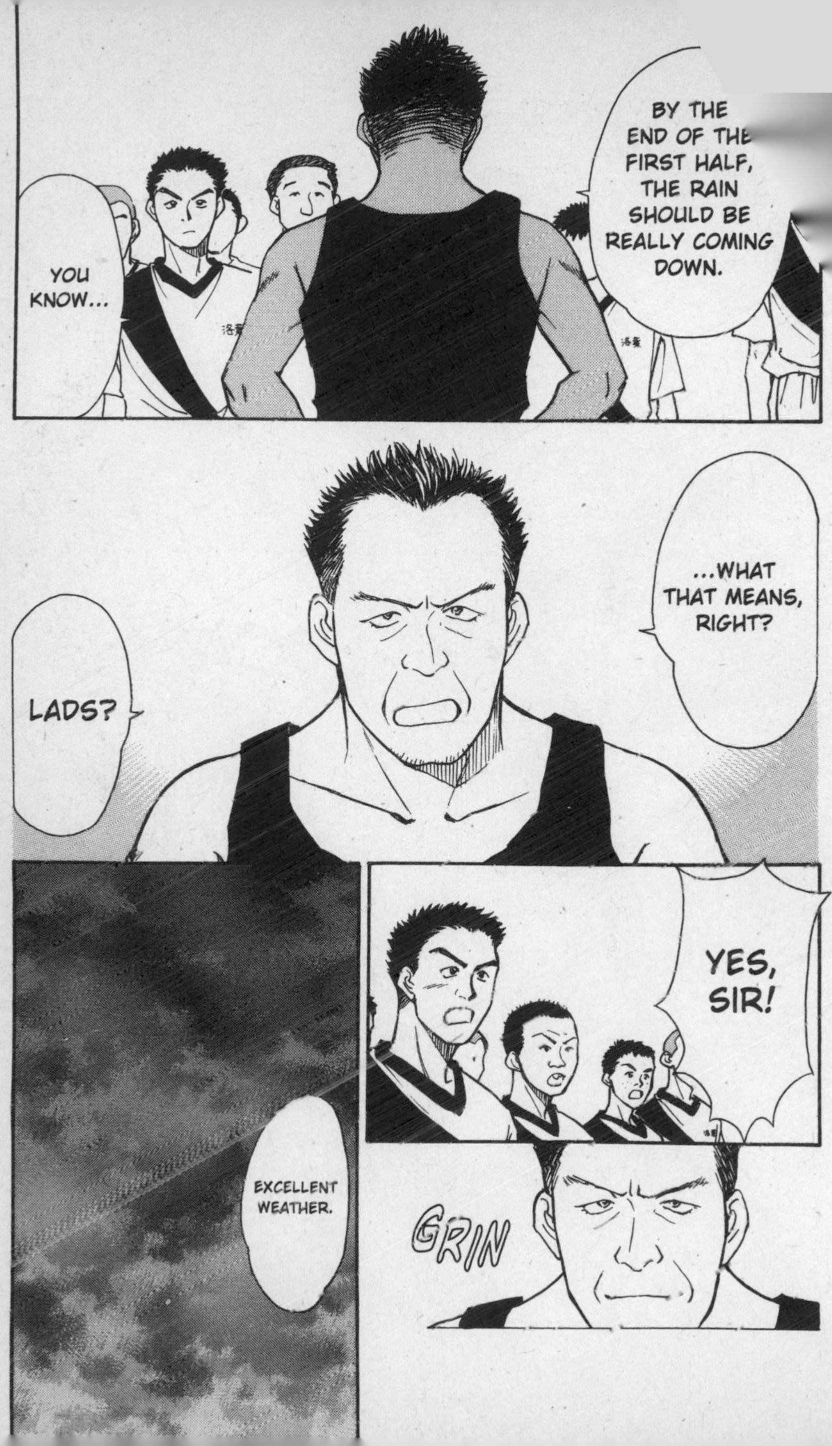
BY THE END OF THE FIRST HALF, THE RAIN SHOULD BE REALLY COMING DOWN.
YOU KNOW...
...WHAT THAT MEANS, RIGHT?
LADS?
YES, SIR!
GRIN
EXCELLENT WEATHER.

WEE-STLE! THEATRE!!

MANGA BY **SEKI**, ASSISTANT S

MAMA SAID SHE'S NOT COMING TODAY.
HOLMES HAS EVOLVED.
TATSUYA
WHINE
HUFF HUFF
HUFF HUFF
WHAT WOULD YOU DO?
UNLEASH HIM
FIGHT HIM
I THINK HIS UMBRELLA'S WEIRD.
SEND HIM TO THE POUND
I MEAN, IT'S NOT HOLMES.

BY AIKO MESO

The Horror

I LOVE THIS TEAM. I LOVE SOCCER.
IF YOU DIDN'T COME TO JOSUI ...
... I MAY HAVE... REMAINED ROTTEN.
JUST LIKE THIS.
NOTE: THIS IS SHŌ.
A PRETTY HORRIFIC FACE.
IN A STATE OF SHOCK
THANK YOU.

STAGE.70
State of Heart, State of Sky

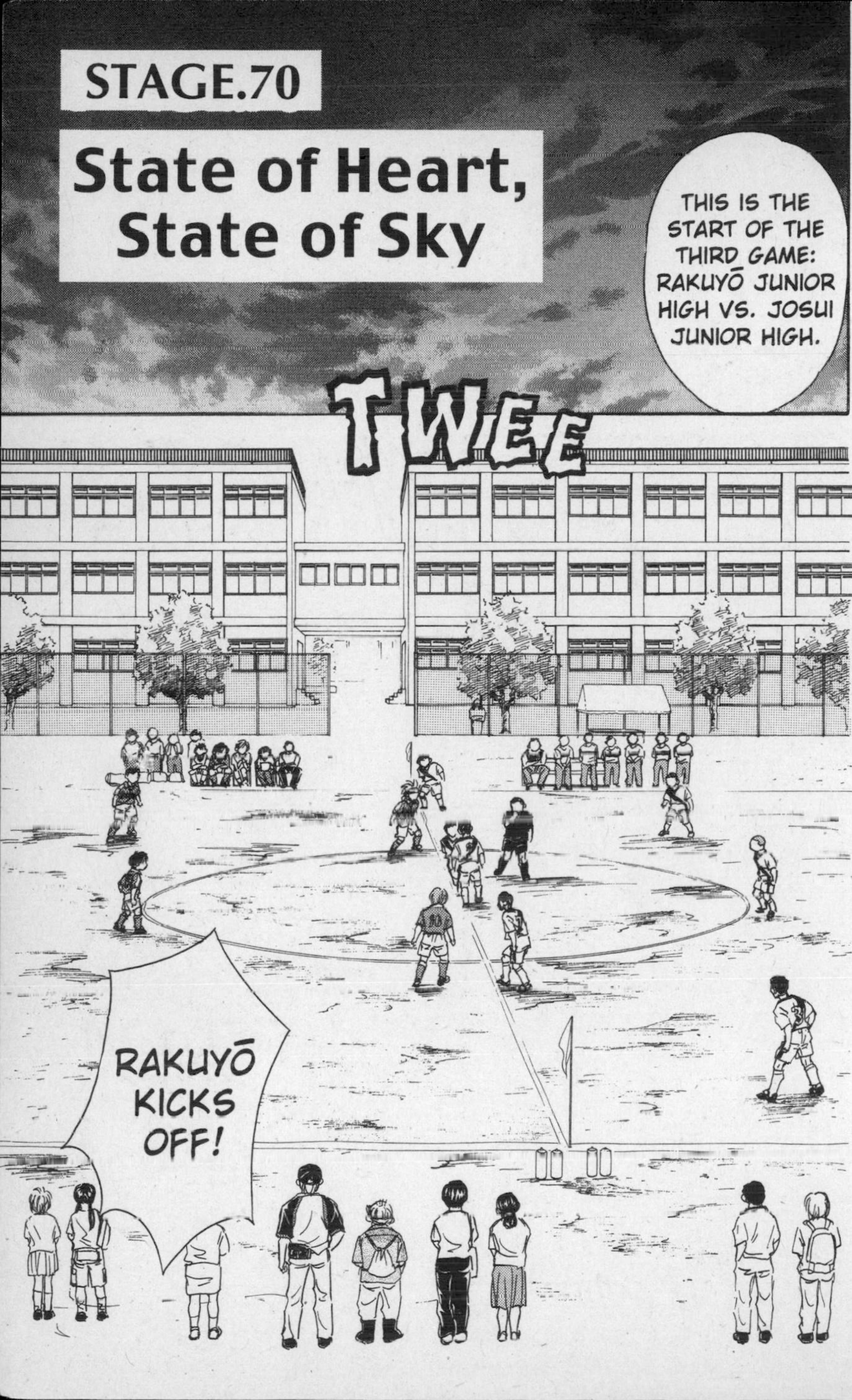
THIS IS THE START OF THE THIRD GAME: RAKUYŌ JUNIOR HIGH VS. JOSUI JUNIOR HIGH.
TWEE
RAKUYŌ KICKS OFF!

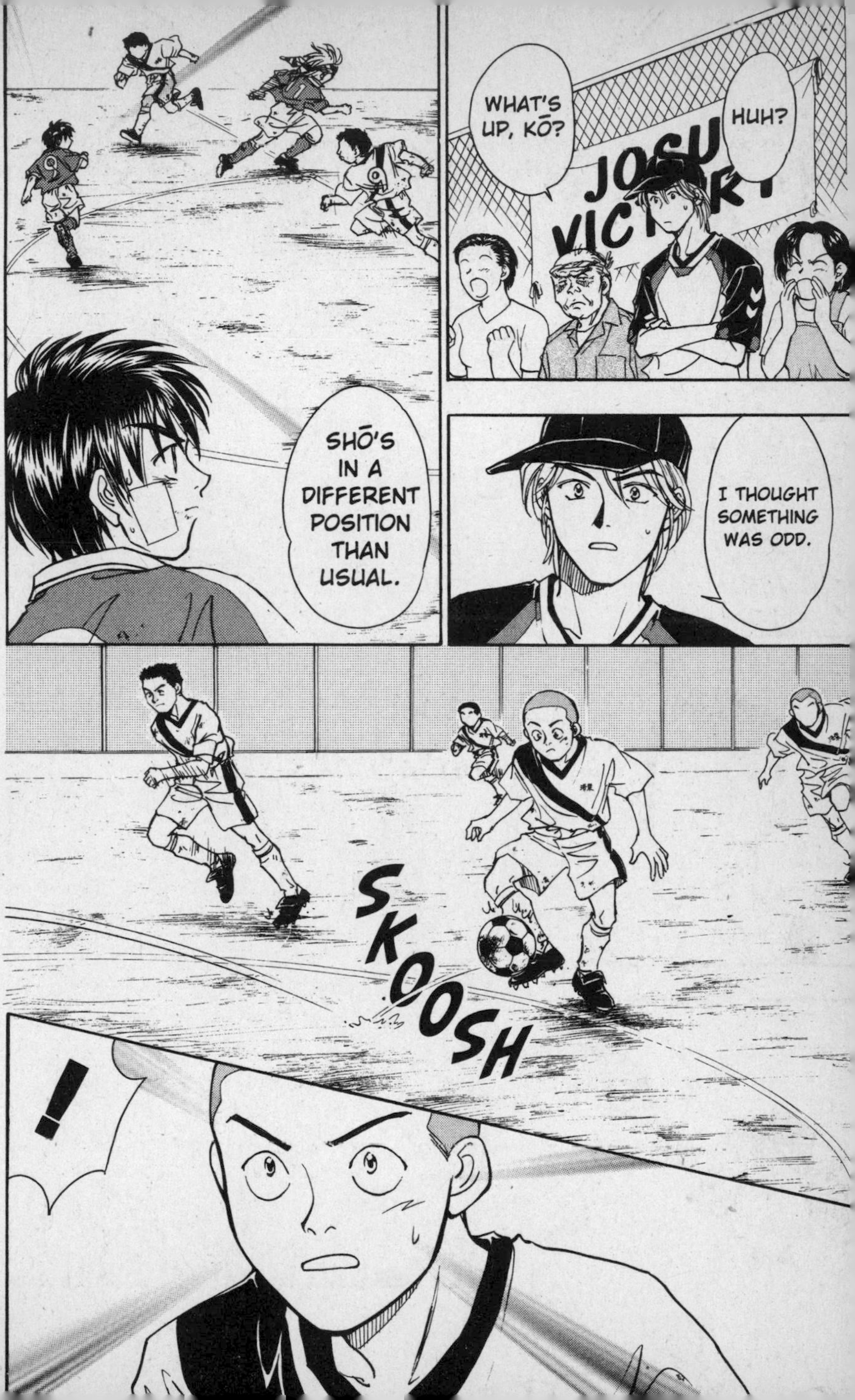
HUH?
WHAT'S UP, KŌ?
I THOUGHT SOMETHING WAS ODD.
SHŌ'S IN A DIFFERENT POSITION THAN USUAL.
SKOOSH
!

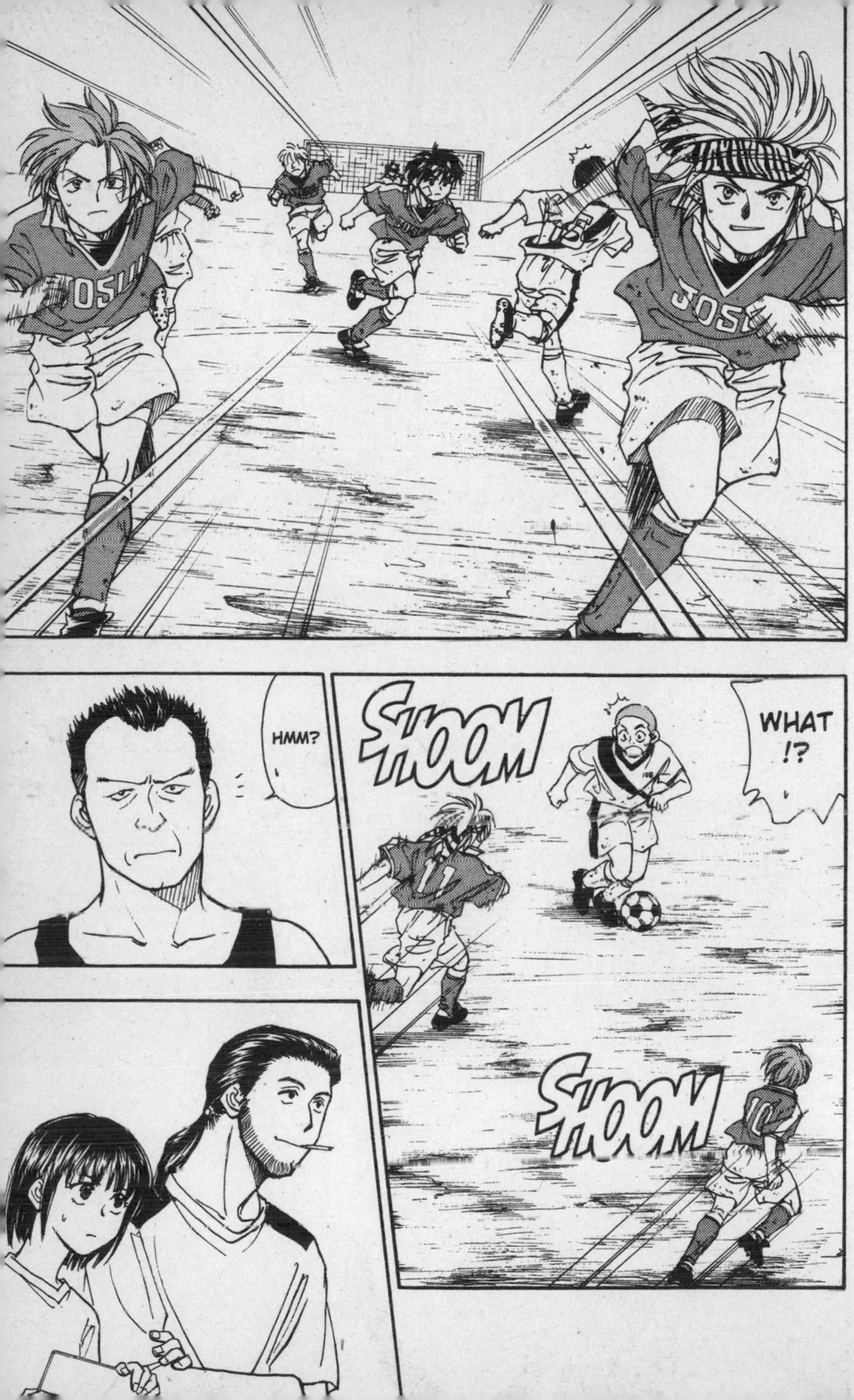
SHOOM
WHAT !?
SHOOM
HMM?

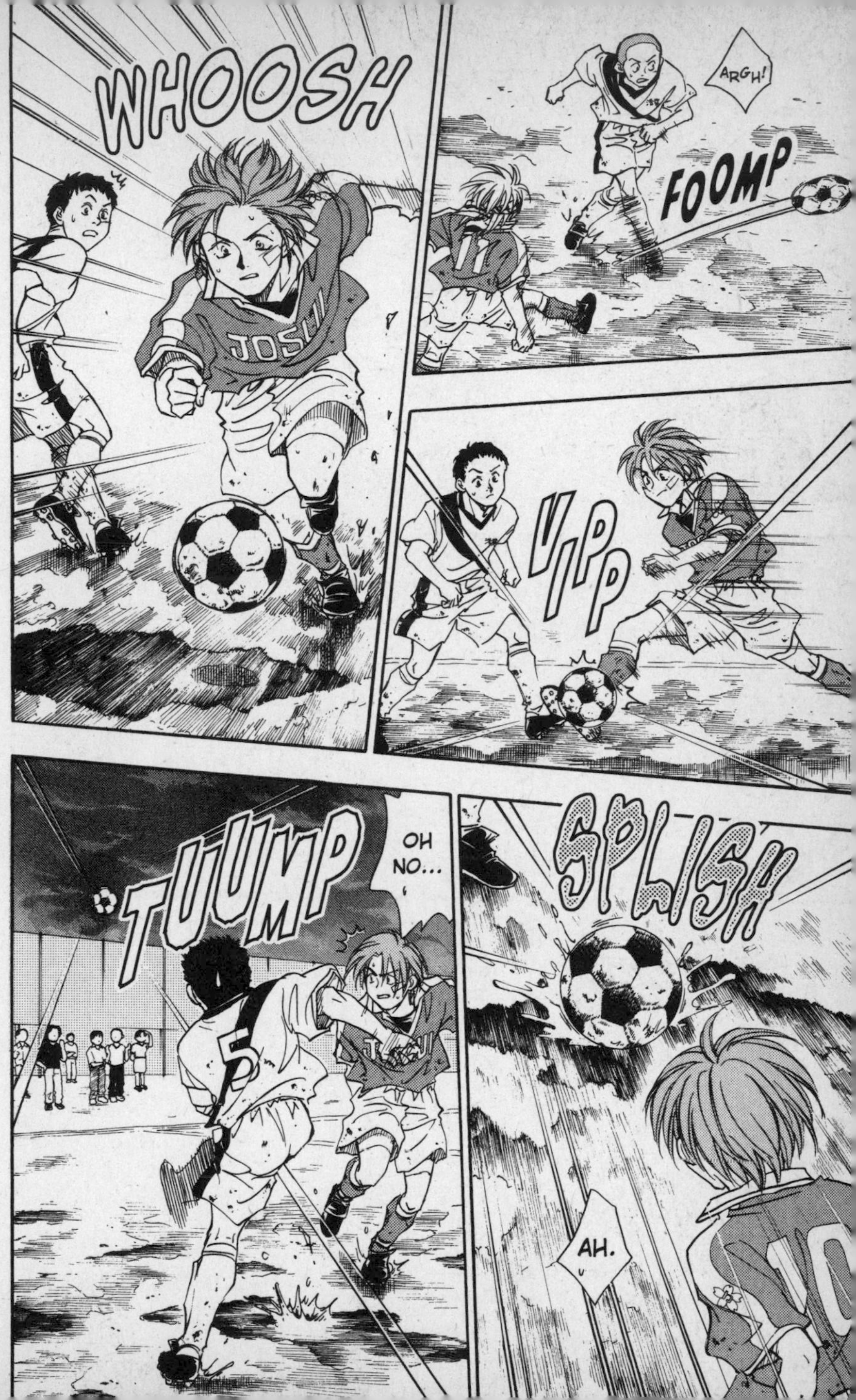
ARGH!
FOOMP
VIPP
WHOOSH
SPLISH
AH.
OH NO...
TUUMP

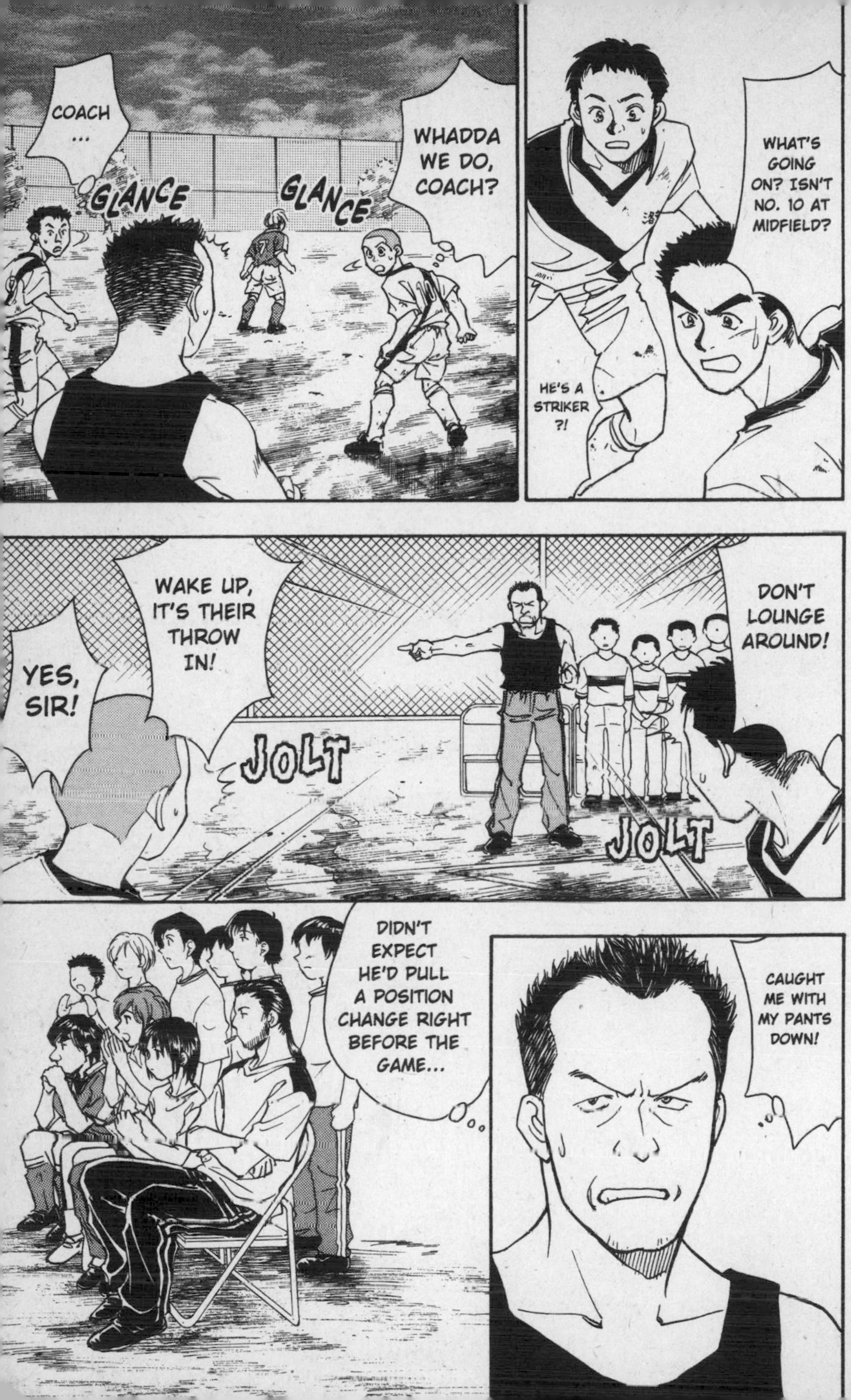
WHAT'S GOING ON? ISN'T NO. 10 AT MIDFIELD?
HE'S A STRIKER ?!
WHADDA WE DO, COACH?
GLANCE
COACH ...
GLANCE
DON'T LOUNGE AROUND!
JOLT
WAKE UP, IT'S THEIR THROW IN!
YES, SIR!
JOLT
CAUGHT ME WITH MY PANTS DOWN!
DIDN'T EXPECT HE'D PULL A POSITION CHANGE RIGHT BEFORE THE GAME...

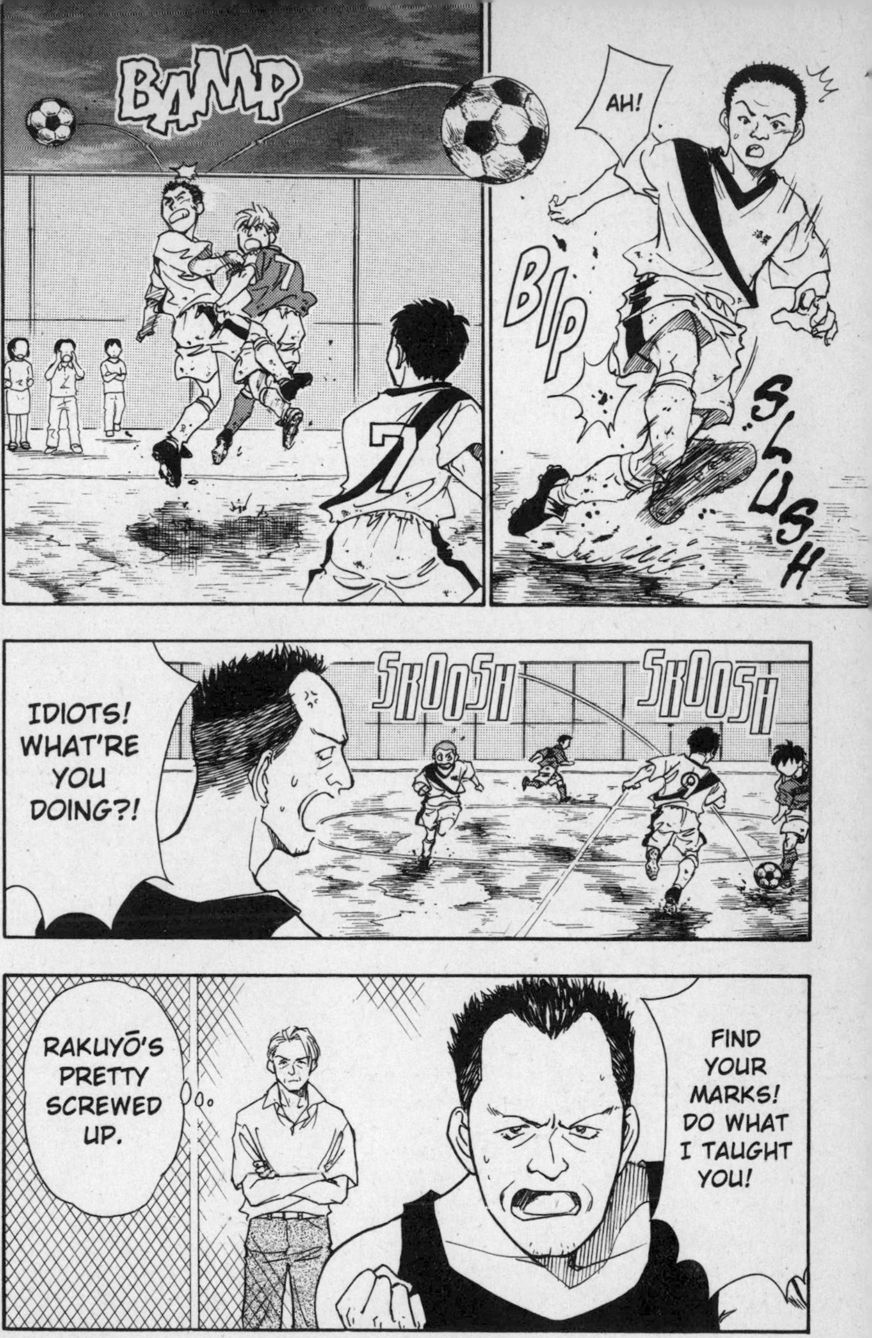
AH!
BIP
SLUSH
BAMP
IDIOTS! WHAT'RE YOU DOING?!
SKROOSH
SKROOSH
FIND YOUR MARKS! DO WHAT I TAUGHT YOU!
RAKUYŌ'S PRETTY SCREWED UP.

READ THIS WAY

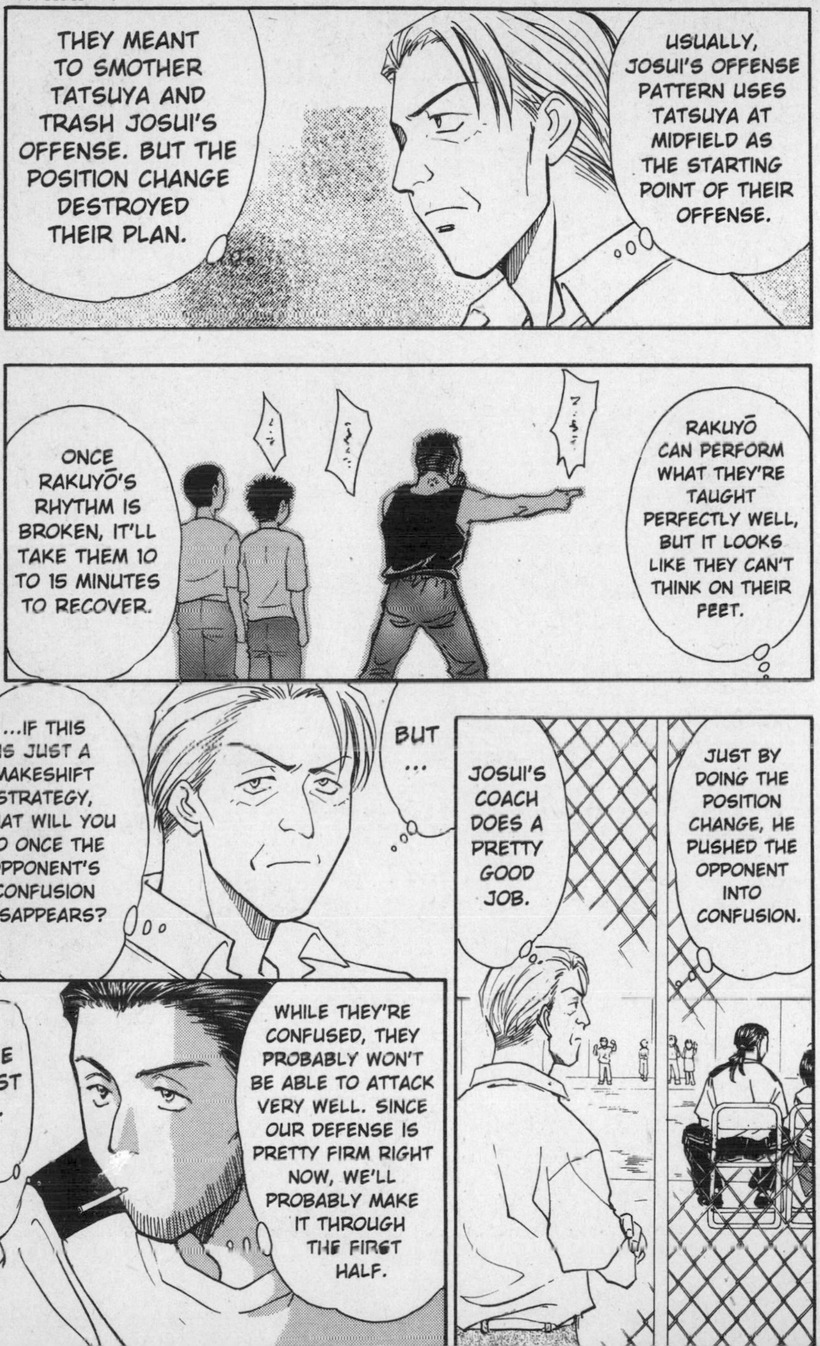
USUALLY, JOSUI'S OFFENSE PATTERN USES TATSUYA AT MIDFIELD AS THE STARTING POINT OF THEIR OFFENSE.
THEY MEANT TO SMOTHER TATSUYA AND TRASH JOSUI'S OFFENSE. BUT THE POSITION CHANGE DESTROYED THEIR PLAN.
RAKUYŌ CAN PERFORM WHAT THEY'RE TAUGHT PERFECTLY WELL, BUT IT LOOKS LIKE THEY CAN'T THINK ON THEIR FEET.
ONCE RAKUYŌ'S RHYTHM IS BROKEN, IT'LL TAKE THEM 10 TO 15 MINUTES TO RECOVER.
JUST BY DOING THE POSITION CHANGE, HE PUSHED THE OPPONENT INTO CONFUSION.
JOSUI'S COACH DOES A PRETTY GOOD JOB.
BUT ...
...IF THIS IS JUST A MAKESHIFT STRATEGY, WHAT WILL YOU DO ONCE THE OPPONENT'S CONFUSION DISAPPEARS?
WHILE THEY'RE CONFUSED, THEY PROBABLY WON'T BE ABLE TO ATTACK VERY WELL. SINCE OUR DEFENSE IS PRETTY FIRM RIGHT NOW, WE'LL PROBABLY MAKE IT THROUGH THE FIRST HALF.
THE REST ...

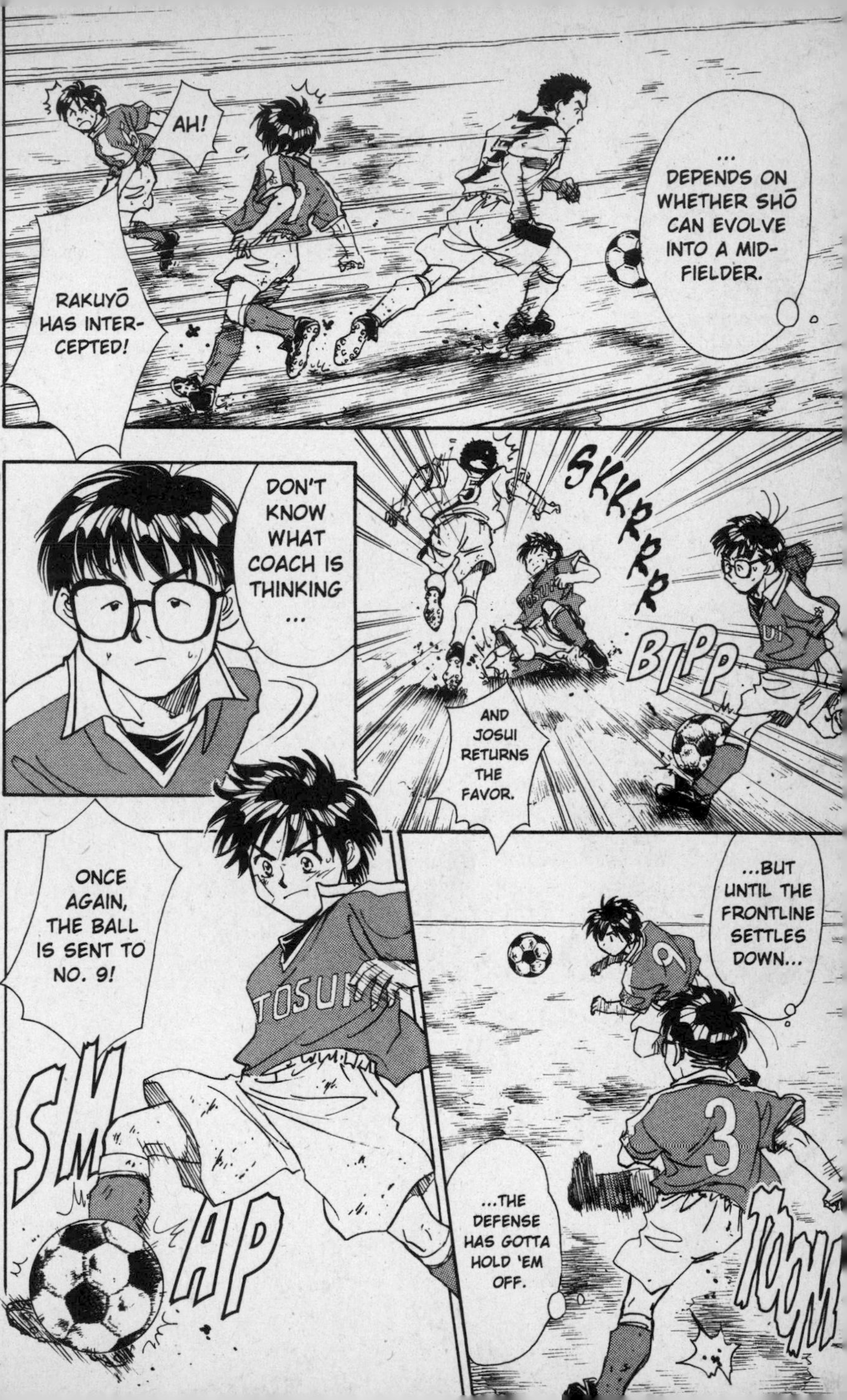
... DEPENDS ON WHETHER SHŌ CAN EVOLVE INTO A MID-FIELDER.
AH!
RAKUYŌ HAS INTER-CEPTED!
SKKRRR
BIPP
AND JOSUI RETURNS THE FAVOR.
DON'T KNOW WHAT COACH IS THINKING ...
...BUT UNTIL THE FRONTLINE SETTLES DOWN...
...THE DEFENSE HAS GOTTA HOLD 'EM OFF.
TOOM
ONCE AGAIN, THE BALL IS SENT TO NO. 9!
SMAP

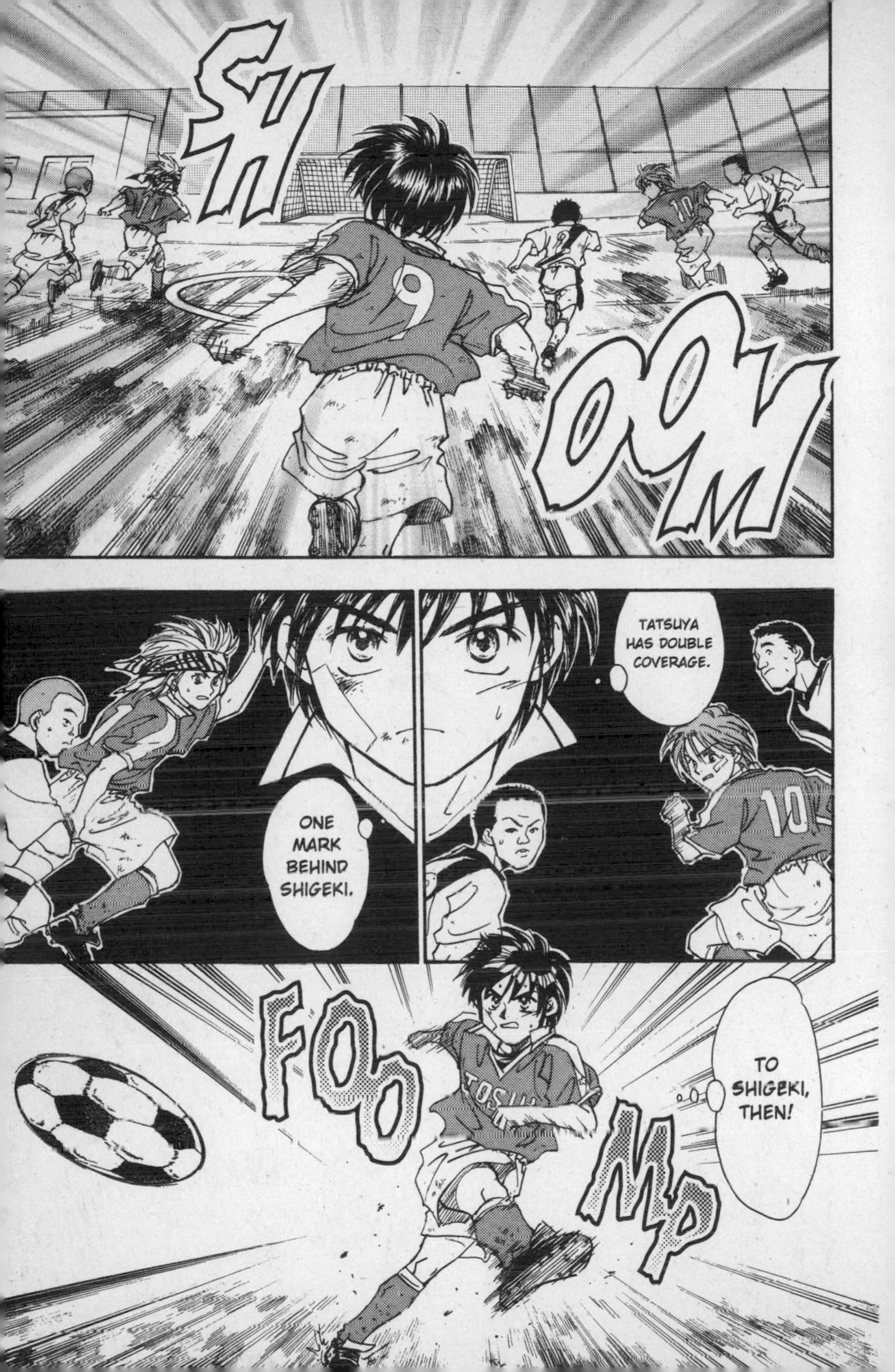
SHOOM
TATSUYA HAS DOUBLE COVERAGE.
ONE MARK BEHIND SHIGEKI.
TO SHIGEKI, THEN!
FOOMP

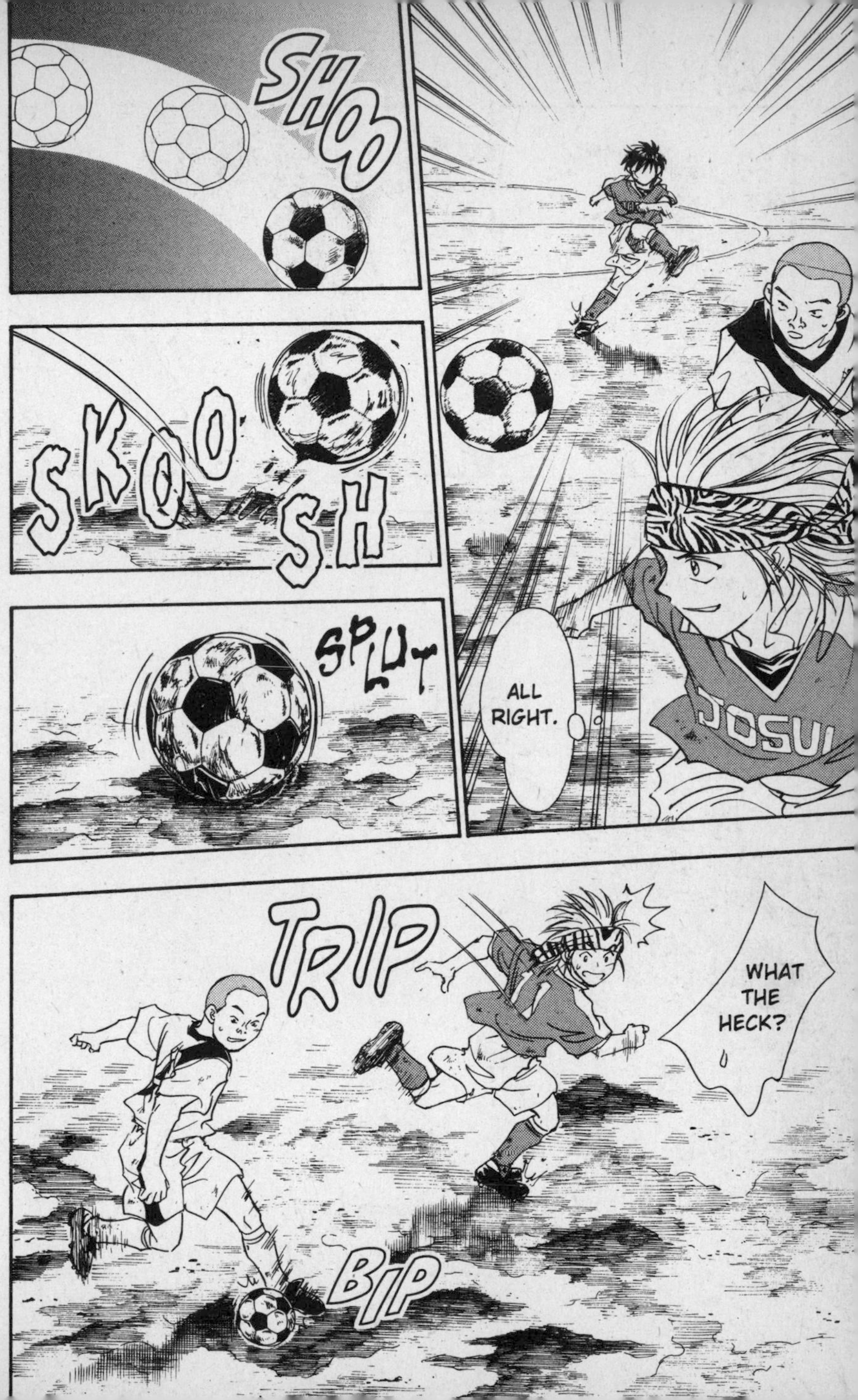
ALL RIGHT.
SHOO
SKOOSH
SPLUT
WHAT THE HECK?
TRIP
BIP

READ THIS WAY

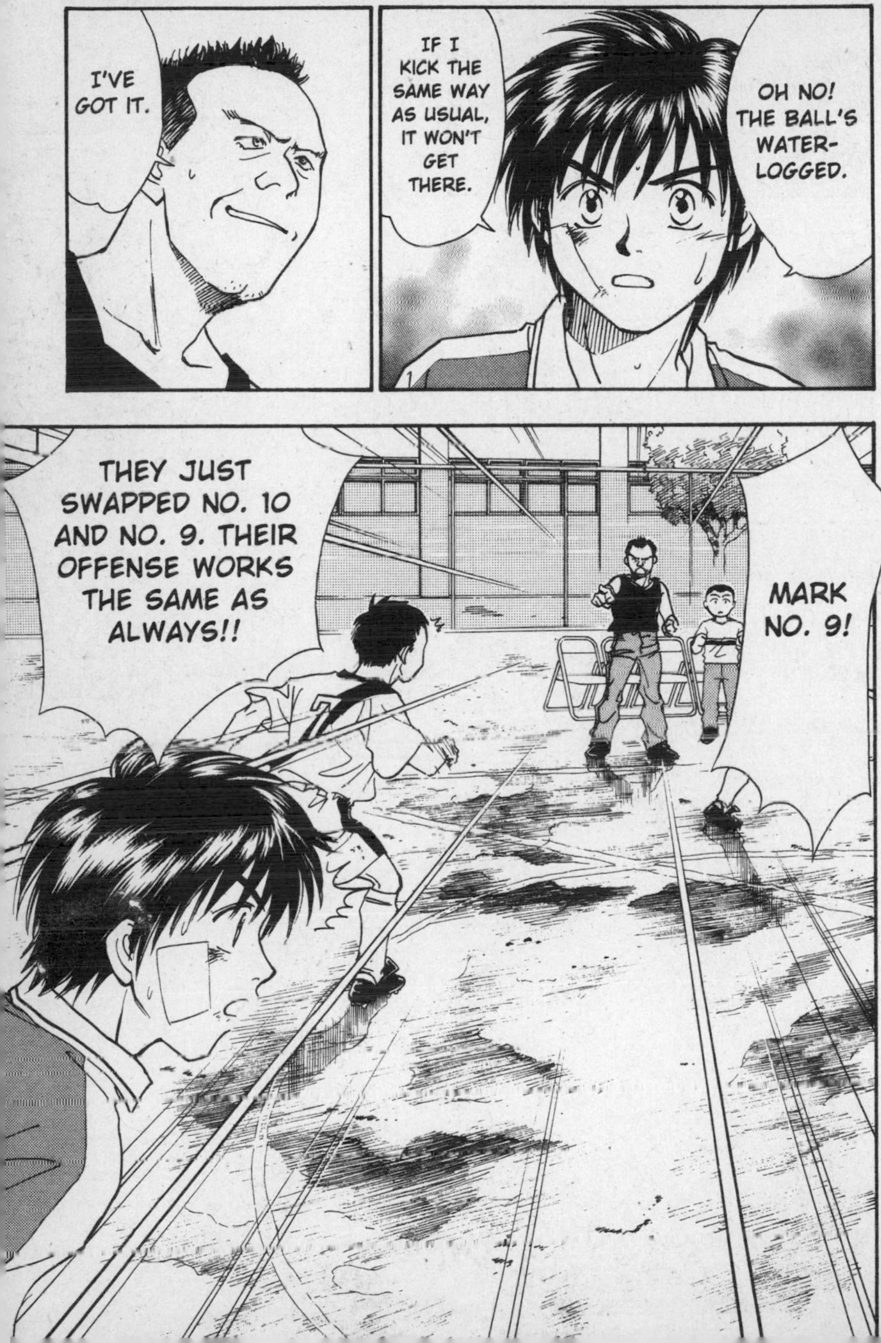
OH NO! THE BALL'S WATER-LOGGED.
IF I KICK THE SAME WAY AS USUAL, IT WON'T GET THERE.
I'VE GOT IT.
MARK NO. 9!
THEY JUST SWAPPED NO. 10 AND NO. 9. THEIR OFFENSE WORKS THE SAME AS ALWAYS!!

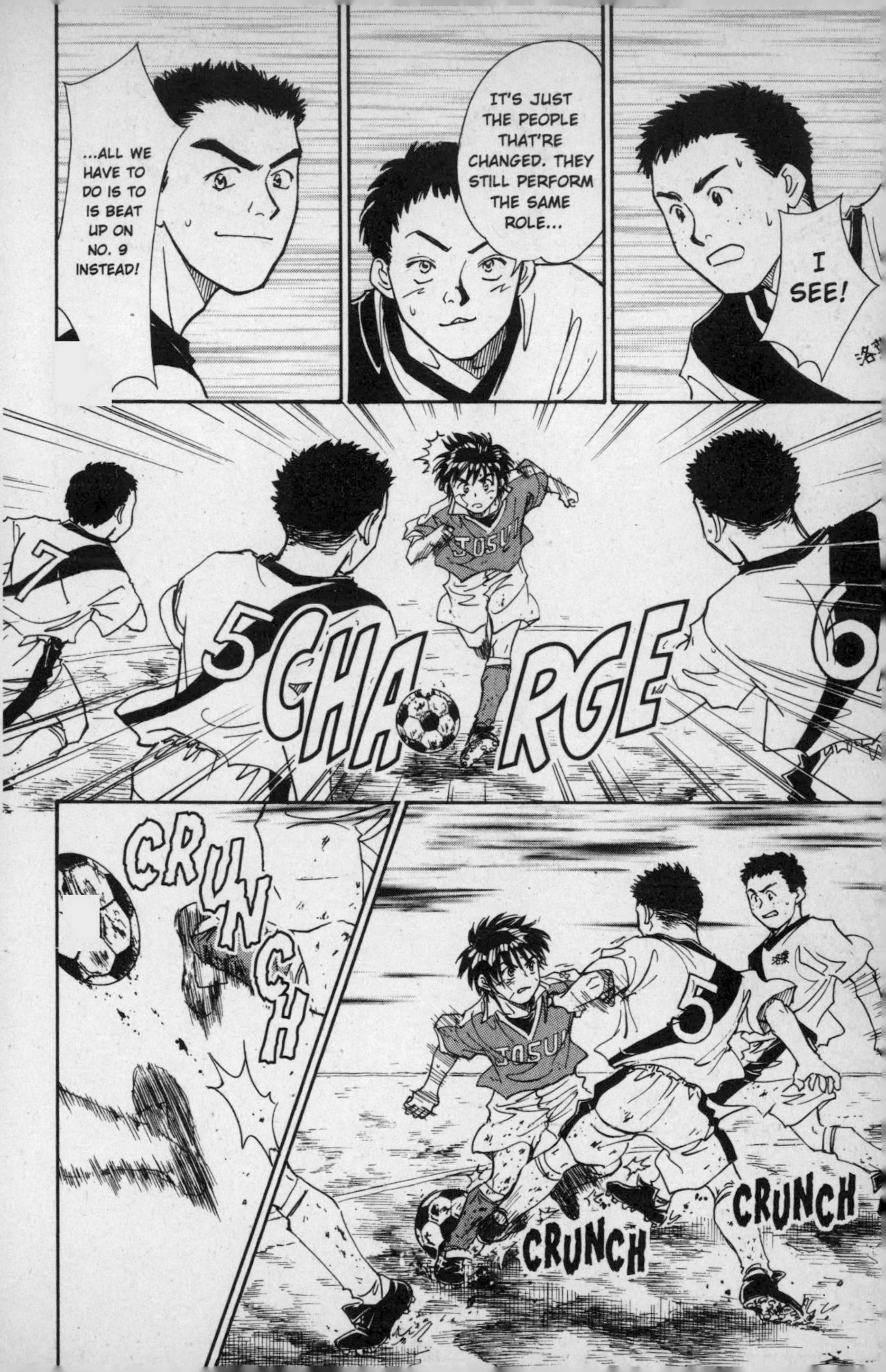

I SEE!
IT'S JUST THE PEOPLE THAT'RE CHANGED. THEY STILL PERFORM THE SAME ROLE...
...ALL WE HAVE TO DO IS TO IS BEAT UP ON NO. 9 INSTEAD!
CHARGE
CRUNCH
CRUNCH
CRUNCH

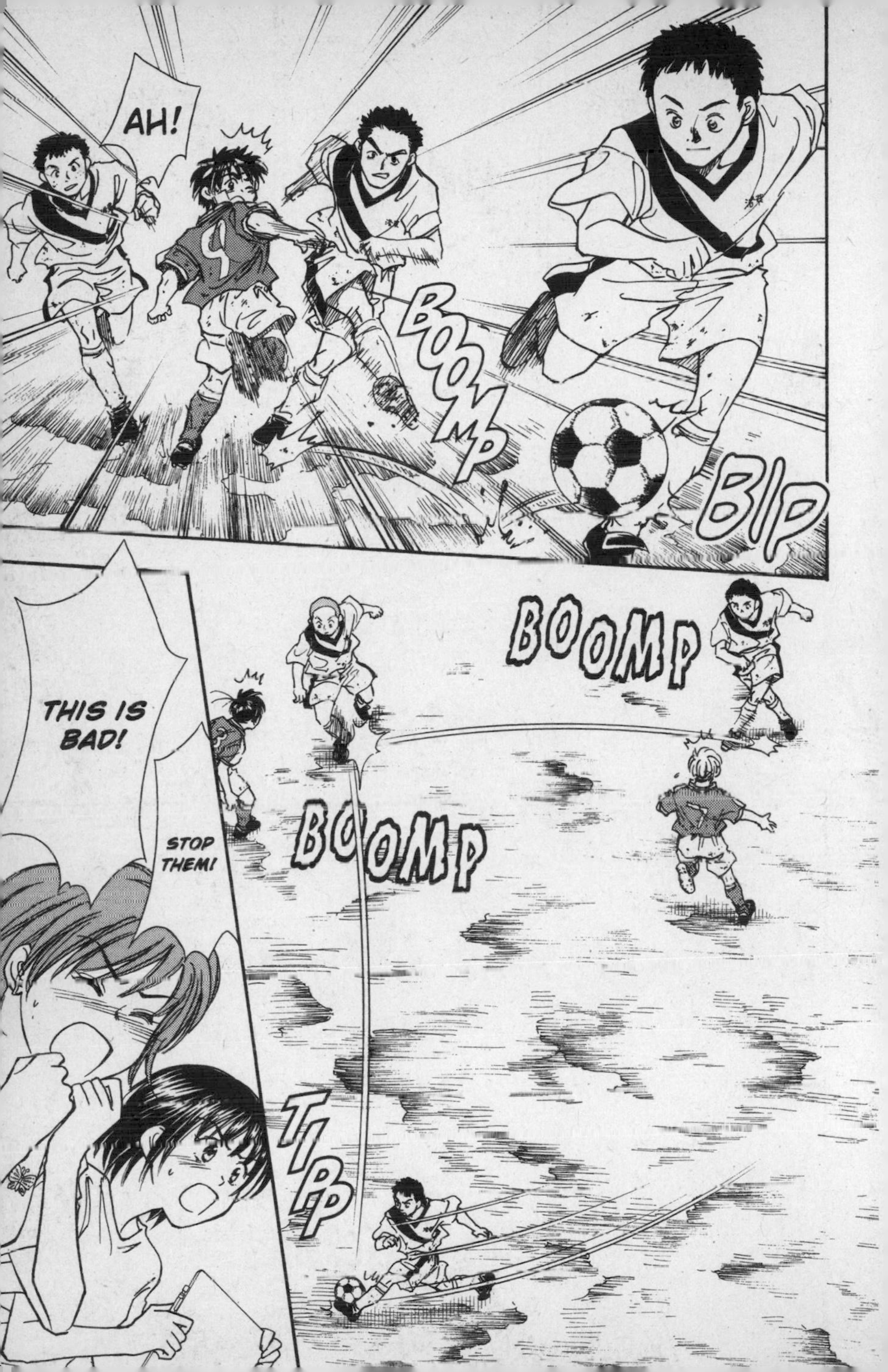
BIP
BOOMP
AH!
BOOMP
BOOMP
TIPP
THIS IS BAD!
STOP THEM!

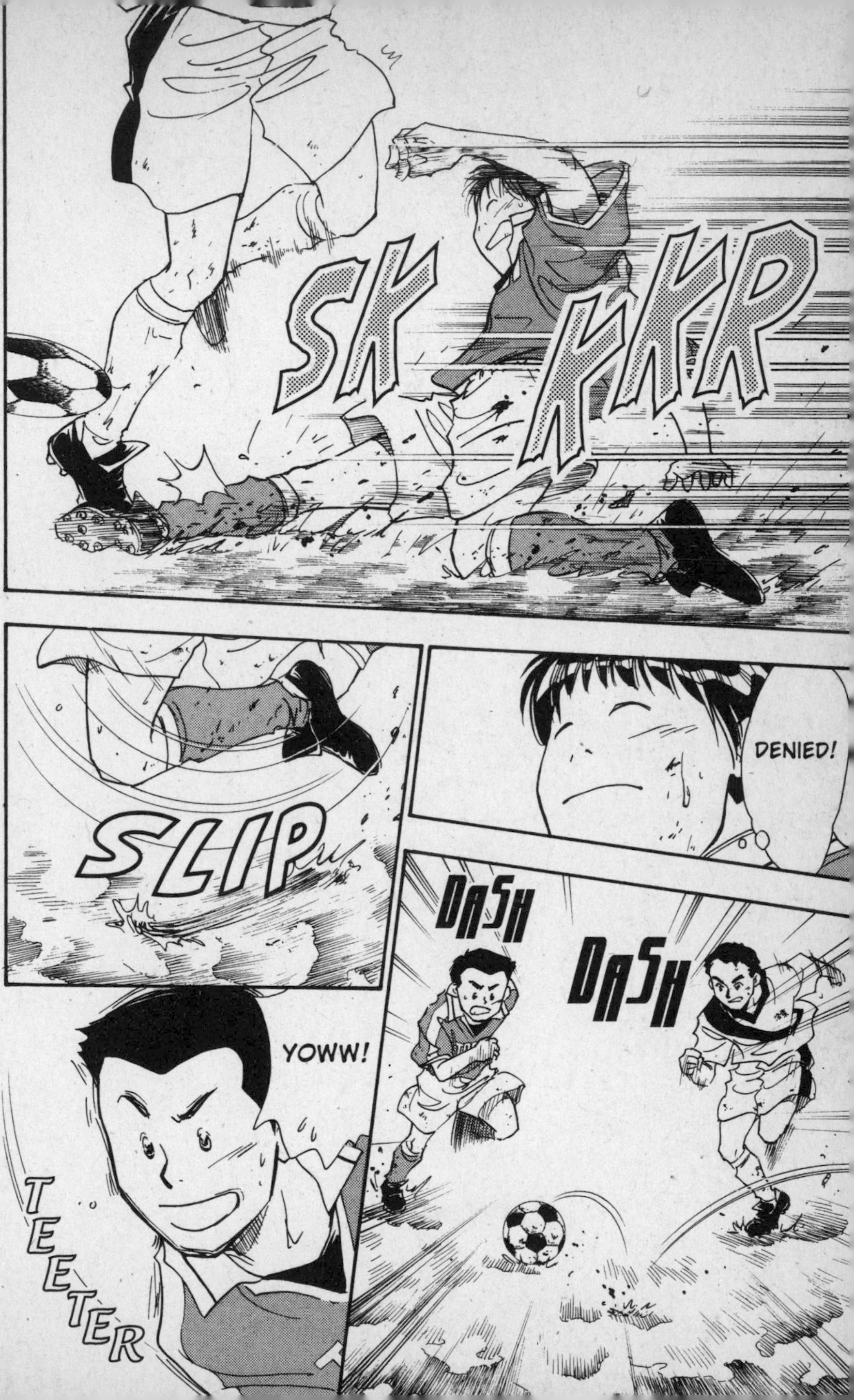
SKKKR
DENIED!
DASH
DASH
SLIP
YOWW!
TEETER

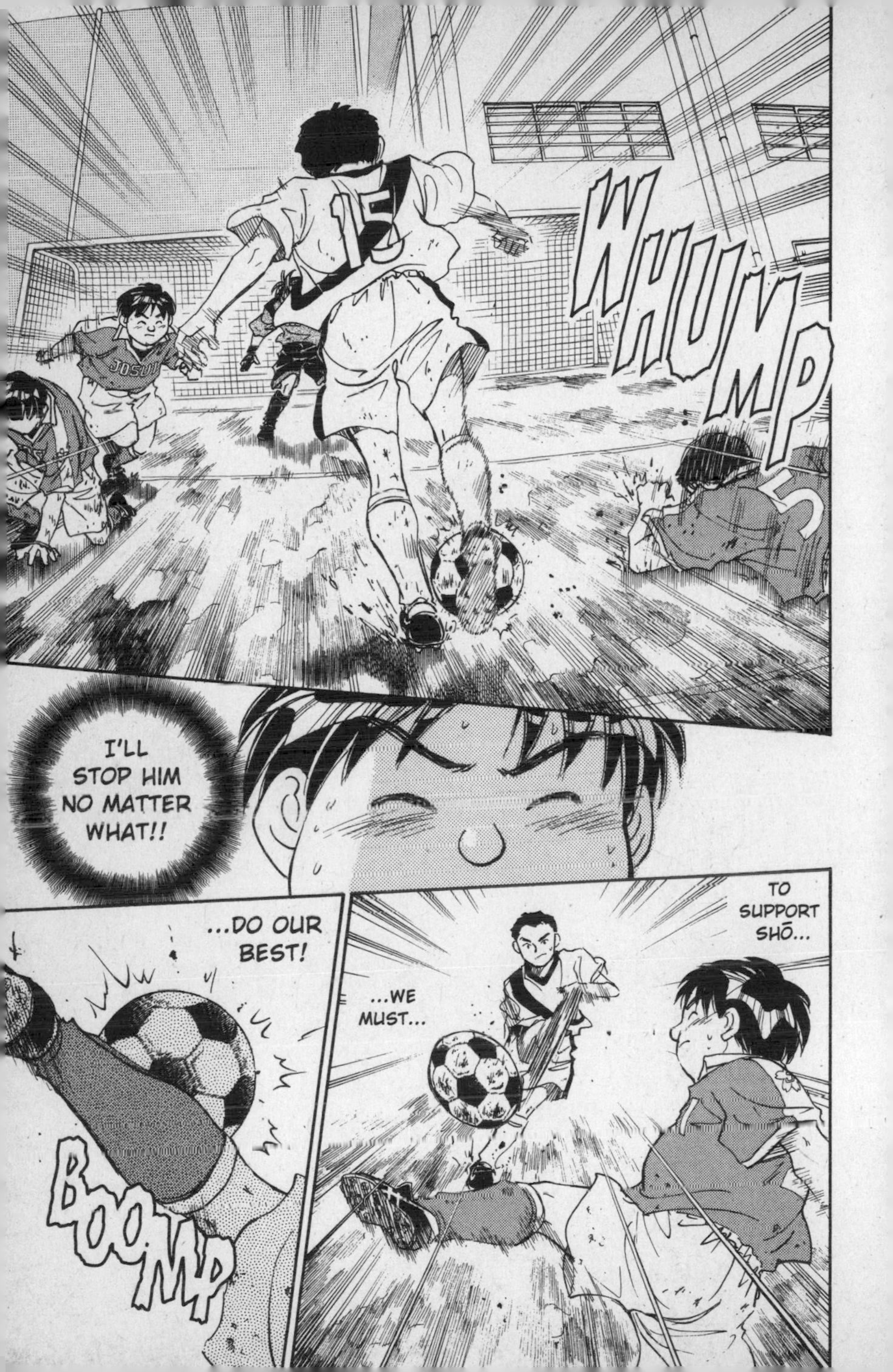
WHUMP
I'LL STOP HIM NO MATTER WHAT!!
TO SUPPORT SHŌ...
...WE MUST...
...DO OUR BEST!
BOOMP

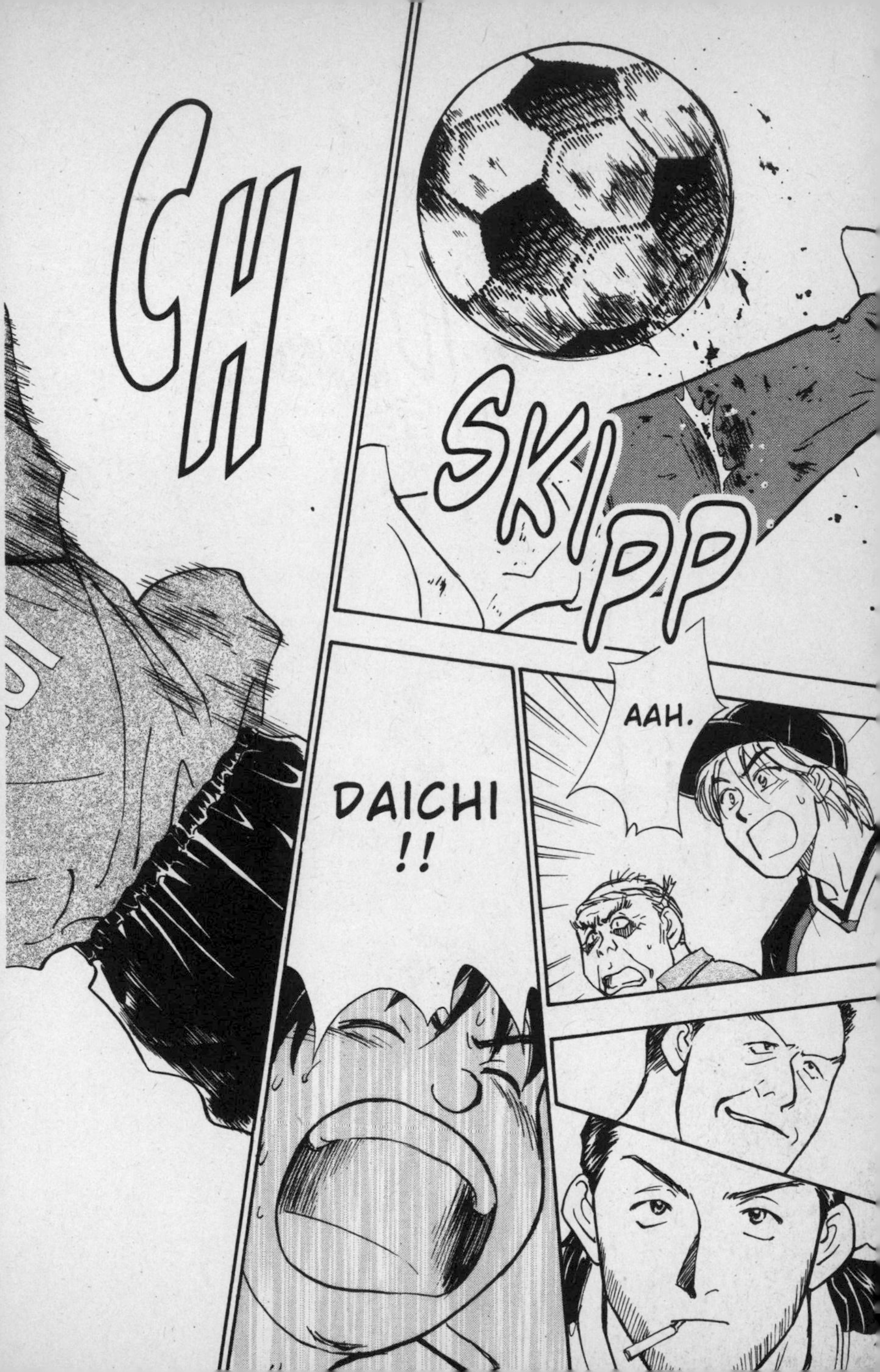
SKIPP
AAH.
DAICHI !!
CH

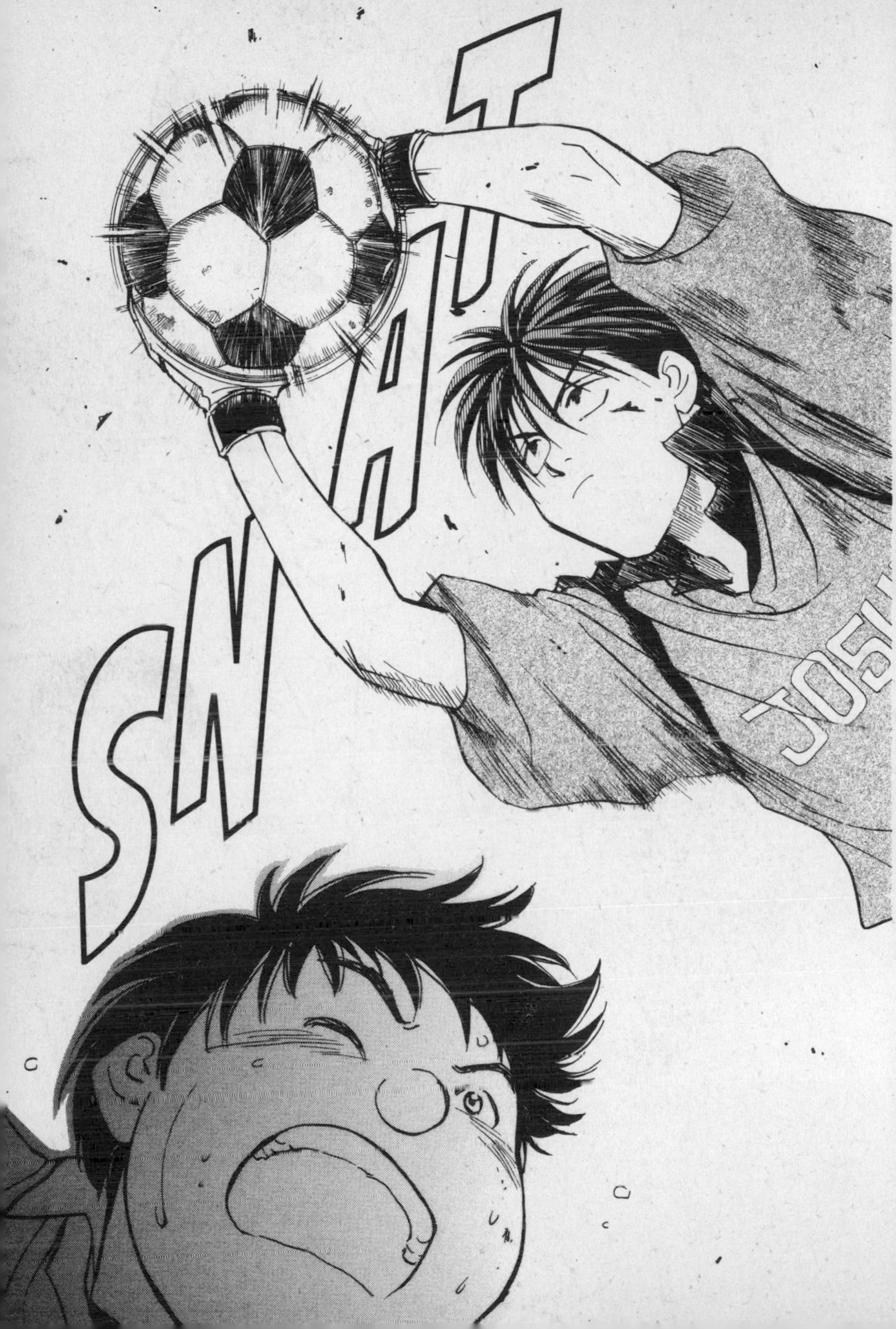

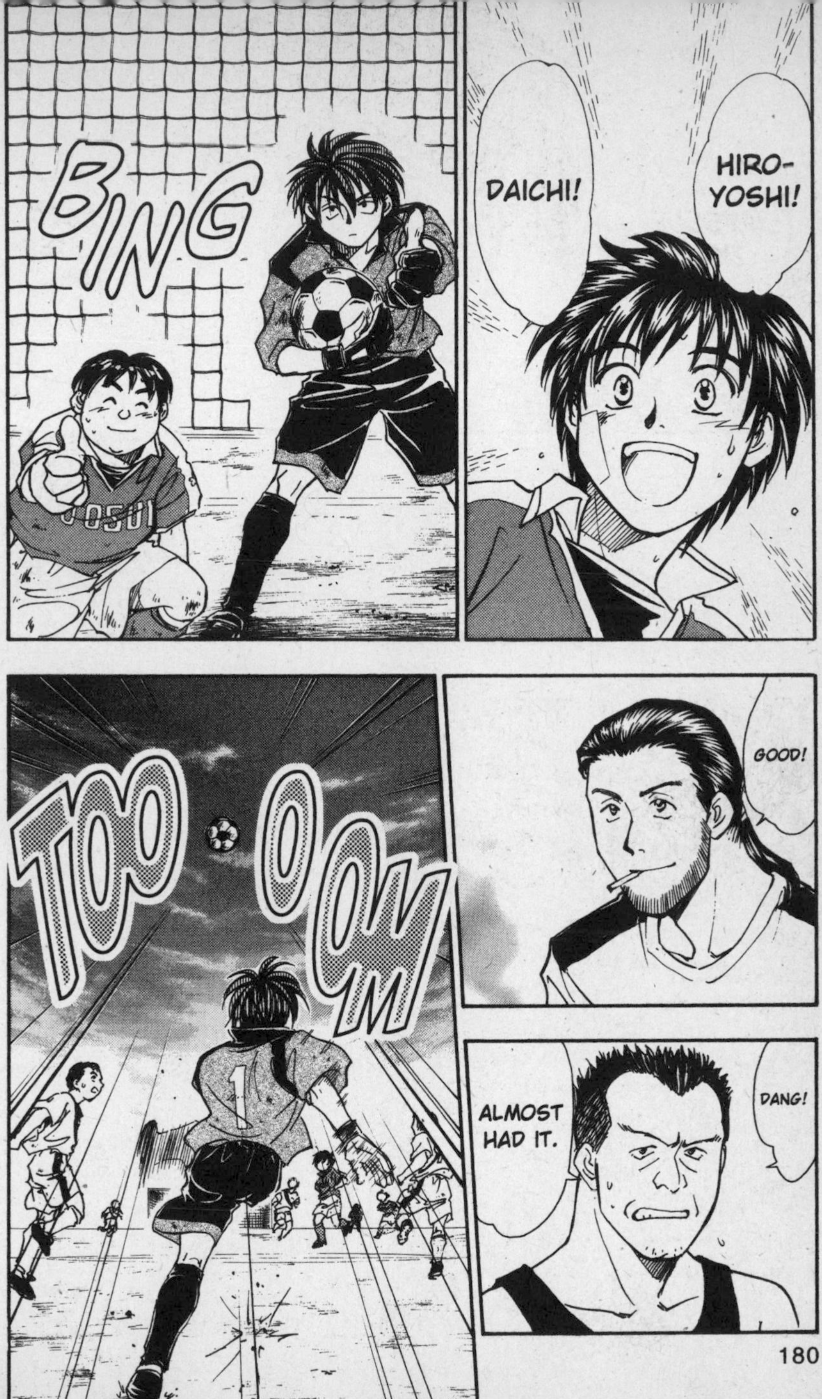
HIRO-YOSHI!
DAICHI!
BING
GOOD!
DANG!
ALMOST HAD IT.
TOOOOOM

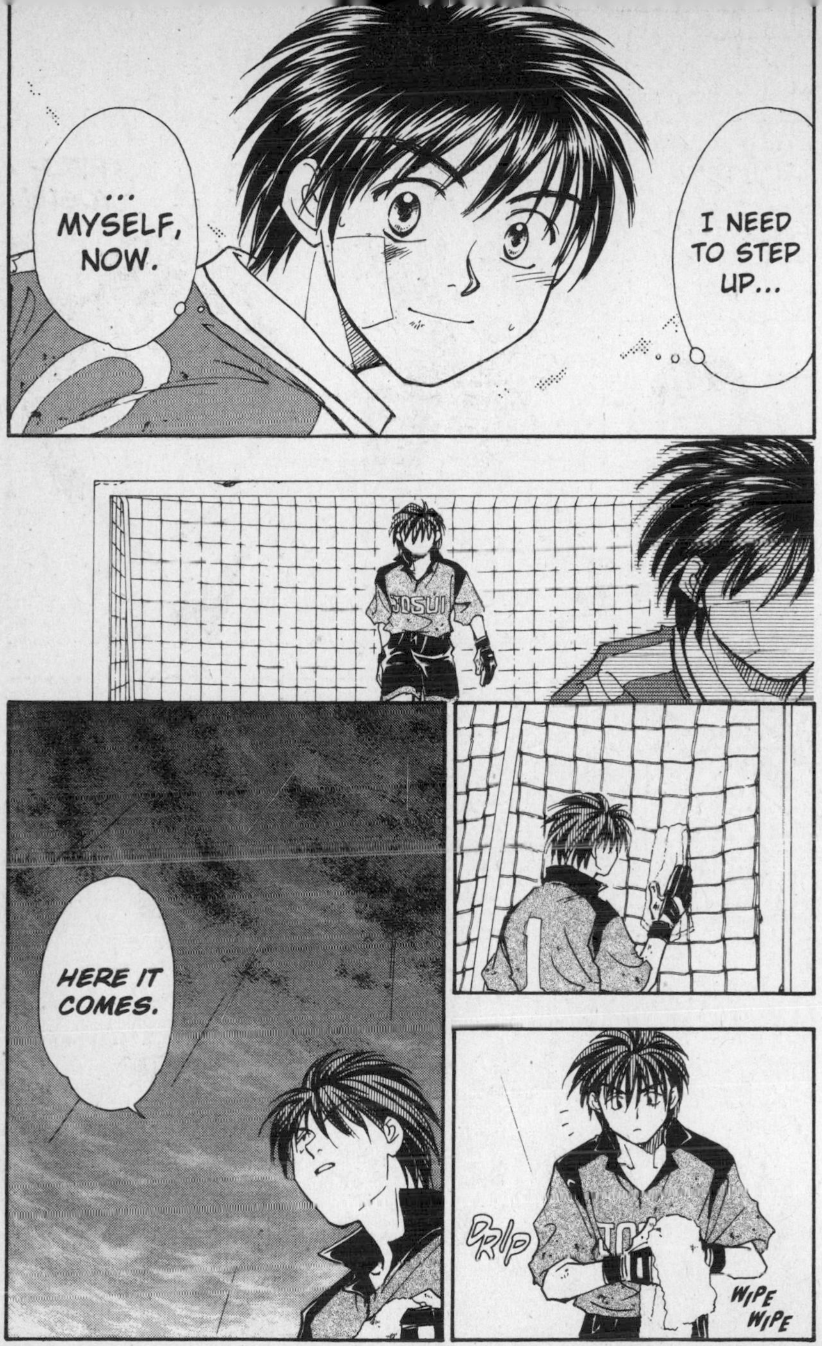
I NEED TO STEP UP...
... MYSELF, NOW.
DRIP
WIPE WIPE
HERE IT COMES.

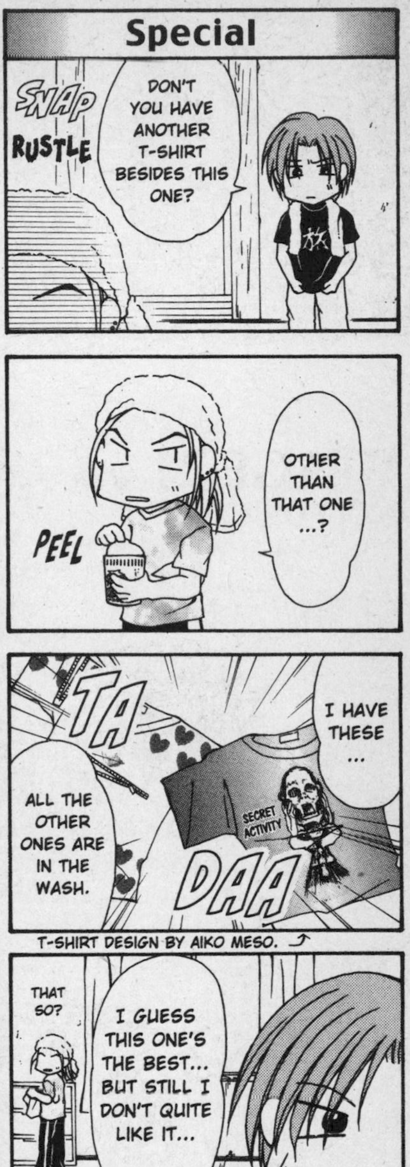
Special
SNAP
RUSTLE
DON'T YOU HAVE ANOTHER T-SHIRT BESIDES THIS ONE?
OTHER THAN THAT ONE ...?
PEEL
I HAVE THESE ...
TA
DAA
SECRET ACTIVITY
ALL THE OTHER ONES ARE IN THE WASH.
T-SHIRT DESIGN BY AIKO MESO.
I GUESS THIS ONE'S THE BEST... BUT STILL I DON'T QUITE LIKE IT...
THAT SO?

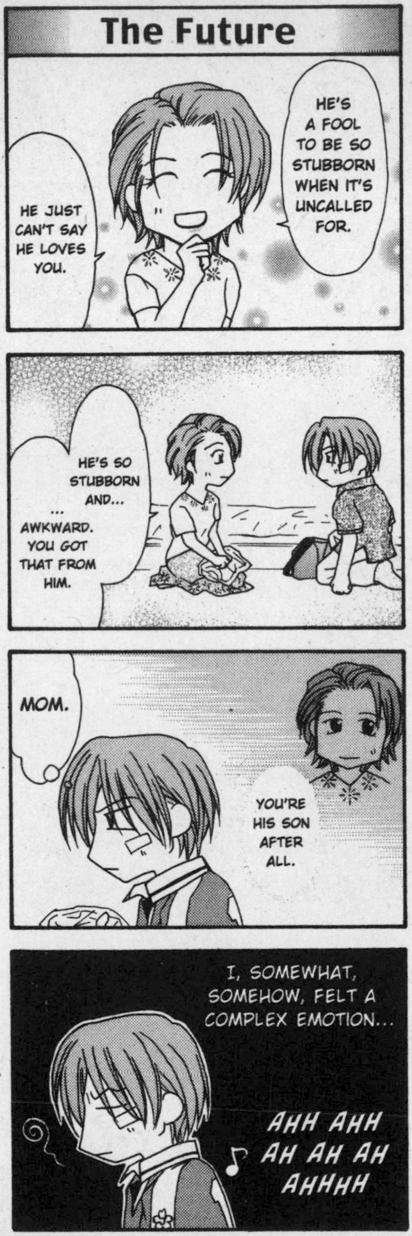
The Future
HE'S A FOOL TO BE SO STUBBORN WHEN IT'S UNCALLED FOR.
HE JUST CAN'T SAY HE LOVES YOU.
HE'S SO STUBBORN AND... ... AWKWARD. YOU GOT THAT FROM HIM.
MOM.
YOU'RE HIS SON AFTER ALL.
I, SOMEWHAT, SOMEHOW, FELT A COMPLEX EMOTION...
AHH AHH AH AH AH AHHHH

PLEASE HUM THE THEME SONG FROM THE JAPANESE MELODRAMA "XX NO KUNI KARA" AS YOU READ THIS.

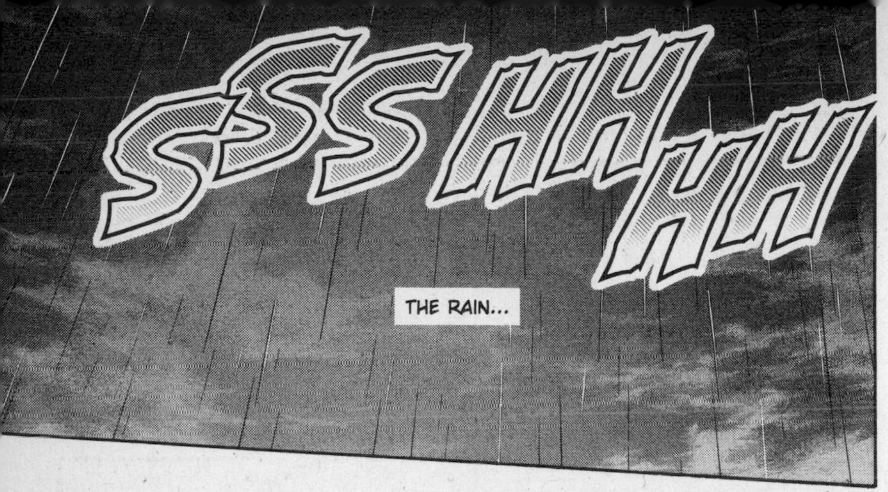
SSSHHHHH
THE RAIN...

STAGE.71 First Half Over

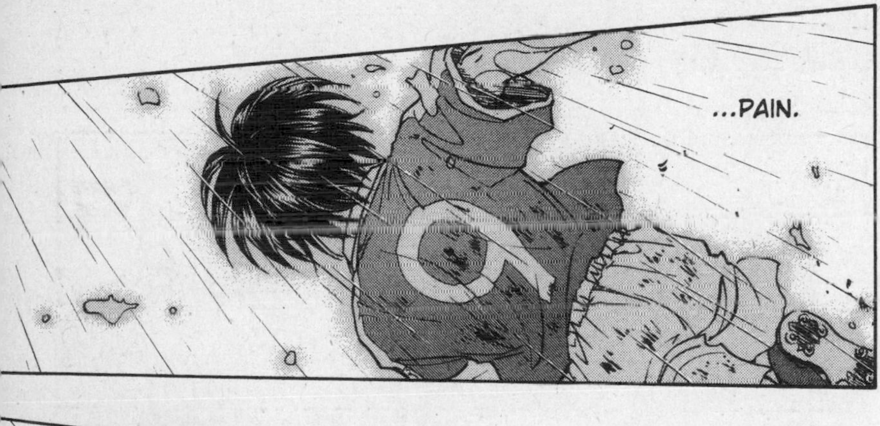
...PAIN.

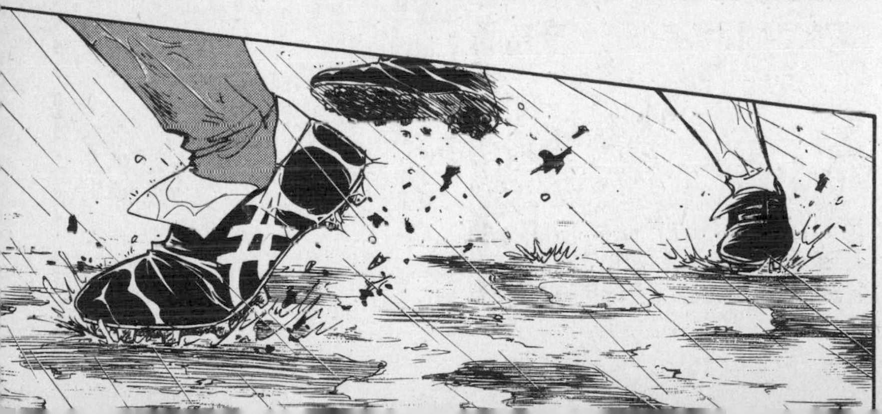

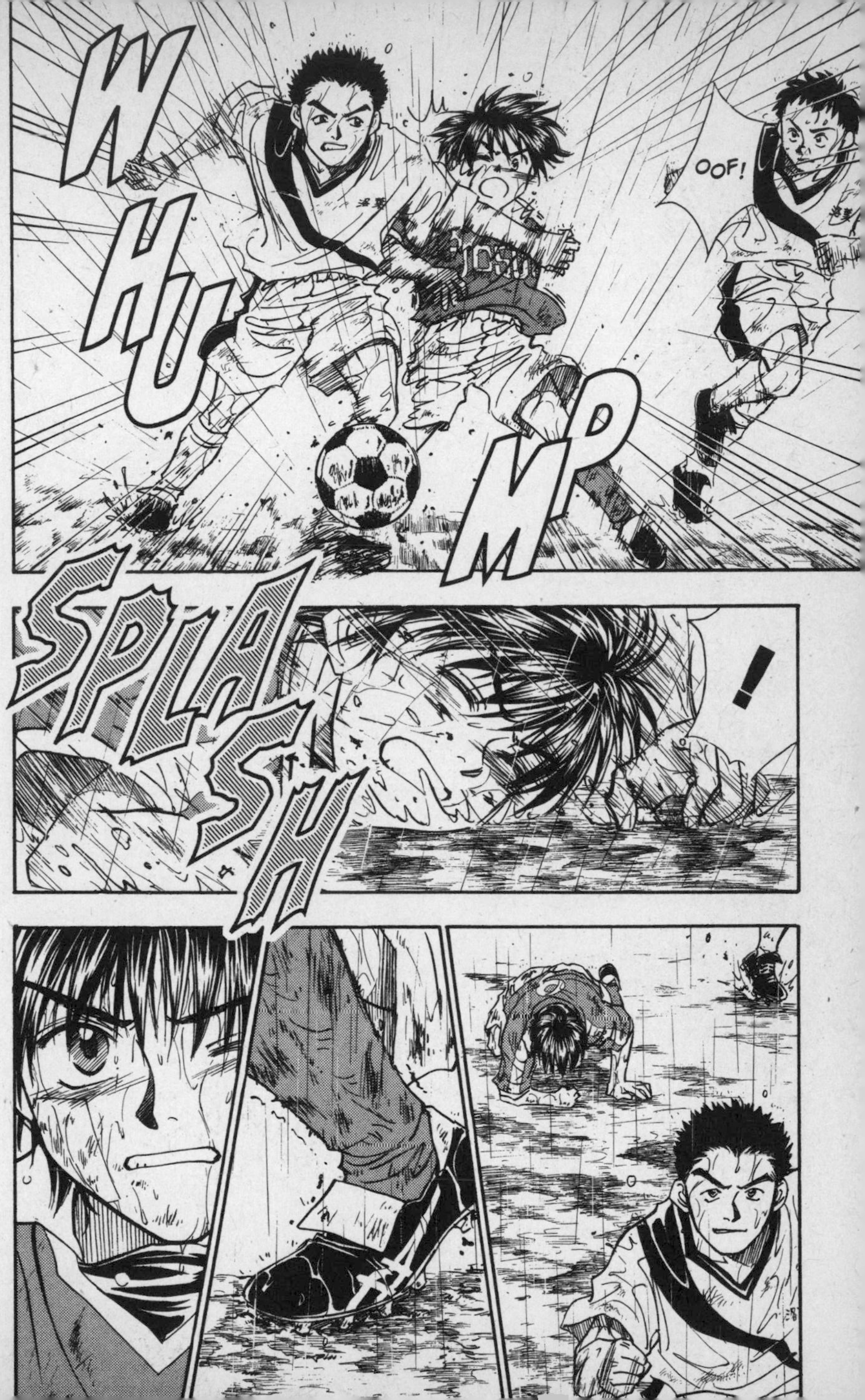
OOF!
WHUMP
!
SPLASH

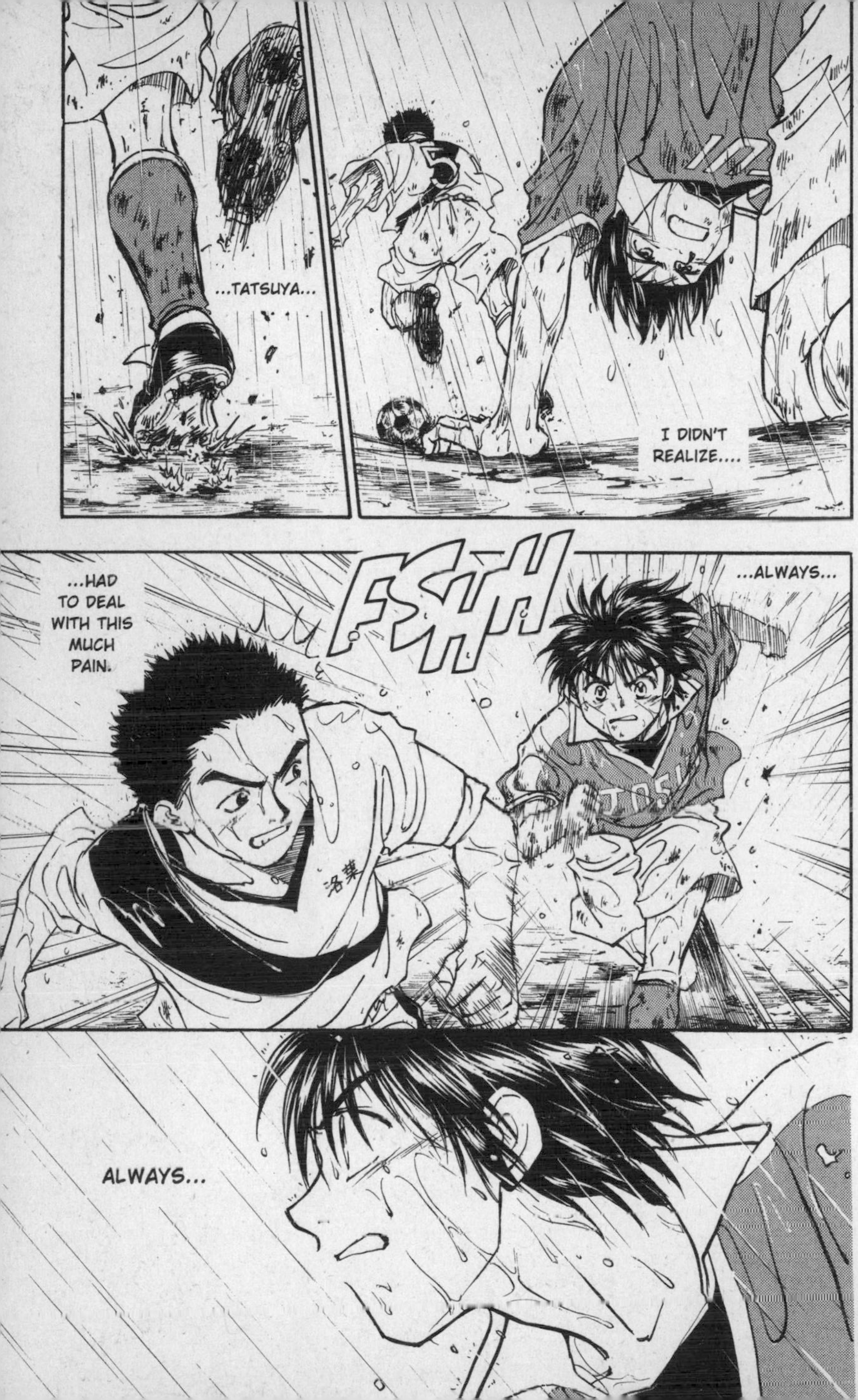
I DIDN'T REALIZE....
...TATSUYA...
...ALWAYS...
FSHH
...HAD TO DEAL WITH THIS MUCH PAIN.
ALWAYS...

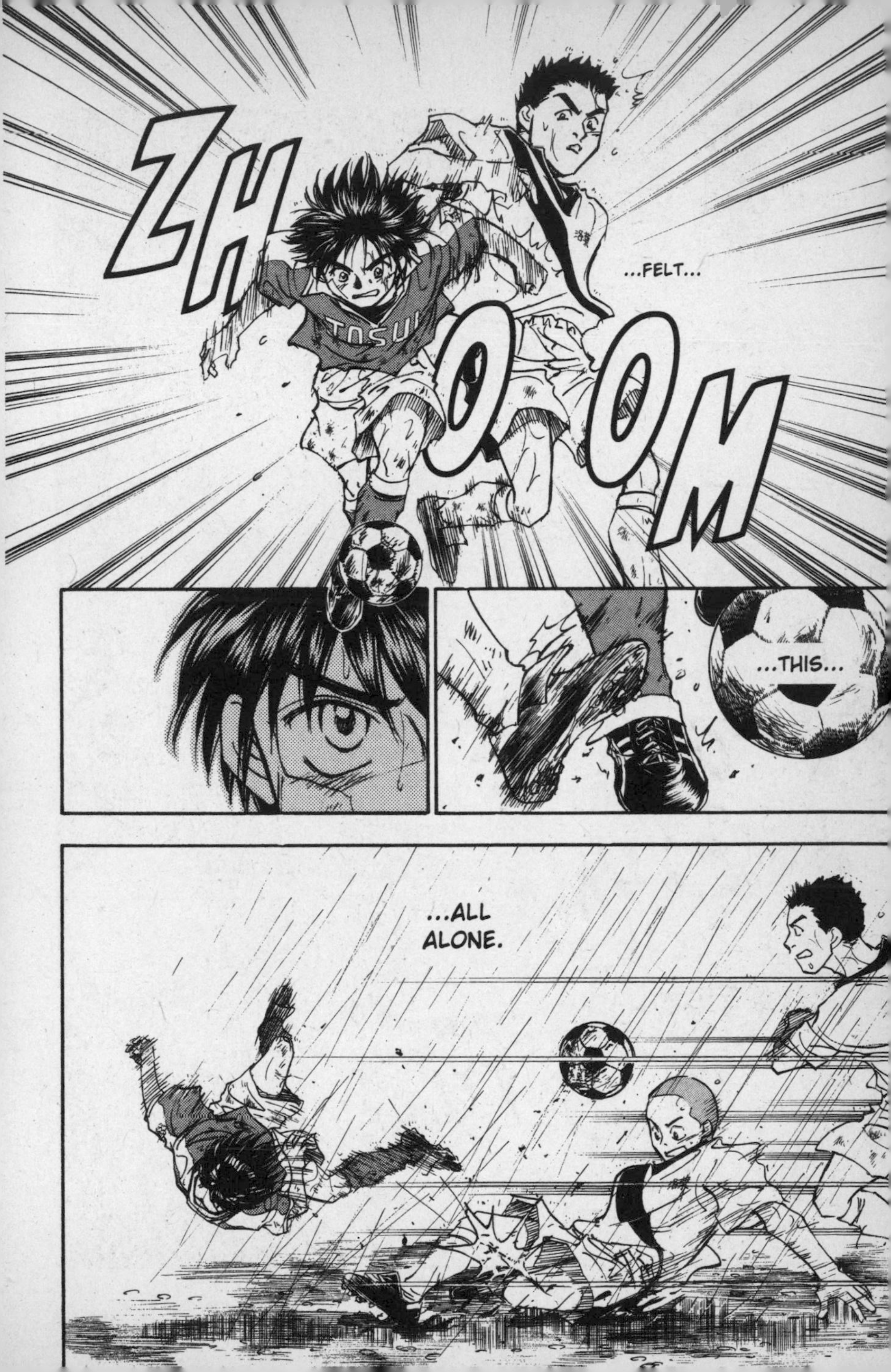...FELT...
ZHOOOM
TOSUI
...THIS...
...ALL ALONE.

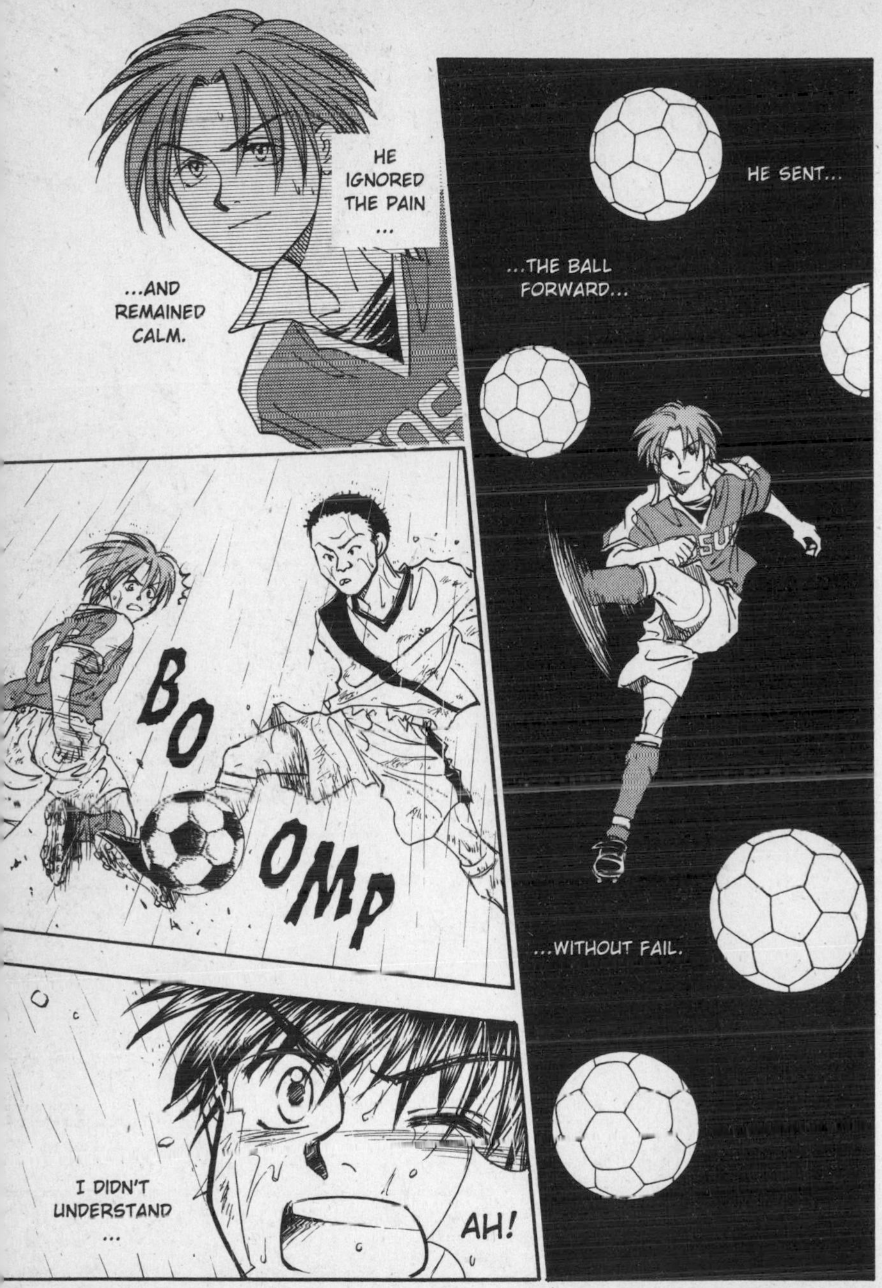
HE SENT...
...THE BALL FORWARD...
...WITHOUT FAIL.
HE IGNORED THE PAIN ...
...AND REMAINED CALM.
BOOMP
AH!
I DIDN'T UNDERSTAND ...

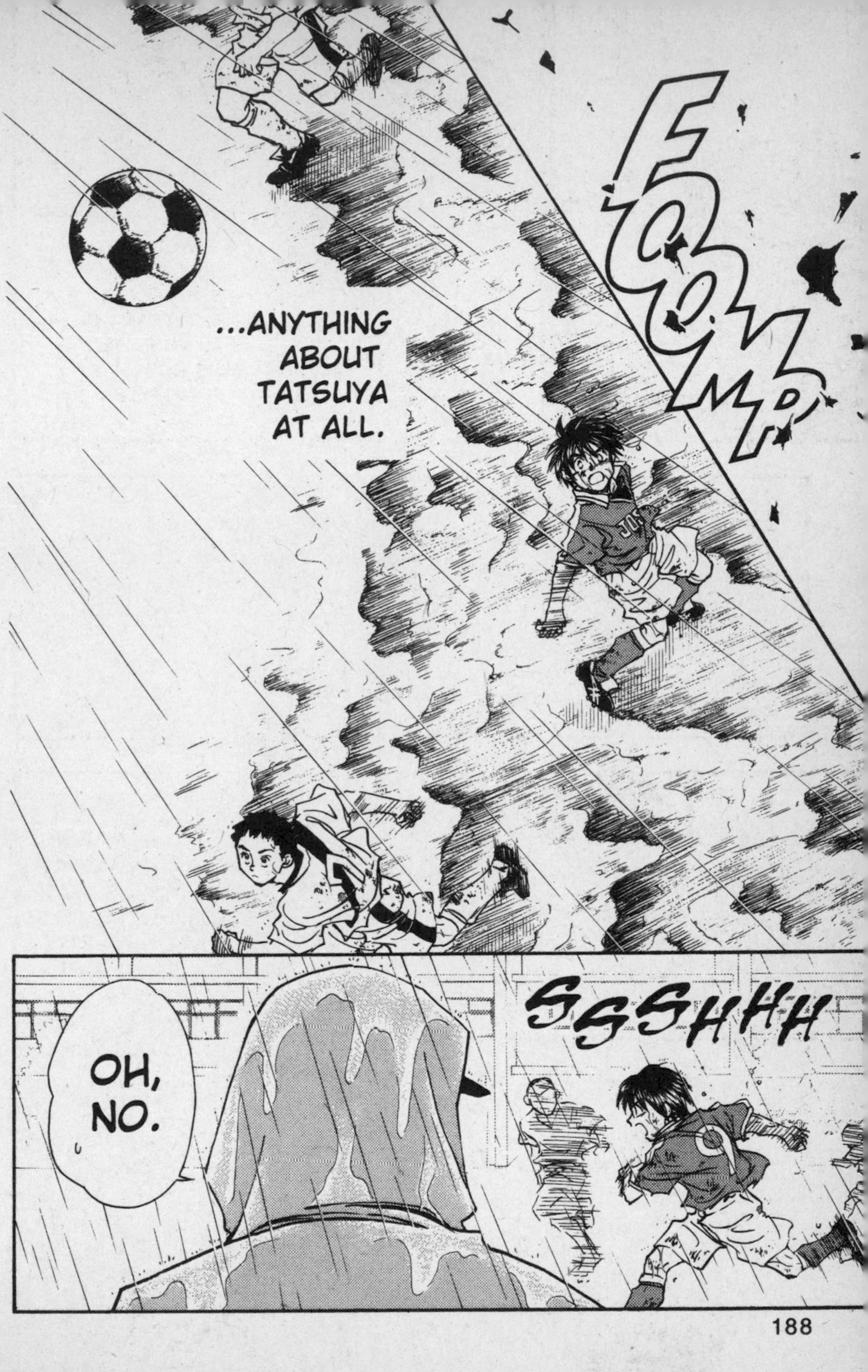
FOOOMP!
...ANYTHING ABOUT TATSUYA AT ALL.
SSSHHH
OH, NO.

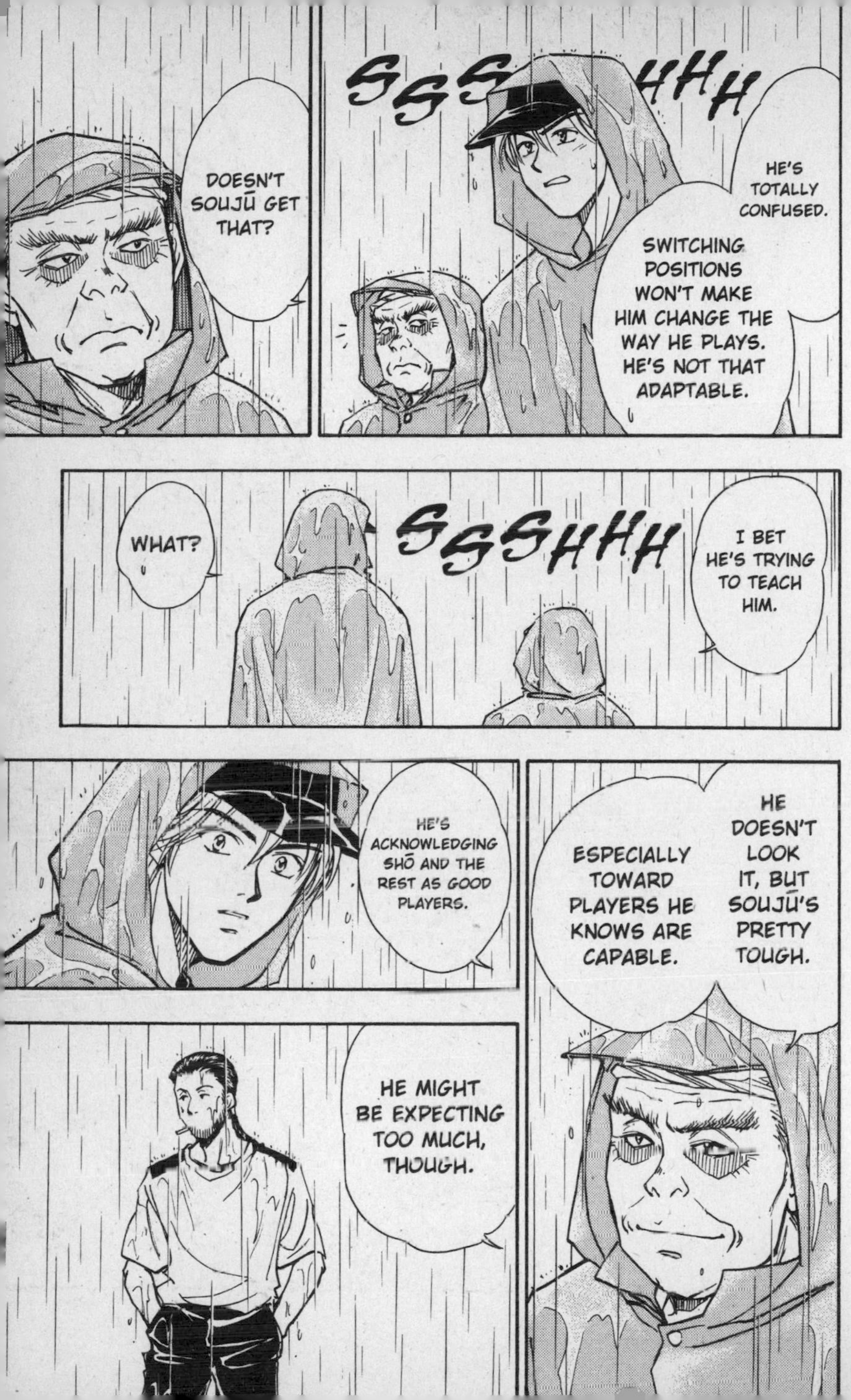
HE'S TOTALLY CONFUSED.
SSSHHHH
SWITCHING POSITIONS WON'T MAKE HIM CHANGE THE WAY HE PLAYS. HE'S NOT THAT ADAPTABLE.
DOESN'T SOUJŪ GET THAT?
I BET HE'S TRYING TO TEACH HIM.
SSSHHHH
WHAT?
HE DOESN'T LOOK IT, BUT SOUJŪ'S PRETTY TOUGH.
ESPECIALLY TOWARD PLAYERS HE KNOWS ARE CAPABLE.
HE'S ACKNOWLEDGING SHŌ AND THE REST AS GOOD PLAYERS.
HE MIGHT BE EXPECTING TOO MUCH, THOUGH.

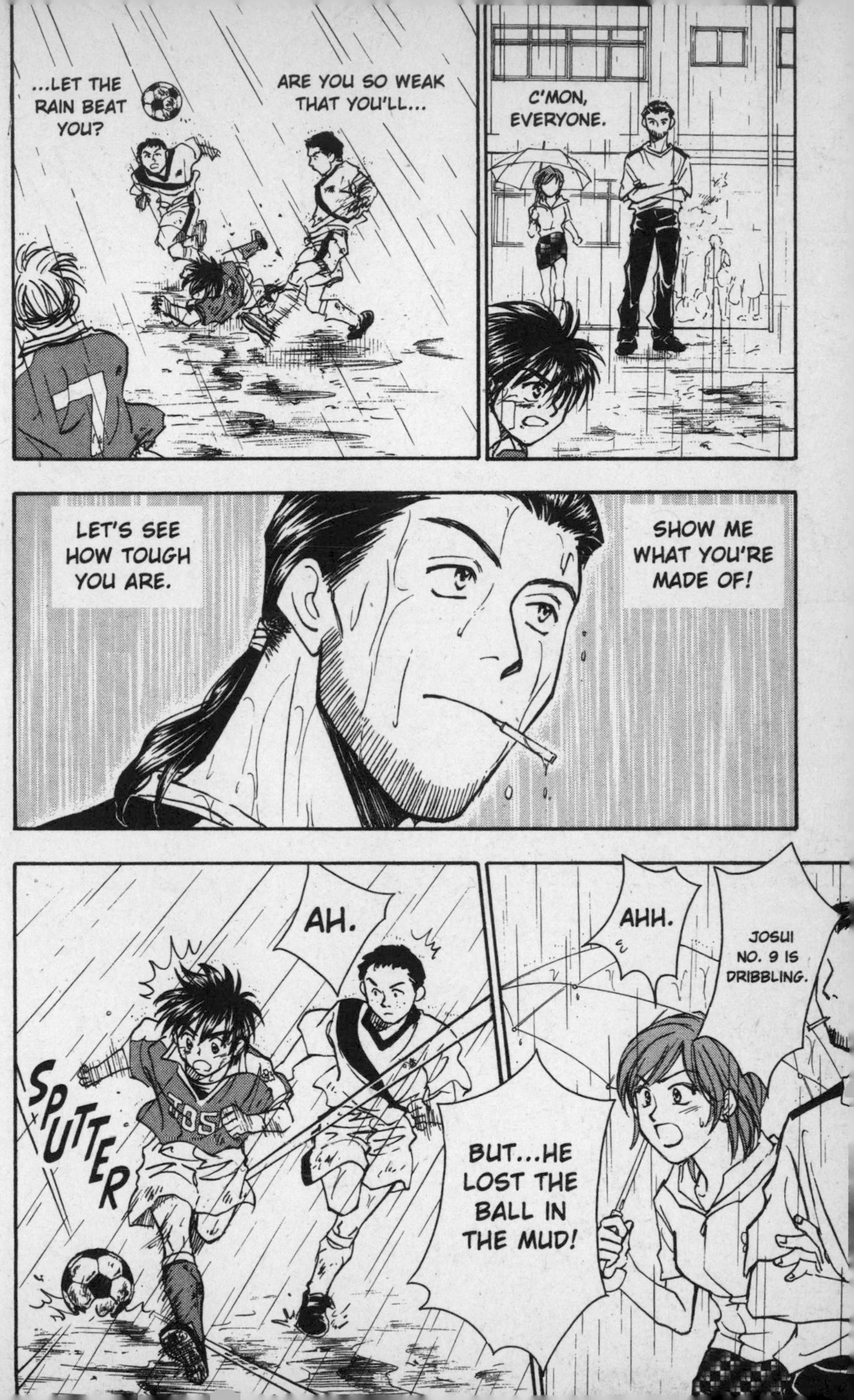
C'MON, EVERYONE.
ARE YOU SO WEAK THAT YOU'LL...
...LET THE RAIN BEAT YOU?
SHOW ME WHAT YOU'RE MADE OF!
LET'S SEE HOW TOUGH YOU ARE.
JOSUI NO. 9 IS DRIBBLING.
AHH.
BUT...HE LOST THE BALL IN THE MUD!
AH.
SPUTTER

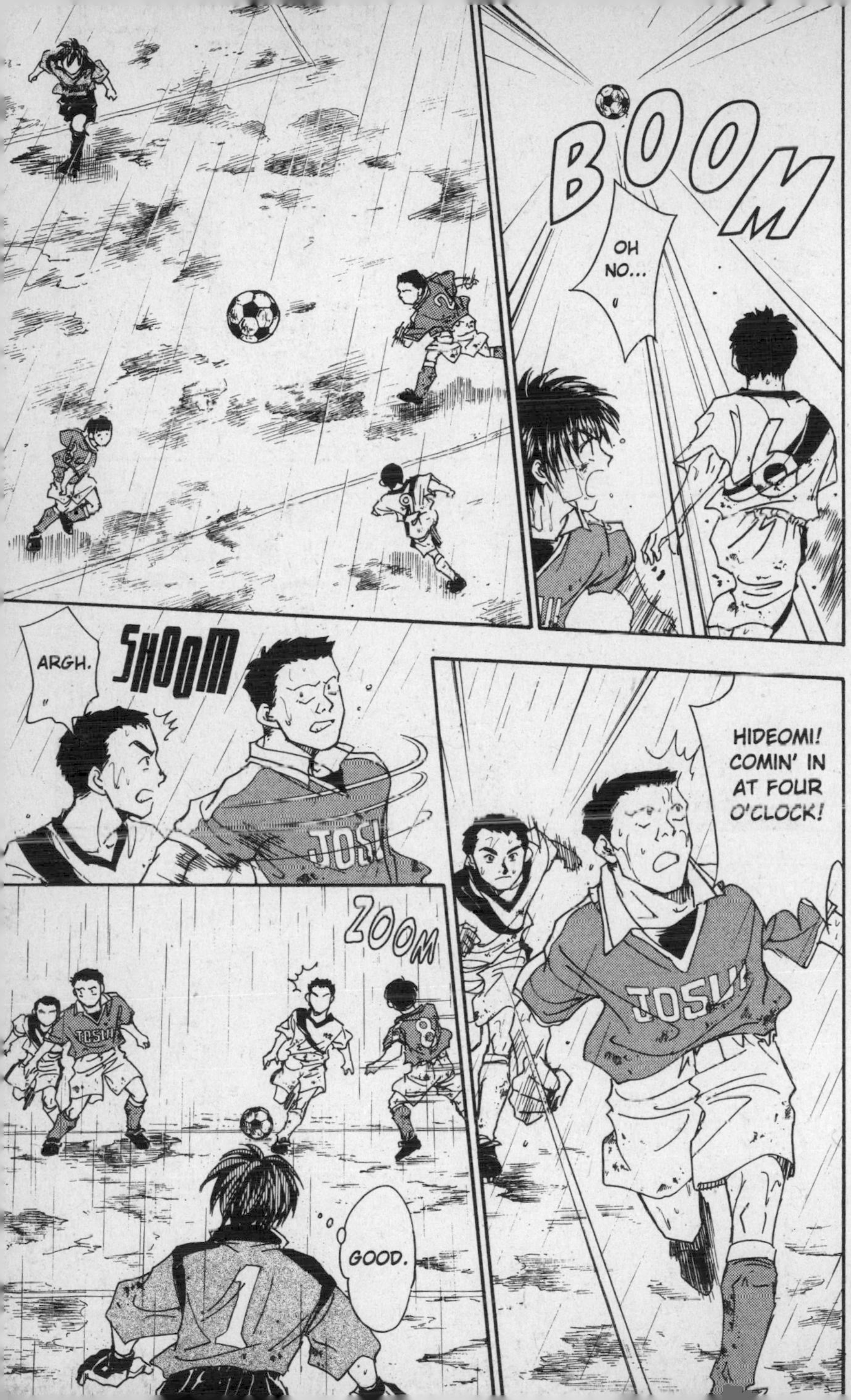
BOOM
OH NO...
HIDEOMI! COMIN' IN AT FOUR O'CLOCK!
ARGH.
SHOOM
ZOOM
GOOD.

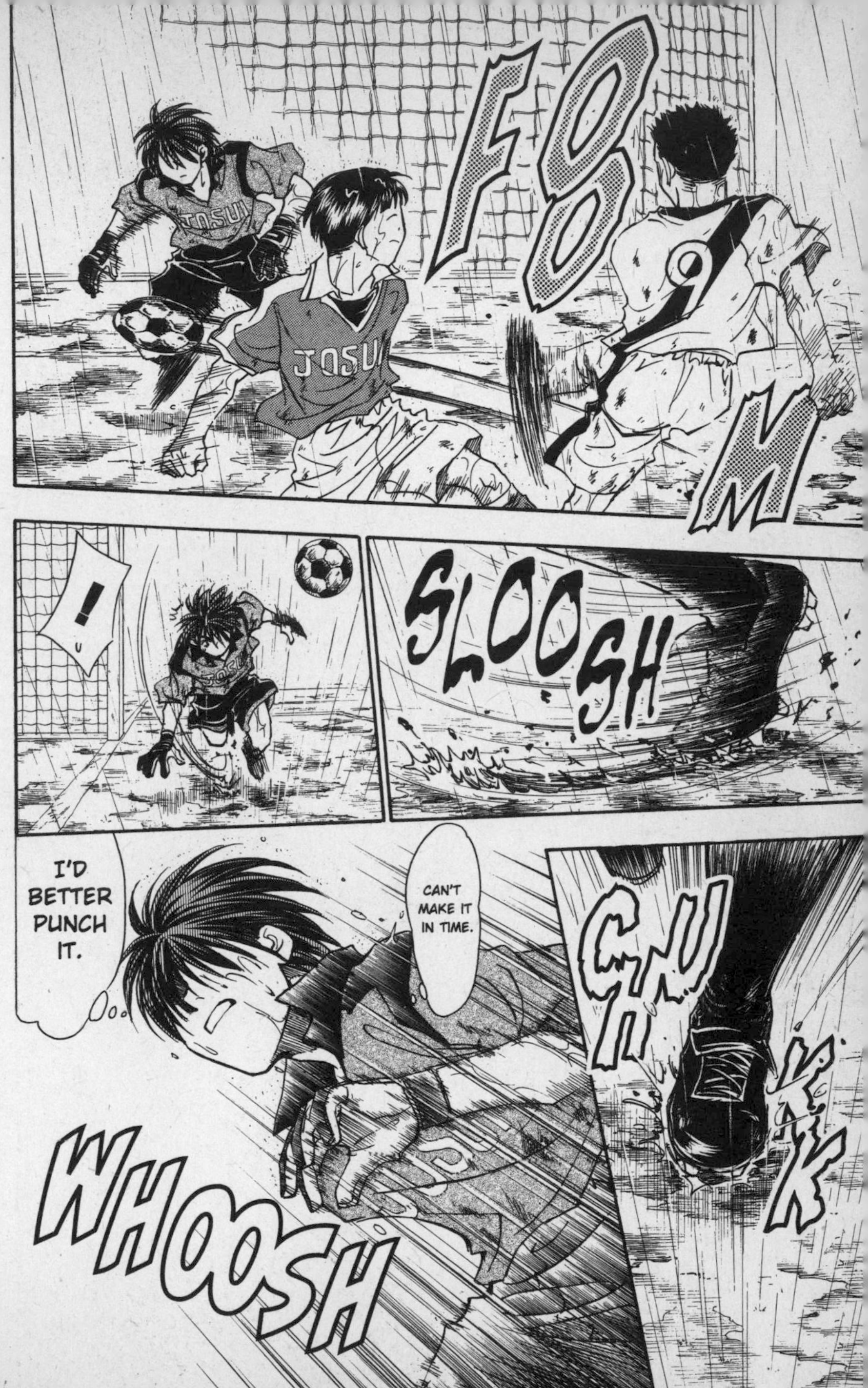

FOOM
SLOOSH
!
CHUNK
CAN'T MAKE IT IN TIME.
I'D BETTER PUNCH IT.
WHOOSH

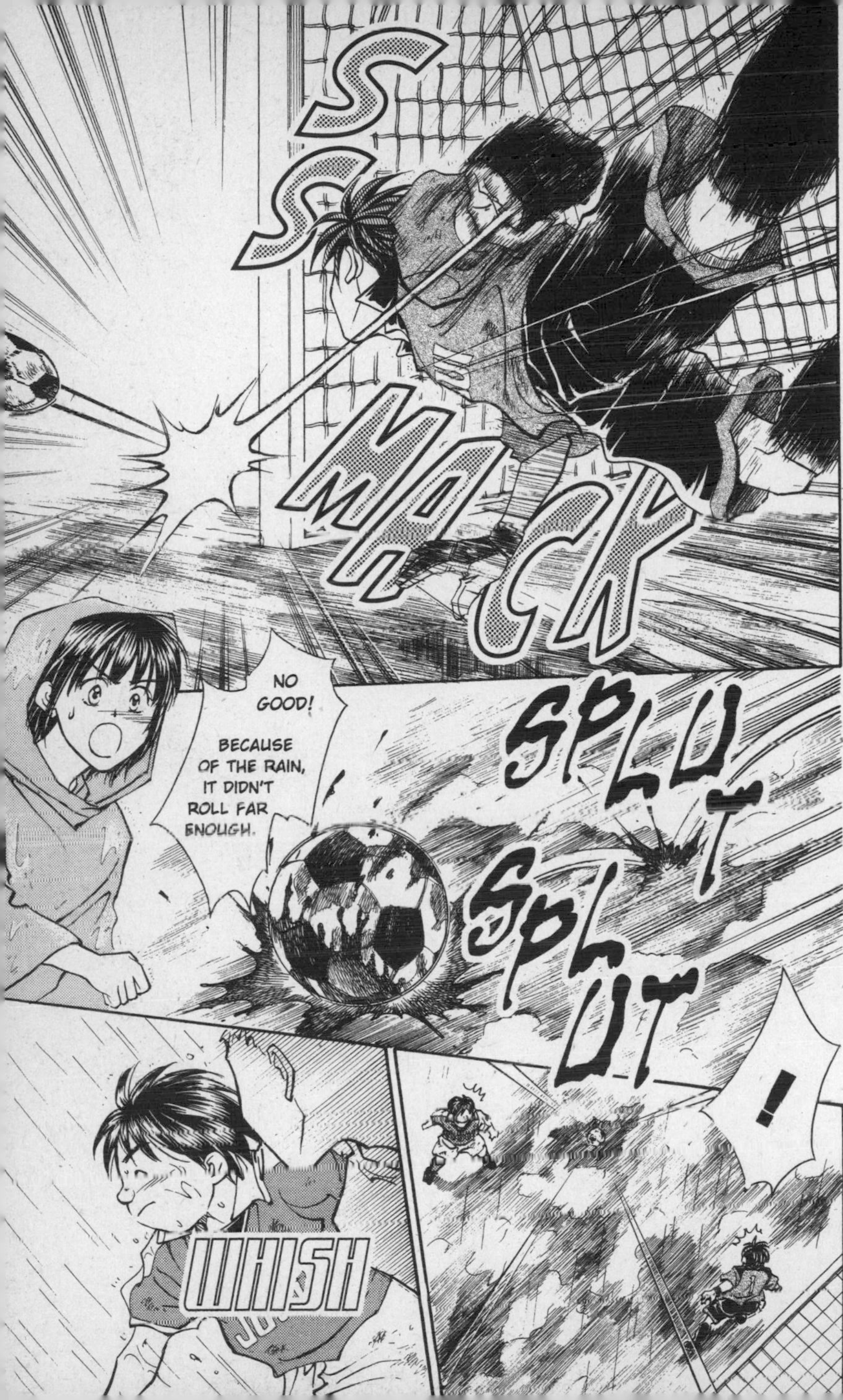
SS
SMACK
NO GOOD!
BECAUSE OF THE RAIN, IT DIDN'T ROLL FAR ENOUGH.
SPLUT SPLUT
!
WHISH

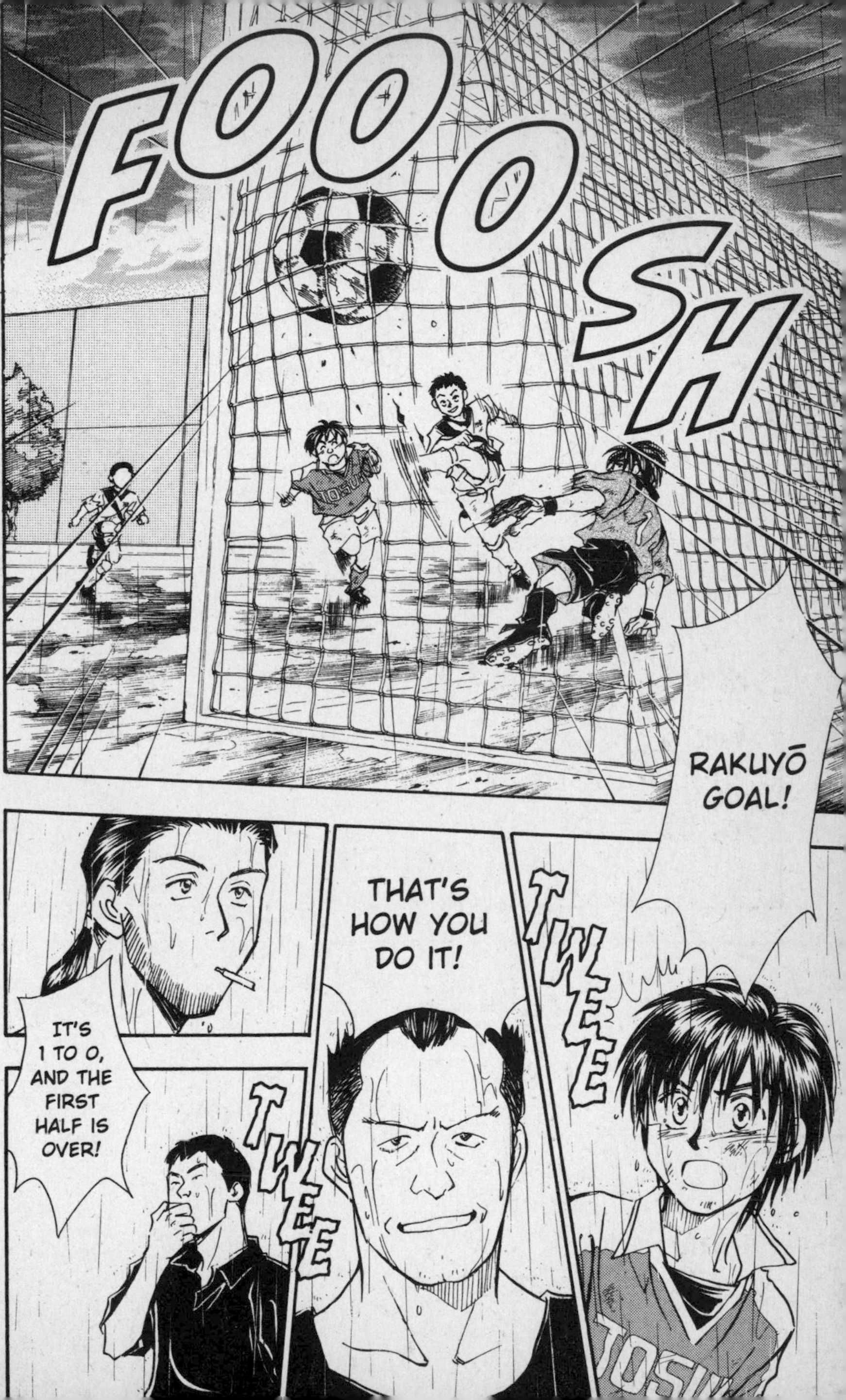
FOOOOSH
RAKUYŌ GOAL!
TWEE
THAT'S HOW YOU DO IT!
IT'S 1 TO 0, AND THE FIRST HALF IS OVER!
TWEE

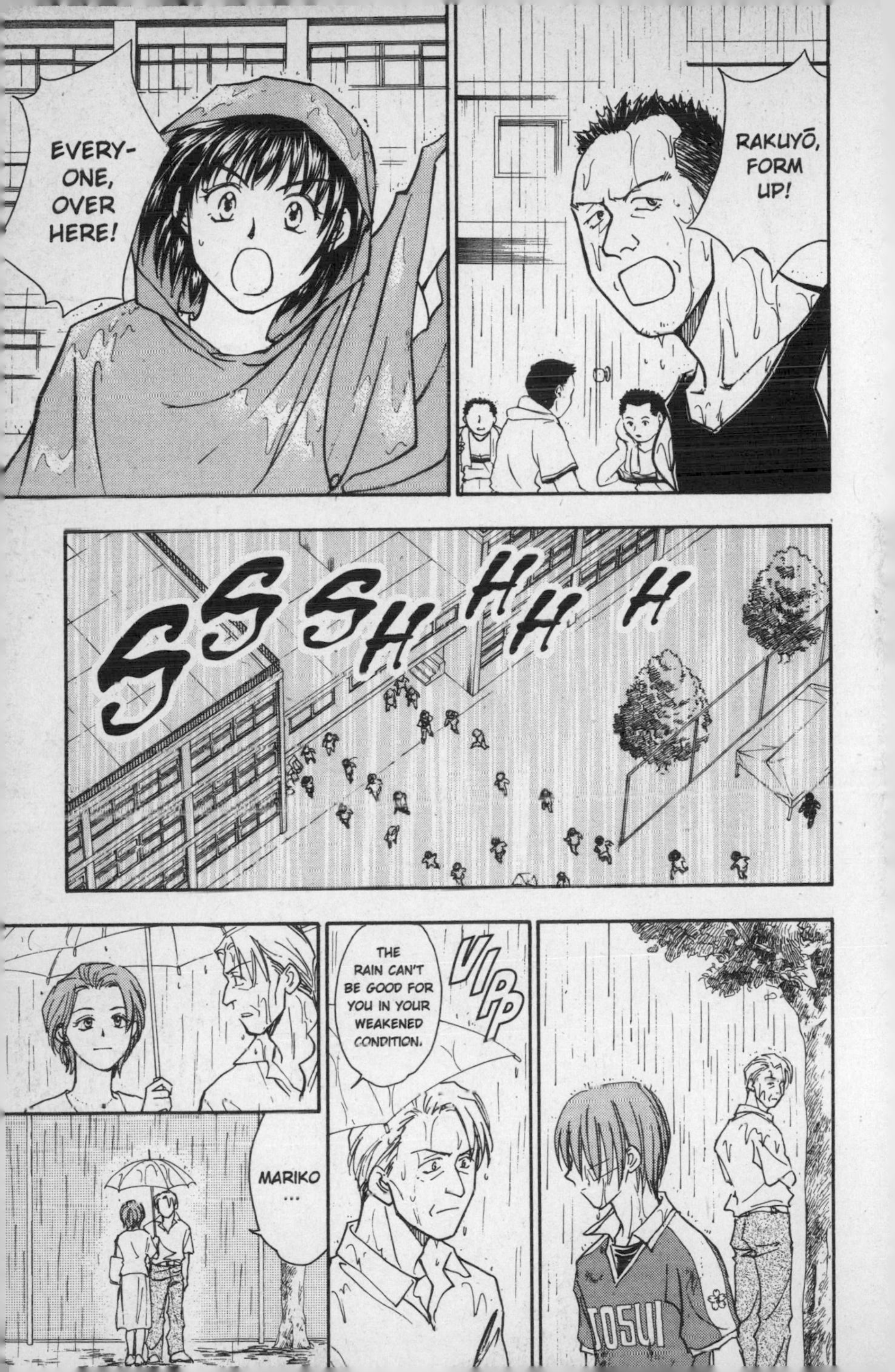
RAKUYŌ, FORM UP!
EVERY-ONE, OVER HERE!
SSSHHHHH
THE RAIN CAN'T BE GOOD FOR YOU IN YOUR WEAKENED CONDITION.
VIPP
MARIKO ...

※ IN GENERAL, WHEN THE REPLACEABLE CLEATS AND MOLDED CLEATS ARE COMPARED, REPLACEABLE ONES HAVE FEWER STUDS AND WORK BETTER ON SOFT GROUND

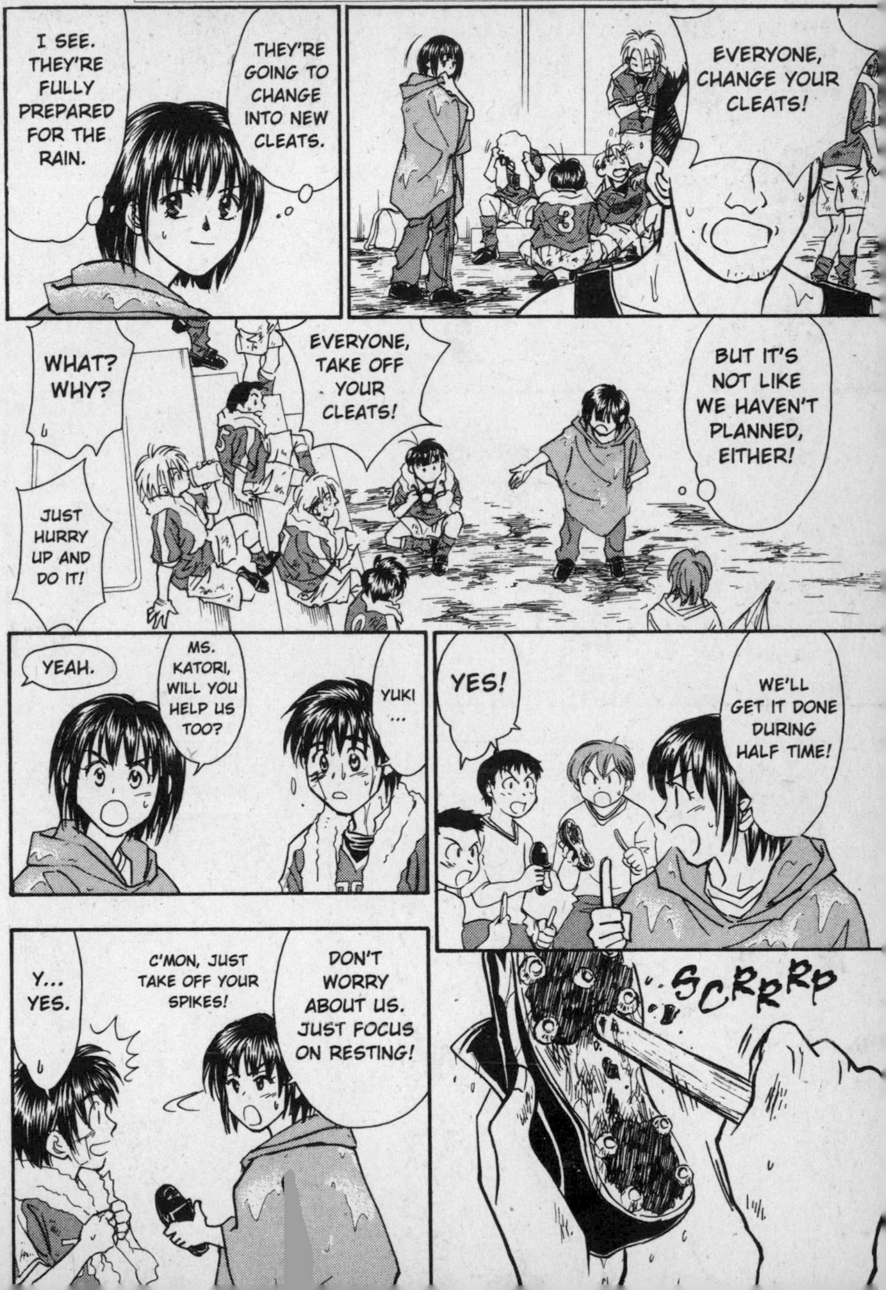
EVERYONE, CHANGE YOUR CLEATS!
THEY'RE GOING TO CHANGE INTO NEW CLEATS.
I SEE. THEY'RE FULLY PREPARED FOR THE RAIN.
BUT IT'S NOT LIKE WE HAVEN'T PLANNED, EITHER!
EVERYONE, TAKE OFF YOUR CLEATS!
WHAT? WHY?
JUST HURRY UP AND DO IT!
WE'LL GET IT DONE DURING HALF TIME!
YES!
YUKI …
MS. KATORI, WILL YOU HELP US TOO?
YEAH.
SCRRRP
DON'T WORRY ABOUT US. JUST FOCUS ON RESTING!
C'MON, JUST TAKE OFF YOUR SPIKES!
Y… YES.

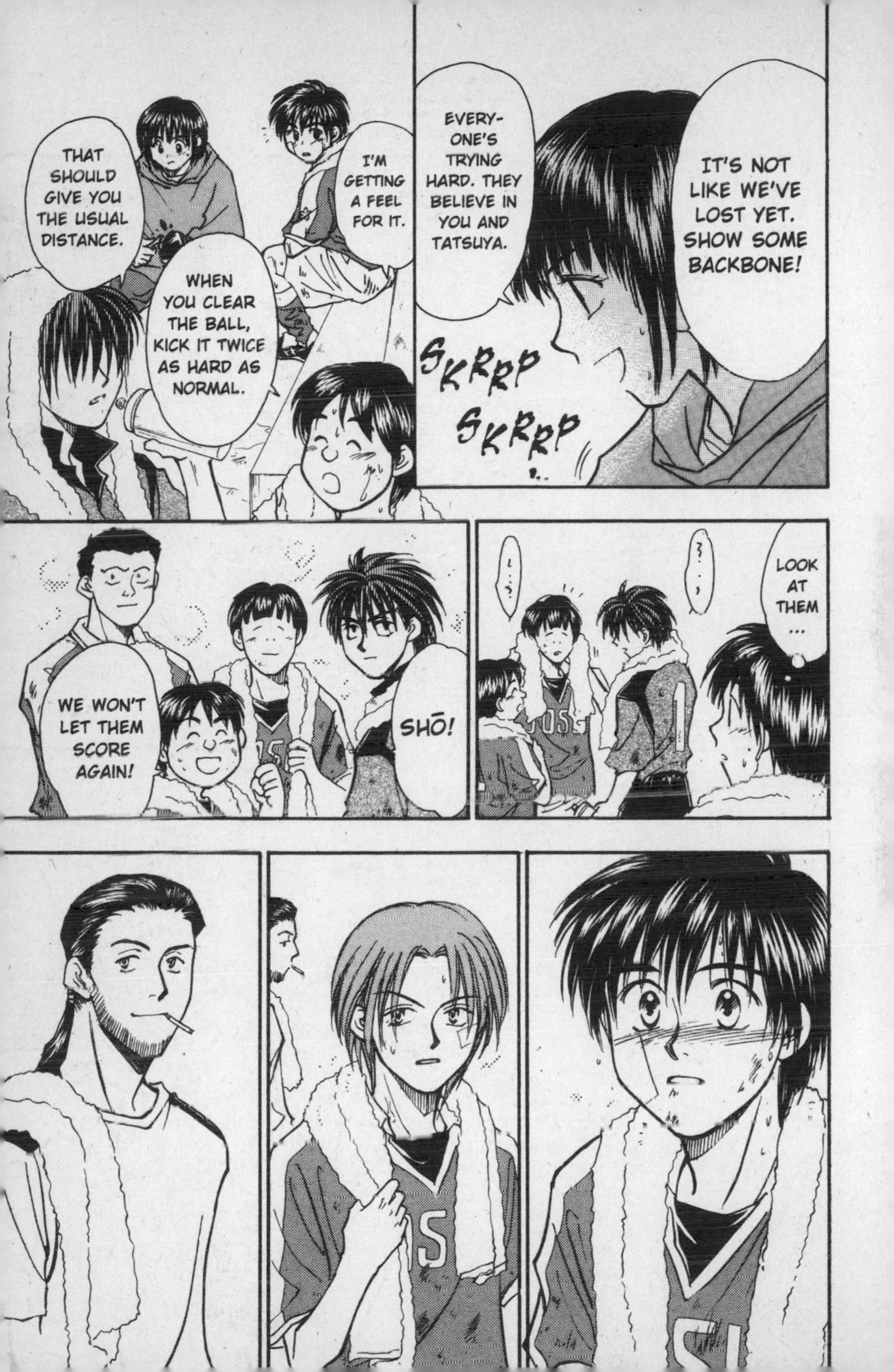
IT'S NOT LIKE WE'VE LOST YET. SHOW SOME BACKBONE!
EVERY-ONE'S TRYING HARD. THEY BELIEVE IN YOU AND TATSUYA.
SKRRP
SKRRP
I'M GETTING A FEEL FOR IT.
THAT SHOULD GIVE YOU THE USUAL DISTANCE.
WHEN YOU CLEAR THE BALL, KICK IT TWICE AS HARD AS NORMAL.
LOOK AT THEM ...
SHŌ!
WE WON'T LET THEM SCORE AGAIN!

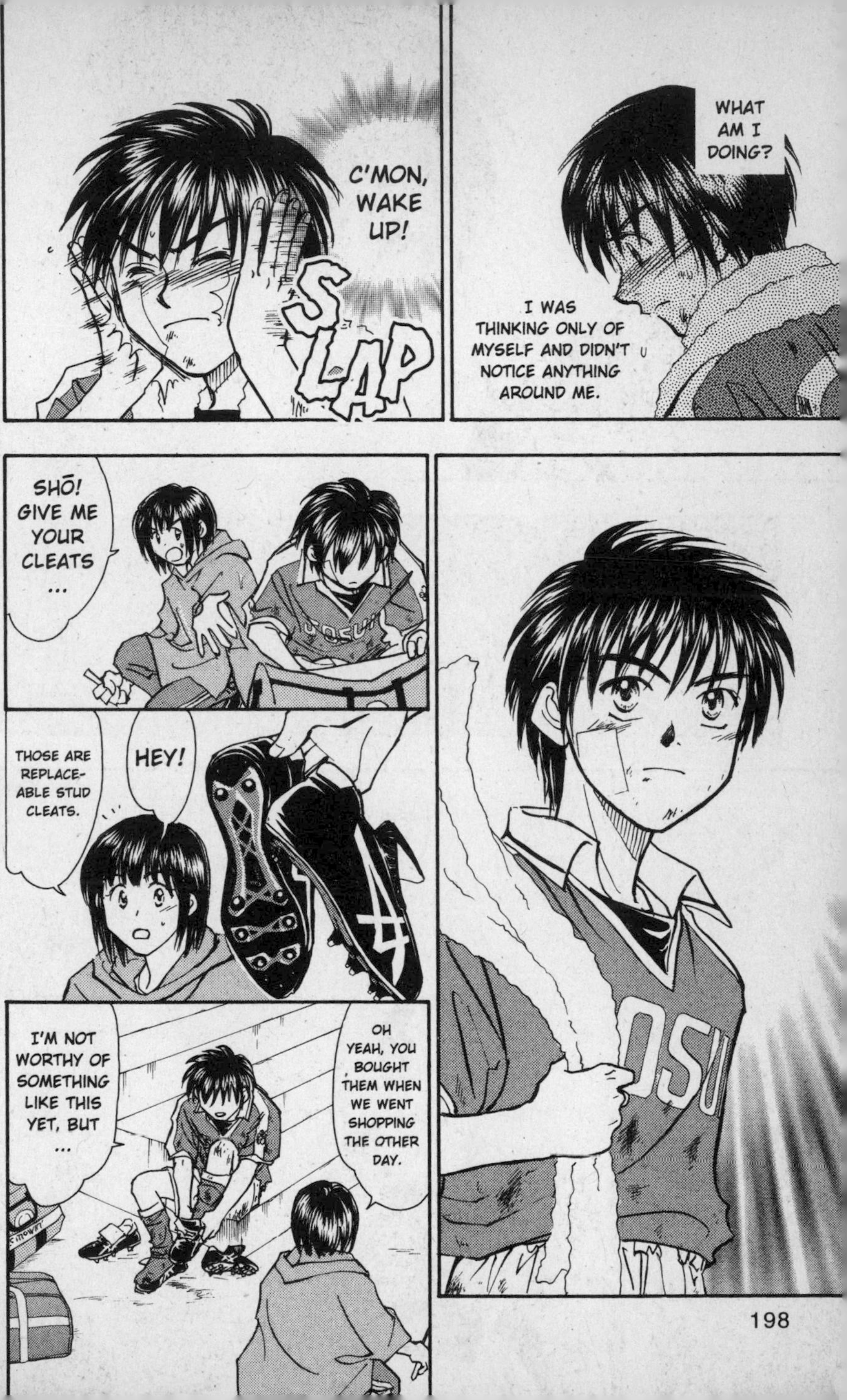
WHAT AM I DOING?
I WAS THINKING ONLY OF MYSELF AND DIDN'T NOTICE ANYTHING AROUND ME.
C'MON, WAKE UP!
SLAP
SHŌ! GIVE ME YOUR CLEATS ...
HEY!
THOSE ARE REPLACE-ABLE STUD CLEATS.
OH YEAH, YOU BOUGHT THEM WHEN WE WENT SHOPPING THE OTHER DAY.
I'M NOT WORTHY OF SOMETHING LIKE THIS YET, BUT ...

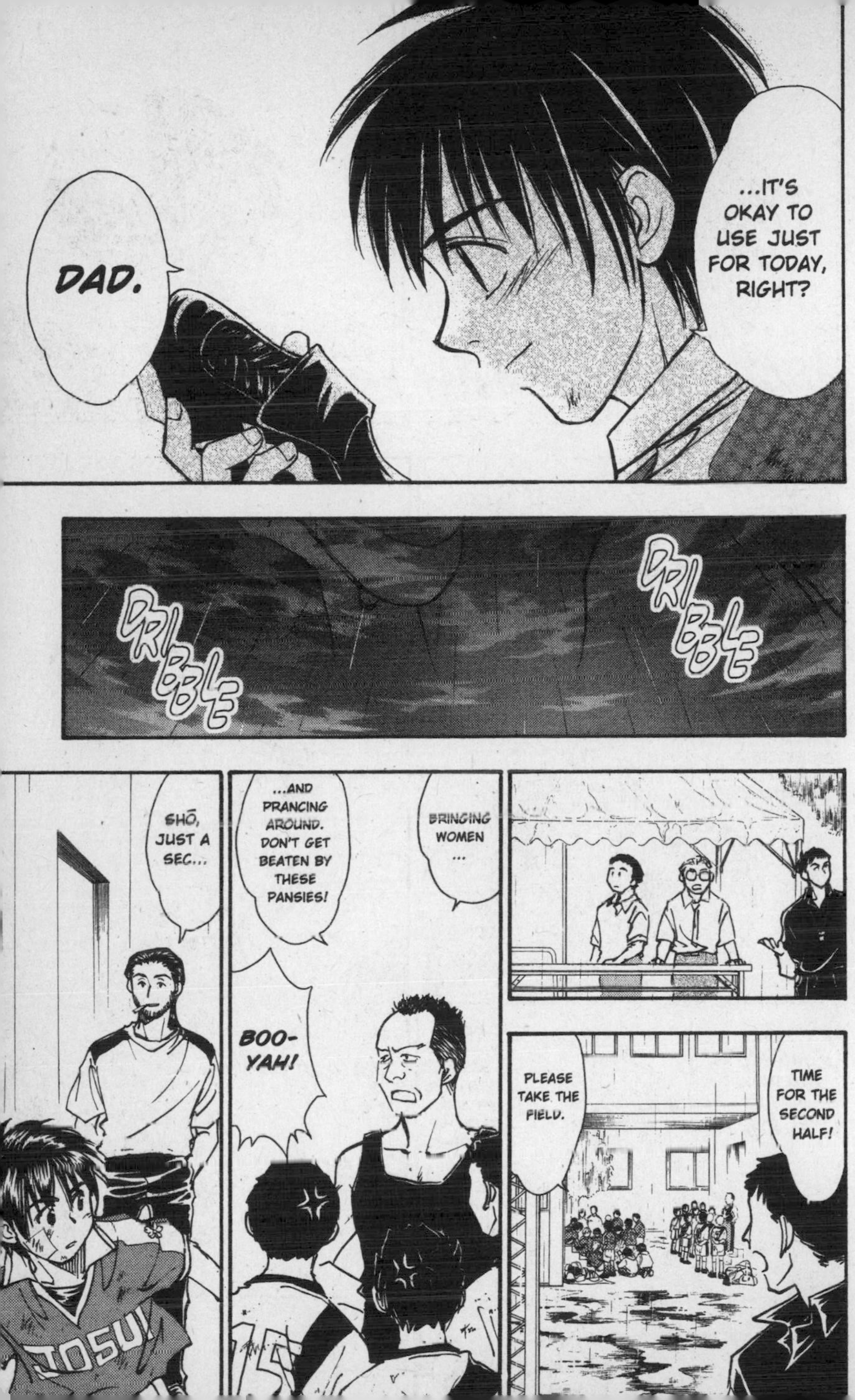
...IT'S OKAY TO USE JUST FOR TODAY, RIGHT?
DAD.
DRIBBLE
DRIBBLE
TIME FOR THE SECOND HALF!
PLEASE TAKE THE FIELD.
BRINGING WOMEN ...
...AND PRANCING AROUND. DON'T GET BEATEN BY THESE PANSIES!
BOO-YAH!
SHŌ, JUST A SEC...
JOSUI

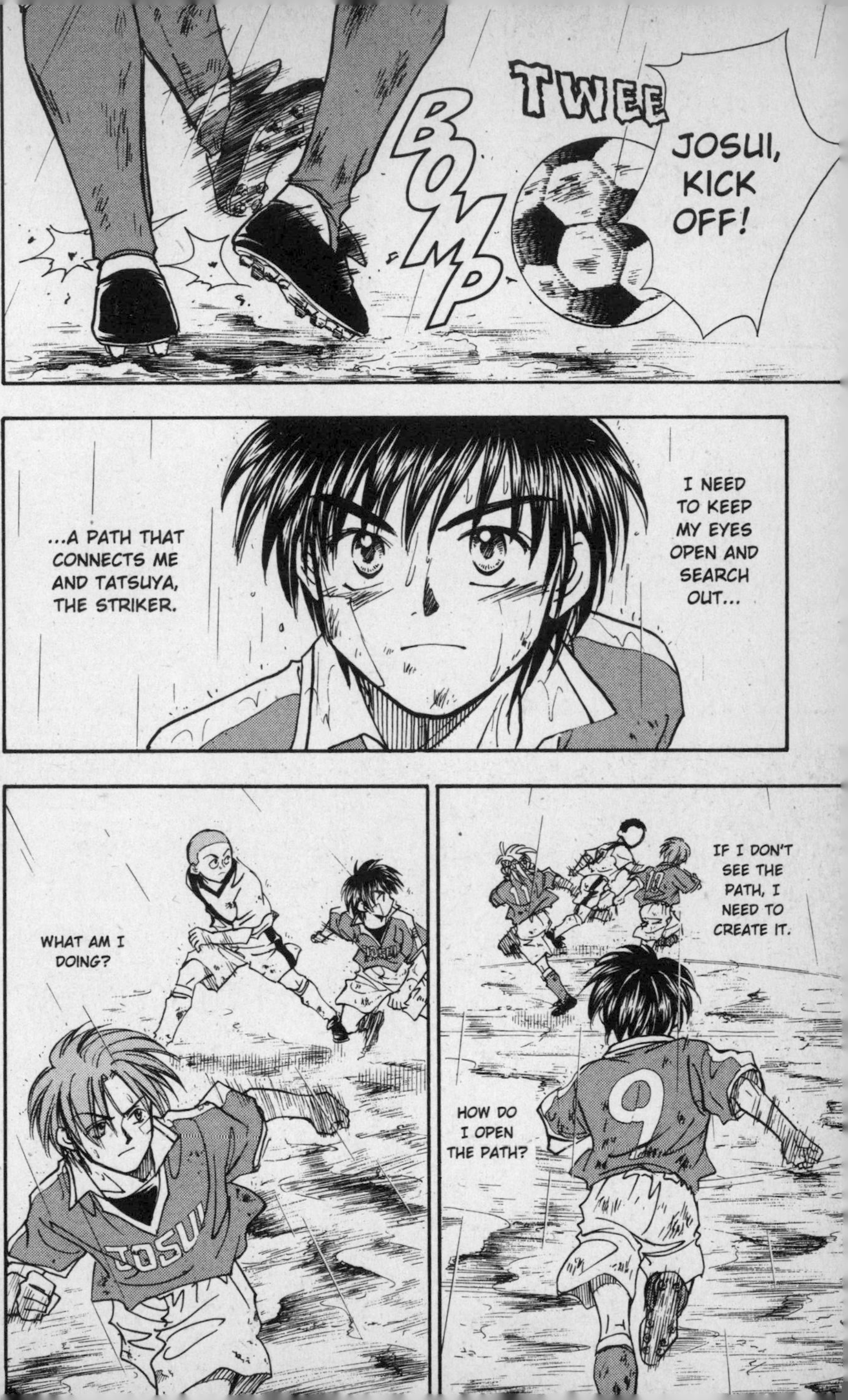
JOSUI, KICK OFF!
TWEE
BOMP
I NEED TO KEEP MY EYES OPEN AND SEARCH OUT...
...A PATH THAT CONNECTS ME AND TATSUYA, THE STRIKER.
IF I DON'T SEE THE PATH, I NEED TO CREATE IT.
HOW DO I OPEN THE PATH?
WHAT AM I DOING?
JOSUI

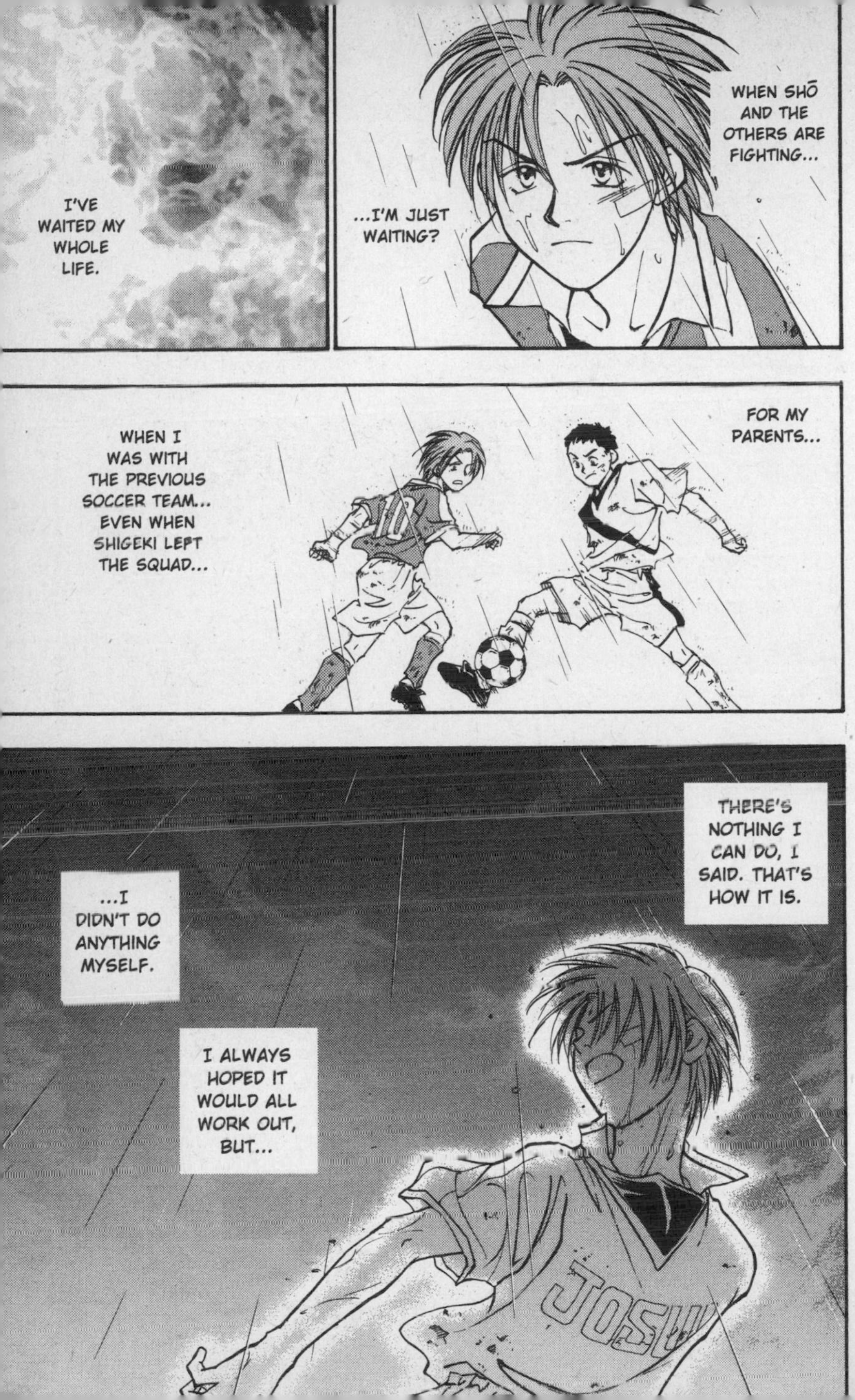

WHEN SHŌ AND THE OTHERS ARE FIGHTING...
...I'M JUST WAITING?
I'VE WAITED MY WHOLE LIFE.
FOR MY PARENTS...
WHEN I WAS WITH THE PREVIOUS SOCCER TEAM... EVEN WHEN SHIGEKI LEFT THE SQUAD...
THERE'S NOTHING I CAN DO, I SAID. THAT'S HOW IT IS.
...I DIDN'T DO ANYTHING MYSELF.
I ALWAYS HOPED IT WOULD ALL WORK OUT, BUT...

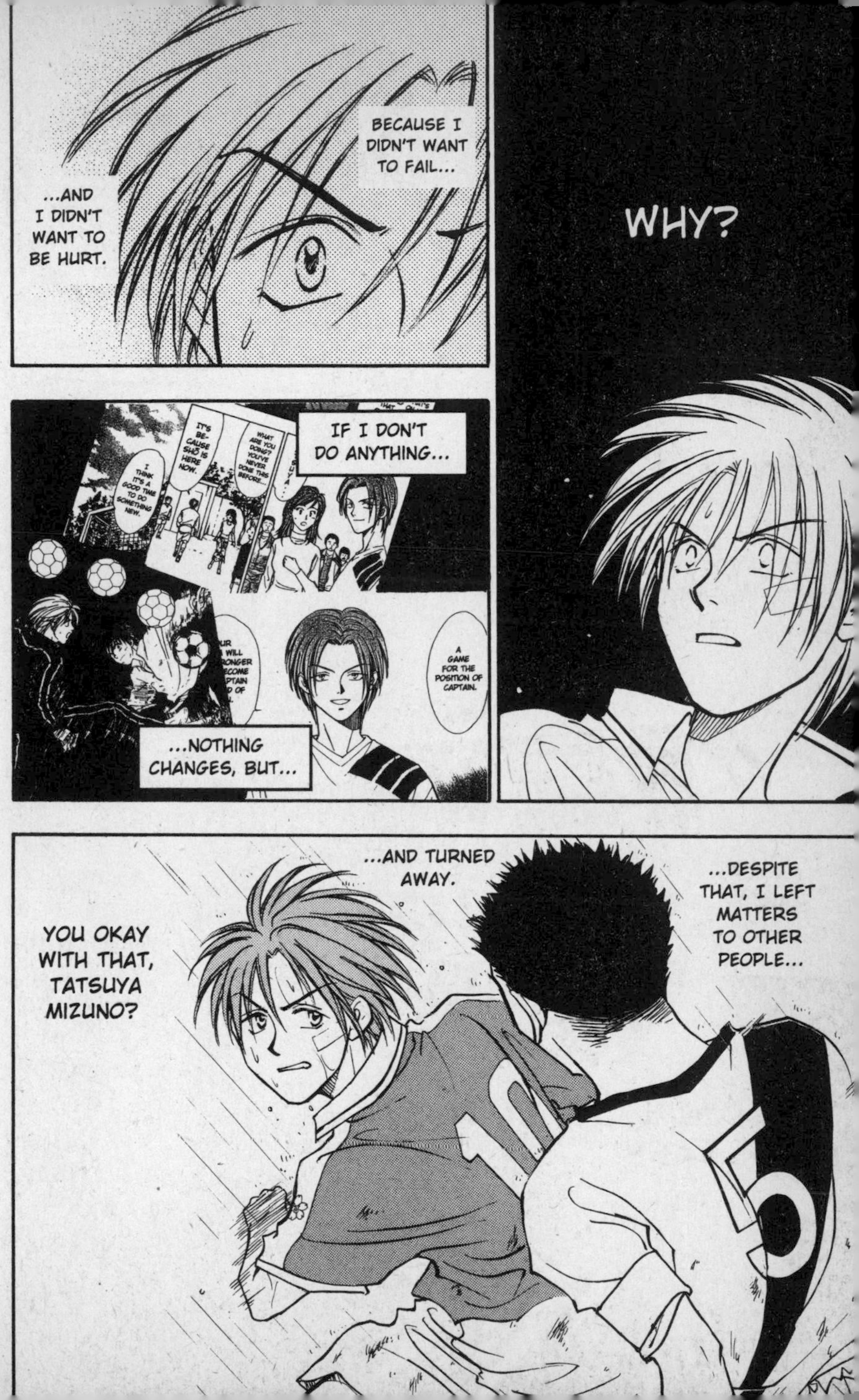
WHY?
BECAUSE I DIDN'T WANT TO FAIL...
...AND I DIDN'T WANT TO BE HURT.
IF I DON'T DO ANYTHING...
WHAT ARE YOU DOING? YOU'VE NEVER DONE THIS BEFORE...
IT'S BE-CAUSE SHŌ IS HERE NOW.
I THINK IT'S A GOOD TIME TO DO SOMETHING NEW.
A GAME FOR THE POSITION OF CAPTAIN.
...NOTHING CHANGES, BUT...
...DESPITE THAT, I LEFT MATTERS TO OTHER PEOPLE...
...AND TURNED AWAY.
YOU OKAY WITH THAT, TATSUYA MIZUNO?

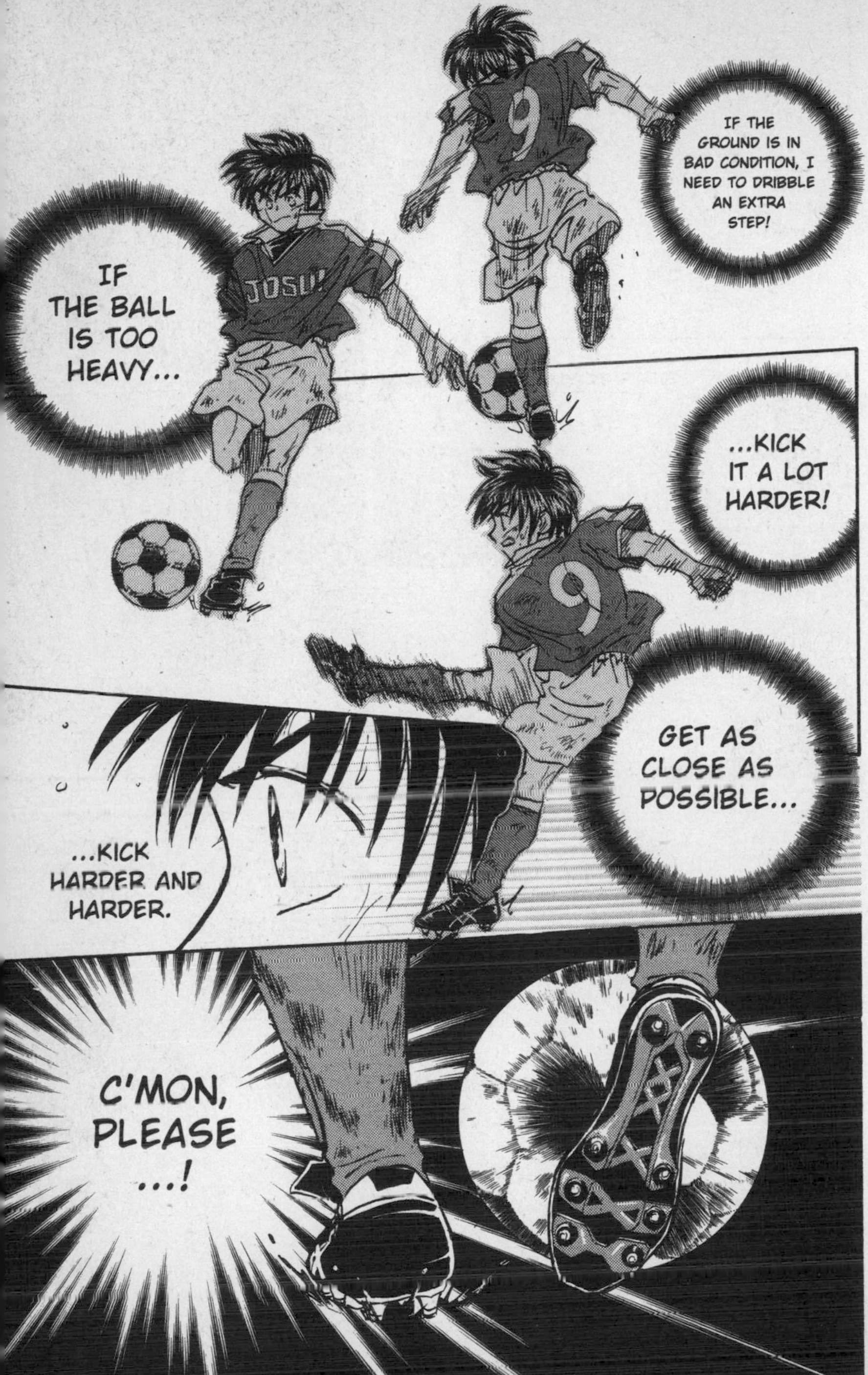
IF THE GROUND IS IN BAD CONDITION, I NEED TO DRIBBLE AN EXTRA STEP!
IF THE BALL IS TOO HEAVY...
...KICK IT A LOT HARDER!
GET AS CLOSE AS POSSIBLE...
...KICK HARDER AND HARDER.
C'MON, PLEASE ...!

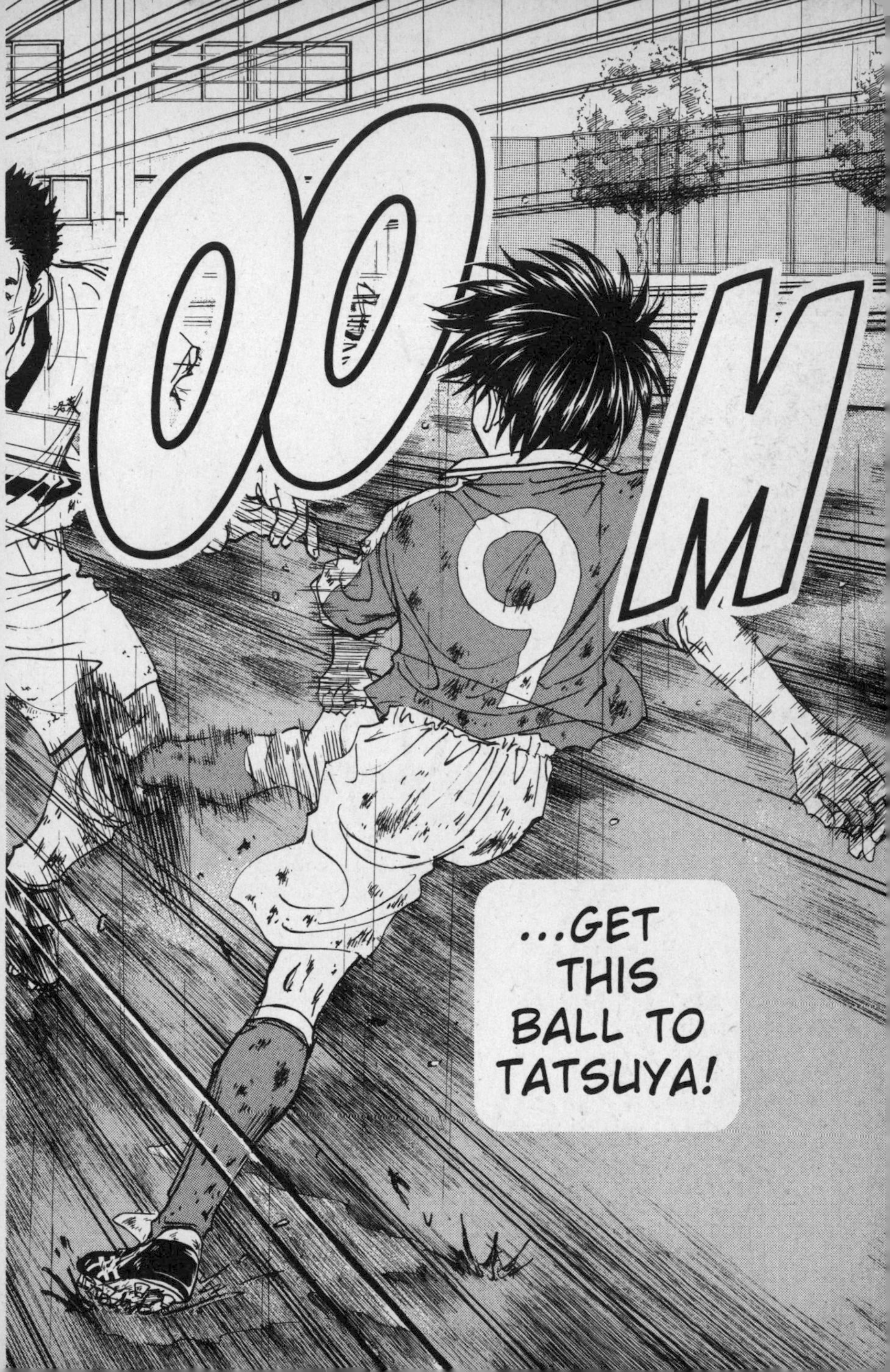
OOOM
...GET THIS BALL TO TATSUYA!

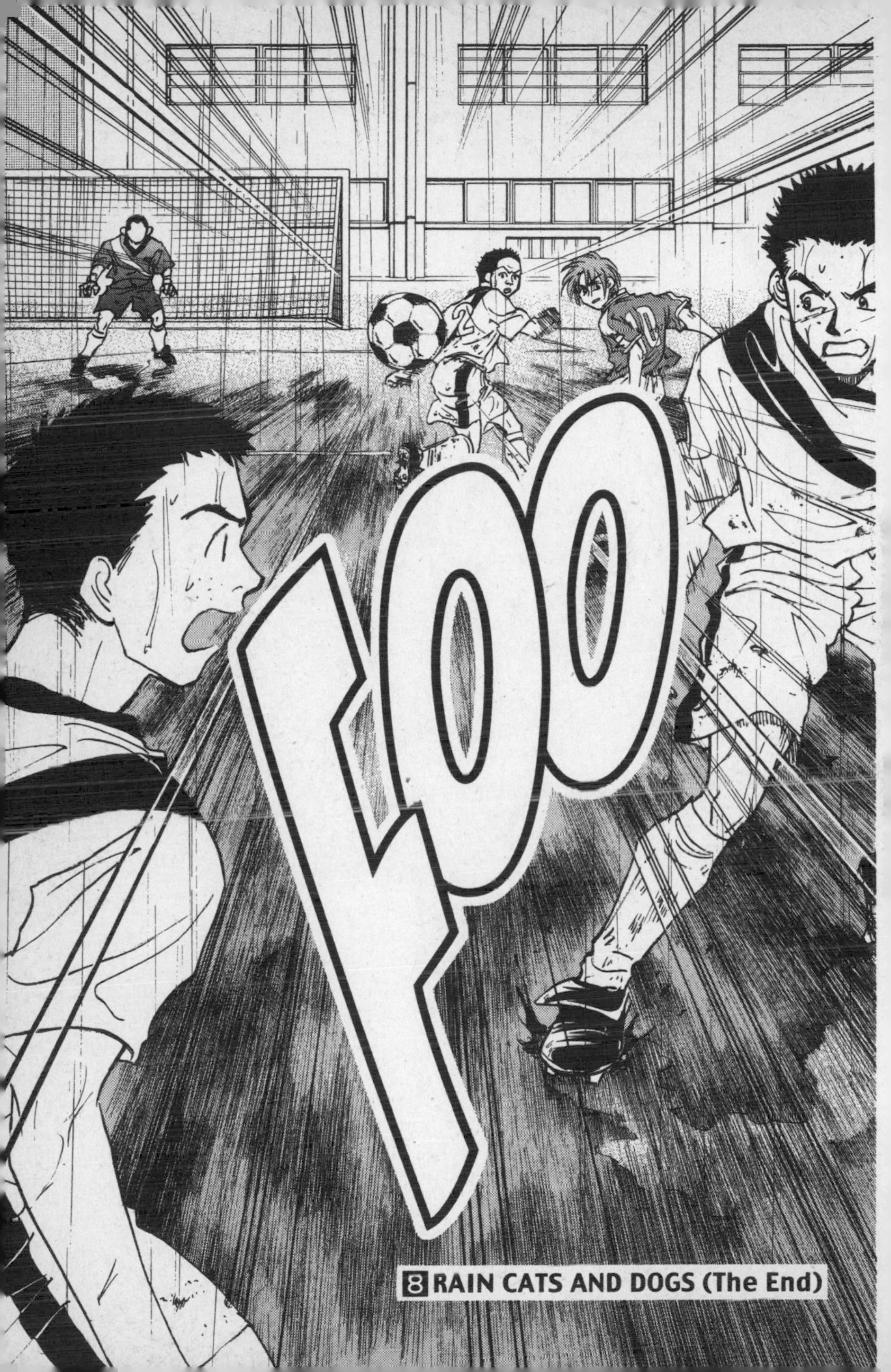
FOO

8 RAIN CATS AND DOGS (The End)

DAISUKE HIGUCHI
MONSTER BODY BIBLE

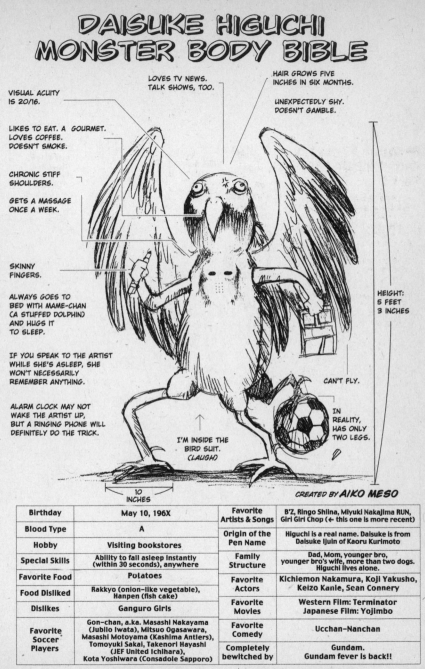

LOVES TV NEWS.
TALK SHOWS, TOO.

HAIR GROWS FIVE
INCHES IN SIX MONTHS.

VISUAL ACUITY
IS 20/16.

UNEXPECTEDLY SHY.
DOESN'T GAMBLE.

LIKES TO EAT. A GOURMET.
LOVES COFFEE.
DOESN'T SMOKE.

CHRONIC STIFF
SHOULDERS.

GETS A MASSAGE
ONCE A WEEK.

SKINNY
FINGERS.

HEIGHT:
5 FEET
3 INCHES

ALWAYS GOES TO
BED WITH MAME-CHAN
(A STUFFED DOLPHIN)
AND HUGS IT
TO SLEEP.

IF YOU SPEAK TO THE ARTIST
WHILE SHE'S ASLEEP, SHE
WON'T NECESSARILY
REMEMBER ANYTHING.

CAN'T FLY.

IN
REALITY,
HAS ONLY
TWO LEGS.

ALARM CLOCK MAY NOT
WAKE THE ARTIST UP,
BUT A RINGING PHONE WILL
DEFINITELY DO THE TRICK.

I'M INSIDE THE
BIRD SUIT.
(LAUGH)

10
INCHES

CREATED BY **AIKO MESO**

Birthday	May 10, 196X	**Favorite Artists & Songs**	B'Z, Ringo Shiina, Miyuki Nakajima RUN, Giri Giri Chop (← this one is more recent)
Blood Type	A	**Origin of the Pen Name**	Higuchi is a real name. Daisuke is from Daisuke Ijuin of Kaoru Kurimoto
Hobby	Visiting bookstores		
Special Skills	Ability to fall asleep instantly (within 30 seconds), anywhere	**Family Structure**	Dad, Mom, younger bro, younger bro's wife, more than two dogs. Higuchi lives alone.
Favorite Food	Potatoes	**Favorite Actors**	Kichiemon Nakamura, Koji Yakusho, Keizo Kanie, Sean Connery
Food Disliked	Rakkyo (onion-like vegetable), Hanpen (fish cake)		
Dislikes	Ganguro Girls	**Favorite Movies**	Western Film: Terminator Japanese Film: Yojimbo
Favorite Soccer Players	Gon-chan, a.k.a. Masashi Nakayama (Jubilo Iwata), Mitsuo Ogasawara, Masashi Motoyama (Kashima Antlers), Tomoyuki Sakai, Takenori Hayashi (JEF United Ichihara), Kota Yoshiwara (Consadole Sapporo)	**Favorite Comedy**	Ucchan-Nanchan
		Completely bewitched by	Gundam. Gundam fever is back!!

COMPILED BY **ASSISTANT S**

Phantom Series No. 3
Early Whistle Concepts, Part 1

TATSUYA'S ORIGINAL LOOK (LAUGH) SIMILAR IN MANY WAYS TO TATSUYA, BUT THE LOOKS AND THE NAME WERE TOTALLY DIFFERENT. LONG-HAIRED TATSUYA! HE'S SORT OF MORPHED WITH SHIGEKI, AND HAS PIERCED EARS, TOO.

YŪKO KATORI SHE WAS ORIGINALLY CONCEIVED AS A CLASSMATE.

SHŌ'S ORIGINAL LOOK THE NAME WAS DIFFERENT BACK THEN, TOO. AT THE TIME, HIS HEIGHT WAS 5'3".

KATSURŌ THE NAME IS THE SAME AS IT IS NOW. THE HAIR WAS CURLING A BIT. ORIGINALLY, HE WAS IN THE SAME SCHOOL AS SHŌ.

Next in Whistle!

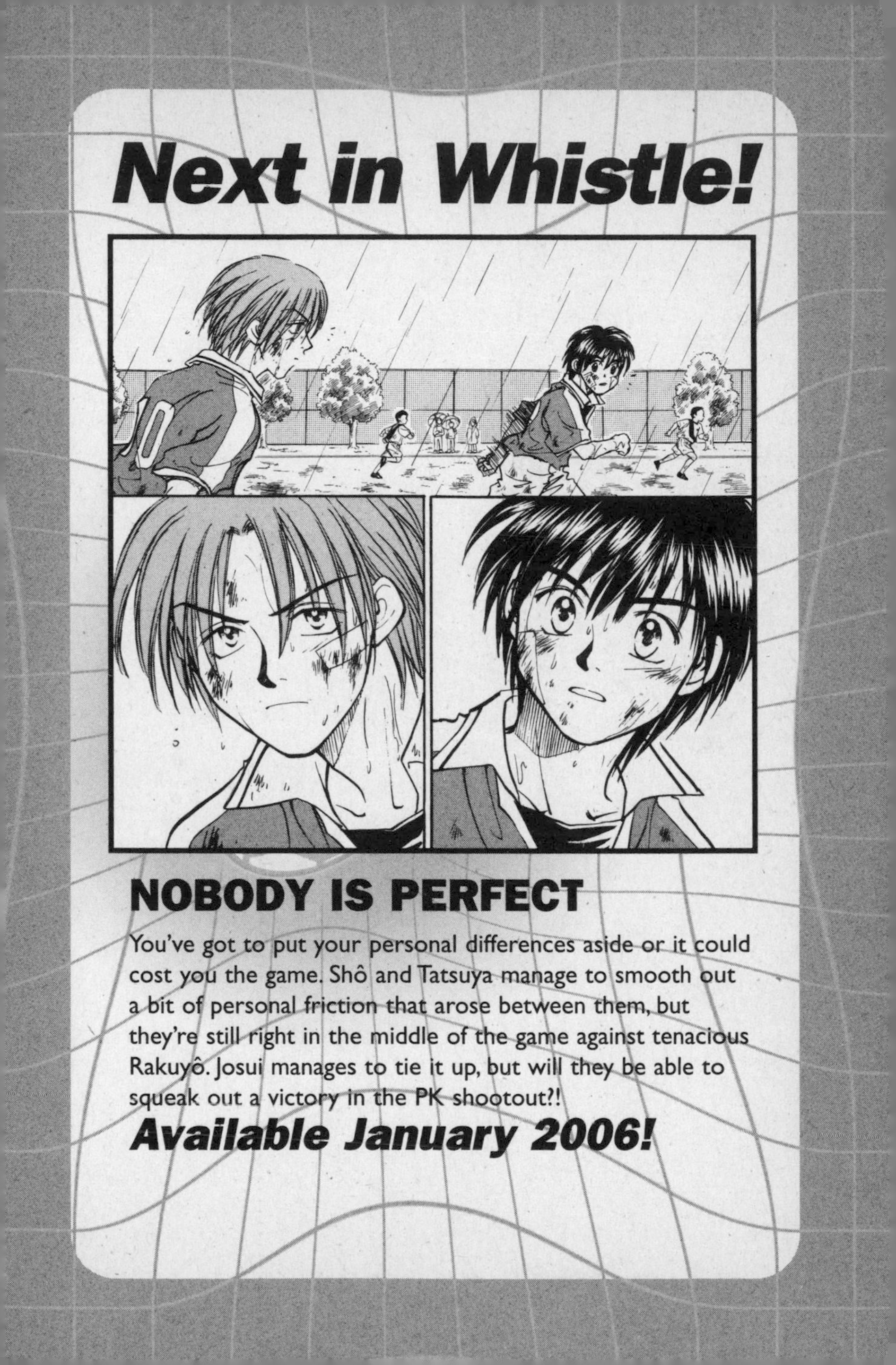

NOBODY IS PERFECT

You've got to put your personal differences aside or it could cost you the game. Shô and Tatsuya manage to smooth out a bit of personal friction that arose between them, but they're still right in the middle of the game against tenacious Rakuyô. Josui manages to tie it up, but will they be able to squeak out a victory in the PK shootout?!

Available January 2006!